Renegades

PETE MARAVICH | MARK FIDRYCH
REGGIE JACKSON | **MY WILD TRIP**
ROBERT | **FROM PROFESSOR TO**
MITCHUM | **NEW JOURNALIST**
JERRY JEFF WALKER | **WITH**
ELVIS PRESLEY | **OUTRAGEOUS**
VISITS FROM CLINT EASTWOOD,
LEE MARVIN | **REGGIE JACKSON,**
DAVID ALLAN COE | **LARRY FLYNT,**
GEORGE ATKINSON | **AND OTHER**
LEROY NEIMAN | **AMERICAN ICONS**
LARRY FLYNT | WAYLON JENNINGS
CLINT EASTWOOD | NGUYEN CAO KY

ROBERT WARD

with an Introduction by ROY BLOUNT JR.

TYRUS
BOOKS

a division of F+W Crime

Published by
TYRUS BOOKS
an imprint of F+W Media, Inc.
10151 Carver Road
Suite 200
Blue Ash, Ohio 45242
www.tyrusbooks.com

ISBN 10: 1-4405-3314-8
ISBN 13: 978-1-4405-3314-3
eISBN 10: 1-4405-3271-0
eISBN 13: 978-1-4405-3271-9

Printed in the United States of America.

10   9   8   7   6   5   4   3   2   1

Library of Congress Cataloging-in-Publication Data
is available from the publisher.

This book is available at quantity discounts for bulk purchases.
For information, please call 1-800-289-0963.

Dedication

This book is dedicated to my favorite editors during my journalism days, all of them brilliant and terrific people. They include:

John Larsen, John Lombardi, Marty Bell, Terry McDonnell, Dick Schaap, Berry Stainback, Roger Director, Bob Asahina, and the late, great Art Cooper.

Without their belief in me as a journalist, and their friendship and support, I would have never had a career at all. Indeed, they were more than editors. They were drinking buddies and close friends. And during those wild creative years I truly felt we were like a band of brothers.

Contents

Introduction from Roy Blount Jr.

Once upon a time—in the much-abused '70s—giants walked the earth, however unsteadily, and stayed out late, and for some reason they suffered certain intrepid reporters to do it with them and take notes. Robert Ward was very good at this. I did some of it myself, with some of the same giants . . .

Well, it wasn't so much that they were giants. Tom Cruise is a giant, but he's not a character. You don't want to hang out with him and find out what he is like. The people Ward was so good at profiling were characters. And characters cry out, by nature, for writers. Capturing characters, back then, took not only an ability to hang, but also an ear for dialogue, a knack for words, and an ability to come off, honestly, as more than just a curiosity-seeker.

Ward's standard statement, to the character in question, of what he was up to—"I want to set the record straight"—was inspired, since characters tend to feel that they have never met the right appreciator. Frequently the character was outraged by the writer's version of him, in print, but I doubt that Reggie Jackson still wants to kill Robert Ward. Ward was too attentive an appreciator, and Jackson too receptive to appreciation. They were a good match, working together.

Ward's piece on Reggie didn't just clear up some Jacksonian history, it made it. And not only did Ward get it right, so did Reggie: he *was* the straw that stirred the drink. He stirred it by saying he was, to Ward.

Sometimes, though, Ward was honorably at cross purposes with his subject. "I don't think we're getting at the real core of me," Leroy Nieman tells him. Maybe not, but they got at his shuck, which was the pertinent layer. Larry Flynt, on the other hand, comes across as an integrated personality, sleazy through and through and no bones about it. Ward got "good stuff"—frequently great stuff—from characters, and he didn't have to rip it off. They wanted him to *know* their stuff.

If there were an equivalent to Lee Marvin today, a magazine writer would be lucky to mine him for grooming tips, relayed by a press agent who had exacted a guarantee that his client would be on the cover. Ward got drunk with the actual Lee Marvin, and talked with him heart-to-heart. Ward also received from Pete Maravich a length-of-the-court behind-the-back pass. If that's not enough to convince you that those were good days to be out and about, how about the fact that the "outlaw country" singer Jerry Jeff Walker lived, as Ward reports, "in a beautiful sixty-five thousand dollar . . . home outside of Austin, complete with modern kitchen, fireplace, sliding paneled doors, swimming pool, and basketball court"?

Granted, we had no Internet back then. So? Do you think you learn anything worthwhile from today's celebrity-hating gotcha-gossip websites? And do you think Robert Mitchum would *tweet*? With Ward's accompaniment, Mitchum blew his own deep, distinctive horn.

~Roy Blount Jr.

Introduction

I was thrilled to learn that Ben LeRoy, major honcho of upstart and super-hip Tyrus Books wanted to put out a collection of my journalistic pieces from the fab '70s and '80s. I mean how many scribes get their perishable magazine and newspaper work collected in book form?

Yep, a collection of my best pieces. Perfect, thought I! That is, until I began to ponder what this endeavor might entail.

Boss Ben wanted me to write a companion essay along with the pieces. Something that might give the inside poop on the life of this particular New Journalist, as he waded his way through the muck and double dealing of the high-powered journalistic world of sharpies, slicksters, and general freaking editorial maniacs.

"Sounds a-okay to me, Ben," says I.

But then I started to write and a sick, twisted feeling spread through my bowels.

The very idea of revisiting my younger self, the mustachioed, cowboy-haired, ill-kempt, bourbon-drinking, wild man who would go anywhere at a moment's notice, meet total strangers, get them to reveal crucial things about themselves, sleep two hours a night, come back home on the red-eye with a filled notebook and then sit down and lash together a ten-thousand-word story over the weekend, while still finding time to play the guitar, go to all-night discos with Morgan Entrekin, Jay McInerney, Bob Datilla, David Black, John Lombardi, Lucian Truscott, Richard Price, Mike Disend, John Eskow, Terry Southern, Rip Torn, Bob Asahina, and anyone else we happened to pick up along the merry way . . . just thinking about that younger version of myself was exhausting. Plus, I'd have to relive the doubt and fear I felt every time I went out on a piece.

The question every freelance journo (without a trust fund) asks himself: "What if I blow it? What if my subject refuses to talk to me? What if all he or she says is, 'We play them one game at a time, Bob.' Or 'I just thank Jesus Christ for my movie career.'" Or, even worse, as one former NFL quarterback once told a friend of mine: "I love playing football and the forward pass is my favorite play." Well, no fucking shit! My friend Hicks then asked his subject to think of something that really made him mad, just drove him nuts, the idea being he might be able to squeeze a soupçon of passion out of this meathead. The QB agreed to try and think of the thing that bugged him, that drove him batshit, like no other. My friend called him back the next day, and the great QB said: "Jack, I got it. I really got it. The thing that pisses my ass off more than anything in this goddamned world!" "Good man," Jack said, getting pen ready to scratch paper. "And what is said thing?" "Careless drivers," the QB screamed. "Careless fucking drivers really make me angry, pal!" Whereupon Hicksie saw his entire piece, career, life fall apart. This was the big reveal? This was what someone would plunk their money down for? Careless fucking drivers?

Holy addled-shit, Batman!

Yes, that was the great fear. Going out into the big world and having the guy/gal/celeb/sports star/murderer just stare at you and mumble clichés. Every time you ventured out, you lived and died by getting "good stuff." No wonder journalists drank, snorted, smoked . . . anything to give them an edge, to shut down the fear that ran through them like an electric cord when they showed up at some total stranger's home and had to become their instant confidant/best friend, if only for a day.

In the end, of course, I agreed to give the essay a shot, but even now . . . for real . . . sitting here thinking about the past, I cannot believe how I did it. Supported myself for years—eight to be exact— as a freelance writer. Never once did I receive a contributing editor's stipend from any magazine, as some of my friends did. See, to get a magazine to give you guaranteed money you had to already HAVE MONEY! If they knew you had a nice bankroll, or your dad was sending you dough from the fund every month, they also knew you didn't have to write for them. You could afford to wait, write your novel, work on a screenplay, or . . . worse . . . write for one of their higher-paying competitors. But if you were a poor muther, like yours truly, you had *no leverage*, and, ergo, you had to take whatever assignments they tossed your way. Everyone knew I had zero in the bank account, and that I could ill afford to turn down any assignment or I'd be living in a phone booth on Forty-second Street. Therefore, as in all things business, it took money to make more money, and I had no freaking dough.

Which meant I had to get the story every month, or I simply couldn't live in New York City. But here's the wildest part: Yes, they had me by the cojones, these slick-assed magazine editors, but even so, I absolutely loved doing it. I loved the freaking challenge. After teaching for six years in Nowheresville, USA, I wasn't ever going back to the dead-assed academic life. I'd get the fucking story even if it killed me (or I had to kill someone else). As the U.S. Marines say, "Failure wasn't an option."

Anyway, I dug the high. The adrenaline rush of making the plane, flying to some unknown place to talk to some cat who had no real interest in talking to me, and, half the time, was barely aware I was coming. Oh, they all knew ahead of time, but guys like ballplayers, cops, actors . . . agreed to things through their publicists, and then forgot about them. More than once, I landed somewhere only to be told my "subject was too busy to talk just now." However, not once did I ever get back without that same guy talking to me. And I usually got "good stuff," too.

Like I say, I loved it all. The sheer juice of it. Hell, I even loved the churning upset stomach, the frazzled nerves, the looming, terrifying deadlines. I dug all of it, and lived for it, and would have done it forever if I hadn't almost died from the trip.

Part One

The Existential Clown

Hello Dear Reader! Ever since I read that greeting in Charles Dickens I've always wanted to use it. Besides it's true. I do have affection for anyone who reads my books, and I hope it's returned. Before I take you on a ride with my Outlaw Journalistic Clan in New York (living on fast food, dope, and booze; catching planes at all hours of the night; battling with editors; making love on the fly; and generally having one hell of a wild time), please allow me a small digression, as I remember how I got into the freelance racket to begin with. After all, people have asked me to tell them how to get into the biz for years. More than one half-defeated wannabe has trundled up to me and said, "I guess I could never be a journalist because I didn't go to any recognized journalist school." My answer is always the same:

"Good for you. Neither did I."

In fact, thinking back on it all, I doubt this book would even exist if I had. Schools teach you the right way to do things, the polite way, and that little lesson has ruined more than one writer, whether journalist or novelist. As for myself, originally, I had no intention of heading into the freelance game. No, no, this working-class kid from Baltimore, Maryland, was on track to live a perfectly nice, normal academic life as a professor of literature at Hobart and William Smith College in the frozen and picturesque Finger Lakes region of Northern New York. Yes, I had a gorgeous wife, named Bobbi (the Bob and Bobbi Show), her two kids from her first marriage, and in thirty years or so I'd be a full professor. I could wear a robe, fumble with my car keys, and act all confused when those darn, meddlin' kids hid my eraser.

Yeah, Robert Ward, novelist and professor, was headed for Mister Chipsdom. Dead on.

Hell, it was only my fourth year of teaching and I'd already published a prize-winning novel called *Shedding Skin*, the wild, comic story of my escape from my drugged-out, dark, harbor hometown of Baltimore, across the fruited plains to the whacked-out, psychedelic, harbor town, San Francisco. To be more precise, a trip to wild and woolly Haight-Ashbury where I took every drug known to mankind; lived across the street from the Grateful Dead; attended be-ins, love-ins; saw the Hell's Angels stomp a guy nearly to death out in front of the Head Shop; hung out with Bill Graham, the great rock promoter; saw Jimi Hendrix play on a flatbed truck in the Panhandle Park, the first time he'd ever played San Francisco (I was in the front row blasted out of my head on Purple Haze); met Janis Joplin and Al Owsley, the actual Purple Haze acid maker; had a total nervous breakdown; and came limping back to Baltimore half dead, seeing psychedelic demons flying out of the toilet.

After recovering, I finished grad school, got married, and ended up assistant professor of English at Hobart and William Smith. *Shedding Skin* came out, won a National Endowment Grant, sold maybe a thousand copies, and my editor, the great Fran McCullough, asked me what I wished to do next.

"Next, haha," I said. "Say, Frannie, I've got a million freaking ideas."

"That's fine, Bobby," Frannie said. "But really you need just one."

"I know. No problem. I'll get right back to ya."

Yeah, a million all right. I took some Dexedrine, smoked a couple of packs of cigarettes, and set my mind a workin'. What *would* I write next?

Then, all at once, I knew.

See, after my *Shedding Skin* days I'd become friendly with many New Lefters, who had all convinced me that I had to get more serious. One of them, Sol Yurick, a then forty-nine-year-old novelist who had written a wonderful, very radical, Lefty novel called *The Bag*, told me that if I was going to be a real novelist I had to commit to The Revolution. He had liked *Shedding Skin*, but admonished me about my comic leanings. "You're a hell of a writer. But you don't want to end up where you are now."

"Right," I said. "Where's that?"

"Bob, you lack seriousness. You're just an existential clown. You skewer everybody but that's not the real you. We're in a serious revolution. Our work has to serve that."

"An existentialist clown." Oh, God, that was the worst thing in the world. All over the world young people were protesting the Vietnam War, fighting evil capitalism, trying to let LOVE flourish, and here I was an existential clown? Why, existentialism was a worn-out, exhausted philosophy for burned-out cases from the Second World War. I didn't want to be associated with them. I wanted to be with my brothers and sisters of the new Revolution. I wanted (God help me) to change the world!

I loved Sol like the father I never clicked with, and decided then and there to write a SERIOUS LEFT-WING NOVEL, replete with evil capitalists, and shining-eyed Leftist idealistic bombers. I wrote and wrote and wrote . . . hundreds and hundreds of pages. The novel was called *Baltimore*. I aimed to show noble Lefties fighting the city government, changing working-class counterrevolutionary attitudes. Lefties would take over the fucking world. My book would be a giant sword of righteousness, stabbing the evil bosses in their fat, plutocratic guts.

The only problem was that most of the Leftist Radicals I'd met at Sol's place in Brooklyn were kind of humorless assholes, rich know-it-alls who had never met a working-class person except maybe their father's chauffeur.

Still, I recall it all fondly. Sitting in Sol's warm, happy Park Slope kitchen we would argue about what the working class wanted. Some of the SDSers I met there were sure they knew. The working class, they said, wanted revolution, they wanted to own the means of production, but due to False Consciousness (Herbert Marcuse's term for Capitalist and Mad Ave brainwashing in his lefty diatribe *One-*

Dimensional Man) they didn't yet know it. The left's job was to raise their consciousness so they understood what they *really* wanted.

It was all so heady. We were going to save the working class from their own brainwashed instincts.

All righhhhht! Righhhhht onnnnnn!

Except for one thing. I had grown up with all these working people in row-house Baltimore, and I was pretty sure most of them weren't the least suffering from False Consciousness. Not only that but I was pretty dang positive that what they really wanted wasn't Revolution at all but something a lot more tangible. Something like, well . . . boats. That's right, speedboats. Which they could race up and down the Chesapeake and the swift rivers outside Annapolis. Yes, they wanted boats and country houses, and RVs, and snowmobiles. Just like the middle class. Okay, granted, maybe working guys wanted speedboats instead of sailboats, but I was pretty sure boats were at the top of the list.

I knew this as sure as I knew the sun was going to come up. So why didn't I say so in Sol's hothouse kitchen? Well, I was younger, and I hadn't gone to Harvard or Berkeley or anywhere important. Unlike me, the clown, these people were committed. Their eyes burned with the passion of True Believers. In short, I was intimidated. Talking to all these Ivy League–educated folks made me doubt *what* I knew. Maybe I was suffering from False Consciousness my very own self!

So when I got around to writing novel number two, I tried. Oh, man, how I tried. I was going to write the great, the ultimate, the most radical of radical novels, stuff that would make Sol's eyes pop. I would be Dreiser, Jack London, and André Malraux all rolled into one. I turned out page after page of Leftist fiction. Serious! Committed! I wrote of giant demonstrations, I glorified union guys and hippies and brave new women!

It was gonna be some kind of wonderful!

Except for the fact that I didn't really believe any of it. My characters were cardboard, talking agitprops, lame knockoffs of Clifford Odets and John Steinbeck. I was never going to be a "good radical" because I didn't believe in Socialism. Of course, I didn't really believe in Capitalism either, which Sol attacked me for. "Which side are you on, Bobby?" he said. ("Will you be a dirty scab or will you be a man?")

After writing about five hundred pages of horrific crap I tossed the book aside. What dreck. What horrific bullshit! My attendant rage from my own stupidity made me probably not the world's best guy to live with at this time. I took speed to hide my depression and disappointment. But speed made me a little cranky. People would walk up to me on campus and say "Hi ya Bob!" and my response would be, "Hi ya Bob? Hi ya fucking Bob? How'd you like me to rip your head off and stick it up your ass? Hi ya fucking Bob that, asshole!" Soon, not only was the book finito but my marriage was too. The gorgeous Bobbi left me for an earnest rock 'n' roller who was going to change the world through music. Together they opened a Leftist vegetarian restaurant known as The Coming Struggle. As I drove by the place I could see all our former friends hanging there. None of them bothered to call me anymore.

A month or so after flopping on people's couches I found myself living in a little cabin on Lake Seneca, feeling like the ultimate loser.

It was all so true. Karl Marx help me, I *was* a mere existentialist clown.

God, the pain of that declaration! That all my earnest reading of Marx, Lenin, Paul Sweezy in *Monthly Review*, Marcuse, Fanon . . . had come down to this miserable, lonely existence. I had let the Movement down. I had thrown two years of deeply earnest, if god-awful, work away. I had lost my family. And what of my students, those who looked to me to do something deeply radical, something brave . . . something that would lead them over the threshold of stagnant bourgeois life to a new and glowing socialist humanism? Yeah, you got it. I'd failed them too.

Clown that I was, I picked up my guitar and played "I'm a Loser" and found myself laughing instead of crying. Bobby Ward, the Revolutionary. What a terrible, pathetic joke.

What's more, I had real material worries too. I had about a thousand bucks in the bank. I was thirty-two years old. I had no future in academia . . . I had failed the Left . . . hated the right . . . God, what a mess I was.

There seemed to be nothing left.

But then, at the very Poe-like pit of despair, I found it.

Even through all the misery of my marriage breaking up, tossing out my book, the kids crying, I had always loved reading, and during those lonely, soul-searching days the only thing that kept me together was The New Journalism. Tom Wolfe was my God. I stayed up all night reading *The Electric Kool-Aid Acid Test* again and again. It was, after all, much like my own novel, *Shedding Skin*. And I felt that Wolfe was nothing if not an existential clown. As were Hunter Thompson, Charles Portis, Joe Eszterhas (before he went Hollywood), Roy Blount Jr., and of course, the genius comic writer Terry Southern. It was impossible to guess which politics they endorsed. Thompson was sort of a Leftist, but more of an anarchist. Wolfe was possibly a hated Republican. But he spared no one his acid wit. Blount was a true comic and even something of a scholar, and Terry Southern found the entire world absurd.

And they didn't have to worry about what subject to write about. America was teeming with change. Rock 'n' roll, sex, politics, art . . . anything you could think of, it was all changing, morphing into something else new, both brave and absurd at the same time. And which novelists were chronicling all these changes and societal explosions?

No one. Not a one.

Okay, Updike sort of was with his Rabbit series, but his suburban generation barely felt the psychic earthquakes. Pynchon was still making up his mythic worlds, which bored me to death. His books seemed to exist solely to exhibit his high IQ. James Baldwin had moved to France and barely wrote anymore, though I still idolized him for *Another Country* and for his essays. The only one who still really mattered to me, Norman Mailer, had moved to journalism and done his best work in that form. More proof that journalism was where it was at.

This, I thought, could be the life for me.

The real world. After all, what was really good about my first novel, *Shedding Skin*, was that it was all based on things I'd lived through or knew about firsthand. I had known gangster teens in Baltimore. I had hitched all over the United States. I had lived in Haight-Ashbury. Yes, the chapters went off into madness and comic exaggeration, but what made them work was that at the core they were real. But all the Radical Political material I had worked into my five-hundred-page opus was second-hand stuff from books. I wasn't a Communist. I didn't come, like Sol, from the Brooklyn Jewish Left. I was a Baltimore boy from a town where your sense of humor was your main weapon in life.

And so I decided out there in my little lakeside cabin that I would start writing journalism. Fuck 'em all. I would make my worst attribute, my clown's view of life, my strongest asset. I would become a New Journalist.

The question was how?

I did a little digging, asking around in New York and I found out my first Catch-22. To get an assignment you needed a clip from another article you'd written. You sent that clip, along with a written proposal, to the magazine you wished to write for. Since they didn't know you and might not even read the clip, you should send your lead—the first paragraph of the piece—along with a few paragraphs of what the piece probably would sound like (I say "probably," because since you hadn't interviewed anyone yet, how the hell would you know what it REALLY sounded like?). The editors of the magazine would then read your clip and your proposal, and if they liked it all they would hire you to write the piece.

But who was going to do that for me? The only clips I had were from years ago, when I'd written for an underground newspaper in Baltimore (the *Baltimore Free Press*, which I had started with Jack Hicks and John Waters!). I became depressed, downhearted. I had to find something close by to write about, some subject I could drive to and observe. Then I'd have to write my lead, send it in, and hope that someone would read it.

I sent a query to my agent, Georges Borchardt. No answer. Fed up with Geneva, my new girlfriend—the gorgeous and brilliant Robin Finn (who later became a great sports journalist for the *New York Times*)—and I drove one weekend to Toronto just to get the hell away from town. While hanging around Bloor Street we saw this new movie called *Dirty Harry*, which blew us both away. The star, this new guy called Clint Eastwood, was the coolest actor I had seen since Steve McQueen. He played a manly killer of a cop: cool, tough, dug jazz, girls fell to their knees when he walked up to them. It was all ridiculous but great fun. Any guy would want to be Clint.

When we got back to depressoville, Geneva, we were both exhausted and famished. We pulled up to an Amy Joy's on Route 5 and 20, and there were three real, live Geneva policemen, all of them the exact opposite of Clint. They were overweight local guys, laughing, drinking coffee, and eating a huge helping of doughnuts. They talked about their kids, sports, and the bad weather. Existentialist clown that I am, I started thinking of a story that would show small-town cops as they really were. I mean what did these guys do all day? Did they, like Dirty Harry, ever solve murders (I had never heard of any in Geneva). Did they have to battle drunks, gangsters on the lam, like in Hemingway's "The Killers"? I had no idea. But I thought it might be fun to find out.

The trouble was I had no assignment, and I couldn't get an assignment without having a lead paragraph to show an editor that I knew something about my story.

Catch-22, indeed.

I thought about it for a couple of days. Then I decided, what the hell, I'll just drive down to the police station, reporter's notebook and pen in hand, and ask them if I could cruise around with them for a few days. If they asked which magazine I was writing for, I'd have to fake it. I decided I would say something like "I have friends in New York who want me to do an article for *Rolling Stone* or this new magazine *New Times*, and if I could just drive around with you a little. . . ." It was the truth but by a nose. My friend in New York wasn't an editor on any magazine but my own agent. A white lie, but a kid's got to get going, somehow.

I shouldn't have worried so much. I learned very quickly that when it comes to being written about most people are thrilled to get a chance to tell their story. Before I could get my request out of my mouth, the chief of police had assigned me to hang out with three teams of cops as they made their rounds.

I left the station house, deliriously happy. I couldn't wait to get out there with the Geneva fuzz. I was back into real life again, finding out what actually happens. Suddenly, Geneva, New York, seemed a hundred times more interesting. Why? Because I would be seeing the place from the cop's point of view, and they knew way more than I did about the world we both lived in. As an academic, high-classed NOVELIST I pretended to stand above the townies and small-town cops who protected me. An easy sense of cultural superiority (i.e., snobbery) kept me from actually learning anything about the very town I lived in. But that was ending now, and I was thrilled to get out and do legwork like a real journalist.

A day later I found myself in the backseat of a patrol car. I was excited, a little scared, but mainly thrilled out of my mind.

Notebook and pen in hand, I started on the ride that a few weeks later would turn into the piece that would be published in *New Times* magazine, under the title "The Yawn Patrol" (a title made up by Frank Rich, one of the founders of the magazine and one which would cause me more trouble than I could have ever imagined).

Here it is then, my first piece: "The Yawn Patrol."

The Yawn Patrol

Serpico . . . *The French Connection* . . . *Magnum Force* . . . tableaus of murder, suave narcotics dealers, massive payoffs, crazed killer rookies . . . bullet holes in foreheads, eyeballs, cheekbones spattered in twilight city streets. . . . These are the police . . . battling the forces of evil, mayhem, insanity that threaten to engulf us at any moment. But wait . . . let us take another look . . . what have we here?

A thirty-year-old policeman named Ed McGuigan of Geneva, New York, is putting on heavy-duty Big Boy Gardner's Gloves . . . another policeman, a big round man named Cring (Richard Cring, partner), is standing there in the dusty old station house with him. Outside, across Castle Street, the tough city bars are quiet . . . McGuigan and Cring are also quiet, businesslike, tense. They are going out on Patrol. Their assignment? They must stop a potential killer . . . a killer who stalks the third floor of one of the plush three-story original American settler Historic Houses that line Geneva's South Main Street. The killer is named Toughy. He is . . . a Persian cat, and he is Out of Control.

"I hope we don't get scratched," says Trickler. "These goddamned animals . . . once they lose their minds . . . you can't tell what the hell will happen."

Cring nods his head.

"Yeah," he says, his eyes bulging. "I know what you mean."

Earlier that day I had talked with Cring about his duty.

"It's not bad," he says. "But what I really look forward to is retirement. I've been on the force six years. Only fourteen more and I can move to Atlanta, get a nice little house . . . play some golf."

That is if that damned cat, Toughy, on Main Street doesn't get him first.

"The main reason I hope it's not too crazed," says McGuigan, picking up a wire hook and a burlap bag, which he tosses jauntily over his back, "is that if he is nuts . . . and I *have* to shoot him . . . Christ, I'll never hear the end of it my . . . wife for one . . . she loves animals . . . and the damned civic groups . . . you can't shoot a cat in this town and expect to get away with it."

Which is, of course, true. You can't expect to get away with anything in a town the size of Geneva, New York (population 17,500). The town is located on Lake Seneca, which runs from Geneva, way down past Watkins Glen, of Grand Prix and Rock Concert fame. But Geneva itself, like many small cities in America, will never gain the fame of Watkins Glen. For Geneva is what is known as a "dying town." Once prosperous in the '20s, once the home of gamblers, a vacation spot for Mafia men who were attracted to the lake (Lake Trout Capital of the World), to the good hotels and the Club 86 where they used to see name stars such as Billy Eckstein, the town has long since been past its Golden Age. Though private and prestigious Hobart and William Smith colleges and the Cornell Experiment Station reside here, the town's main economic booster, the Sampson State Air Force Base, has been gone since the Korean War. With it went Shuron Optical, though the uninhabited building still stands next to Shuron Baseball

Park, once home of the minor league Geneva Twins, who themselves have disappeared. Also listed among Geneva's casualties are the Patent Cereal Company, the Andes Range Company, the U.S. Radiator Company, and finally the Geneva Market Basket. All of them were bought out by bigger corporations and moved to more lucrative, less isolated cities.

When one rides around Geneva (as the police do), one begins to feel that all that *is* left in the town are bars: those bars mostly inhabited by working-class whites; the black bars; the funkiest and strangest of Geneva's bars, Moon's, which features poor whites, blacks, Puerto Ricans, and several transvestites; bars like Tiara's, where Geneva's first murder in several years took place last summer; and the Central Hotel, which even the police don't like to walk by, in the town's "Butt End." Many more, without names or signs, are just storefronts with taps serving Genessee and Utica Club to the tired, sweaty blacks, Puerto Ricans, and rednecks who work at the few places left to work at in Geneva—Libby's and the American Can, or the Geneva Foundry, a hideous smoke-belching building that blasts forth excrement into the sky night and day.

This torpor then, which pervades every aspect of the town, is the atmosphere in which the Geneva Police must work. The boredom, the feeling of exhaustion, of almost a twilight sleep, is as real an enemy to the police as the fights, marital spats (their most dangerous call), and burglaries that the Punch Patrol must combat.

On my first day cruising with the Geneva Police, I ride with Jim Trickler, twenty-six, who has served two years on the force. We have been riding his route—the Northwest Area of town, out Highway 5 and 20, past the Twin Oaks Restaurant, a hangout for Hobart kids, past the Town and Country Plaza and back again—for three hours and not a trace of anything has happened.

"It's like this," says Trickler, taking off his blue cap and running his hands through his hair. "Sometimes nothing happens for so long you wonder why you're getting paid at all . . . but that's when it can get very dangerous for you . . . because when it does happen, it always happens fast . . . very fast . . . and if you've let the boredom get to you, you could react in the wrong way . . . or maybe not react at all . . . which could be fatal."

Notes While Riding: Friday

It is eight o'clock on a Friday night and Officer McGuigan, thirty-two years old, married with two children, is telling me about his most memorable evening as a policeman: "I was off duty and I was trying to catch some hookers down on Exchange Street," he said. "It was right outside of the Paddock Bar. . . ."

He is smiling and his eyes twinkle. Though his nickname among his fellow cops is Barney Fife, he looks more like a thin Steve McQueen, blond, friendly, and boyish.

"Anyway, we were down there to get this whore . . . me and a couple of the other guys . . . a couple of them were real bad actors. They just didn't have it right . . . I mean they stood out on the corner just leaning on the parking meters saying, 'Hey, baby' . . . stuff like that. . . . I figure there's only one way to get this baby . . . you got to drive up to her and come on from the car. I get the unmarked car . . . the one that works, most of the cars don't work, a couple of the engines are literally held together by bailing wire . . . anyway, I ride up to her and I say, 'Hey, how you doing.' . . . I don't ask her to go with me, 'cause that is entrapment . . . but sure enough, she comes right over . . . and soon she's in the car.

"Anyway . . . these colored broads all got old men . . . pimps . . . and you don't want to have to mess with some of these guys . . . jeez . . . so anyway, we get going, now I'm tryin' to get her to take me to this motel outside the town, where the cops are waitin', you know . . . but she don't want to go . . . so we start going out 5 and 20 . . . right along here . . . and she finally says, 'Hell, whitey, I gonna give it to you right over by the car wash there . . . yeah right over there by the car wash across from Loblaw's. . . . and I'm thinkin' . . . 'Ohhh boy, maybe I ought to knock off a piece free and make the city pay for it,' you know? But I don't do it. . . . Anyway, we get over there and she takes off her dress, right there in the car wash, man she just whipped that dress off . . . and she no sooner had it off than she looks at me and says, like she can smell me or somethin', 'You're a cop. You are a cop, you mutherfucker.' Well, I had just given her the money . . . that's very important . . . it was ten bucks . . . and I said, 'That's right, baby . . . and you are under arrest.' Well, she started screamin' and yelling, and she laid one on me almost put me through the window, wham, she punched me in the head, knocked me every way but loose. I didn't want to hurt her. She's a girl, right? But what you gonna do? I finally grabbed her, and held her down. Well, she sees where I'm takin' her and she says, 'No you don't, you muther' . . . and grabs the wheel. I couldn't believe it. Then, she manages to get over next to me, and slams her foot down on the gas pedal. Oh, that was it. I thought, 'Well, Ed, you've had it now, baby.' We were going across the parkin' lot about eighty miles an hour, and I'm holding her, slapping her with the back of my hand now, with one hand, and trying to steer with the other, and we were headin' right at the big lights . . . zoom zoom . . . just whizzin' past' em . . . By Jesus, I thought, this is it, Ed . . . and finally I whacked her a good one and said, 'You cool it or I'll put you out with some Mace' . . . and I started trying to take her in. It was a hell of a struggle, I'll tell you . . . and I felt weird . . . I mean a naked black chick in my car . . . riding down 5 and 20. Christ, what a night."

He is in high spirits now, laughing and looking at me.

Soon, however, the car falls into silence. Though the radio is always on, and we are receiving calls from the Canandaigua Sheriff's Department and the New York State Troopers, one learns not to really listen to it. It's like a low Muzak in the back of one's brain.

"I wish something would happen," McGuigan says, apologetically. "Some nights it's like this. Christ, we been ridin' five hours and not even one high-speed chase." We drive up 5-20, past Carroll's, Home of the Club Burger, and past McDonald's, Home of the Big Mac.

"Do you like to go to bars when you get off?" I ask.

"Forget it. Practically every time I try something like that some jerk starts in on me, 'Hey you . . . cop . . . what chu doin' here?' You have to either punch your way outta the place or jes turn around and quietly leave. I drink in the Men's Club downtown now. It's a drag. A real dead place, but at least I don't get bothered."

He is quiet for a minute, listening to some jockey on the radio. Then he turns toward me, and nods his head.

"You know what it is," he says. "It's my face. That's what it is. I got this youthful face so every son of a bitch in Geneva thinks I'm a punchin' bag. It's my face."

Notes While Riding: The Next Friday

At the wheel is a heavyset officer named Don Cass. His parents own Cass TV and Records out at Town and Country Plaza. Cass, twenty-three, has been an officer for just ten months.

"I love it," he says, as we ride up South Main Street. "Some officers go home and forget it . . . but I love it. I'll work any time they want. . . . Last year when we had the murder downtown, I was a rookie, and I was off duty . . . well, my parents have a police band radio and so do I. But I was asleep at the time. My mother heard that Trickler had taken the man in from the Tiara Club, and she called me. I went right down there, and guarded the prisoner's cell all night. I mean I was new on the force, and it was a murder . . . you wouldn't want to miss something like that."

"GD-10 to GD-4."

Cass picks up the microphone. He has big hands, and the mike disappears in his fist. When he talks, his heavy jaws move to the side in a chewing motion. He seems to enjoy talking over the mike.

"GD-4 to GD-10."

"There's a stabbing reported at Geneva General Hospital. Go up there and check it out."

"Check GD-10."

Cass steps down on the gas. He drives with two hands on the wheel, talking pleasantly as we shoot toward the complaint.

"I would rather be doing this than anything," he says. "On what other job can you be outdoors, help people and see so much action?"

We pull into the Emergency Room Entrance at Geneva General.

Inside a young, muscular black man with short-cropped hair sits on a cot. A doctor is sewing up two slash marks just above his left temple just above his ear. The patient turns and stares at Cass.

"Aw-oh," he says. "It's da cops."

Cass waits until the doctor is done, and asks the patient his name.

"Smithson," says the black man. "Donald . . . but I don' wanna start no trouble. . . . Ya see it was jes one my frens . . . he and me we had dis little disagreement . . . and he got excited and I guess I musta been wrong, 'cause I was de one got stabbed. I don' wan press no charges. Jes a little dis'greemen'."

At that moment a short, dark man with slick, black hair comes in the door. His name is Detective Simon, and he is well-known in Geneva as the only cop who has been involved in two shootings.

"Stabbed, huh, buddy? He stabbed you?"

"Hi, 'Tective Simon," the black man says. "I don' wanna press no charges. He my fren . . . no trouble."

"Jes a pal of yours, huh?"

"Dat's right."

"Okay, you have it your way."

The black man smiles. He seems greatly relieved.

"I tell you what though," he says.

"What's that?'" says Simon.

"I want to be a dee-tective jes like you, Dee-tective Simon. You let me be a dee-tective, and I get *all* the dope pushers."

"Sure, pal," says Simon.

"You gimme a ride home, Detective Simon?"

"Sure."

Simon looks at Cass.

"When you make out this report," he says, "don't play up the stab wounds . . . call 'em scratches . . . ah . . . suffered when the patient and his friend had a 'misunderstanding.' All right?"

"All right," says Cass.

An hour later I sit with Cass in the Chalet Coffee Pot in the Greyhound Bus Station on Lake Street, right across from the Tiara Club. I ask if he has ever been hassled by former Geneva High School mates who may resent that he's a cop.

"No, well, there was one guy, the first week on the job. I saw there was a warrant out for this guy I went to high school with for being AWOL. And so, I was coming up Castle Street, right there on the corner of Castle and Main, he's standing there hanging out in front of the sub shop. I had to arrest him. It didn't bother me when I did it . . . but later I thought about it . . . and it *was* strange."

We sit and drink our coffee. The blond waitress keeps smiling at Cass as she had at Trickler and McGuigan the night before.

Notes from the Station House: Saturday

The station house is a small, cramped room in the back of City Hall. There is a desk at which the sergeant sits, and around the desk are some shelves that the police built themselves. The desk sergeant calls the squad cars from here. Now, in his one hand is a copy of *Penthouse*, and in the other is the microphone. On the table next to him is a bugging device that picks up signals from bugs placed inside Geneva businesses that are likely to be robbed.

"If anyone talks in any of these places, we got 'em," he says.

While I am looking over the buggers and the police radio, two officers come in from the patrol for a break. One of them is laughing and telling the other one about a potential bust.

"You know Girelli, the kid who drives the white Continental?" says the first officer.

The other one nods his head.

"Well, when you see him, I want you to nail him. Grab his ass and if he starts in giving you any of that search warrant jive, tell him the search warrant is up in the sky, and so will he be if he doesn't shut up."

The other cop laughs, and goes out past the Wanted Posters (Wanted: David Donald DeFreeze . . . drinks plum wine and may be wearing tinted glasses) to the men's room.

I approach the first officer and ask him if what he just stated isn't illegal.

"Maybe," he says. "It depends on the way you do it. You can't search his car without a warrant, right? So, you get him to harass you, and arrest him for harassment. Then you can search his car nice and legally."

Notes While Riding: Monday—5 P.M.

I am again riding with Jim Trickler. We have been riding since three o'clock, and I have noticed that many people wave to Trickler.

"Why do people wave?" I ask. "Do you know them all?"

Trickler talks in his closed-mouth, Alan Ladd fashion.

"No . . . I don't know all of them. A lot, but not all. Some people just wave because you're the police."

We ride up Pultney Street past the professors' well-kept houses. We watch a group of long-legged, pink-and-blue-sweater William

Smith coeds riding their ten-speeds across the intersection. They look at Trickler and myself with their big beautiful eyes, but I have a strong feeling they do not see either of us.

"They don't wave," said Trickler. "But I love coming up here . . . and staring at them. It's enough to make your mouth water. . . . There are some really good-looking girls on this campus. Sometimes I feel like I missed my generation," he says. "I guess these kids are having a ball, aren't they . . . free love and all?"

Trickler started as a factory worker out at Libby's. Like many of the police, he moved from the factory to the force, which is a great leap up in town social status. But the world of William Smith and Hobart, with all its advantages and seductions, lies just outside of his reach. His only contact with the colleges comes through busts or disturbances, such as the famed Tommy the Traveler riots in 1970.

We turn up St. Clair Street and more William Smith students walk by.

"They walk differently than the girls from the town," Trickler says.

I watch them through his eyes, and feel his yearning and perhaps a little of his bitterness. "You know," he says, "except for the danger . . . this job is exactly like what I did while *I* was in high school: ride around and wave at girls."

Notes While Walking the Beat with Bob Verdehan: Saturday Night

While working with Trickler, McGuigan, and the other officer, one name came up over and over again. The name was Verdehan. The younger officers' respect and admiration for Verdehan bordered on hero worship.

As Trickler tells me: "If you want to meet a tough old-fashioned cop, Verdehan is your man. He's been on the force for over twenty years, and he's seen it all."

I meet Verdehan at the station. Desk Sergeant Jabara is watching an old Cagney film, and Verdehan is showing some photographs to another officer, Jay Covert, known as the Hippie for his long blond hair and gentle manners. I had ridden with him the night before down Geneva's Butt End. While we stood waiting in the cold, he had confided to me that he planned to leave the force as soon as he could get his Elementary Education Degree. Now the two officers stand there chatting, a perfect study in contrast. Unlike Covert, Verdehan exudes the image of "the cop." Though he is no bigger than Covert, he "feels" bigger. He stands straight, wears his cap to one side of his head, and puts his huge rugged face close to yours when he wants to emphasize a point.

"Look . . . look," he says. "Here's some pictures of my vacation to Florida."

He sees me watching and calls me over.

"That's a beach," Verdehan says.

"Oh?" says Covert, smiling at me. "Is that a beach?"

Verdehan misses the joke. His big gnarled hands slide to the next picture. "That's the new modern airport they got there in Daytona," he says.

"Planes land there, I'll bet," says Covert.

Verdehan shuffles through some more pictures of trees and beaches. Then he comes to his "criminal pictures." He puts his big face close to mine and says: "See that. I'll bet you don't know what that is, do you?"

I look down at a very conventional hookah.

"No," I say.

"Jeepers," says Verdehan. "That is a bowl . . . they call it a bowl. It's what they smoke marijuana out of. I got this picture on a good bust I got a couple of months ago. Got two ounces."

Soon we are walking up and down Exchange Street. The bars are humming.

"I love this work," Verdehan says. "I give any guy a break. But if he takes advantage or tries to use force . . . forget it." Like all the other members of the Punch Squad, Verdehan is fond of telling stories about his most violent fights. He gets halfway into one (". . . so I get him in a chicken hook, and start pulling him down Exchange . . .") when the radio crackles.

"GD–10 to Portable-3."

Verdehan takes out his pocket radio, pulls up the antenna and answers the desk.

"Bob, get down to the old Temple Theater . . . quick, somebody just drove a car through the window, and there's a big mob out front."

We make it to the top of the alley and look down Exchange Street. Three blocks away there is a white car on the sidewalk, its hood stuck inside the Temple Theater. Shattered glass and pieces of wood lie all around it.

"Let's go," says Verdehan.

We start running again, down past the Paddock. A few town women with teased blond and brown hair come out of the Paddock and raise their glasses to Verdehan.

"Hurry . . . we're safe," one shouts. "Big Bob's here."

Verdehan doffs his cap, and we run across Castle Street to find Covert, Trickler, and Steve Pesarek (Verdehan's nephew, who had told me Verdehan was "like the Marines to me when I was a kid, which is probably why I joined the force") talking to the crowd.

"Anybody hurt?" Verdehan says.

"No," says Covert. "They grabbed the girl and took her up to the station. The car belongs to these guys."

Two black men about eighteen came toward us.

"We was jes in Moon's drinkin'," says the young one, "when this friend of ours comes in and says, 'Didn't I jes see you go by?' I said, 'No, we been in here.' 'Well, somebody has got your car then,' he said. We went outside and there it is . . . she's coming down Exchange

Street, and she is jes going round and round and round . . . and then wham . . . she takes off across the pavement, takes off this fire hydrant clean, and smashes right through the building."

I walk around to the driver's side of the car. The doors are bent into a V. Inside the Temple Theater are a couple of barber chairs. Sitting there next to the front fender of the car they look like some kind of junk sculpture.

Suddenly from behind me, Detective Simon is on the scene. He bounces around on the balls of his feet, snapping pictures with his Polaroid camera. The crowd circles around, pouring out of Cliff's and Moon's. Two girls, with ratty looking bleached-blond hair and shiny looking miniskirts revealing their fat white legs come forward out of the crowd.

One of them looks quite upset.

"Where did you guys take our friend, Patches?" she says. Simon doesn't answer. He keeps snapping pictures.

"I said where did you take her?" the girl says loudly.

Simon, who is noted for his hot temper, turns and tells the girl that her friend is in the station and to go away.

"You can't keep her there," the fat blond says.

Behind her a black man tries to pull her arm and calm her down.

"Let me go, Sugar Bear," she snarls. "I want Patches. These white mutherfuckers can't keep her in jail. She didn't do nothin'."

"Look," Simon says. "She's in the station, which is where you'll be if you don't keep your mouth shut."

"You can't scare me. I'm only asking a question," the girl says.

"Go home, or you'll be up in the station," Simon says.

"I can ask all the questions I want," says the girl. "You don't scare me."

"That's it," says Simon, his eyes popping out. "You're going up to the station. Let's go."

He drops the camera on the roof of the battered car and goes after her. She tries to pull away but he catches her and is dragging her toward the door.

"You white mutherfuckers," she screams. "You white assholes."

She hits Simon in the side of the head, and then digs her nails into his temple. Blood flows from his scalp. Trickler and Covert grab her from behind and struggle with her. People pop out of the tenement apartments above Demming's Hardware.

"You rat finks . . . we'll get you all," they scream from their windows. "Especially you down there taking notes."

Suddenly I feel like the police; what was only a routine investigation of a rather un-routine car wreck has become a possible riot situation. But who had caused the riot?

At the station, while the two girls screamed, "White mutherfuckers" at the police, I asked Simon if it had been really necessary to arrest the girl.

"Yes," he says, in his short-breathed Cagney manner. "She was harassing us. You let one harass you and you got a riot on your hands."

"Yes," I say, "but she was really only upset about her friend. I don't understand why you just didn't ignore her. She was just badmouthing you, showing off."

Simon doesn't answer me. He takes the two boys who claim to own the car into his small office for questioning.

Inside the desk room, the police are laughing it up. They seem happy to have been involved in the scene. Most of the concerned townspeople are filing out now, and order of a sort is once more restored. I look at Trickler and Verdehan and Covert, and they all smile at me.

"I told you," says Verdehan, sticking his big, handsome, brutal face close to mine. "There ain't nothing like this job. I wouldn't trade it for anything in the world. You got your outdoors, you're doing one hell of a public service and you got the action. I like that most of all. I love the action."

Postscript

I was happy when "The Yawn Patrol" came out in barely established *New Times* magazine. I was paid $1,500 for it, which, when you consider I was making $12,000 a year teaching, wasn't bad. The sad part of the whole deal, as far as I was concerned, though, was that very few people read *New Times*. I doubted anyone outside of my own little world would see it at all. But at least I had a "clip" to send to another magazine. Little did I know what would follow.

It started two days after the pub date. Though not one newsstand in Geneva sold *New Times*, somehow the Geneva police had the issue at once. How did I know? Because at the end of a typically freezing cold day, after teaching a course in Southern Novel, I walked from the classroom to the faculty parking lot where two of the cops I had written about, Jim Trickler and Ed McGuigan, were waiting for me.

And they didn't look happy.

"Hey, Robert," McGuigan said. "You are a real asshole."

I didn't say anything, but my stomach turned as I tried to look innocently puzzled.

"Yeah," Trickler said. "That remark you said I made about those rich girls' legs . . . that got me the last three days sleeping on the couch."

Now I felt sick. He was referring to his comment about how the rich girls walked like they had money and how he loved looking at them.

"How could you write that?" he said.

What could I say to him? They'd told me anything they said was fine to write about. They'd seen me taking notes in the back seat.

"Look," I said. "It was such a great line. It shows the class differences [my radical training was of some use after all!] between you and the people you serve. It delineates the line between men and women and. . . ."

"Bullshit," McGuigan said. "That's all bullshit."

"Yeah," Trickler said. "Tell that to my wife."

They glowered at me, and headed back to their patrol car.

"Well, you have a nice night, out at the lake all by yourself, Robert," Trickler said.

"What's that supposed to mean?"

They both smiled in a snarling, knowing way, and I felt real fear zapping through me.

And with good reason. For the next month I got strange phone calls in the middle of the night. When I picked up the phone, there was a very scary silence. I hung up, and lay there in the dark waiting for two cops to come bashing through my doors. I sent my girlfriend back to her dorm room for a while. It was just too creepy to think about her out there in the lake house with me.

I wondered if I should get a gun. I had dreams of myself getting blown away like Fred Hampton of the Black Panthers. Maybe I would become a Radical Martyr! Then Sol wouldn't dare call me a clown!

How could they be so goddamned vindictive? It was just a harmless little article. But, I had to admit, it was easy to see it their way too. They let one of the school professors come into their lives and he turns out to be exactly the kind of rat all townies thought he would be.

So, on top of feeling frightened, I felt guilty. I hadn't lied. I hadn't thought twice of writing what I wrote. But maybe I'd screwed up a guy's family life. These were small-town people, not used to publicity or complexity. Maybe his wife would never trust him again and it was my fault. I had come from a neighborhood in Baltimore with three cops in it, and if you crossed any of them like I had the Geneva cops you might find yourself, at the very least, beaten to a bloody pulp. Or at the bottom of Baltimore Harbor.

Christ, all for a magazine piece. This New Journalism thing was a lot trickier than I had imagined.

The days slipped by, and the phone calls stopped coming. Snow fell on the town and I saw the cops digging people out, helping drunks get home, and I felt lousy about what I'd written, but at least the excitement had died down.

Then a funny thing happened. That spring, Tom Wolfe was invited to the campus to speak. I was thrilled. My hero. Tom Wolfe!!!

I was determined to meet him, to hang out with him . . . and in fact, it couldn't have been easier. I threw a big party for him at my little cabin. It was a decently warm day and I had my buddies in the rock band White Trash come out and play. Tom was there dressed, of course, in his white suit. I showed him my novel, *Shedding Skin*, and told him about "The Yawn Patrol." He said he'd seen it and would read it. I was insane with happiness. Tom Wolfe would read my work! It seemed impossible. I told him about feeling guilty about what I'd written, and he smiled and said: "Look, you're new at this. And you will have those feelings. But you have to see this as your job, from now on. You have to take it as seriously as those cops take their job. If they're bothered about what you said, too bad. It's your job to report it. Once you leave here this will be what you do. And if you're any good as a reporter, you'll report the real stuff. So forget all about it. You did the right thing."

I was stunned by his tough, professional attitude. And I knew he was right. This was going to be what I did from now on. I was there to get a story, not to be the cop's friends. Trickler's line did show the tremendous gulf of class and desire that separated the cops from the wealthy girls at William Smith. I was right to include it.

Tom gave me his address and his phone number and told me to write him, and said that we would see one another in New York.

I drove him back to the airport in Rochester the next day and he told me all about Joseph Smith and the Mormons, and what northern New York had been like a hundred years ago. These were facts I should have known myself but had been too lazy, too superior, to find out.

Meeting him was the turning point in my life. I knew from then on that I would be a journalist for as long as I could.

As for the local cops, well, I was still uncomfortable when I saw them riding by me. But I figured it had all blown over and nothing more was going to happen.

The whole thing was history. I'd met my hero Tom Wolfe, and on top of that I had received good news. I heard from *New Times*. The editor-in-chief Jon Larsen loved the piece and promised me they would come up with a new assignment for me as soon as possible. I was deliriously happy. The existential clown was making money, getting published, and was heading for a whole new career. In New York!

Interestingly enough, many of the people who had sided with my wife in our breakup began to talk to me again. Proof that the old saw, "Everyone loves a winner," is all too true. But I didn't give a damn. I was leaving, and if I never saw any of them again it was okay with me.

I felt so good that I decided to splurge and treat myself to a good meal. I went out one night, had a steak at the Bellhurst Castle, the town's only good restaurant, and then headed down to Causey's bar, a student hangout. I liked Cosmo Fospero, the proprietor, and thought I'd just have a few Jack Daniels to celebrate my good fortune.

I showed up at the bar around eight, and quickly drank two Jack Daniels, then felt so good I had two more. I was fast getting bombed when the back door to Causey's private party room opened. I had never seen anyone come out of that room before, and I was so loaded that at first I didn't recognize them.

By the time I realized who was walking toward me it was already too late.

It was the two cops who hated me most, Jim Trickler and Ed McGuigan. They were dressed in their black leather jackets and they looked dead-bang serious.

"Well, well, if it isn't our old friend, Bobby Ward," Trickler said.

"Hi, guys," I said, trying not to panic.

"You're coming with us, Bob," McGuigan said.

"The hell I am," I said. "On what charge?"

They didn't say anything else, but grabbed me by the arms and pushed me toward the back room.

Oh, shit, I thought. This is it. This is where I get the beating of my life. I thought about running but my feet wouldn't move. I was drunk, disoriented, and terrified.

They threw me into the room, slammed the door behind me. Then they pushed me into the middle of a circle of people. I looked down at the floor, and waited for the first kick or punch.

But nothing happened. I looked up, expecting to find all the other cops I had written about, but instead I was standing in a circle of . . . middle-aged women.

Women? What the hell? Who were they?

Then they started in on me:

"You rotten bastard."

"You piece of shit."

"You made my daughter cry."

"You ought to be beaten until you die."

"Asshole!"

"Shithead!"

Their faces were twisted with hate, while behind them six Geneva cops roared with laughter.

Oh, God, I was in a circle of cop's wives. And they were having the time of their lives!

"What do you have to say for yourself?"

"I'm sorry," I said. "I really am."

"To hell with you!"

"Fuck you!"

And then it occurred to me. This was the perfect revenge for my piece. Just as I had humiliated them for living in a fantasy world while doing mundane little tasks, they had humiliated me by scaring me to death and then showing me that their humanity was larger than mine. They would make me think I was in a great noir '40s drama, the tragic, noble hero about to be beaten and thrown off the pier into Lake Seneca.

But that's not what happens to an existential clown.

He's not a beaten, brave hero, at all. He's no Philip Marlowe. Only, once again, a joker and a fool.

They pushed me out of the room a few minutes later and as I wandered out into the snowy night I heard them laughing so loud I thought the sound might knock down the dusty old bar.

I staggered to my car, and drove home. Humiliated, beaten and alone.

Two months later, I was walking by the school, heading for the English offices, when a cop car stopped next to me.

I looked over and saw Trickler and McGuigan.

"Bobby," Trickler said. "Get in the back."

"Oh, come on, you guys," I said. "Enough's enough."

"Don't make us come out and get you," McGuigan said.

I shook my head and got in. Jesus, I thought, maybe this is it—the day they really do kick my ass. I was so tired from all the harassment that I didn't much care.

We drove along, heading out 5 and 20, toward the edge of town. There were deep woods there, a good place to drop a dead body.

But we never made it to the tree-line. Instead we stopped at the Amy Joy Doughnut Shop, the very place where I'd first seen them.

Trickler parked and they turned around and looked at me. Then they held up the magazine.

"You were a fuck to write this," Trickler said.

"Yeah, I know," I said.

"But on the other hand," McGuigan said. "It's the best thing anyone ever wrote about cops. It's just . . . hilarious. We just got done rereading it this morning and we laughed so hard we were crying."

"You were?" I said, in disbelief.

"Yeah," McGuigan said. "All that stuff about the cat . . . that was just right on the money. Great work. Hey, what kind of doughnuts you want?"

"How about glazed?"

"Only one?" Trickler said. "C'mon. Have two and some coffee. On us. You're a hell of a writer. We just wanted you to know, no hard feelings. Okay?"

"Yeah," I said, smiling. "Right. Okay."

We all laughed and Trickler and I ran through the funniest parts of the story again, while McGuigan went in and got our doughnuts and coffee. We sat there for a half hour, then eating, drinking, and laughing. Then they drove me back to the school in time for my American Classics class, shook my hand, and wished me good luck.

I left them feeling good about my work and amazed how forgiving and kind they really both were. Great guys in a small town with a heart bigger than I'd ever given it credit for.

My very first piece and I'd had more drama in my life in the past six months than I had in the last six years.

The Passing of Baltimore's Block

No sooner had I survived the Yawn Patrol than I had to start on my first *Penthouse* piece, "The Passing of Baltimore's Block." Having been raised in a very moral and church-going family, I felt weird about writing for *Penthouse*. On top of that I was a recently converted good Lefty pro-feminist dude, though I scarcely acted like one. I talked to my agent, Georges Borchardt, about my reservations. How could I, a bona fide Left Wing Clown, write about strippers for a sleazy magazine like *Penthouse*? His attitude was interesting. He told me that if I wrote well I would be filling up the pages with intelligent commentary instead of another display of skin, so it was my duty to write for anyone who would pay me. He also said it would help me pay the rent when I left teaching and moved to New York, which I was planning to do at the end of the school year.

I found both these arguments persuasive.

Besides I did have a love/hate relationship with the sleaze of Baltimore's block. Though it was filled with clip joints, hookers, and bad men, it was also my last connection with the Old Baltimore of my youth. My grandfather, Robert Roland Ward, was a ship's captain out of old Pier I in Baltimore. Squat, built like a tank, Cap, as he was called by everyone, was as tough as the ships he guided down the Chesapeake. His last ship, the old *Port Welcome*, took people on pleasure cruises down the Chesapeake Bay to Betterton and Tolchester, fading beachfront destinations (broken down Ferris wheels, half-speed carousels, balloon shooting stalls, and throw-the-ring-over-the-bottle scams) on the Eastern Shore. I went with him as an ordinary seaman and wiper, perhaps the worst job aboard a ship. The wiper wiped oil on the engine so it didn't overheat and blow up. The engine room was about ten thousand degrees, or so it seemed, when you were down there for five or six hours.

In spite of the tedium of the job I loved "shipping out" with my granddad, even if it was only a day run down the bay. Sometimes I would sleep over on the ship and Cap would come down and pat me on the head, and say, "What a good boy!" I was very close to his wife, my grandmother, Grace, one of the finest people I've ever met. But I barely knew Cap at all. So these trips gave me a chance to get close to him, and to find out that he loved me, dearly, something the rough-hewn guy would never admit out loud. To tell the truth, I often wondered if Cap really even loved Grace. She was a teetotaler; he was a heavy drinker. She was a civil rights leader; Cap couldn't have cared less about any of that. He was away for months at a time when he was younger, running tankers all the way down the Eastern Seaboard and around the Gulf of Mexico. She was home with the kids: Robert, my dad, and her daughter, Ida Louise, who grew up to become a powerful woman in the department of Health, Education, and Welfare. Finally, she was a serious church woman, and I doubted if Cap believed in God at all.

My question concerning my grandparents' love for one another was answered one day when I was at a bar with my grandfather. We had just come off the ship after a week's work and received our pay in a white envelope from the paymaster, who sat in a battered white shack on the old, swaying dock. The crew of the *Port Welcome* then went across Pratt Street to blow their money at the Wishing Well, a tavern built there for just that purpose.

I had just turned eighteen, and my grandfather invited me to come along. I was shy, and not much of a drinker. But the idea of drinking with "real seamen," especially Cap, was too exciting to turn down.

The Wishing Well could only be described as a serious waterside dump. There was a bar, some crude tables, and battered chairs. But on a Saturday afternoon it was filled with seamen. Now every Tom, Dick, and Lawyer has a tattoo, but back then sailors got them on their adventures in foreign ports. The place was filled with guys who looked like they had come out of *Treasure Island*. Old salts with grizzled faces, missing half their teeth, guys with broken noses, and scarred throats from knife fights.

I bellied up to the bar (which had no stools) alongside Cap and we ordered boilermakers. Beer and a shot of whiskey. I watched as my granddad downed his in one toss and did the same. The whiskey burned and I had to turn away, and hit my chest to keep from coughing. Seconds later, another shot appeared in front of me. Cap put his big arm around me and said, "Well, ain't this a day!" I was exhausted from all the sun on the bay, and the engine work, and now the booze took its toll on me, pronto. I smiled and hugged him back. Then I noticed a new guy who had slipped in on Cap's other side.

"Hey, Rob," he said.

"Hey, Masters," Cap said. "Want you to meet my grandson, Bobby."

"Hey there, kid," Masters said. He was a big guy with a face like a lopsided football.

I nodded hello.

"How you doing, Cap?" Masters said.

"Good. Just got our pay. First time I been here for a while."

Masters laughed in a knowing way and looked at me.

"That's 'cause of your grandmother, kid," he said. "She tells Captain Rob to stop drinking, he stops."

I nodded and smiled but said nothing back. I felt disloyal saying anything negative about Grace, whom I loved more than anyone in the world.

My grandfather seemed to pick up on my discomfort. He turned to Masters and said:

"Now don't start badmouthing Grace, Masters. I won't have it."

Masters belted back another shot and looked a little dazed.

"Ah, Rob," he said. "Why do you defend that old bag?"

I literally froze at the bar. "Old bag"? This was Grace Ward he was talking about. I felt such a fury at his words that I could barely speak. Which was fine, because Cap spoke *for* me.

He turned to Masters and said: "Don't ever talk about my wife like that. You hear me? Never!"

But Masters was already belting back another whiskey and laughing. "C'mon, Rob. You gotta admit. That old broad has got your number."

"Hey," I said. "That's enough of that kind of talk."

"Hey, listen to the tough guy," Masters said. "Your grandmother is a mean old bag, boy. High time you knew it."

He looked as though he might want to continue his speech but he never got the chance. My grandfather punched him in the nose so hard that it looked like a squashed tomato. Blood flew all over Masters's shirt and he fell like an anchor to the barroom floor.

The whole bar became deathly still and people moved away, as though the two men were having an Old West gunfight.

"Don't tell Grace, Bobby," he said, as he reached down to help Masters up. "She hates it when I get into a brawl."

"Don't worry," I said. "You think he's all right?"

"Oh, yeah. He's always getting into fights. Tough guy too. That's why I hit him first. Anybody tries to bully you, always get the first blow in."

He half carried Masters to a table and sat him down in a chair. An old grizzled guy looked at him and laughed.

"That was quite a shot, Rob," he said.

My grandfather laughed and patted Masters gently on the head, like he was petting a dog.

"Let's get out of here," he said. "I know a better place."

We walked out onto Pratt Street. Across the cobblestones was our ship, the *Port Welcome*. Gulls dove to the rotten old pier, picking up some popcorn an old rummy had left for them. There was a bum panhandling just outside the Wishing Well door.

"Hey," he said. "I was once an officer and a gentleman, Cap."

"I know that," Cap said, and peeled off a twenty, and handed it to him.

"Gee that was a lot of money, Cap," I said.

"He was a good man before he got onto the booze. We went through a lot of scraps together."

We headed up to Baltimore Street, and all the strip joints. I was in shock. I had no idea my grandfather knew about any of this. But then it made perfect sense to me. He was a seaman, a drunk, and a man's man. I was really so incredibly innocent. My friends and I had gotten into a few scrapes but basically we were good kids.

My grandfather was another type of cat. Another kind of man. The kind you don't meet in polite middle-class society.

We walked down tawdry Baltimore Street, past neon lights. The Club Troc. Girls, Girls, Girls. Each club had a doorman who laid out his rap to get you inside. "See things here that you can see nowhere outside the Orient. C'mon in. Two for one on well drinks."

We finally came to the Gayety Theatre, Baltimore's oldest and finest burlesque house. The strippers there were once world famous.

Now burlesque, like the *Port Welcome*, was a fading business. People watched television, went to the movies. Live strip shows, in a theatre, with comics and an orchestra was something out of the '20s. Only a few of the old places were even operating anymore. There was constant talk in the papers of a moral crusade to tear the Gayety down.

There was a small bar in front of the theatre, the Gayety Bar, and my grandfather sat me down on a stool. Within seconds an older woman bartender named Ruby came up to us.

"Hi, Cap," she said. "Who's this youngster?"

"My grandson, Bobby," he said. "He's my mate now."

God, I was so thrilled to hear those words. *My mate.* Even writing them down now I feel a thrill inside, though all of this happened over forty years ago.

Soon we were drinking and laughing with all the local characters at the bar. There was a skinny guy who sold watches, and another big, hairy guy who sold ties. He had them inside his overcoat, which seemed about two sizes too large for him. They all obviously loved my grandfather, who became even more popular because he bought everyone there drinks.

I had another boilermaker, and looked hazily at the pictures of the girls inside.

I wondered if he knew any of the girls. It seemed likely, of course, but I still couldn't quite believe it. My grandfather had this whole other life away from the family. And now, for the first time, I got it. It was tawdry, cheap, and exciting as hell down here. We had a couple more drinks and then another shipmate named Sparky John wandered in. Sparky was a nomad. He worked on ships in the summer and in the winter went to Florida where he was a clown and a roustabout in rodeo shows. He was a big guy, with a bulbous nose with a scar running across it. He told how he'd gotten it saving a couple Dobermans that had were fighting in the water. When he tried to pull them back to safety, the dogs had panicked and clawed him across the nose. But he had saved the dogs. On board ship he was a mate, but his actual job was to dress like a clown and entertain the young passengers with his magic tricks. I loved him, like I loved everything in those days.

My grandfather bought us all more drinks. I could barely stand up.

Sparky started to tell us all a story about meeting Elvis Presley on the movie *Roustabout*. I was stunned. I didn't know mere mortals could even meet Elvis. I loved his records so much that he seemed like someone from another planet. I tried to be cool, but finally blurted out: "You actually know Elvis?"

"Sure," Sparky said. "He's a great kid too."

Elvis, a kid? That threw me too. I guess to Sparky, who was in his fifties, he was. To me though, Elvis was God.

We had a few more drinks, then my granddad smiled and said, "Well, Bobby, I gotta get home to Grace. You coming?"

"Why don't you stay around a while?" Sparky said. "If it's all right with you, Cap?"

My grandfather looked at him and shook his head. "Well, yeah. I guess so. But you take care of him. I don't want him getting sick."

Sparky looked at me and smiled. "Don't you worry. I got this covered."

My granddad looked at me and shook his head. "My big grandson. You take care now. And never say nothing about this to Grace."

"Don't worry, Cap," I said. We hugged one another then, and I could smell his chewing tobacco.

He walked out of the bar and down the street. His legs were bowed, seaman's legs, my dad called them. He looked a little like a silent movie clown. Chaplin . . . but with the build of Jimmy Cagney.

"Your granddad's a great man," Sparky said. "He gives an old mate a chance."

"Yeah," I said. "He is."

We had another drink and traded our histories, though my own was so skimpy that I barely knew what to say. Sparky had been an orphan, hitchhiked around the world by the time he was twenty, and become a circus clown, after being a dishwasher, a security guard, a farmer, a logger . . . the list went on forever.

He was like someone out of a Woody Guthrie song. He had been all over the world, didn't have a dime, and seemed a happy man.

After one more beer, he said: "You want to meet some of the girls?"

"Girls?" I said. I wasn't being coy. I didn't understand what he meant.

"Inside. The peelers?"

"Oh, the peelers?" I said. "Sure."

I knew peelers must mean strippers, but like him knowing Elvis, it just didn't seem possible. I had come to the Gayety with a fake ID and seen the women taking off their clothes before but there was a magical barrier between the stage and the audience. No one like me could know them.

I mean in a way they were unreal, like . . . like movie actresses.

It seemed impossible and yet, here we were, talking to someone at a side entrance and going backstage . . . and there they were, vaudeville clowns, and this fantastic stripper named Tempest Storm. She was cheap and overpainted and her red hair was too shellacked but she was also the most beautiful woman I had ever seen in my life. She smiled at me and said: "Hello, Bobby. Any friend of Sparky's is a friend of mine. Are you in college?"

"Uh-huh," I said, like a dead man. "Yeah . . . I go to Towson."

"That's great," she said. "Have you ever seen the show?"

"Uh, no," I said. I couldn't tell her the truth. I was ashamed that I had looked at her naked before. Even though that's what she did for a living. I felt a complete fool.

"Well, this should be fun for you. You boys can watch from the wings."

She batted her eyes at me, pressed my hands with hers, and went off to her dressing room.

Sparky and I walked to the wings, and peered out. The place was half empty.

A comedian was on the stage, doing a doctor and nurse bit with a blonde with huge boobs and the world's shortest nurse uniform. The jokes were terrible, but when they came off both of them seemed happy.

"Went over good," the comedian said.

He looked at me, and I nodded and smiled enthusiastically.

"Great," I said.

He pinched my cheek and waddled in his big shoes toward the back.

We stayed for a while more. Waiting for Tempest. The way it worked was that the older strippers came on first. Up close to them I could see their wrinkles and how much makeup they needed to appear young. On stage, they took a beating as they peeled away their clothes.

"Put it back on, baby!"

"Ugh. Don't make me look!"

But as each of them came off, they all smiled and kept a perky attitude. One of them said, "I killed them." She was lucky. Only one or two people had thrown candy boxes at her.

Another old stripper came on a few minutes later. She had her clothes half off, when she winced. Something had hit her, but I couldn't see what it was.

"What the fuck?" she said, as something else hit her.

Sparky pointed to the stage.

"Guys are shooting paper clips at her," Sparky said. "With rubber bands. Old trick."

"Man, that must hurt."

The girl winced again.

"Be right back," Sparky said. "You wait here."

"Uh-uh," I said. "You go, I go."

He shrugged and we took off around the outside of the curtain and soon found ourselves out in the audience.

There, in the middle of the theatre, were three tough-looking teenagers with Duck's Ass pompadours, long hair piled high, like black pasta. In New York they were known as gang members, or JDs for juvenile delinquents, but in Baltimore we called them "drapes." They wore slick, cheap-looking suits, and black shoes with three-inch Cuban heels. They were tough guys.

We watched as the oldest of the three lined up his rubber band, and shot a paper clip at the elderly stripper.

He hit her on the leg and she screamed and looked furiously out at the audience.

Sparky John moved with the quickness of a pulling guard. I followed behind him. I was scared but told myself I'd rather die than chicken out.

We came upon the three of them as they were getting out a new box of paper clips.

"Get out of here," Sparky said. "Now."

The tough boy stood up, and stared at him.

"Fuck you, scar nose," he said.

Sparky pushed him back down in his seat. Another boy stood up, and I pushed him back down. I could not believe I had done this.

The three boys looked at each other. They weren't afraid, and they weren't backing down.

"You shoot that woman again, and you are going to disappear, kid. I mean forever." Sparky said. He reached into his old, filthy overcoat, and showed the handle of a gun to the young hoodlums.

I felt my pulse racing but it was all over. The three seemed to lose all their confidence.

"We already paid for our tickets," one of them said.

"Leave now and I won't shoot you in the face," Sparky said.

The three of them got up and left in record time. They practically ran over one another trying to get out of the place.

Sparky and I sat down in their seats.

"Don't tell Cap about this, Bobby," he said. "He'd fire me for sure."

"Don't worry," I said. "I'm not going to say a thing. That gun? Is it loaded?"

"Hell yes," Sparky said. He pulled it out and aimed it at me. Then shot me in the head with a stream of water.

"Jesus," I said.

"Every clown needs a water pistol," he said.

Then we both cracked up and watched Tempest Storm take off her clothes.

"Hey, Ward-o, this is Mike. Let's go down the Block tonight, whatya say? They got Chili Peppers, yah know, didju see her last time? She gets up onna stage, cups her hands over her breasts and says, in this incredibly sexy voice, 'Heeeeey Beeeeeg Boyyyyys, cooooome up here, with Chiliiiiii, nooooo?' She drives you outta' your mind. Look, my folks are comin', I'll meet you and Spencer down at Arundel at nine."

And then comes the lying, and the cajoling, and the champion riffing. "Ah, Mom, I gotta go to the library for a while. Yeah, I gotta go study up on the . . . ah . . . Crimean War. It's real interesting. Lotta people got massacred. See you later." Then I'm off to meet Mike and Spence who will take us in his '56 two-tone Willy's down to the Northwood Liquors, where we will pay off Jim, the shopping-cart collector, two dollars to buy us a pint of Sloe Gin. Ah, so silky smooth, gives you quite a buzz, friends. Just right for the occasion, for tonight. Soon we were tooling down Loch Raven Boulevard past the veterans' hospital, and I thought of them in there all coughing and hacking away with the bad TB, and I felt sorry that they couldn't be with us. Couldn't drive with us down to Baltimore Street, our city's two-block strip of sin. Ah, the Block, with its Club Oasis, and Club Troc ($1.75 a beer), and that unspeakable armpit, the Miami Club ("Live Rats on Stage"). And then there's our true Shangri-la, the ancient Gayety Burlesque House, with its golden pillars and rococo stage with the plaster nymphs peering out of the eaves. And on that stage, in that green-blue-indigo spotlight, were our saints of the Block: Ms. Chili Peppers, Ms. Candy Barr ("A Little Piece of Southern Hospitality"), and Ms. Virginia Bell ("and her Fab 44s"). Oh, we came as a gang, but we went away like a congregation who had seen the light. And you might say it was chauvinism, and you might yell it was one-dimensional, but what a dimension. For this was the real '50s, that era we worship as secure and safe and fun. But for those of us approaching or waving good-bye to thirty, the '50s was, above all, the Age of Horniness. Legs you could not see, but only imagine. Breasts that pushed out from V-necks, huge breasts of Pam Hooper and Diane Conway, eighth-grade Wonder-women. And necks and backs and piles of stiff starched hair piled on the head in beehives. And what did they keep in those hollow cones, what instruments of delicious torture?

And the questions, the endless questions:

"Didja hear about Mole? He got tit offa Sandy Franklin."

"No, I don't believe it."

"No, he did. He's straight about it. He coulda maybe scored a home run, but her old man came in."

And, Dear Readers, we were not, let me emphasize, we were not those '50s Innocents, with the pathetic bebop lingo. Oh, we spoke that scan every once in a while, but there was always the parody. The self-parody, which itself was full of hope, and full of worship for the female form. Tit, for God's sake, impossible, unreachable, invisible. And Ass, and the Other, which you didn't even think about. Oh, sure, you were a tough dude, with your pink jacket with "Four Aces" stitched on the back, and you were ready to support the Greeks against the Remington Avenue Drapes—but THEY were still out there, those perfect girls, like "Diana" by Paul Anka, and the "Queen of the Hop," who turned away when you came near, as if you smelled strange. And we scowling mean-assed kids who rode around Loch Raven Reservoir mooning the necking couples . . . we could not be released.

And so we went instead to the Block, to see our fallen angels. These women, these strippers, these exotic dancers, were, to us pim-ply, mumbling, and pathetic youths, the real girlfriends, saints, and artists of our world. And it was a fine art, friends. Ask the man who came to the blue light of the Gayety, a *Baltimore News Post* ("IKE SAYS NO TO KOREAN DEMANDS") rising, rising mysteriously off of his lap. And ask Jack D., the toughest of the Greeks, whose chiseled features melted, widened, and spread with joy at the sight of Candy Barr's long cowboy-booted legs. And ask Michael Spencer, who cursed and hooted when we had to wait for the dead-eyed rummy comics to finish their bits:

"Don't yell at me, boys. Are you wif or agin me?"

"You're as funny as a fart inna space suit."

Which is no way to act around Billy "Cheese 'n Crackers" Williams, who is doing his damnedest to make us howl.

But we were not amused. We were waiting for the royal entertainment, Blaze Starr bustling out on stage, with that apple-red hair and those huge, buoyant breasts. We wanted Chili Peppers who came on, and lay on her red bench, and lifted her one black-meshed leg to the spotlight, and began to tickle that same leg with a peacock feather, and then let that feather work its way ever so slowly to the dark V in between those perfect thighs, and then slowly took off those hose, and worked that feather around and around in there, and let out with those little ecstatic apostrophes to nature, love, and sex, well, let me tell you, folks, we *believed* in the Act. . . . This wasn't any cheapo strip routine . . . this wasn't any top-heavy Irma the Body bouncing her jugs at the boys in the front row, this here was class . . . and the moment of revelation, the revelation of the mystery of sex and the essence and the torture of major teenage lust!

The idea, friends, was Adventure and Romance. The reality was my grandfather, Captain Robert Ward, at seventy-four the oldest sea captain in the Baltimore harbor. He managed to get Michael and me jobs as ordinary wipers and deckhands on a broken-down old tourist boat named the *Port Welcome*. This was not *Trader Horn*, friends, nor the *Queen Mary*. This tub's route consisted of a leisurely, not to say dull, cruise down the Chesapeake Bay, with stops at Tolchester, Maryland, a seaport distinguished mainly by its stinging sea nettles, and Betterton Beach, which featured a clapboard fortress called the Hotel Betterton—a construction that leaned at a sixty-degree angle over the lapping waves.

So it was not the Arabian Nights, but it was romantic all the same. Sparky, the ship's clown and alcoholic *extraordinaire*, kept us alive and excited with his tales of loose women and card games in the Virgin Islands. A huge, powerful man with kinky black hair and a bulbous Karl Malden nose distinguished by a long scar that crossed the veiny bridge and ended at his short mustache, Sparky became our Long John Silver, our Wallace Beery, our newest Brother in the ongoing struggle against our own middle-class roots. We loved him with the desperation of the young.

He loved us in return, and took us to every club on the Block, where we were now accepted as regulars. He introduced us to Tempest Storm, a red-haired beauty who, we were told, was involved with the Long family of Louisiana. He shared his wine with the paraplegic Arky the Bagman, who rolled up and down the Block on a platform screaming *Ahhhhhh Ahhhhhh*, his blue eyes rolling around helplessly in his head. He took us down by the docks, where we sat and drank Jim Beam, and he told us of how he had been in Florida on location with Elvis Presley, shooting one of the Great E's horrible movies. On those mornings when he wasn't totally sick (and they became fewer and fewer), he woke us up and dragged us on deck to see the sun. We were embarrassed by his romanticism and his sentimentality, but his courage and generosity won us over. I remember the night we sat in the Gayety watching Candy Barr, and Sparky turned us on to some hash and told us about his nose scar. Two Dobermans had been fighting on the beach at Bermuda, and their scrap had sent them out into the water. Soon they were out too deep, in danger of drowning. Sparky dived in, fully clothed, and tried to separate them. For his efforts, the panic-stricken dogs had both turned on him and nearly bitten and clawed him to death.

"But I saved those bastards," he said.

And we believed him. Like Blaze and like Chili, we believed in his Act, and we were happy to have been able to bring some species of love into his rough and troubled life. One of the last nights Michael and I ever saw him (the summer was ending and he was going off to Florida to make the carny circuit) he took us to the Two O'Clock Club, which was now owned by Blaze Starr. Before we realized what was happening, we were sitting at the back bar with Blaze herself. Sparky was telling her about two sailors who had robbed and beaten another member of the *Port Welcome*'s crew, an old sailor named Gene, who was famous on board ship for being able to hand-roll his cigarettes faster than anyone else.

"They try to rob me all the time, honey," Blaze said in a hoarse voice that sent shivers up my back, "but I do just like you, Roy, I kick their asses." Then she gave a deep rich laugh, and Michael began to shake his head.

"She's wonderful," he said. "She's like a cross between Lucille Ball and Mae West."

"And better than either of them," I said, patting my friend on the back.

"Hey, you two," Sparky said, "I'm outta cash. How about buying a round of drinks?"

"They're on me," said Blaze. She smiled at us and nodded her head.

"Thank you," we said, feeling small and intimidated, but very good.

"It's nothing," she said. "I treat my friends good, honey."

In June 1973, a young man, fresh out of his second marriage and deep within the dream world of his own miseries, his new novel, and his newly freed angst-terror plans, made the trek from upper New York State, down superhighway 81, past the mountains and steel towns in Pennsylvania, finally stopping at the old shingled house on Woodbourne Avenue in Baltimore, Maryland.

On my second day back in my old city, I spoke with the current mayor, Donald J. Schaeffer, and the commissioner of Housing and Community Development, Robert Embry. Both of them were justly proud of the plans for Baltimore, and both of them sounded a bit amused, and at the same time concerned, about what would happen to the Block, which would, if it stayed where it is, be right in the middle of the new progressive downtown.

"We don't want to tear it down," said the mayor, "if it were only located someplace else. You know, if the Block owners could get together, and maybe agree on where they would like to go."

Embry, a short, stocky man, said the same thing:

"We don't want to get rid of the Block. Hell, it's an attraction. But it's going to seem a little odd sitting there next to the new district police station."

Yes, I thought, that would be more than a little odd. But I kind of liked the idea that in the middle of all that beauty (stainless-steel variety; the new central police station has golden one-way windows, architect: Franz Kafka) and progress and security would be the little old ugly rundown funky con artist, whore-loving, exotic-dancing Block. A constant reminder of what we were all about. Like the newspaper article I had seen in the *Baltimore Sun* just the day before, "Father Stabs Son to Death over Crab Cake." When asked how he could do such a thing the man had replied, "Well, there was only one left, and I was damned hungry." Oh, yeah . . . the Block in the midst of Eden. It was an idea worth considering. . . .

And so . . . so . . . they are going to demolish the Block. In another year or two there will be no tawdry strip houses, no strippers. And what's more, when I am in my right mind (and we must be in our right minds sometimes, friends), I suppose it's inevitable. Who needs it anymore? Who is willing to . . . ah . . . suspend the disbelief? I mean you can go to Fells Point and get that college nooky baby, and there ain't no teasing going down. But I still have this thing, see. I still believe in the Block. Or do I just believe in my own past, or want to believe in my own past? These things become difficult, they sorely do. And so, the next night, I found myself sitting once again with Ms. Blaze Starr in her Two O'Clock Club, across the street from the old Gayety, which burned down in '71.

"For the insurance," says Ms. Starr. "They got a *lot* of insurance out of that, honey."

I smile and drink my Scotch and look around the Two O'Clock. It is a class place, black leather everywhere, and a huge horseshoe bar with the stage and the runway in the center. Right now the girls are starting to come in, and Blaze tells me to talk to them while she takes care of her finances.

"You know," she says, "I'm one tough businesswoman, honey. I'll be the last to go on the Block. And when they start closing the other places, I'll triple my profits. Not that I wish the other owners any trouble, you understand. They're my friends, but, honey . . . well. . . ."

She gives that smile. Oh, Mae West, forget it. In fact, oh, Virgin Mary, and Saint Teresa of the Roses, you can bag it, too. Blaze, Sister Blaze, is the main woman.

Next I talked to Miss Exotica 1973, whose Christian name is Ms. Terri Lawrence, and she comes from Highlandtown.

"Yeah," she says, nervously working her hands over her curlers and chewing some gum, "I was working on the day shift at Procter and Gamble, you know, all that assembly-line work. The most boring job in the world, honey. And my friend Viki, she's a dancer. Well, she says, come down here and try to be an exotic dancer. And I said I couldn't. I mean *strip* in front of a bunch of men? But I saw what kind of money they were making, and I tried it . . . the first night, I almost died. Some guys were drunk and yelling, and I had heard about what happened to Candy Sweet the day before. Some guy came out of the crowd and started to strangle her. But it was all right . . . it went over, in fact, a lot of guys really liked me . . . they cheered me . . . you know. . . ."

I knew. At least I think I knew. I knew what it was like in old row house Highlandtown, in those drab, endlessly dull summer nights. The only diversion was the Walt Disney flick or the bingo game. And I felt something new about these women, something beyond the romance of my youth, or my later super-political Brothers-and-Sisters-All consciousness. I now felt that what they were doing was, in its small way, heroic. They had opted for self-expression, for recognition, which most of us only dream about. They were willing to risk being laughed at, hooted at, even strangled rather than to go back on the assembly line.

A moment later, I was talking to Candy Sweet herself, a thin dark-haired girl of about twenty-six, with a rather pronounced overbite. She was shy and nervous, and like Terri Lawrence, played with her split ends while we chatted.

"I'm from Remington Avenue," she said.

I was shocked and delighted. Our old enemies the Remington Avenue gang was without doubt the most feared of any gang in Northeast Baltimore. Behind the Marine Hospital and plush Johns Hopkins University were the old frame houses. The families came from West Virginia, and the deep South. They arrived in Baltimore with few skills, and tried to dig out a living. Everyone I had known from that area, except one boy who got a scholarship to the University of Maryland, had ended up on junk, on booze, or in jail. Or they were dead.

"I love Blaze," said Candy Sweet. "She keeps the bums and the hustlers out of here. She don't make us do nothing we don't want to do."

"Like what?"

"Oh . . . like the other bars . . . they aren't as nice. They don't have any class, you know . . . like a girl will have to give a guy head in a back room if he buys her champagne . . . or jerk him off under a table. We don't have to do that here."

Now, in spite of all my worldly experience, I felt a bit shocked. Saint Chili giving head in the back room. Oh, no, sir. Her appeal, after all, was that she was red-hot sensual, but also ice-cold unreachable. Myth. Perfection. Platonic sex. Head jobs in the back room? Ugh.

Candy left to get dressed, and Blaze returned.

"They treating you good, honey?" she said, patting me on the leg.

"Yes," I said, "everyone's been very helpful."

"Well, I want them to be that way. Mr. Goodman—that's Sol, honey, he was my agent when I was touring—he taught me how to get along, how to save my money. Next year, if they start tearing down the Block, and I know they will, honey, seven clubs are going to get their eviction notices this year. . . . Well, I plan on moving to Glen Burnie and opening Blaze Starr's Country Cooking. I wanted to move this year, but they were afraid down there. I told them I didn't plan on moving the *club* there, but they were nervous. I think they thought I was going to have topless chickens or something, so they kept me out. But I told them, honey, Blaze'll be back . . . you hear me? I come a long way from Pole Creek, West Virginia, and I got a long way more to go."

"How did you start dancing?"

"I started when a date took me to Washington. I was a waitress at the Mayflower Doughnut Shop for thirty dollars a week. Then I met Mr. Goodman, and soon I was making . . . well, a whole lot more than that. I was free."

There it was. Freedom. None of us had thought much about that before. They danced and stripped because it gave them a kind of freedom they couldn't find in their straight lives. I took a look around. Women behind the bar (Blaze's sisters, I found out), women as dancers, a woman emcee. The Two O'Clock Club was liberated in the classic Marxist sense of the term. Women owned and ran the works.

"You know, honey," Blaze said, "I love what I do. I think all the girls who work here really love it. This isn't a porno movie . . . this is burlesque . . . I mean, it's a very personal thing, dancing. Take my act. I don't do a regular strip, nothing dirty in it . . . I do a comic strip. I've got a whole act."

"I see," I said.

And I did see, for I had caught her act a couple of times. It was very funky, very funny burlesque. She came on wearing a gown, and then lay down on a red chaise longue and sprinkled powder all over herself. I remembered her promenading up the runway, dropping her feathered boa with the insouciance of a queen, parting some sailor's hair with her breasts. It was all done with consummate style and good humor: It was entertaining, and it told us something about Ms. Blaze Starr. About her courage, her ability to survive, and her comic vision of sex. Porno movies had nothing to say to any of us except that sex could be exhausting, and as dull as accounting.

"Now here's someone I really want you to meet," she said. "My co-feature, and don't you think she'd really be nice for the center spread in *Penthouse*? Miss Sandy Shores, the baby doll of burlesque."

I turned, and I'm sure my mouth dropped open a bit. In front of me was the most sensational-looking woman in the club. Black hair, red hot pants, and long, perfect legs. Oh Chili, oh Virginia Bell, I'm sorry to forsake you, but. . . .

"Hellllo there," she said, in perfect stripper's hoarse-throated wonder. "Do you have any questions you'd like to ask me?"

Oh, many, many, I thought, gnashing my teeth. Michael, you should not have died.

I asked Sandy and Blaze what they thought of women's liberation.

Sandy Shores said, "Sure, I want equal opportunity in jobs. I tried to get an apartment in a high-rise downtown because it was closer to work, but they wouldn't give me one. Not because I was a woman, but because I was a dancer. But, as for acting and dressing like men, well, what can I tell you, I'm a lady."

Blaze handed me a copy of a booklet called *Blaze's Booby Book*, which features photos of her and two original country and western songs, and said, "Well, honey, if they really knew it, women have always been free. Nobody ever stopped me. I just used what I had and went out and did all right."

"Yes," I said, "but what about the charges that what you and Sandy are doing is somehow demeaning to women, makes them look like sex objects?"

"Look, honey," Blaze said, "These are mine."

She put both her hands over her breasts.

"I do what I want with these," she said. "And I used them to free myself."

I considered the subject closed.

Blaze went off to take care of her business again, and I chatted with Sandy Shores (that is, when I was able to speak properly—I still get very nervous in the presence of beauty, sex, and passion). She wanted to be an actress, she wanted to appear in *Penthouse*, she wondered if I could take her home.

"What?" I said.

("Heeeeey Beeeeeg Boooooy, you wan come up weeeeeth Chili?")

"Would you like to take me home tonight?"

"Yes," I said, "that would be nice."

"I hope you like my act," she said, lifting her perfect leg and crossing it, rubbing the stockings together.

"I'm sure I will," I said.

"I've got to go backstage."

"Yes," I said.

And so I had another drink, and another, and watched Miss Exotica 1973, Terri Lawrence, go through her act. And as I watched, what

Blaze had told me began to make more sense. I thought of Terri in Highlandtown, thought of that slow, repressive life-on-the-line at Procter and Gamble, and I saw all her hurt and anger come out when she moved slowly, sullenly through the dance. Her mouth was curled down, partially in submission and partially in real defiance. And when she went to the floor and spread her legs, it was slow, powerful, and commanding, and yet painfully self-conscious. She was wounded, this big strong woman, but she was also in the process of healing herself. I watched her with a new fascination, with the fascination one has when one finally learns about jazz or painting.

I began to understand that there was real intelligence of the most personal kind behind what these women were doing. The strip, like the blues, tells us something about the dangers and fears of life.

Knowing that, I understood more when Sandy came on. She came whirling out of the blue lights, twirling her feathered boa, and wearing a long see-through blue negligee. I thought of what she had mentioned to me about her life, her wealthy Jewish parents in Pikesville, her dropping out of college. She was dancing and twirling about, doing splits and leaps: She was the Jewish Princess gone to the outlaw world, she was an actress who had chosen to live on the edge. Her dancing celebrated the facts of her existence, her youth, her beauty, and her attempts to be free of the suburban dredges. She whirled, teased, laughed, and grew sullen. She was young and turned on to her own body, turned on to her body in the midst of her own drama; a drama that redefined the body and the self, made her transcend her personality and her past, and that finally transcended even sex itself—for sex is always defined in relation to your partner, but the body in a strip is defined only by the extent and the ability of the dancer's fantasy life. Of course, that fantasy life has itself been shaped by events, people, money, and family. But the dancer has the ability and the freedom to determine how these obsessions will be patterned and so the exotic dance, the striptease, if you will, is, in the hands of the ladies of Baltimore Street, the most personal of mediums.

Or maybe the fuck not. Did I mention I am a philosophical drunk?

I watched, very happy for her happiness, as she whirled once again in front of me.

Then she leaned over the bar, did a split, caught my eye, and stuck out her tongue in a lewd, ancient, sexuality that stirred me, turned me on.

I laughed and held up my drink to her, to Terri Lawrence, to Blaze Starr, and to the whole grand dying Block itself—the home of the saints I had worshipped as a child, revered romantically as an adolescent, and now loved again, as any man loves sex, art, the body, and the courage to try to extend the tightly bound limits of our short, blunt lives.

Postscript

Rereading this piece I'm struck with how romantic it is. How sentimental. As you can see, I was still influenced (and rebelling against) my recent trip down Revolutionary Road, and wanted to see something more in stripteases and barroom girls than mere sleaze. I debated whether to include this piece. It's so full of Left-Wing academic jive, but what the hell . . . I kept it in because it catches some of the real spirit of my old hometown before it was taken over by the slick-assed publicity boys. The Gayety is still around but is no longer a burlesque house. Just another Hustler Club, which is ironic, for later on in this book you'll meet none other than Larry Flynt.

In any case, it was an early piece and I was anxious to prove that I wasn't wasting my time writing about strippers. There was something of the Good Boy in me that I didn't want to violate. What would my church-loving grandmother think of what I was doing? (Even though she was deceased.)

I felt funny about writing about these people, slightly guilty, and I was anxious to make them seem better than they were.

On the other hand, I still believe what I wrote may be true. For a person working in a soap factory, stripping is a way of gaining freedom. Even if feminist middle-class women might find it just another form of female slavery.

An energetic piece anyway, and I did get to go out with Miss Sandy Shores. We had a nice couple of days and nights together and then one night, while we were sleeping together she said I'd have to leave early that night.

"Why is that?" I said.

"Because my girlfriend is coming home, baby. And the last guy she caught me with got a stab wound in his back."

I kissed her on the head and got out of there half dressed. I drove away from her and the Block and haven't been back since.

The Mount Kisco Sting

*How the good guys dreamed
they won (and finally did)*

Imagine this: a 1940s movie, directed by Frank Capra, starring Jimmy Stewart, Spencer Tracy, Edward Arnold, and Akim Tamiroff. The plot involves an international gang of gunrunners who descend on a sleepy town called Mount Kisco. This gang happens to run into a guy named Vinnie, whom they assume to be a Mafioso. Vinnie tells the gang he has a friend named Tony. Vinnie hints that if the gun boys think he's a hard case, they ought to meet Mr. Big himself, Tony Stagg. The gunrunners are an oily crew who have sold illegal arms to the Arabs, the Israelis, the Greeks, the Serbs, and the Kurds. . . . Soon the arms merchants are meeting regularly with Big Tony, Vinnie, and other "mobsters" at a Mount Kisco restaurant. A deal is arranged, which includes the U.S. State Department, Guatemala, the military commander of El Salvador, and thirty million smackolas worth of illegal rods. The day for the big transaction is set. The gunrunners are drooling. . . . But lo and behold, the "mob" they met, the mob that seemed to control Mount Kisco, is not a mob at all! What the baddies are up against is a clever assemblage of local yokel police, a couple of feds, and the brilliant acting of some guys who aren't even police, but just wanted to help out. The town is completely ordinary.

The slickers from the big cities and south of the border have been hoodwinked by good old American Small Town Togetherness and Know-How. . . . Sound ridiculous? Don't we know that nobody helps the police? That small suburban towns are mere pits of alienation, alcoholism, and adultery? Too corny—even for Frank Capra?

The trouble is, the above is no fantasy. What we have here is a true tale, which took place in March 1976, in Mount Kisco, New York, an ethnic suburb of Manhattan.

Mount Kisco locals were led by an undercover cop buff named Tony Stagg. Stagg is a huge, dirigible-shaped man in his forties whose consciousness has been fried by gangster movies and TV crime series. With police chief William J. Nelligan and U.S. Attorney Robert Fiske, Stagg was primarily responsible for the convictions of seven defendants in one of the biggest illegal arms sale cases in U.S. history. He completely conned the arms merchants, a weird assemblage of tatty businessmen, crazed Latins, and terminal bumblers whose own imaginations were as media-maimed as his own, into believing he was a kingpin Mafia don who was going to introduce them to big-time American crime.

Tony "Big Bear" Stagg sticks his derringer into his neat little holster, which is in one of his cowboy boots. It's tough getting down there below his stomach, which has ballooned up even larger of late, and the sweat runs off his shiny forehead. Still, he manages gracefully. Like Sydney Greenstreet's, his bulk is imperial, swaying regally as he cruises a room, pops his gum, swivels his head, checking out the turf. The gun clips in with an authoritative snap that makes Tony smile. His smile is cockeyed, ambivalent, warm yet utterly distant; his teeth and eyes shine promises at once charming and dangerous.

"Hey," says Tony, "you like these boots? I got these boots for the Bicentennial, baby. You see, 1776. Nice, huh?"

Nice indeed. Blue leather and white stars and the American Eagle looking up at you like Marlon Brando in *Julius Caesar.* Tony is wearing a western jacket and safari hat. His Volkswagen features giant eagles on the front framed by huge white numbers against a blue backdrop: 1776–1976.

"This is where it all went down," Stagg says, cruising through Mount Kisco with a proprietary air. "You know what dey say when they talk about Mount Kisco? They say, 'Hey, nothing ever happens here.' But it did, you see. It did happen. Capice?"

Next to us, a red-faced kid with blond hair and an L.L. Bean jacket is straddling a BMW. He looks like he is in no hurry, may remain at the light indefinitely.

Tony looks him over.

"Stoned. Stoned out of his mind. I can spot 'em, baby. If I was still around we'd have his ass in the can in a month. We done a lot of cases, baby. They say nothing ever happens here. Yeah, right."

Listening to Tony, one has an uneasy sense of déjà vu. *Baretta*, *Kojak*, *The French Connection.* He has invented himself, assumed a crazy quilt of All-American tube gestures, voice inflections, habits. He admits it: "That's it, man. I study those shows. That's how I got to be the kind of cop I am. It's how I put it over on those gun dudes."

Somehow, this all seems right. Mount Kisco is a familiar place, and after a bit, it makes you feel uneasy, too. Republican. Population 9,000. Home of such talk-show entities as Arlene Francis and Robert Goulet. The perfect place to retire. . . .

Stagg landed in Mount Kisco after a period of wandering. He'd flunked as a police candidate (the great disappointment of his life), made a half-hearted attempt at the construction business, and finally became a bodyguard to various pop singers as a means of compensating for his lost police career. One of them, Rudy Isley of the Isley Brothers, owned a club in Mount Kisco. Tony had a look at the town, liked all the Italian-Americans he saw, and settled in. . . .

Soon he'd made himself the premier "character" in town, had befriended the local cops and was helping them with small busts, dope entrapments, etc. He could fulfill his fantasy world, one that craved action, adventure, danger, and at the same time be on the right side of the law.

"You know the Bear," Stagg says, pulling into the Northern Westchester Health Club, "the Bear hates crime. He hates dope. He hates punks with guns. Me, I'm an American. A government man all the way."

Which, in some ways, makes Tony the perfect citizen of Mount Kisco, which is itself a victim of TV ennui. Stagg seems to be a man who lives by myth, by code, in a theater of the self that inexorably draws people in. Gunrunners, cops, and bored businessmen were all too "American" to resist.

The Beginning of the Case

"I was a flashy dresser and my last name was Coppola," Vinnie Coppola, one of Tony's prime actors in the Mount Kisco Sting, says. "A lot of people thought I was related to the Mafia don in New York, 'Trigger' Mike Coppola. I never denied it, though I never said I was either. But occasionally people would mention something about my 'Family,' and I'd just nod, or play along with them. Jim Grey was convinced I was a Mafia hood. I didn't discourage him."

Jim Grey was himself a frustrated salesman. A small man, bored with his dull job, he had fallen into a relationship with Bob Michaelson, of Wittington Investments, Ltd. Michaelson, a heavy man with connections in the South American coffee and hemp trades, a successful businessman who was dying to do something illicit and glamorous, one day told Jim Grey he had a list of guns that he wanted to get into the "right hands." Grey took a look at the list, and his brain reeled. This was it. Big Time. Gunsville. Hoodland. *Mean Streets. Serpico.*

Excited as the Road Runner, Grey called Vinnie Coppola, whom he'd known and admired since high school, and told him he had something that might interest the Family, if Vinnie knew what he meant. Hanging up, Grey felt terrific. Things were moving.

Vinnie met Grey at Kennedy Airport, and received a list from him. Oh, Foreign Intrigue! Coppola put on his dark glasses to look at the list. It was hard to believe. The ultimate Movie Scenario Dream List. Uzi Machine Gun, M-26, IA hand grenade, 9 mm Sten Gun, bazooka (bazookas in Mount Kisco! Crazed killers hitting the Dairy Queen, ski masks on: "Give it to us now, Red! Three triple snow cones with sprinkles or we'll blow your ass off! . . ."), M-79 grenade launchers, .38 caliber pistols. Rockets, tanks, tanks for Chrissake—what are we gonna do—blast the Weight Watchers? Coppola was so excited he felt like hijacking a 747. . . .

Cut to Mount Kisco. Tony Big Bear is handling the list. He turns it over and over. This is weird shit . . . this ain't Johnny-Too-Late-for-the-Revolution popping reds and speed and trying to get off on Black Sabbath at Stepinac High School. This ain't the track coach who decides to dynamite his wife's Tupperware party so he can run free over the hurdles of life . . . this here is Trouble. . . . Across the deck is Chief Nelligan, who looks like George C. Scott. The jutting jaw, the lines on the face from too many years of meeting his private friend, Johnnie Walker, but now Nelligan is caught up, too . . . not so much as the others, for he has savvy, but he can feel the Big Wave, the Big Case fever. . . . Should they do it as they had before, using the Organized Crime routine? Should they risk it all by themselves, keep the case away from the fucking FBI who always try to horn in and grab all the credit? . . .

"So what we do," Chief Nelligan says, fingering the sign on his desk that says THE BUCK STOPS HERE, "we get in the ATF [Alcohol, Tobacco and Firearms, a small, easy-to-handle federal bureau], get Joe Kelly, who is a good man, works well with Tony, then we set up the scam. . . . Tony is the kingpin; Bobby Cercena [a Mount Kisco detective] plays his adopted brother; Joe Kelly plays a gun expert recently brought into The Family." The other Mount Kisco cops, men like Ralph Hyatt, Big Jerry, and the only black on the force, Duke McKenzie, would play supporting roles. The invisible figure is Poppa, Tony's old man, who lived in Vegas.

"The reason for Poppa," says Tony now, "was if we needed a time lag. We got to check with Poppa first. That gave us a day to figure out strategy."

Of course, the ruse wouldn't work with just the cops. If the gun people really were big time, they would have to see palpable evidence of Tony's power. . . . They would have to see snapped fingers and doors opening. They would have to see big shiny limos that moved through the frosty air like mechanical panthers, underlings ready to pounce on the small-time dude who failed to show Tony "respect." In short, if this episode of hometown *Baretta* was to get the right ratings with the crooks, then there would have to be a real set. To do this, the townspeople, the people who owned and controlled Mount Kisco, would be crucial.

Nelligan never questioned *why* the gunrunners thought they could unload heavy artillery on the Mount Kisco branch of the mob. Criminals, in his experience, were crazy.

So Tony fell by the local Caddy dealer, Martabano Motors, grabbed Marty Martabano and said, "Hey, Marty, you done us a little favor before, lending us the cars when we needed them to impress that asshole who had the dope. Well, we need a couple of limos again." And, because things were a little slow, Marty was only too happy to get in on the action.

So was Frank D'Allura, owner of the Northern Westchester Health Club and the Pepper Tree Restaurant & Lounge. . . . "Hey, listen, Tony, you come in here and you got the run of the place. No problem. You wanna little Chicken Francese, you got it. No problem, Tony.

You and Bobby. You want to act like the owner, then, hey, you are the owner. Capice?" Glenn Modlin of the Holiday Inn helped, and so, eventually, did half of Mount Kisco.

The First Meeting—March 21

Ten o'clock in the morning. Joe Kelly was outside of the Pepper Tree, wiring himself for sound. Kelly watched as Tony sat down inside. Almost eerie working with that guy. Nobody knew enough about the crazy bastard. Tony himself had been busted in some kind of bizarre federal insurance case, Kelly knew, but had gotten off with one day's probation. The best goddamned undercover cop in the world. In a class with Serpico. But who was he? So many voices coming at you at once. So many gestures. Eerie.

Earlier that morning Stagg had gotten them prepped: "We ain't no faggots, baby, but we will all be holding daisies if we make a mistake."

A little weird being led around by a guy like this. But he was good. Maybe the best. But still. . . .

In truth, Kelly wasn't the only one who had doubts about Stagg. So many "buts." Strange displacements of personality. People felt like they were being taken over by Tony. He was so—weird. He looked like a Don Martin character, some mad prince who kills pigeons in the park. He often wore a little bolero coat that came only to his waist; a huge belt buckle, real jade and silver, sticking out like knuckles on a giant fist. And dark, plum-tinted glasses, so you could never see his eyes. The glasses swept back greasy strands of hair, combed straight. A fat Valentino. Sometimes you wanted to chuckle at the guy . . . only . . . only . . . you didn't.

Not that any of this bothered Stagg. He went about his business like a howitzer, blasting his way through a thicket of complaints and doubts. While the rest of the cast waited for the show to begin, Stagg would be thinking "tactics."

"Bobby," he would say in a hoarse, New York hood rasp, "you know . . . it might be good to break some ashtrays. You know da bit. . . ."

And Cercena would comply.

The broken ashtray ploy was something Stagg had picked up from *Baretta*. . . . One night on *Baretta*, Stagg saw a hoodlum look down at his table, notice an ashtray with a crack in it and throw the object across the room, smashing some whiskey bottles behind the bar. Well, he wouldn't do anything that dramatic. He would just quietly look down, and stare regretfully at the ashtray as if he, in his magnificence and regal Mafia splendor, had been slightly offended, ticked off ever-so-minutely, nothing for anyone to get real upset about. Only don't ever let it happen again! Show the don some respect!!

"Hey, Bobby," he would say, shaking his huge, dark head slowly. "Hey, Bobby, you see dis ashtray? You see it, baby? Well, don't let me see it like dis no more, you unnerstan? I don't like broken tings, you see? You start traveling with broken tings, pretty soon you got broken people . . . when you got broken people, you are nowhere, you see?"

Stagg would deliver this speech slowly and mournfully, with so much threat in it that whoever the mark was, whatever his questions as to Stagg's legitimacy were, he would soon be overwhelmed. What use were questions in the face of Mister Big?

On the afternoon of March 21, at lunch, Stagg, Kelly, and Vinnie met a fat man with many chins. Michaelson. They hated him immediately. Michaelson's small grayish eyes stuck out of his face like peas in a frozen Swanson meat pie. He was dressed in an expensive dark suit with food stains on it. He was a slob, yet not without intelligence. Wittington Investments gave him over one hundred thousand dollars a year. "But," he said, "I like to live high. I like to live on the money. After taxes, there's never enough. . . ." And so he had met some people in Guatemala, and they knew some people in Spain, and they knew some people, nice people, who owned a casino in Greece, and all of them knew very nice people in Chile. . . . Michaelson paused: "I understand you people are interested in some guns?"

Stagg came on warily. *Maybe* he was interested. He would have to see another, fuller list. Michaelson had brought the list, and when he showed it to Stagg, Kelly, Cercena, and Vinnie, they all felt the same electric shock. This was for real now. Michaelson was talking howitzers. . . . But Tony never flinched. "What the hell," Tony asked grumpily, "*is* an M-79, exactly?" Bobby and Vinnie almost cracked up. Michaelson quickly said he himself wasn't sure what M-79s were, but his people, all very professional, good people . . . *they knew* . . . because they'd "sold guns to both Israel and Egypt. You could see 'em right on TV at night. . . ."

Tony said nothing. He just stared at Michaelson through his black glasses. Michaelson began to sweat. Maybe he should have stuck with the illegal coffee shipments . . . ha ha . . . this was a bit much . . . this big, bald guy. . . . At one point, while Michaelson was trying to listen to Kelly, Tony said in his gruffest voice, "Hey, are you *really interested?*" And Michaelson, in his high-pitched falsetto, said, "Sure, why?" And Tony looked down sadly at his feet, as if thinking this hurts me a lot more than it hurts you.

Now Michaelson was starting to sweat a little more. "What in the hell have I done to offend this guy?"

Then Tony said, softly, like a snowflake falling on a dying child's head, "You was looking the other way when I asked you a quesh-on; so I asked you again, but you was looking the other way again, you know?"

And Michaelson can't say anything. But he is thinking. His brain is sending out alert signals: "Got to get this deal through, and split. This guy isn't kidding." He looks at Tony and says weakly, "I'm sorry." And right there, Tony knew he'd gotten his claws in good.

The Next Meetings

During the following weeks, Tony, Vinnie, and Bobby Cercena lived like functional schizophrenics.

"Not only did I have to be Tony's partner, ready to roll at any time, but I was also investigating burglaries in town here," recalls Cercena. "So one minute I'd be in court testifying about a robbery case, and a second later one of the gunrunners would show up unexpected and I would get a call from Tony, or someone else on the case. 'Get up here fast . . . bring a Cadillac.'"

And Bobby, dour-faced, heavyset Bobby, who likes to say, "I'm the happiest guy in the world, I just never smile," Bobby would wheel up to Marty Martabano, ask for another Caddy limo, and Martabano would deliver. Only, truth to tell, Marty was starting to get a trifle worried. The lid was starting to come off just a little . . . like the time he was down at the Dairy Queen with his wife and he looks up and there's this strange black limo sitting next to his. *And then he realizes it's not his limo!* Inside are these heavy-looking dudes with big-business suits, and these are definitely not, no way, Mount Kisco boys. . . . These guys were big time, for sure, and Martabano's wife is getting a little jittery . . . like maybe the death threats will come in and there will be a horse's head sitting on her bed some night. Marty thinks this is bullshit, the *Godfather* isn't *real,* and it wasn't that he didn't have confidence in the boys, these are good boys . . . but . . . good *local* cops, see. What if they are dealing with heavy heavies, not just your average light-heavy gun nut, what if it's like the show he saw on *Kojak,* where the guy helps the police and finds his wife tied with a cord and plugged into the place where the waffle iron usually goes? Stuff like that went through his mind. At times, because of his wife you understand, he thought about taking a gracious bow out. It crossed his mind . . . but then Bobby would come around and say, "Hey, remember back at grade school, the time we had Lucille Funguzi, and . . . bip bop bam. . . ." The upshot would be Bobby would drive out with yet another Caddy limo, and Marty would go home and try to explain to his wife that "after all, the boys had the situation in hand." But at night, Lord, at night, after the *Kojak* reruns, he would sit up in bed and do a couple of quick Hail Marys just for insurance. . . .

Certainly the boys who showed up at the Pepper Tree during the next few weeks were heavies. They were heavies in the sense that they had done deals in the past, they had access to huge shipments of burp guns and C-130 attack planes, all weird shit like that, yet, everything about them seemed . . . well, *light* instead of heavy. In fact, there was a definite buffoonish aspect to them that Stagg and his friends hadn't anticipated. Take Raymond Geraldo, the Midget, for example. Geraldo is about five-three, slightly porky, with a friendly teddy bear quality. It was hard to imagine him as the Merchant of Death. On *Kojak* or *Police Story*, a guy in his role would have forty-five inches of acne scars, Lee Van Cleef eyes, and a voice from the Big Gravel Pit. Geraldo, however, had a pleasant, soft voice. Instead of wanting to put him in the Big House, Bobby Cercena began to feel he was a pal. . . . They were all in a game together . . . the game of cops 'n' robbers. . . . Even Tony, who "hates punks and scumbags," had to admit feeling sort of mellow about Raymond: "The boy had charm." Indeed, he should have, for his background was not a poor-boy-from-slums-goes-bad number.

Actually, the Midget's father was an American military man who had acted as an adviser in Guatemala. Geraldo had grown up there in a fine house, and through his family had "made many friends among the generals from South American countries." He'd learned that the ways to power and money were many and varied, but all had one constant—the United States. The good old U.S. could be counted on in various ways to support its "friendly neighbors." He told Tony these facts in quiet, lovable syllables, and Tony, warming to the lad's story, told him about Poppa. While the theme song from the *Godfather* played on the jukebox, Tony movingly recited the Poppa Story:

"Poppa lives in Vegas. You ain't ever gonna see him, but he is waiting, watching. He has heard good things about you. He knows you are right."

As for the shipment of the guns itself, Geraldo was not to worry, for as Tony put it, "Poppa owns the Westchester County airport, you unnerstan' what I'm telling you?"

The Midget smiled, his brown eyes flashed. He was caught, wired in, entering TV Cop World. He thought of what he would tell his friend, Miguel Celis, his buddy in El Salvador's Department of the Exterior. Here it was at last. Not merely a gun deal but an in to organized crime. There could be no stopping them if they made the Big Connection. The Midget was so happy he broke out in a rash. Guns were only the beginning. He said his friends controlled "Nomad missiles" that could wipe out entire cities. Tony kept his cool, smiled.

How Would You Like a South American Country?

The following day Geraldo showed up at the Pepper Tree Lounge with Dominick Cagianese of Dix Hills, Long Island, and Michaelson. Cagianese, a big man with a thick, blunt body and a worried expression, had been a beer-truck driver for twenty-two years, until he hurt his back. Now he worked for Mott Haven Truck Parts, in the Bronx, the place where Geraldo said some of the guns were stored. Cagianese was introduced as a gun expert. At this meeting everyone was happy. Tony was so happy, he played the *Godfather* theme ten times.

"I figured they was going for it," Tony says. "I'll lay it on. The whole Poppa bit had been taken from the *Godfather* anyway, including the adopted son. . . . We use most stuff from television because it's already inside a criminal's brain."

But Cagianese, for all his working-class background, was a little cagier than terrified, greedy Michaelson. He asked a few preliminary questions, answered a few technical questions about the weapons, then smiled and wanted to know what the guns were going to be used for.

It was a bad moment. *Godfather* theme or no, what possible rationale could even a powerful Mafia gang have for such items as C-130 attack planes? Negotiations at this point were for $2.8 million, with extensions up to the $3 million range if everything worked out. Still, the question was well put. What the hell did the mob want with what amounted to war weaponry? Tony smiled, looked down at his cheese sandwich, then held it up.

"You see dis cheese," he said. "Every time you see dis cheese, I want you should think of me. I control cheese like you wouldn't believe." He laughed, a rare thing. Everybody looked expectant. "Maybe you hearda a place down south, I mean *way* down south . . . where there are some poppy fields. . . . Maybe you hearda the trouble we have there. . . ."

Amazingly, Cagianese and Michaelson (Geraldo, at this point, was already Tony's greatest fan) went for it. The skimpiest of explanations. A place down south. The trouble. The reason they went for it was television. Things had already been filled in by Geraldo Rivera. A week before on Geraldo's show, the hipper-than-thou TV journalist had taken his audience "to the strange and wild borders of Durango, Mexico," where the poppy growers were being resisted by a new government that was trying to reform the heroin situation. . . . Two ten-minute segments had emphasized the fact that the gangster forces were stocking up on weapons in order to fight the government boys. Cagianese, like millions of other Americans, had heard about the story, and put two and two together.

Subsequently, the talk became expansive in the extreme. Geraldo warmed up over a few drinks and the good food of the Pepper Tree. He was now offering Tony and the boys "houses in Guatemala. Over the sea. Beautiful places." He had enough friends in South American countries to "take over most of them," but he didn't have enough money yet to pull it off. Geraldo drank Cinzano and spoke of the value of tourism in his homeland:

"You know they are opening Guatemala up to tourism . . . there is no reason why you couldn't put up a few hotels there, with a few, uh, diversions. . . . There's a lot of land there, and very, very friendly people."

Stagg nodded, ate his cheese, snapped his fingers, asked for "Stardust" on the juke box, countered with a joke:

"You know why they shaped Italy like a boot?"

"No."

"Because you can't stuff all that shit into a sneaker."

Shades of *The Godfather*. The gun boys roared.

The Feds Find Out

During the next few meetings Tony and Bobby and Kelly discovered that working with Michaelson was one Frank Alvarez, another Latin hustler. Alvarez and Cagianese had office space in the Mott Haven Truck Parts warehouse in the Bronx. At the warehouse were brochures, pictures, and Alvarez himself, so Tony decided to pay the man a visit.

Things were set with the technical backup unit. Pictures and tapes of Tony and Alvarez together would be invaluable.

At first the scheme seemed to work perfectly. Tony, dressed in a hat with peacock feathers, his dark suit, and wine-colored tie, went into Mott Haven and entertained Alvarez with tales of his youth and checked out the arms brochures.

He was about to take Alvarez to lunch, so his men could take photos, when he received a phone call from the Westchester County DA. The DA had no idea Stagg was working on the Mount Kisco scam, and wanted to have Tony testify for him in another case. He'd called the Pepper Tree, and was told by an employee that Tony had left the number for Mott Haven Truck Parts. Tony, of course, had left the number for Bobby. Unfortunately, Frank Alvarez answered the phone and heard: "Assistant DA of Westchester County calling for Mr. Stagg." Alvarez, completely fooled by Tony's act, froze. Stagg, watching Alvarez, felt his entire body turn to ice. Now, more than ever, it was like a movie. When he was shot he would be like Fearless Fosdick, walking home with Swiss-cheese holes in his gut. . . . Alvarez was looking at Tony strangely, but all he did was meekly hand him the phone and say, "It's the DA calling for you." But Tony just grabbed the phone and said, "Hey, baby, forget it! You can reach me if you can catch me, baby!" Both men stared at each other, while outside the trucks roared by.

"The DA is an asshole," Tony said. "He's trying to serve me with a subpoena. Can you imagine the idiot? He won't ever get elected again. He'll be on welfare."

The two men went outside. Tony hugged Frank Alvarez like a good Don should. Across the street, the Mount Kisco cops took nice, clean pictures.

The End Use Certificate

Since Stagg's "underworld" had chosen to buy Bushmaster Automatic machine guns, weapons made in America, the only way they were able to buy them legally was to pretend the guns were being shipped out of the country, to a friendly nation. U.S. State Department policy does not permit a domestic group to purchase machine guns, but the Staties are more than happy to help some South American country that might be in the throes of a Communist takeover.

And since many South American countries are in this state, it's only a matter of finding the right general in the right country. The South American general would sign a document called an end use certificate, a document issued by our State Department.

"Once the friendly South American general has signed the paper," Geraldo explained, "it's simply a matter of putting ten thousand Bushmasters down as 'arms needed to defend our country against invasion.'" The guns would then be bought from the Bushmaster people in Vermont and shipped to the Mott Haven plant. Once there they could be taken out of their boxes and given to the "Mount Kisco Mob."

So Geraldo went off with Tony Stagg's blessings. But not Bob Michaelson's. In fact, by this time Michaelson was beginning to sweat again. Here he was, flying to Guatemala and El Salvador, wining and dining people . . . and it was all on his own dough. This Mafia don character, Tony Stagg, might be a big, bad-assed mother, but, truth be told, he had yet to put up one cent. They had talked millions of dollars, huge future deals involving Bell Cobras and Christ-knows-what, but the Mount Kisco boys hadn't shown a cent. Perhaps they didn't have that much money. Perhaps they planned on waiting until the day the guns arrived, and then they were simply going to waste everybody. Stagg certainly looked capable of it. Now Michaelson began to worry for the safety of his family, for his own life. He *had* to see some money. He had to know there was a pot of gold.

Soon Geraldo was back, with wild stories. He had found a wonderful man named Montenegro. Montenegro had been willing to sign the end use certificate. They would all have liked Montenegro. A giant of a man. Unfortunately, he wasn't going to be able to help. Just a day before he was to meet Geraldo, on his way to a lavish lunch with some of his junta compadres, some careless revolutionaries had driven by and filled Montenegro full of holes.

But, said Geraldo, never fear. Where there is one Montenegro, there are many. All friendly to the U.S. Beautiful people. There is another wonderful man, a man called the Colonel. Colonel Manuel Alfonso Rodriguez, the military commander of the country of El Salvador. This wonderful man, said Geraldo, was an invaluable friend.

He might be able to do not only this deal but many others. The thing was, the Colonel's reasoning sounded a little off to Michaelson and the cooler heads. For example, if he signed an end use certificate asking for ten thousand machine guns for El Salvador, a country with only five thousand people in the army, it might sound like he was getting one machine gun for each arm of every soldier. If, next year, he came back with another end use certificate for, say, a Bell Cobra with attack configuration rockets, it might look a little hairy to even the most jaded of the State Department boys. True, said Geraldo, but in that case we'll simply go to a bigger country. Chile is always good. But meanwhile, said Geraldo, the Colonel will do just fine, and he will only cost seventy-five thousand dollars. No problem, Tony said. But Michaelson was definitely sweating now.

He felt vague fear about everything. He began to pressure Tony. "We pay for all these expensive trips to South America. We even flew Joe Kelly down to South Carolina to shoot some guns. We've done everything, but we have yet to see any money." Tony tried his heaviest intimidation, but it was obvious the Mount Kisco gang was going to have to come up with some bread. That night, after the gun boys left, Chief Nelligan appealed to the ATF to come up with fifty thousand dollars.

"We simply assumed a government agency would have the money handy," he says now. But the ATF is really a poverty-stricken little federal bureau. They couldn't come up with that kind of cash, so once again, the chief, Tony, Cercena, and company had to improvise. First, they tried a local stationery store, Fox & Sutherland's, run by Kal Fox. In the past Fox had assisted the police by telling them who was buying small, glassine envelopes . . . the kind junkies use for heroin. Fox had to come up with fifty grand by six o'clock that night. The money had to be in cash, and he had to trust the police to use it, to bandy it about and impress the arms boys . . . and then pull it back before the bad guys could take any. It was a risky business, but, like Martabano,

Fox came through with as much as he could, thirty-five thousand dollars. That left Tony and the boys fifteen thousand short. Martabano might be good for it, but Richard Martabano, the elder partner, was out of town. His son couldn't make the transaction without dad's approval. Finally, the National Bank of Westchester, in conjunction with the Village of Mount Kisco, agreed to loan the police the entire fifty grand. Now all Tony had to do was not blow it.

The next day's meeting was in the main office of the Northern Westchester Health Club. Tony, Vinnie, Cercena, Kelly, and ATF agent Waxman were under the heaviest pressure they had yet seen. Michaelson, Alvarez, and Cagianese were furious. They wanted to see money, they'd had it with talk. Yet the police couldn't possibly let them *take* the money. . . . Tony went into his act, which was made somewhat easier by his 103-degree temperature. He had pneumonia.

He shouted for two hours. He stomped around the room. He slammed his fist and glowered. He tried every trick he knew. It was like orgasm. Finally, he opened the bottom drawer of a desk and pulled out all fifty grand. Making a grand gesture, he flung the money at the gun boys:

"You want to see money?" he said, screaming at Cagianese. "You want this money? You got it. Here."

He stood up, sweating and straining. The message was clear: If you take the money you have shown me great disrespect. Of course I'm good for it. I have always been good for it. Your doubting me shows that you are without class. Without respect.

It was a huge gamble, but it worked. The gun merchants stared at the money, tantalized. They touched it and fondled it, and then finally placed it back on the desk and left the room. The Mount Kisco Gang was okay in their books.

It was time to wind things up. The Big Payoff was scheduled for the Pepper Tree, then changed to the Holiday Inn. Tony had promised Michaelson and the others a "banquet you would never forget." He had promised them women . . . well, not exactly women—"escorts." The police got quite a kick out of that, but then Tony changed his mind. He didn't have much use for policewomen. In fact, he was dubious about broads generally. He once told Dominick Cagianese: "In the old days you give a broad ten bucks and a wagon and she gets to California. These days you give her a Cadillac and fifty grand and she can't get over the George Washington Bridge." Cagianese laughed loudly, but had a strange feeling that he'd heard the line before. Which he had. The joke had been from a Redd Foxx party record. In the end there were no women in the Katonah Room at the Holiday Inn, and there was no banquet either. The police just set up fruit cups. Beautiful fruit cups in a sweet semicircle, which the gun boys were to admire, but never eat.

In addition to the banquet, Room 101 was set up for the Big Conference. And adjoining 101, the feds and the Mount Kisco locals waited with their videotape equipment, ready to record the whole transaction for posterity. Unfortunately, the two groups were at this point not best buddies. As with any cop show, locals and feds were vying for control. Chief Nelligan was very anxious that his men be given full credit. He cited the fact that Tony Stagg had always worked with him in the past, and in effect was one of the force. The feds noted that, technically, Tony was on their payroll. Stagg, listening to all of this, felt a strange glow. He was no longer just an undercover cop. He was a Superstar.

After a hassle in the chief's office, during which the Mount Kisco boys threatened not to go to the bust, peace was made. Paul Malagiero of the Mount Kisco police went to Mott Haven to pick up Frank Alvarez. Michaelson drove himself to his funeral. Bobby Cercena went to Kennedy to pick up Geraldo and the Colonel, who'd flown in for the climax. Waiting by the gate, Cercena felt he was inside a cloud. . . . When he arrived, the Colonel had a hole in his shoe. His toes stuck out absurdly—a large smiling man in a dark suit who was suffering from gout.

One of the treats of the Payoff was to be the appearance of Poppa, and the Colonel and Geraldo were as excited about meeting him as they were about the deal. Poppa was the central fantasy. . . . As Cercena drove through Mount Kisco, he pointed out the Catholic church, the old buildings, and finally the police station. Inside, Chief Nelligan was as tight as a fist, but he couldn't resist walking out and looking as the car cruised by.

"Oh, look," Cercena said, turning to catch the Colonel's attention. "That's the chief of police." The Colonel answered in Spanish: "He must have very little to do in a small town like this." Everyone laughed heartily.

At the Holiday Inn, everyone gave the Bear the respectful hugs he had accustomed them to and then, after a brief drink and a look at the banquet room, Tony promised each of the men "escorts." "They'll be here after business," he said, winking broadly.

Inside Room 101, the men talked about future plans. Carefully, the police asked the Colonel question after question. "You have ordered these guns?" The Colonel nodded his head and said, "Yes." Joe Kelly opened a briefcase, and took out seventy-five thousand dollars. Tony looked at the Colonel. "He's getting seventy-five thousand dollars, right?" Everybody nodded. The Colonel nodded, too. Carefully, almost boringly, the police rehashed the details. On videotape, the scene plays slowly. Unlike *Kojak*, there is no real action at all, only meticulous attention to detail. But in scene after scene one can't help but notice that Stagg and the police look a little sorry that things are coming to an end, and the criminals look uncomfortable. No braggadocio at all. "Let's get out of here with our lives," their eyes say. Finally, after handing over the money, Tony says, "Now I am going to get Poppa."

He opens the door and detective Ralph Hyatt of Mount Kisco comes in. Tony hugs him and Hyatt pulls his gun and says, "Up against the wall, you are under arrest." Everything seems even slower, as in a dream. Michaelson, unlike movie criminals, does nothing. He is very still, a zombied spirit. He allows the cops to frisk him, sit him down, then cuff him. As Tony Stagg turns to go, there is no look of satisfaction on his face, just a dreamy stare. Then his face takes on a look of sorrow . . . as if he is afraid to leave the order of police work for the small terrors of everyday life. The last lines spoken on the tape are, "Handcuffs? Who the hell brought the handcuffs? Has anyone seen the cuffs? Somebody should have the cuffs."

And so the Mount Kisco case closed. All of the defendants were convicted. Robert Michaelson was given five years for aiding and abetting a crime. The Midget, Raymond Geraldo, was given four years. Frank Alvarez got five. And the Colonel now resides in our prisons, serving two consecutive five-year sentences.

The Vortex of Synchronicity

A few months after the case was solved, the town of Mount Kisco held a Mayor's Award Presentation. ABC-TV filmed Stagg and the concerned citizens and cops receiving gold medals. Stagg told his story to the nation, took calls from *60 Minutes*, chatted with national reporters.

In the next months there were rumors of death threats on Stagg's life. The threats were vague, but Tony was placed under the protective custody of federal marshals, and is now living somewhere in the West. In Mount Kisco, sentiment runs to pathos. "Poor Tony. Look at what he did, and look at his reward. Uprooting his family, losing his home." Bobby Cercena: "Nothing much exciting happens now. We miss him. In a way, I guess we miss the case."

And now, the case is about to happen again. Paramount Pictures has bought rights to the story, and, if things go as expected, Stagg will be coming at the nation, full of juice, making the talk show circuits, hustling, improvising himself, creating from his own bizarre imagination a celluloid reality, which was itself inspired by Hollywood fantasies of the underworld. In short, Tony Stagg's natural progression from old-movie fan, to cop buff, to ace undercover agent is nearly complete. In another year—even if Gene Hackman plays him—Tony Stagg will have become a public myth, like Popeye Doyle. His fantasy, which was the gun hustlers' downfall and which changed the face of Mount Kisco, is about to become a waking dream.

Postscript

What I didn't add in the body of this piece was the deal I made with Paramount to write the script for King/Hitzig Productions. During the next year I worked like mad on this project. The script was done, Paramount liked it, but for reasons unknown to me the entire project was dropped. A few years later there was talk of reviving it, but those plans too were scrapped. This is the way it is in the film business. Great plans, big meetings, stars like Gene Hackman and Dustin Hoffman are said to "be involved," and in the end, the whole thing is dropped for some other project. I think this is a highly amusing piece, and it showed I could write about very involved facts without losing my grasp of the narrative. I loved working on it and still think it would make a great film. Tony and Vinnie are still living under the Witness Protection Plan I suppose. Though I have no idea where. But they were wonderful subjects to write about, and not unlike the Yawn Patrol, they revealed the remarkable connection in the American Psyche between real cops and their show business counterparts.

Marshal Ky Amongst the Roses

The Butcher! The Killer! The Playboy Assassin! Leaping from the cockpit of his fighter jet in a heroic black jump suit, his lithe body strung like a bow, his lavender silk scarf trailing war mythology like a Sam Peckinpah dream . . . the day he nearly got it leading the bombing raid but the guy next to him took the bullet, spilling his guts like Beefaroni . . . the time he buried his comrades with his own hands and then, drunk on good French wine, sat all night in a Saigon disco staring at the wall with beautiful Miss Mai on his arm. . . . Lord, the tales the man has lived, and oh, the troubles he has seen. The Viet Cong, who had this thing about firebombing his house (they tried seven times and made it twice, but he was out rocking and rolling); the Buddhists, who pretended to be a bunch of bald sweeties, interested only in the White Light (never political, those Buddhists), but who wanted to take away his power as surely as Ellsworth Bunker or President Thieu did; the American press and students, those misled Com symps, who pictured him as the Butcher, the Killer, the Man Who Invented the Tiger Cages, the Adolph Hitler groupie in the first place. . . .

Nguyen (pronounced "win") Cao (pronounced "cow") Ky is the former air marshal, former vice president, former strongman of Vietnam, hated equally by liberals, radicals, right-wingers and good folks everywhere. He was prime minister of Vietnam at thirty-five, a job that lasted for two of the bloodiest years of the war, 1965–1967, back when we still thought we could win, but he was ousted by Nguyen Van Thieu; Ky then served the last seven years of the war as VP . . . and when he finally did leave (on the next to last day of fighting, April 29, 1975), he was purported to have made off with a huge amount of cash. According to the popular tales, Ky has (a) salted away his bucks in Swiss/Caribbean banks, (b) laundered them, (c) invested, through his wife, Miss Mai, in Hawaiian land deals. But the fact of the matter is that Marshal Ky has settled, amid a huge colony of poorer Vietnamese ex-patriate, in Huntington Beach, California, the surfing capital of America, just south of Los Angeles, and is about to open a liquor store. Reluctantly, he is trying to adjust. . . .

Creeping Gilliganism

Marshal Ky cruises the living room of his new $107,000 stone home. His living room is tastefully furnished. A glass-top coffee table with chrome legs, a classy-looking abstract painting, a huge white sofa. Chic, monochromatic, in the manner of the waiting room at the William Morris Agency. The only contrast is Marshal Ky himself. It's been ten years since his jump suit days, but he still cuts a dashing figure. He has on a black leather jacket, a blue turtleneck, handsome cotton and silk pants tapering down nicely to hundred-and-fifty-dollar Spanish boots. . . . But Ky looks troubled. His movements have a predatory quality. Strange depressions come to him. Sometimes he will walk back and forth across his rug thirty or forty times . . . walk down past the kitchen and the TV room where his daughters or son are watching *The Munsters* or *Gilligan's Island* . . . and he will open the sliding door, and go out back and stare at his roses . . . the sight of them makes him feel an insufferable joy. For though he has grown them himself, in the warm California sun, the truth is he cannot look at them without thinking of the flowers of Vietnam . . . and then he knows such longing, such loss, that he must go back inside and call Tony Lam, his PR man, or Big Jack Hanshaw, the liquor king of Huntington Beach and his financial adviser and best American buddy, and ask them if they still plan on playing tennis that afternoon . . . though he already knows they do.

Today, his depression has been particularly rough. He is not only nostalgic, but worried about the future. Miss Mai is over at Hanshaw's Liquors working eight hours with Big Jack so she will know the business when they start running their own liquor store. Marshal Ky isn't sure Miss Mai can handle the chores and still be a mother to his children. He wonders if they shouldn't have taken the car wash business after all. At least the hours are regular. Deep gloom: "How can I end up in Orange County, selling liquor to Americans?"

Two years ago Marshal Ky lived in the vice presidential palace in Vietnam. He had ten servants, four drivers, five official cars, a private tailor for himself and Miss Mai, a private chef . . . the list goes on. Now he is about to run a liquor store. But he is not without a sense of humor. What would make the bastards laugh? Air Marshal Ky's Cut Rate Liquors? Plastique Liquors? Oh, the haplessness of it. Still it's better than hustling burgers.

Jive Talk

Talk about your mid-life crisis. Marshal Ky is a forty-six-year-old deposed dictator with a Negro growing in his living room. Each night now, Ky watches his son Dat, twenty-one, change from a nice, polite, traditionally minded ruling-class Vietnamese lad into a crazy-quilt kid, neither Vietnamese nor American. Ky is not rigid. He expected his children to become somewhat Americanized. He even told Tony Lam: "We must blend in here, or we will be crushed." To that end, he changed his daughters' names. Van, eleven, is now Jennifer; Tuan, fourteen, is now Jackie. But this other stuff! Marshal Ky didn't know how frightening the process would be. He didn't know Dat was going to be talking trash like some badassed muther from down de block. Ky didn't think the day would come when he would say: "Dat, my son, what are you doing tonight?" and Dat would answer: "Hey, I'm going up de club wif my man Jack, you dig, Marshal Ky, baby?" My God! All of Ky's liberal social attitudes, the ones he's tried so hard to cultivate, get swept aside when he hears such talk. And it's *how* Dat is picking up this stuff. It's not as if the boy knows any blacks. Huntington Beach isn't exactly integrated. Dat is talking black because he watches *Good Times* on TV, and has subconsciously picked up Jimmie Walker's jive. . . . Marshal Ky's big fear, the one he doesn't even like to think about, is that TV is wiping out hundreds of years of tradition easier and more absolutely than a million Viet Cong ever could. And not only is Dat talking like J. J. Walker, but his way of carrying himself, his slinky bopping and prancing through the house suggests . . . the Unthinkable . . . the kid isn't even turning into a *real* black man, but into a television ghost of a ghost . . . and that way lies true madness. . . .

The Battle of the CB

Marshal Ky is in the car with his family. They are driving into the Huntington Beach hinterlands, like any red-blooded American family. They are going to the Sizzler Steak House for dinner. Marshal Ky likes the Sizzler. You get a nice meal, and it's quick and efficient. Sitting on the benches with his family around him, Ky feels the blues shaking away. Except to get to the Sizzler you have to fight the Battle of the CB. Once on the Freeway, Dat likes to get on the citizens' band

and make all kinds of bizarre noises. And the girls go crazy, too. Seeing all his kids hanging on that damned toy, talking to the rednecks, really gets Ky:

"This here is Red Dragon old buddy. . . . Yeah, Red Dragon on the horn. There's a beaver where? . . . Down at the corner of Golden State standing outside of Oscar Wilde's? Check, old buddy, Breaker Five."

When Marshal Ky hears this stuff he begins to feel a freezing sensation . . . the Red Dragon! That might have been the name of a fighter jet. Now it's the name of his family car. When your car becomes the Red Dragon, what can that mean? Dat defends the CB on the grounds that it puts him in touch with "what's happening" in town, what "excitements" are going down. . . . Ky doesn't even know how to reply. The incredible *ease* with which Americans can be introduced to strangers, to aimless, promiscuous Fun, goes against everything Vietnamese. One huge gulp by the red, white, and blue dragon of goofiness and Dat is gone. One day a Negro, next day a redneck. Ky's face grows as grim as a bomber pilot's.

At the Sizzler, Marshal Ky tries to relax. He goes through the line, gets his steak, his baked potato, and sits down, preparing to Eat American. But just as he is about to pop that first juicy bite of steaming Sizzler into his mouth, he looks up and there is a little girl next to him. She is standing there looking as cute as an advertisement. She is smiling shyly. Marshal Ky puts down his fork. Behind the little girl are two middle-aged Californians wearing identical pale green leisure suits.

"Go ahead, Julie," the man says, his glasses reflecting blue Sizzler lights in weird angles, strange patterns.

"Gosh," says Julie. "My granddaddy says you are President Ky. I would like to have your autograph."

Marshal Ky smiles and looks around at Dat and Jennifer and Jackie. They are all beaming at him.

He signs a wet napkin and the little girl smiles and rushes back to her grandparents. They smile, wave and the man says:

"Welcome to California, President Ky."

"Why, thank you," says Marshal Ky, suddenly looking young and dashing.

The two people and their granddaughter leave. Ky feels a lump in his throat. He looks at his son, who is smiling and acting neither like a redneck nor a Negro.

Ky takes a mouthful of Sizzler. It is moments like these that rekindle his belief in America.

How Are the Fish on Route 66?

Tony Lam has come to visit Marshal Ky. Lam is a short, bouncy man who has worked for many Vietnamese-American groups. He has worked for AID, for Rand, and has helped relocate thousands of Vietnamese on Formosa. Lam is always ready with a joke, and when he laughs he squeals like a child. He is a successful insurance man and Ky's main liaison with the eleven thousand Vietnamese who live around Huntington Beach.

Today Ky is especially glad to see Lam. The morning was bad. Miss Mai was out working with Hanshaw, "learning" the cash register. Ky had no luncheon engagements, so he thought he'd work on the lawn. Except the lawn was dead. The entire thing looked like Khe Sanh after the Tet offensive. Months of careful seeding and fertilizing had yielded overcooked bacon. The stubble Ky assumed was "natural," which the guy in the store *swore* was only a phase, was clearly permanent. The "fertilizer," Ky realized, was some kind of poison. Or else he'd used too much. Or else . . . anyway, the grass was lost. Ky had gotten very upset. He'd even begun to see the lawn "symbolically." Then Tony Lam showed up:

"You think you have problems, Marshal Ky? Listen to this. . . . There were a couple of Vietnamese fishermen—this happened just last week—who had eaten dinner and decided to go for a walk, as they used to do in Vietnam. Well, they walked and they walked and pretty soon they came to a huge path, a huge white stone path. They had never seen anything like it before . . . So they decided to walk *up* the huge white path, and pretty soon it seemed to flow into an even wider path, which had these strange white walls in the middle of it."

"Oh, no," says Marshal Ky, slapping his leg.

"Yessssss," says Tony Lam, starting to squeal a bit. "Yes Yesss. They were on the freeway. . . . the San Diego Freeway, and they ended up screaming, stuck on the traffic island out there with huge trucks and cars zooming by at a hundred miles an hour. Have you ever heard of anything like that? God, it was awful. . . . The po-leese had to come to get them off. . . . Ohhhh. . . ."

Lam is squealing hysterically. Marshal Ky knows Tony is not laughing because he thinks what happened to the two fishermen is funny. Tony is laughing because he is afraid. He is afraid for his friends and for his family, and even for Marshal Ky. Tony Lam is a good friend, and makes Marshal Ky feel better. But there is a sadness to him. His stories are always entertaining, but after he leaves Ky often finds himself depressed.

"Can you play tennis today?" Marshal Ky asks.

"I will try," says Tony Lam. "But you will butcher me as usual."

Ky tries to smile.

God and Ky at Yale

When his Buddhist fatalism fails him, Ky thinks of his Yale lecture. Here was a moment as good as the best moments of his life as flyer or air marshal or vice president of South Vietnam. Last year Ky went to Yale University, promoting his book, *Twenty Years and Twenty Days* (Stein & Day, 1976), knowing full well he'd be meeting a liberal audience with no love for him. Before he could begin, a bunch of kids held up signs that said: "Send Ky to North Vietnam," "Yale Doesn't Need a

Murderer," etc., etc. But during his talk he managed to retain his cool and his dignity. Ky explained to the students that he was not a butcher at all, that during his regime he had let most unduly charged political prisoners out of jail. He had attempted to get rid of corruption. Indeed, even liberal journalists like Ward Just and Frances Fitzgerald had publicly acknowledged his honesty—it was legendary. He had a military man's pride in a clean-running machine, he said, even if the machine was a government. He went on at great length, then stopped and asked for questions.

Question: "Sir, you misled the Americans. Weren't you responsible for the United States staying on after the war was lost?"

Ky: "Do you really think I could have misled all the American generals? I told Johnson at the beginning: 'This is Asia. Asians fight forever. We believe in destiny . . . we accept life fatalistically. We will fight for twenty years if necessary. If you come at all, you must prepare yourself for that kind of battle.' Johnson, of course, didn't listen. You are an impatient people. You think you can simply overwhelm a country with money and men."

Question, from a long-haired student who strikes a defiant pose: "What about corruption? The Communists weren't corrupt like you were."

Ky: "We were in total chaos. There had been ten coups since 1963, when Diem fell. I took *over* amidst much corruption, I only had two years in power and during that time I made many mistakes. I was never primarily a politician. My programs, the Strategic Hamlet Program and the Land Reform Program, were revolutionary, but were opposed by both the Americans and the corrupt government bureaucracy, so they failed. . . . As for the Communists, your left-wing press and your movie stars romanticized them. People like Jane Fonda knew about the corruption on our side, which I do not deny, and they assumed it simply had to be better on the other side. In a way I don't blame them. It's a human mistake. But let me tell you a story:

"Rice prices were spiraling out of control. Rice, as you know, is essential to everything in Vietnam . . . without it, there would be starvation, total economic collapse. . . . Well, I investigated and found that eight men really controlled the rice market. One especially, a Chinese, ran things. So I had him arrested and tried and he was found guilty, which he was, and he was sentenced to die. That was the law I instituted. If you were guilty of treasonous crimes, you were shot. Well, his parents came to me, Chinese ambassadors came to me, and they offered me many million millions to save him. But he was shot as scheduled. Still, rice prices did not fall. They were dumping rice into the rivers to keep prices high. So I called the other seven men into my office. I remember the day so well. I stood behind my desk and I told them, 'Price of rice must come down. I know what you are doing. You are bad citizens. You have seen one of your members shot, and still you persist. So now we will play a game.' Then I took off my hat . . . my *military* hat . . . and I tore up strips of paper, and I said, 'Now each of you will write your name on this piece of paper and you will put it in the hat, and next week we will have a meeting, and at that time I will draw the first name out of the hat, and whoever is chosen, I will shoot personally, right here! This will happen, I assure you, unless price of rice goes down *below* the minimum I have set. . . . It is up to you.'"

The student body had grown quiet. Ky was smiling and shaking his head.

"Within twenty-four hours," Ky said, timing it, "price of rice dropped dramatically."

When the laugh came, Ky rode it out. Then he continued: "Your movie stars and press knew little of Vietnam. And they knew nothing of Communism. They didn't know how the Communists enlist children to spy on their parents. I come from the North, and I have seen it with my own eyes. I have seen a child turn in his father for the 'crime' of being a landlord. The man was shot the next day. I have seen thousands of people put into 'reeducation' camps. These camps are concentration camps. What do you know of such things? Would any of you here at Yale like to live under such a system?

"You must understand my position. I had to fight the Americans as well as the Vietnamese who wanted to kill me. . . . I am speaking of ambitious people in my own government. Not to mention VC. All this, and I was only thirty-five years old, inexperienced as a politician. Perhaps some of you are over thirty. Could you rule a country?"

In the end Ky got a standing ovation. When the student body president drove him to the airport he said, "We thought you were so evil, but we are just beginning to understand how complex the situation was."

Later, Ky received a lifetime membership in the Yale Student Union.

War in the Blackboard Jungle

Talking to Americans is a little bit like war, and war, as Marshal Ky frequently points out, is all he's known since he was nine years old. It's built into his nervous system. But war gets tiring.

This afternoon, Marshal Ky is going to the Circle View School for a parent-teacher conference. He will discuss how Jennifer, who is in the fifth grade, and Jackie, who is in the ninth, are adjusting.

Despite her age, Jennifer's personality is more highly developed, and Marshal Ky assumes she is doing very well. Still, her outgoing, friendly demeanor worries Ky a bit. He wonders if she is perhaps not too forward. He recalls his own school days in Vietnam at the lycée. One did not fraternize, one did not presume with one's teachers, as he sees Jennifer doing.

The three teachers who meet with Ky are in their early twenties. There is Mr. Painter, who teaches science, Mrs. Mosher who teaches Jackie, and Mr. Oberle, who teaches Jennifer history.

Mr. Painter looks like someone who stepped out of an orange juice commercial. His hair is golden and combed surfer style over his forehead. His skin is ruddy and smooth. He smiles a lot when he talks: "You don't have to worry about Jennifer, Mr. Ky. She's good people. Yessir."

Ky reacts to this by nodding his head slowly. He does not smile at all, so Mr. Painter smiles a little for him.

Mr. Oberle, a big, healthy-looking man, says: "I'm very impressed with the way the girls handle themselves. Really. They don't rip books or write on desks. They have such a manner with them. All the Vietnamese children who come to our school do. It must be the Vietnamese education system."

Marshal Ky nods his head again and stares at the three teachers as if he has seen a pale horse.

"No," he says. "Is not the schools. It is tradition. And culture. I am very concerned with the way my Jennifer acts."

"Well, I wouldn't worry about Jennifer," beams Mr. Oberle reassuringly. "But *Jackie* is a little shy. When she wants to know something she should just see me. Rather than go through Mrs. Mosher."

Marshal Ky nods his head very slowly. "No, that has to do with culture. In ancient times we had girls taught only by women. So we kept girls and boys apart. This tradition has been handed down . . . thus women are shy. Jennifer is the one who worries me."

Mr. Oberle laughs and shakes his head: "Really, *I* don't think she's got a problem."

Then Oberle stops. Ky looks pained. "Well," he says, trying to lighten the mood, "I'm glad it's not *me* that's making Jackie shy."

Everyone laughs politely. Even Ky. Then he clears his throat. "There is one problem," he says. "Next year Jackie is leaving your school to go to junior high. We wonder if Jennifer could go with her."

That would mean Jennifer skipping two grades. The teachers speak up, hesitatingly, but in accord. Bad idea. The junior high is too big.

The kids are so much older, more socially sophisticated. That would mean adjustment problems for Jenny.

"I was just thinking," says Ky, "that, as it is now, the girls can come to school together . . . they are safe. But if Jennifer is alone . . . well, it's just that we have heard so much about kidnapping."

Mr. Painter has stopped smiling. Mr. Oberle is nodding seriously, and Mrs. Mosher is talking: "We said right in the beginning of the year, Mr. Ky, that we must always keep an eye on your children. They should never be left alone on the playground. They should never be allowed to run off on their own at lunch hour. We can promise you they will always be watched every minute they are here. But, of course, there is still the problem of them coming here."

The two male teachers agree. One would not like to see the children of Marshal Ky kidnapped by a madman. Perhaps Ky will come in again next week and see the principal? Ky nods, shakes hands.

"It is very frightening," Ky says, driving home. "I have no money. I took nothing. . . . But people all assume I have many million millions. If one of the people who think I have such money were to find out about my children . . . there are so many *nuts* in California!"

"Sometimes I Feel Like the Lonely Ranger"

The next afternoon I arrive early at Marshal Ky's house to talk with Miss Mai. She is just back from a morning at Hanshaw's. It's hard not to remember her as the Asian beauty with the model's body who appeared regularly in *Paris Match*, who learned to cook at the Cordon Bleu, who roared through Saigon in sleek black limos. Now she dresses in a yellow pantsuit.

"We are poor," she says, "but please don't write it. We never knew what poverty meant before we came here."

"You live in a hundred thousand dollar house," I say. "That is not exactly poor."

"No. Not by poor people's standards. But compared to what we had in Vietnam, the huge house, the drivers, the cars . . . we are very poor indeed. There are seven of us in this house, including my mother and my aunt. It is crowded. Everyone thinks we have so much money, and in truth I wish we did. I wish Ky had stolen money so we could live like our rich friends. I used to believe it was wrong, but in America no one cares how you get your money, only that you have it. I am constantly embarrassed socially by our lack of money."

Miss Mai joins her mother and her aunt (who speak no English) in the kitchen and begins dinner. She says she enjoys cooking, but that she is very tired from the liquor store.

"Nothing is as easy or as much fun as it was," she says. "Today, for example, I would like to fix you a really good Vietnamese lunch, but I must prepare *Chao Tom* for the tennis party at the Hanshaws tonight. So we are just having some raw fish. You will probably not like it. Americans always like things with rich sauces.

"I cook *Chao Tom* for the Hanshaws for a change. I mean I like steak and baked potato as much as anyone else. I really do. But after you've had it night after night . . . at every house you go to . . . well, you long for something with a little different taste."

Miss Mai smiles sweetly, but her voice is brittle. Efficiently, she strips away the outside of a sugarcane stalk, cuts it up, dips it in a light sauce made from various oils and spices. Next she wraps a jumbo shrimp around the stalk and fries two at a time in a small pan.

"This is a delicacy," she says. "I want you to try it. I only wish I could fix another for your lunch.

"It will be better after we get the store started, and hire some people. . . . I love family life. That is what I'm used to. Of course I miss Vietnam terribly, and worry about my friends there. . . . I send money to one friend every month . . . whatever I can afford."

She reaches into her purse, as if she has to prove this to me, and pulls out a check made out to a Vietnamese woman. The check is for fifty dollars.

"Don't print her name, please," Miss Mai says. "She would get in trouble with the Communists. . . . They are terrible."

"Are you glad to be here?"

"Slowly I am getting used to it," Miss Mai says. "Now that Ky is better."

"Better?"

"Last year, he was very very depressed. He would sit up late at night all alone, and grow quite sad. It was awful. . . . He worried constantly about money, also. But now things are a little better. Oh, the shrimps are done."

A little later Ky and I are having lunch. We are eating raw fish and noodles.

"What she told you is true," swears Ky. "We have little money. I know no one will believe me. You probably doubt me."

"I must confess I do."

"I don't blame you," Ky says. "Everyone thinks I steal. They say power corrupts and absolute power corrupts absolutely. But on the contrary, it did not corrupt me. You see, I had absolute power, and I could have made many million millions. But I am honest, which is why I was never a good politician. I should have been more like your American politicians. Like Nixon, or the others."

"What of Carter?" I say.

"He is just the same as the others. Jimmy Carter the president is very different from Jimmy Carter the candidate. He said he was going to change the government, but look at the men he chose. Many of them are very familiar names to me . . . I remember them too well from Kennedy's administration."

Ky smiles and shakes his head: "If you must know, I view my life as a tragedy. The Americans called me a butcher, said I didn't care about 'democratic ideals.' But there was no time for democratic change then. We were in war, in crisis, and strong decisions had to be made. . . ."

I ask about Ky's famous Hitler quote—"Did you say 'What Vietnam needs are two Hitlers, not one'?"

Ky laughs, but the sound is brittle, like Miss Mai's.

"Do you know how that quote came about? We were sitting around the barracks one day. A group of flyers and myself. There was one reporter there. We were talking about how the nation desperately needed a strong leader. We were all noting that whenever countries got into trouble, a good strong leader made them tougher. We all mentioned names. Hitler was one, true. But so was Franklin Roosevelt and Winston Churchill and John Kennedy. We weren't talking about whether the man was good or bad, merely if he was forceful, not afraid to make decisions. Because up to that time in Vietnam we had had nothing but weak leaders who couldn't withstand the coups. Anyway, what happened was the reporter quoted me as saying, 'What we need is Adolph Hitler.' . . . They tried to make me seem like a devil. I think it was because I was never pro-American . . . and because of my style."

"Perhaps that's true," I say. "I remember the pictures of you in your jump suit and your lavender scarf. People got the impression you didn't really care about anything but yourself."

Ky looks incredulous. He waves his hands as he speaks: "But all the officers wore jump suits. As for the scarf, I *liked* it . . . and I like pretty women. What man doesn't? The question should be why did they pick on *me* for these things? In America good clothes and the company of beautiful women are considered marks of distinction. . . ."

"You're saying the rap against you was because you were Vietnamese?"

Ky nods enthusiastically: "That is exactly right . . . as were the attacks on me for being a 'butcher.' I did what had to be done in war.

I do not believe laws are made for criminals. I believe laws are made for good citizens. I do not believe in coddling criminals."

"Actually, a lot of people I know in New York, who claim to be liberals, privately would like to see muggers drawn and quartered."

"And they are exactly right," Marshal Ky says. He eats his soup and nods his head. "You know, I look at Westerns on TV, and I feel like the hero. . . . I feel like the Lonely Ranger. . . . I feel very much like the Lonely Ranger."

He stops, grows silent, and his mouth curls up in an odd way.

Later we drive to the home of a Mr. Von Thon in Villa Park, where Ky is to meet with twenty Vietnamese ex-soldiers, currently eking out livings as fishermen. Father Ha, a radical priest and leftist journalist, is scheduled to show up, too, to "debate" Ky on how the large community of Vietnamese ex-patriates can best adjust to Americanization. On the way, Ky explains that he is not against the meeting, but is afraid for the Vietnamese. "Our position here is fragile," Ky says. "'We cannot afford to offend people. It would take only a couple left-wingers or hippies to come and start a fight, and what would the papers say: 'Vietnamese start trouble,' and other bad things. Father Ha is just a crazy priest. I have always had trouble with priests."

The twenty ex-soldiers are waiting, standing in a semi-circle, drinking cheap red wine. Several still have their army jackets. All are smiling broadly. Meeting Ky in this way is a rare pleasure, equivalent to Jimmy Carter just dropping in before dinner. Ky shakes each man's hand and begins talking rapidly. The men talk of war, telling Ky he is a hero, how people thought he would "save the country." One man says: "Even now people say that you will come back to South Vietnam and save us all."

Ky responds emotionally: "There is nothing I wanted more," he says. "You do not know. I could do nothing, though. Mr. Thieu took my power. He had my hands tied. I stayed until April 29, the next to last day of the war. I offered to lead a bombing mission even then. But Thieu would do nothing. He is brilliant, but only thinks of himself."

The fishermen nod their heads. Another man speaks, a Mr. Tinh: "I do not wish to brown-nose you sir," he says, "but I must tell you, you are a brave man. I respect you. I do not respect many of the other leaders. . . . Now I hear that the Communists are eliminating people who originally came from the North and fought against them in the war. All are being sent to camps. It is very bad."

"That is why we must speak out," says another man.

Ky stares at a poster on the wall: HUMAN RIGHTS FOR POLITICAL PRISONERS IN VIETNAM. "That should read just 'Human Rights,'" he tells the fishermen. "Then it will fall under President Carter's human rights campaign." There is a pause, but no one asks Ky to elaborate.

"I am trying to do things even though you do not see me," he says. "Last night I had dinner with Mr. Antoni, the supervisor of Orange County. I asked him to work out a plan to help Senior Citizens Training, to start a Vietnamese Service Center. I want to help you in any way possible. If you have problems, come to me and tell me."

The men look delighted. Ky goes on: "I understand you have had trouble here."

Several men tell a tale of community tensions. Over one hundred and fifty Americans who live in the Villa Park area signed a petition saying that the Vietnamese were "filthy, living fifteen in an apartment, unsanitary." The landlords of one apartment complex, where many poor Vietnamese live, publicly denied the allegations, however, saying, "We had more trouble with the whites who lived here before. The fact is, for a poor people, the Vietnamese are incredibly neat."

Marshal Ky nods. "I told Mr. Antoni we are a people willing to work and to learn. Many of you have never seen an inside toilet before you came here. We must be given a chance to learn."

The men nod and drink and tell more stories about Vietnam. Ky suddenly looks very tired. "Father Ha did not come," he says. There is some relief and some regret in his voice.

Marshal Ky sprawls on a huge couch at Jack Hanshaw's mansion. The couch makes him look very small. His thinning hair is matted, his mouth is curved down, and he is sweating. Tony Lam offers to get him some juice. Miss Mai, still in her tennis skirt, proffers a tray of shrimps. Next to her is Jack Hanshaw. Hanshaw is a well-conditioned forty-five, tall, tanned, with light blue eyes and a big toothy smile.

"Boy, you took some time," Hanshaw says. "We've been waiting for you for some time."

"Well," Ky says, sighing deeply, "they don't like to let you go. I expected to stay no longer than an hour. If they had their way I would have been there all night."

"Well," says Hanshaw, smiling at Miss Mai, "I'll tell you what. We all need to play some tennis and relax."

Ky nods and disappears into the bedroom. I go with Hanshaw and sit by a huge pond stocked with giant gold fish.

"Very nice place," I say.

Hanshaw is still smiling. He even manages to smile while he talks, like Ed McMahon.

"We've got quite a nice place here," he says. "Very few places like it in this area. Our pool is terrific. You saw our pool, didn't you?"

"Sure," I say. "Nice pool."

"Well, that's a sixty-five-foot pool," Hanshaw says.

As he talks he watches Miss Mai and Tony Lam playing tennis.

"How are people responding to the Kys?" I ask.

"She came in at six A.M. today," Hanshaw says. "Worked all day. I'll tell you, business is up twenty percent in the two weeks Mai has been in my store. If they are accepted that well in all phases of their life, I'd say they are going to be a big success out here. Actually, I'm putting Ky in a good spot [Hanshaw is selling Ky one of his fifty-six liquor stores]. It should easily bring him sixty thousand dollars a year. That's good money. Mai says they want a string of liquor stores . . . get a house like mine."

"Very nice place you've got," I say.

"Seventy thousand square feet," Hanshaw says. "Did you see my rabbits?"

On cue, some rabbits come bounding out from beyond the palm trees, and right behind them is Marshal Ky. He is dressed in a spiffy red tennis suit.

"Yippee!" says Marshal Ky. "I'm ready now!"

He opens the gate to Hanshaw's tennis court, and begins hitting the ball to Tony Lam. His strokes are smooth, and he has a strong forehand.

"He learned to play with Ellsworth Bunker," Hanshaw says. "Quite a good player. Ky was kind enough to bring the champion of South Vietnam by last week. . . . We played for hours. . . . Ky beat her in two sets. He's really athletic. Would you like a drink?"

"No thanks," I say. "I guess I'll be going."

"Take a beer for the road," Hanshaw says. "Have a Coke or something. You ever see fish like these?"

Nguyen Cao Ky is really into his game now, smashing backhands at giggling, diving Tony Lam. He is sweating and grinning, truly at ease.

"I'll go get the Coke," Hanshaw says. "Take a look at those fish. You won't see fish like those everywhere."

Postscript

This interview came as a total surprise to me and is one of my favorites. I walked into Ky's place with all the usual left-wing assumptions. I'd done quite a bit of research to get ready for the interview and thought I already knew many of the answers to the questions I posed to him.

I knew nothing. Ky struck me as an amazing person. He was strong, brilliant, fearless in battle, yet sensitive and kind. Yes, he could have been putting on a show for me, but every person I talked to—many more than I was able to get into this piece—said the same things about him. He was universally respected.

I didn't get it in the piece but at one time he began to cry and said, "You people talk of war. All I know of life is war. I've been in war all of my life, even as a kid."

Perhaps I am still naive but when he died a few months ago I felt a deep sorrow. He was one of the most impressive people I've ever met.

Grossing Out with Publishing's Hottest Hustler

(or Flem Snopes in Skinland)

I had done a few pieces for *New Times* when editor John Larsen called me up one day and said: "We need a story on the hottest guy in publishing, Larry Flynt, and you're our guy." I was thrilled to hear those words. I was "their guy"! Hooray! The only problem was that I had no idea who Larry Flynt was. Never heard of the man. I didn't want to tell Larsen that, though. I was afraid he'd think I was out of it, some kind of hick who still lived in Geneva, New York, and wasn't the hip guy he'd thought I was after all. But there didn't seem any way around it.

I told him and prayed he'd still want me.

"Larry Flynt is the hottest thing in magazine publishing," John said. "He has this magazine that outgrosses *Playboy*. I mean that literally and figuratively. It's called *Hustler* and it's incredibly gross. He's killing *Playboy* at the stands too. We've set up a deal for you to go out to Columbus, Ohio, and interview him. Stay as long as you want. I think he's going to be a good interview. He's this redneck guy who loves to drink and tell stories. You're going to love him."

"Right," I said. "When do you want me to leave?"

"In two days. We're overnighting you some *Hustler*s so you can get acquainted with the magazine before you go. You aren't going to believe what you're looking at. Outrageous stuff."

"When do you need the piece?" I said.

"Oh, a week or so after you get back."

"No problem," I said.

I hung up, so wired with excitement that I couldn't finish my lunch. A new assignment. Great! If I could just keep it up, get a name, I would actually be able to quit teaching and move with Robin to New York City.

The next day five copies of *Hustler* came by Federal Express. I opened the package and starting reading them. Or should I say "scanning them" since there was nothing much to read. The pictures were gynecological shots of open vaginas. The articles were amateur hour, but I didn't think *Hustler's* clientele was into reading anyway.

I was stunned by the magazine. It was so gross, so dumb . . . and yet there was something funny about it too. Redneck humor, outhouse guffaws.

Two days later, I got a pal to teach my course in American Novel and I was on my way to Columbus, Ohio, to interview the wildest character I'd ever met.

Then or since.

With Hustler *magazine, Larry Flynt has proved an old adage: No one ever lost money underestimating the intelligence of the American public.*

Burly Larry Flynt is sitting in his French Provincial chair, staring meditatively out of the fourteenth-story window of the New York Hilton. Below him are the winking, blinking red, yellow, and blue lights of the bankrupt Big Apple.

"This here is some city," he drawls, barely moving his mouth and with a reptilian glimmer in his eyes. "This is the kind of a place where you would expect a Bob Guccione . . . or a Hefner. . . . The big city. Me? I'm just a farm boy from Kentucky, you see? That's the truth. Quit school in the eighth grade. In the army at fourteen and out at sixteen. Spent *most* of my childhood looking up a mule's ass."

"Oh, Larry, stop moving," says Flynt's girlfriend, Althea Leasure. "I've got to get this hair done. We're gonna be late for the dinner!"

Larry Flynt shuts his heavy-lidded eyes, hangs his big belly yet another notch over his midnight-blue cotton pants, and lets Althea work his Roman curls up into a nice soufflé.

Althea is dark-haired, country-girl pretty, with just a few pounds of the bulge starting to pop out of her chiffon dress. She smiles a lot, a very appealing toothy grin, which makes her look at once innocent and vaguely malicious.

"Larry's not always this . . . particular, you know. But this is a rather special occasion."

"You see," says Flynt, "it's not every night that the publisher of *Hustler* magazine gets to eat with the publisher of *Penthouse*, the big, phony creep. I'll bet when they give him the award, he doesn't mention one thing about all the ass shots and wide-open beavers. That's Guccione's whole problem. He and Hefner won't admit that their magazines are turn-ons first. Editorial content comes second. That's why *Hustler* magazine is going to run them off the market. Wait till you get to Columbus and I show you the sales stats. We're wiping them out. You know why? Because we know how to appeal to our readers. We'd rather have ten truck drivers reading *Hustler* than one college professor. We're the only men's magazine that tells it like it is. Our magazine is a turn-on. You see? And our magazine responds to what the people *are,* not what we'd like them to be. That's why they love us so much."

Which, all things considered, is the literal truth. Since its inception a mere eighteen months ago, *Hustler* has become the third leading contestant (circulation of 1.4 million) in what is politely called the Men's Magazine Trade, trailing only *Playboy* and *Penthouse.* Arthur Kretchmer, editorial director of *Playboy*, and Bob Guccione, editor of *Penthouse*, both consider Larry Flynt's magazine an abomination, a virtual encyclopedia of bad taste and vacuous content. And both deny that *Hustler* is making any impact on their sales or editorial policies. On the first score, at least, they're telling the truth. *Hustler* is so lowbrow, so tasteless, so essentially moronic that one is tempted to write it off as a put-on. What can one make of a magazine that, for instance, runs a monthly column entitled "Asshole of the Month"? The total mindlessness of the magazine is astounding: A majority of the profiles are about other smut kings; the poorly drawn cartoons are the kind of thing junior high school kids find funny. (An old man and woman are in the kitchen. The woman is on the phone, the man is undressed and sticking his penis into a turkey. The caption: "Yes, honey, Granddad is stuffing the turkey this year.") The fiction is written by rank amateurs from the Dick and Jane school of creative writing, and the photo layouts are simply gross caricatures that dehumanize everyone involved. (Butch, a black man with an enormous member, sticks it to Peaches, a white Southern belle; a teenage girl hops into bed with an inordinately ugly middle-aged goon.)

Still, after all this is said, one is left with the astounding fact that *Hustler* appeals to about one and a half million people every month.

What's more, Larry Flynt's goofy, inane, and tasteless features (a centerfold of a fifty-year-old woman; thirty photos of Jackie Onassis swimming in the nude) have pushed both *Penthouse* and *Playboy* closer to hard-core porn—though both magazines deny it. Check inside either *Playboy* or *Penthouse* and you will see the mark of Larry Flynt. *Penthouse*, once considered an upstart in the skin business for showing pubic hair, is now coming on strong with "wide open beavers," "female masturbation," and the whole boatload of once taboo "erotica." *Playboy*, according to editorial director Arthur Kretchmer, "will never be a magazine as low and tasteless as *Hustler*." But one look at the November issue gives the game away. There, in good old-fashioned heterosexual *Playboy*, is a very suggestive lesbian motif. In short, both *Playboy* and *Penthouse* may be feeling the hot beer and sausage breath of the Flem Snopes of Skinland—Mister Larry Flynt.

In fact, the heat is getting so intense in the skin world that *Penthouse* publisher Bob Guccione is starting a hardcore magazine (*Bravo!*) to compete with Flynt's "raw" publication. And in the coming months, newsstand browsers may expect to be inundated with several new sex publications; in addition to Guccione's venture, there will be *Gallery*'s offspring *Pub* and *Dawn* (a magazine for women). There are even rumors that *Playboy* (circulation six million) is starting a hard-core magazine, though *Playboy*'s Kretchmer stoutly denies it. As *Dawn* editor Gay Bryant put it, "Larry Flynt's *Hustler* has caused a revolution in men's magazines. He's dropped the bottom out of the business."

Moreover, skin-magazine fans can expect to pay higher prices than ever for their vicarious titillation. *Playboy* and *Penthouse* have gone up from $1.25 to $1.50 for their regular issues; $1.75 for their holiday issues. *Hustler* sells at a regular price of $1.75 and soars up into the ethereal ranges of $2.25 for its holiday issue. Just a cursory look at some magazine racks is enough to make one think we are truly living in the last stages of the Roman Empire. At one small and rather poorly stocked newsstand in the Chelsea district of New York City, I perused the following publications: *Hot Sex, Swing, Pornocopia, Pussycat, San Francisco Ball, Fetish Times, Smut, Hooker, Pleasure, Screw, Orgy, Swingers Yellow Pages, Skin, Eat (For the Oral Minded), Sex, Gay Scene, Dick (The Magazine with Balls)*. Now, to be sure, most of these are what people in the skin-mag business call "garage publications," but remember, friends, *Hustler* was once merely a two-page house organ for Larry Flynt's Ohio Hustler Clubs. With a little capital and with the stiffly erect banner of *Hustler* successfully sailing in the wind, who knows how many of these small-time smut-mongers may decide to "go national." In short, if *Hustler* is the success Larry Flynt and many others (not all) in the skin-trade business think it may be, then we may expect to see the geometric growth of these rags on every news-stand in the United States. One may imagine a day when there are over a thousand slick national sex magazines, filled with no stories at all, only endless color pictures of endless couplings, endless suckings, giving rise to endless ennui.

Flynt, however long he lasts, has succeeded in exposing the grimy exploitative foundation of all the other men's magazines by merely embodying, and unconsciously parodying, all of their most base values. If Hefner shows big, melony breasts, Larry Flynt shows severed nipples. If Guccione gives the reader a big, wide swath of curly, black pubic hair, Larry Flynt finds the pinkest, most yawning cavern he can buy and spreads it all over a four-page pull-out centerfold. In short, *Hustler* is a prod, a critique, and an unconscious parody of the exploitation, stupidity, and tasteless mediocrity of all the men's magazines.

Scene: *The Annual National Publishing Industry Dinner in Support of the Brandeis University Scholarship and Fellowship Program.*

Larry Flynt, Althea Leasure, and I are sitting in the back seat of a cab that is parked in front of the St. Regis Hotel. Larry is paying the driver and eyeing the procession of angry, sign-carrying women who are circling the pavement in front of the entrance. Flynt is just finishing explaining to me why *Hustler* magazine is the "biggest publishing success since Henry Luce came on the scene with *Life* magazine."

"You see," Flynt says, fishing in his pocket, "it's like this. The American public don't respond to repressive, ah, things. I mean take, for instance, the two biggest successes of the last year in the movie world. What were they? I'll tell you. See, it was *Jaws* and *Godfather.* Why? Because the American people identified with Al Pacino because he wasn't repressed. I mean the character he played wasn't repressed. See? The same with *Jaws.* That shark wasn't repressed. The American people don't like repression. What the hell is this?"

Larry is shutting the door to the cab and staring at the nine women who are marching around yelling things like "We don't want Guccione's money. Dirty man. Dirty money. Bob Guccione is a male chauvinist pig. An exploiter of women."

Larry shakes his head and stops one of the girls.

"Are you a student at Brandeis University?" he says.

"Yes," the girl says. In her two hands she clutches a big sign condemning Guccione.

"Well, don't it cost a lot of money to go to school?" Larry says.

"Yes," the girl says politely.

"Well, isn't Bob Guccione going to give Brandeis University one hundred and fifty thousand dollars for their scholarship fund? And won't that make it easier for some kids to go to school?"

"Maybe so," says the girl. "But we don't want that kind of money. Do you realize that Bob Guccione made his fortune exploiting women? *Penthouse* is a sexist rag, and I think it is disgusting that my school is groveling to him by offering him an award as Publisher of the Year."

"*Penthouse* is sexist, huh?" says Larry.

Althea is standing there in her pink chiffon dress. She is staring wide-eyed at the girl, as if she is looking at a recently landed alien.

"Well, lemme ask you this," says Larry Flynt in his soft Kentucky accent. "Would you think it was wrong if *Ms.* was offering you the money?"

The girl stops and assumes a thoughtful look. "No, that would be all right. *Ms.* is a good magazine."

Flynt opens his eyes a shade more. *"Ms.* isn't sexist?" he says. He stares at Althea, who immediately starts to smile her big-toothed, country grin.

"*Ms.* isn't sexist, huh? Gloria Steinem isn't sexist? That's good. Hell. . . ." Flynt wants to go on with this, but an older woman in the protest, a NOW member, comes up and gets the Brandeis students marching again.

"Harvey," Larry says, as a middle-aged couple walks toward us. "Harvey, I want you to meet Bob Ward. He's here to do an article on us. Harvey Shapiro, Bob. He's our circulation man. I stole him away from the *National Enquirer*. He put them over the top . . . got them from two million to four million. This is Harv's wife, Bob. Babs, Bob. Bob, Babs."

"Hi, Babs," I say, and we start up the steps to the St. Regis.

The dinner is sponsored by the National Publishing Industry, a trade association of magazine publishers, retailers, and circulation people. Each year Brandeis and the NPI honor some prominent figure with the Publisher of the Year award. This year the golden Justice Brandeis plaque goes to *Penthouse* publisher Bob Guccione, who just happens to have recently contributed to the Brandeis University Scholarship and Fellowship Program.

As we enter the lobby, we are surrounded by a weird assemblage of people: dapper-looking academics and administrators from Brandeis and little munchkin people, short little guys with balding heads and large pots. These are the retailers, jobbers, and executives from the NPI. They are dressed in tuxedos but have the lines of the street in their faces. We are all flowing by the check-in desk, waiting for the elevator. A very uneasy marriage, this alliance between the Smut Kings and the Academics. Larry Flynt chooses this moment to vent his opinions on the women who are protesting this affair.

"Did you see them out there?" he says to Harvey. "They told me that *Ms.* magazine isn't sexist. That Gloria Steinem isn't sexist! Can you believe that? Bunch of filthy whores! You know what my ultimate dream is?"

"No," I say. "What is your ultimate dream?" Around us the faces fall apart. People are gazing desperately at the elevator dial, as if they are looking at a votive light.

"My ultimate dream is to take Butch—you know that big, black stud we had in the last issue of *Hustler*, the one with the fourteen-inch cock? I want to take Butch over to Gloria Steinem's and get him to ram his huge organ up that bitch's ass. That's my ULTIMATE DREAM!"

Harvey smiles and shakes his sad-eyed Dopey Dog head.

"Did ya hear that, Babs?" he says. "Larry . . . you are such a kidder."

Babs looks a little faint but manages a nice, appreciative smile. Everyone else rushes for the elevator, as though they are trying to get away from an earthquake.

The St. Regis Room

Gore Vidal is standing in the exact center of the St. Regis Room. He is sipping a drink and talking earnestly with Al Goldstein, publisher of *Screw*. Vidal, impeccably dressed and using his Victor Mature eyebrows to show his patrician disdain for one and all, explains the problems of "making the big leap" to Al.

"You'll never get on the Carson show, Al," Gore says, raising the eyebrows. "It's not that you wouldn't be good. It's just the name of your publication. Johnny would come on and say, "And now we have Al Goldstein, editor of. . . ." And that's it. You're through!" Gore turns his head slowly, rolls his eyes and arches his eyebrows a few more times.

Goldstein laughs and runs his hand over his silken, poodle, wide tie, which hangs like a dead turkey neck from his tight blue body shirt. Though Al had been animatedly talking with Larry Flynt about circulation problems and his upcoming trial (Goldstein is under indictment in Utah and claims he could go to jail for "six hundred years"), Al is now silent, and his eyes take on a doe-like quality. Here he is, a nice Jewish smut merchant from Brooklyn talking with a world-famous author. Al and Gore trading tidbits! Who woulda thought it?

Before Al can answer Gore, their conversation is interrupted by Herald Fahringer, a lawyer who has made his name by defending people like Goldstein, Larry Flynt, and Monique Von Cleef, the "Torture Queen" who ran a "House of Pain" in New Jersey. Fahringer is so slick, so distinguished (in the Rossano Brazzi mold) that he and Vidal look as though they are having a contest. Actually it's *nolo contendere*, for once Fahringer speaks it's obvious that he is deferring to Vidal's greater fame.

"I just loved your book *Burr*, Mr. Vidal," Fahringer says. "I found it to be so . . . historically accurate! Just what are you doing here? It's such a thrill to meet you!"

Vidal makes his eyebrows go up and down in double time. "I'm here with The Big Gucco," Vidal says in his 1950, FBI documentary voice. "The Big Gucco and I are doing a movie together *Caligula* . . . but not Camus."

Althea Leasure speaks up.

"Oh thaat," she says. "Larry and I saw thaat. . . . It wasn't thaat good."

Vidal eyes Althea and exhales a short snort of breath. A second later he wanders off in search of the Big Gucco.

Al Goldstein looks at Larry Flynt and Herald Fahringer.

"He's tremendously important," Goldstein says. "A literary giant!"

Flynt nods his head and smiles. At that moment the great teeming crowd of academics and members of the National Publishing Industry head into the main dining room. Dinner and Culture shall be served.

Big Gucco's Award

After nibbling at the fat-laden roast beef and playing around with the Brie and the sherbet (this tasteless gunk cost $150 a plate?), the great assemblage of magazine people, smut kings, and Brandeis officials is introduced to a whole rash of speakers, all of whom think they are on the Catskills' Borscht Belt Circuit. One speaker after another gets up and tells a bad Yiddish joke. However, only one is bad in a truly interesting way. A short, pinched-voice representative of the school gets up and looks out at the audience:

"This reminds me of a story," he says. "A man goes to the rabbi. The man has his dog with him and says to the rabbi, I would like to have my dog bar mitzvahed." The rabbi looks sternly at the man and says, "We don't bar mitzvah dogs here." The man persists. He says, "Look, my dog is thirteen and I want him bar mitzvahed." The rabbi is just as stern as before. "I told you once already, we don't bar mitzvah dogs here." Finally, the man gets a glow in his eyes and says to the rabbi, "'I'll give you $50,000 for your building fund." The rabbi smiles and says, "Funny, I didn't know your dog was Jewish."

That particular joke is met with an uneasy laughter, and the speaker receives a dark frown from the Big Gucco. Surprisingly, the joke is not lost on Larry Flynt, who leans over to me and says:

"See, them teachers and them professors are just the same as everybody else. It's money that makes them move. Just a bunch of whores."

Althea smiles and looks down at her sherbet.

"This isn't sweet," she says. "I just love sweet stuff. I can't wait until you come to Columbus, Bob. You're gonna have such good food. There's a lotta stuff out there that's really good."

The great moment has come, and the Big Gucco is given the big golden plaque: the Justice Brandeis Award for the Publisher of the Year. He nods and talks in a gravelly voice, reminiscent of the Godfather.

"Thank you from the bottom of my heart," mumbles the Big Gucco. "Dis is da most touching . . . the most moving thing that has happened to me since circumcision. . . ."

Now that's FUNNY! Larry Flynt and Al Goldstein laugh with much abandon. Al looks serious and says, "Class. You got to give it to him. He has class."

"Yeah," says Flynt. "But you watch. He won't mention one thing about the wide-open beavers. He don't want to admit that he's selling tits and ass just like the rest of us."

"Yer right there," says Goldstein.

And indeed Big Bob Guccione doesn't mention it. Rather he dwells on the plight of Vietnam veterans and how much the cause has personally meant to him. All humble, the Big Gucco says he took on the cause in the first place because "it seemed right." He would have us believe he is a noble savage, one strong man rising up from the urban wilderness. And as for the "so-called exploitation of women," the Big Gucco claims that the protesters "don't fully comprehend how much Penthouse is behind women. We support the ERA, for God's sake."

Larry shakes his head and plays with his tie—black silk with white polka dots and red roses. But he does seem impressed. Could it be that L.F. feels just a touch of admiration? Not on your life!

"I'll bet when he's sitting in bed getting head from Kathy Keeton," Larry says, "he doesn't talk about the Viet vets. I'll bet he talks about how *Hustler* is showing more pussy and better pink shots than *Penthouse*, and how they better get that old beaver open or they'll get blown off the market!"

"I'll be glad to get home," says Althea. "Then we can have sweets and Bob can meet Wendall."

"Who's Wendall?" I say.

"Wendall is the grossest person in the world," Althea says. "He can make musical notes with his farts. I'm not kidding. He can play tunes with 'em. And he's so accurate he can let one fly and blow out a candle!"

Jimmy Flynt's Tale

At the Columbus airport I am met by Larry's brother, Jimmy Flynt. He is copublisher of *Hustler*. He is wearing a dark blue cotton suit and black pointy-toed Italian jobbies with scarlet red heels. The shoes clash violently with the hayseed image of the suit, making him look like some kind of strange cross-pollination between Puerto Rican hipster and Kentucky Bible salesman. It isn't until later that I realize this bizarre hybrid defines Larry Flynt and Althea Leasure as well as Jimmy.

"We ought to stop in here at the airport newsstand a minute," Jimmy says. "Then we got to get right in and attend the editorial meeting. Larry wants you to see it."

"Great."

At the newsstand Jimmy turns on the old country charm.

"How's it going, darling?" he says to the woman behind the counter. "*Hustler* selling well?"

"Yes, it is," the woman drawls. "It's doing fine . . . outselling *Playboy* and *Penthouse*."

Jimmy smiles and squeezes the woman's arm. She smiles like Olive Oyl and goes back behind her cash register.

On the way out to the car, Jimmy is critical.

"That's a sloppy operation there. She's a good girl but just doesn't have the manpower to move *Hustler* like she could. Man, they sell out of there as fast as we can get 'em in. The damned distribution problems are terrific. We send in ninety a month, they sell out in two days, and then they can't get no more of 'em."

We throw my bags in a big, white Chrysler and pull out of the airport. On the way to Columbus, Jimmy tells me about his childhood in Kentucky.

"We weren't born with a silver spoon in our mouths. We were down in Lakeview, Kentucky, in the Appalachias, man, where there was nothing. We knew we had to get out of there or we didn't stand a chance. I was at the Hazel Green School, this boarding school, my father was a pipe welder, but he hits the juice too much, and Ma was up in Dayton running a country and western club. Larry was gone off into the Navy on forged birth certificates at fourteen. I couldn't sit still for class. It didn't mean nothing. I remember the day I left there. The teacher told me I could go to the barn and get a beating with a rod, or I could leave school. I said, 'Hell, that ain't no choice at all!' I went home, packed my bags and started hitching for Dayton the same afternoon. I was up near Covington, Kentucky, coming into Cincy, when I got a ride with a man named Joe Jet. He was a nice guy at first, but then a bulletin comes over the radio that says they are hunting for him. He's an escaped con! We started going about a hundred miles an hour then, and when we got up near Warren County, a cop starts in chasing us, and, man, we was going around curves and everything, and we slammed into a ditch, and I bashed my head on the windshield, and this huge welt comes up right up here, above my eye. They caught him but let me go, 'cause I was just a kid. I don't ever go back down there now if I don't have to."

"What happened to your father?"

"Dad? He works in the mailroom now, along with our stepmother. They open mail and love it. *Hustler* is really a family success story."

Home Is Where the Pink Is!

From the outside, on Gay Street, the *Hustler* building is a seedy-looking dump, the exact kind of place one would imagine a hard-core sex factory to operate from. The building, ugly gray stone, is situated next to an alley, and the *Hustler* sign, which hangs over the street, looks like any cheap, gaudy bar neon. As we go inside, Jimmy Flynt tells me this is all about to change.

"Larry's doing everything," he says. "He's going to blast the bricks. One side of the building is going to have a kind of 'Chicago look,' and on the other side we're adding wrought-iron balconies, to make it look like New Orleans."

I nod and wonder why it would be considered advantageous to have two different looks on what was going to be one office-club complex. Like Jimmy's strange clothing combinations, the building itself would become a kind of crazy quilt of incompatible styles, a palpable embodiment of the various forces that drive the Flynts: hippies, hillbillies, smut kings, and capitalists. A strange pastiche of conflicting selves, and not a little unsettling.

The Editorial Meeting

On the walls of Larry Flynt's office are giant centerfolds of the *Hustler* Honeys. All of the girls have a country look, and many of them are staring down at their genitals with open-mouthed astonishment, as if they are seeing themselves naked for the first time. The ones who aren't staring at themselves are touching themselves and staring off into a far horizon. In their eyes is a mystical dreamy look, and though it's easy to put the photographs down as moronic, it is perhaps instructive to note that the looks in the women's eyes are the same magical mystery look that used to be on happy hippie love posters of the late '60s. Sentimentality and simple-mindedness rule the roost in more places than *Hustler.*

Behind his massive oaken desk, Larry Flynt is sitting in an open-necked silken shirt. Around his neck he wears an ornament of some kind, a silver ornament that looks familiar to me but that, upon first entering, I cannot name. Directly behind Flynt is a poster that shows the ultimate *Hustler* Honey, a blonde space cadet who looks suspiciously like Barbarella; in her hand is a Luger and under her right leather, knee-length boot is a squashed *Penthouse* turtle. Beneath her long, muscular left leg is a murdered rabbit; there are blood stains on the *Playboy* Bunny's stomach and its eyes are crossed in surprised pain. In front of the desk, sitting on couches, is the *Hustler* staff. Flynt introduces me to Bobby Flora, the art director, a young man of twenty-two with a neatly blow-dried shag and a reindeer sweater. Next to Bobby is a middle-aged bearded man named Jimm Grady, the cartoon and humor editor. Beside Grady is Steve Hanley, a recently signed on associate editor; Jack Sharp, the *Hustler* ad director; John Hegenberger, another associate editor; and Althea Leasure, who holds the grand title of associate publisher and executive editor. All of these people shake hands with me and then give their complete devotion to Flynt, who begins with this speech:

"Bobby, you know I'm going to be Asshole of the Month. . . ."

Bobby Flora nods and swallows a bit. He looks nervous.

L.F. turns to me and turns on his slow sidewinder's smile.

"What happened, Bob, is that the retailers all said I should be Asshole of the Month because in the last issue I called them all cocksuckers. So, I'm gonna do it, though I really think it should be Jamaica Airlines . . . but we'll work that up, too. . . ."

Larry turns his majestic head back to Bobby Flora. It occurs to me that when Flynt moves his head, he rarely moves anything else, so one has a sense of almost Romanesque grandeur, as if the king must not weary himself with excessive movement. The only thing lacking in Flynt's Roman motif is muscle or bone structure in his face. While his profile is suitably striking, a full view of his face reveals him to look more like a baked potato with red hair on the top than an ancient emperor. Still, an impressive sight, this slow, grave rotation.

"Now for the cartoons," says L. F. "Has everybody seen this cartoon?"

Larry hands a cartoon around the room. Each editor looks at it and nods.

The cartoon is a picture of Bob Guccione cast as a nudie photographer. In front of him is a pair of open legs, and next to the legs is a whole case of Vaseline petroleum jelly. Gucco's face shows astonishment as a blond, strongly resembling Kathy Keeton (the Big Gucco's real-life "Living Associate"), comes to the door.

"What we need is a cutline on this cartoon," Flynt says. "Something funny!"

Althea starts to say that she doesn't think the artwork is really "first rate," but Larry Flynt is adamant.

"I said I'm satisfied with the artwork, so there's no point in saying anything about that. Now I want a funny cutline. Can anyone think of one?"

Steve Hanley speaks up:

"Ah . . . how about 'Still using that greasy kid stuff'?"

Everyone gives a small, tentative laugh. They are waiting to see if the Boss laughs. Larry nods the head but does not stretch the mouth.

"Well, that's pretty funny," he says, in the tone of a grave digger. "But I've seen it someplace before."

Althea chirps up: "How about having Kathy say, 'If you're good enough for Bob, you're good enough for me'?"

Everyone laughs at that one. (When the Boss's girl makes a joke, everyone laughs.)

"That's pretty good. Yeah . . . but we better think about it. Jimm, see if you can come up with something."

From the doorway, Jimmy Flynt pops in: "Say, Larry, did Linda Lovelace call you up yet?"

"Yes, she did," says Larry, pursing his lips a little in displeasure. "She said she would not fly all the way out here for an interview. So I told her agent the hell with it, and he said, 'Well, do you want some pictures of her anyway? I could send you some,' and I told him, 'No, I already got pictures of her,' and he said, 'Which ones,' and I said, 'The one where she's fucking the dog, and that's the one we're going to run.'"

Larry looks at me and smiles. Machiavelli of the porn kingdom. Step on the Godfather of Smut with your fancy Hollywood ways, and you end up underneath a giant King Husky!

The editorial meeting goes on and is uneventful. Larry hands me a pile of letters just recently delivered to *Hustler*. Like many people, I've always naively assumed (and hoped) that the skin mags make up their letters. Unfortunately, this is not so. The first letter I look at is written on a piece of torn, yellow legal paper. The correspondent pays no heed to such things as keeping each sentence on a single plane. Rather the words run up and down the page with reckless and desperate abandon. The first half of the letter is a celebration of Butch Williams's fourteen-inch cock; the second half is in the form of a request. Could *Hustler* please induce Butch Williams to part with a piece of his underwear, which would provide the reader with great "smell thrills"? I open another letter, which is addressed to Larry Flynt himself. The writing in letter two is nearly as bad as in the first, and the message is just as bizarre. The writer claims that Larry Flynt is the only man in the world honest enough to run for president, "because Larry Flynt tells it like it is."

Suspicious that Flynt is feeding me the more "baroque" letters, I request that I be able to look through a group at random. Larry agrees, and soon I am seated outside in an office with a huge stack of letters, all of which have come in just this morning. In a few minutes I am trapped inside a whirlpool of lust, yearning, and mindlessness that seems bottomless: endless letters from soldiers describing what they would like to do to a certain *Hustler* Honey. Letters from housewives in Kansas saying what they would like to do with Butch Williams; a letter from a man who begs *Hustler* to show women nude, with their legs open, smoking cigarettes! A letter from a man who claims to be in his late sixties but "hung like a horse"; he wants to "get in touch with a certain *Hustler* girl named Donna." And letters from several men asking Larry to set them up with Althea Leasure. After a half hour of reading these letters, I become groggy. At first they had been amusing, then depressing, and finally one had no reaction at all. I am amazed how quickly my feelings have become blunted. In forty minutes I am no longer astonished by any of it. Not even a letter from a man demanding that *Hustler* show nude women "doing housework," "show them nude making beds, cleaning filthy ovens" has much effect on me. I put the pile aside and think that I have really learned my first lesson. That is, after entering into the world of skin shocks, all moral and social distinctions tend to blur.

The Cartoon Session

Jimm Grady and Larry Flynt are sitting side by side in Flynt's office. They are going over the cartoons that have come in for *Hustler*. Flynt considers the cartoons one of the most important features in *Hustler*, perhaps as important as the *Hustler* Honeys. In the language of a layman, *Hustlers* cartoons are "gross." By design, they are at the opposite end of the cartoon spectrum from, say, the *New Yorker*. Where a *New Yorker* cartoon makes one smile and gives one the "shock of recognition" (real life problems of upper-middle-class people recognized and skillfully parodied), *Hustler* cartoons make one hold one's hand to one's head and say, "Oh, my God." Even though the intent is lowbrow, there is nonetheless a recognizable aesthetic at work. Where the *New Yorker* might say, "Elegance needs no defense," *Hustler* might counter with a parody of Wallace Stevens, "Grossness is all."

"Do you get a lot of freelance stuff?" I ask Grady.

"You wouldn't believe it," he says. "We can't get them to hit hard enough. There's always too much restraint used . . . they just won't be *really* gross."

Flynt picks up a cartoon and smiles. "Lord," he says, pushing out his breath. "Where in the hell did you get this? It's unbelievable."

Grady smiles and leans over toward Larry. "It's a beauty, isn't it? That's the one I'm most happy about. It's terrifically drawn, too. It's almost a *woodcut.*"

"Yeah," says Flynt. "But it could get us in big trouble. I mean if those Southern bigots ever haul us into court and we have something like this in the magazine . . . they'd never let up on us. We can get away with the open pussy shots, but they'd pass right by those and fry us if they saw this."

Grady shakes his head and rubs his hand over his goatee. "Aww, come on. I want to fight for this one. I mean this one really does it." Flynt hands the cartoon across the room to me. "What do you think, Bob?"

I look at the cartoon in disbelief. Pictured is the Crucifixion. We see Jesus' body from the waist down. His penis is hanging out of his loin cloth, and around the head of his cock is a crown of thorns. Beneath him, two Roman soldiers are staring at his member and saying, "He may rise again, but that thing sure won't."

"Well?" says Larry.

"Christ," I say. "Are you gonna print this?"

Grady slaps his fist into his open palm. "We have to, Larry! That's hard-edged. That's the kind of thing our readers want."

The Phone Call

Flynt and I are sitting in his office going over some sales statistics. While Flynt likes to talk about anything concerning the magazine, his favorite topic of conversation, one that he returns to again and again with monotonous regularity, is the way he is cutting into *Playboy* and *Penthouse*'s markets.

I am nodding my head but not really hearing. Rather, I am entranced by the silver medallion that I had seen the first day but could not recognize.

"Larry," I say, "that, ah . . . thing you are wearing. It looks like a . . ."

"A cunt!" Larry says. "I make them nervous with that. A little old woman cashier in the Hilton started fondling it and saying how pretty it was. 'What is it, young man?' she said. I said, 'That's a cunt, lady.' You should have seen her jump!"

As Larry begins to laugh, the phone rings. "Hello," he says. "Yes . . . Oh, yes, how are you? Tonight? Dinner? Well, sure, I'd like to have dinner with you tonight, but you see there is this reporter here from *New Times* magazine. He will be with me tonight, and if you don't mind him coming along, then fine . . . what? . . . wait, I'll ask him."

Flynt puts his hand over the receiver and addresses me: "There's a man on the phone who wants to see me tonight. He's going to be on the board of directors I'm setting up. But he's got very close ties to the legal and social establishment of Columbus, and he wouldn't want any publicity. Can our meeting be off the record?"

"All right," I say. I figure I'll get something out of it, even if I can't use the guy's name.

Larry goes back to the conversation:

"Yeah, it's all right. He says he won't use your name, and I'm sure you can trust him. What? You'd rather not? Well, I'll be tied up all week. Call me next week and we'll have dinner then. Right. Goodbye."

Flynt puts down the phone, gets up and stretches his leisure suit.

"See, I'm setting up this board of directors. I can't have all sexual fiends on it. I've got to have some good legal and business minds, and unfortunately most of those kinds of people are conservative. Bunch of goddamned hypocrites. They want a piece of the action in a winner like *Hustler*, but they don't want anyone to know about it. That's the whole fucking problem with this country. It's like what I was talking about the other night. It's repression. They are just a bunch of whores, like everybody else."

Lunch with the Major-domo

Around a big circular table in the back of an old Columbus hotel sit Larry and Althea, Lee Henry (a well-known Columbus restaurateur), a PR man with a local restaurant newsletter, an architect named Bill (who is looking for Flynt to give him some work), and myself. The architect is trying to get a few words in edgewise but for the most part is being snowballed by Larry, who wants to tell me about his own sex life.

"Well," says Bill, tossing his head around like a spring doll in the back of an automobile, "I had a dinner date with Joey Heatherton. Just a dinner date. That's all."

"Too bad," says Larry. "I ball most of the girls who come in to model for the magazine. I get them in the office and I ask them if they want to model and if they have any inhibitions, and then they say no, and I take out my Polaroid camera and tell them I'll have to take a few test shots, and they take off their pants and I just start posing them, and pretty soon I say, 'You're getting pretty horny aren't you, honey?' and I can see they are, and then I just lock the door and pile on!"

Bill makes this odd little clucking noise in his throat. Could it be that he's just a bit repulsed by this grisly story of mutual corruption? If so, he gets himself under control. He wants to finish his story.

"Well, that sounds like fun. Haha. I wish I coulda done that with Joey. But, you know . . . it was strictly business."

"Bob," says Larry, totally ignoring Bill, "I'll tell you. I am dead serious about repression. Now you take me. The key to my success was reading Napoleon Hill's *How to Make a Million*. The most profound book I ever read. I got to this part where it was called 'Why Men Are Seldom Successful Before Forty,' and lights went off in my head. In there Hill says that all great men have a huge sex drive. George Washington and Abraham Lincoln. But they learned to channel their sexual drive into their work. Well, that really hit me, because when I owned the Hustler Club all I did was structure my work around all the pussy I was getting. I would ball so many girls that I would have to ask Althea when a girl came into the club, 'Say, have I balled her yet?' And Althea would tell me. Anyway, when I read Napoleon Hill, I realized that if I channeled myself into my work fifty percent and my balling fifty percent, then I would be a success. I mean with *Hustler* there is plenty of pussy, but it is not like the bar business. Besides, having come from Kentucky, and being dirt poor, I went through a stage when I had to have the finer things. But now that I'm thirty-three I'm beyond that. I understand why I had to have them things. . . . Hell, in Kentucky I remember sitting on a bridge looking down at the water. I wore Anvil Brand overalls, polo shirts, and I had holes in my shoes. And my mother had started crying because she was so sorry to see me have to go out in the snow without shoes to school. And I thought right then, 'I'm going to get rich someday and then my mother won't have to cry no more about me not having good shoes.' Anyway, I was in the navy at fourteen and got sent overseas to Italy. Then they found out I was underage, and they threw me out, so I forged some more birth certificates and joined the army. And after I got out of there, when I was eighteen, I got married. Man, I was bankrupt once and married twice before I was even twenty-one. I even worked in a mattress factory. Then I started my tavern business. The first one was Larry's Hangover Haven. I met every con man in the world. If we didn't have two or three good fights every Saturday night we didn't consider ourselves a success. From there I got some other clubs, like Larry's Hillbilly Heaven. All in all, I've owned over forty clubs. *Hustler* started off as a house organ in one of the clubs. Two pages . . . just to tell you which girls was appearing in which clubs, stuff like that . . . but it wasn't until I read Napoleon Hill that I learned to channel my sex life."

"And I'm sure your good woman had something to do with that, Larry," says the PR man.

"Yes," says Larry. "Althea has been a great help to me. But that don't mean she's the only pussy I want. I don't mean to say I've settled down yet. I mean, I took her out when she was a dancer in the clubs, and I balled her, and she started hanging onto me, you know . . . and . . ."

Althea, who has been talking with Lee Henry, stops and gets a look of mock indignation on her face.

"Larry," she says, "I did not hang onto you."

Larry smiles. "Now you know you did. I mean you liked it, didn't you?" Althea rolls her eyes and changes her look to mock guilty.

"Anyway," says Larry. "I told her right then and there that no one pussy, even if it was lined with gold, was going to be enough for me!"

"Satin's not good enough for you?" Althea says.

Next to me, Bill is making that odd clucking noise. He is turning pale. The PR man is smiling this big puppet's smile, as if he is just hanging on every word, but his eyelashes are going up and down like windshield wipers in a shit blizzard.

"What if Althea wants to sleep with someone else?" I ask Larry. "Could you handle that?"

Larry smiles and looks super sincere.

"If she wanted to, it would be all right with me. But she don't have them kind of desires. She's not like that."

"Not with men anyway," Althea smiles. "If I'm going to sleep around, I'd rather make it with women."

"Are you serious?" I say.

Althea happily nods her head. "I like any kind of sex, but I really prefer women."

Bill's clucking takes on the sound of the whole henhouse. The PR man's eyes go all hazy, and even dapper Lee Henry looks a bit ruffled.

I look for some reaction from Larry, but he is merely laughing and shaking his big belly. He reaches over and gives Althea a tender, loving squeeze.

The Mail Order Game

"This here is the Fulfillment Room," Larry says. "We started off the mail order business first because we knew we'd have trouble with advertisers. We wanted *Hustler* to be totally self-sufficient, so we sell our line of Leasure Time Products. It brings in an amazing amount of money."

We walk through the long, ugly mail order room. About fifteen long-haired teenage boys are packing away posters and cardboard boxes filled with what Flynt calls Fulfillment Items.

"What the hell is all this stuff?" I ask.

Flynt smiles, opens a cupboard and pulls out a couple of plastic bags filled with stuff that looks like marijuana. One package is called Volupte, the other Fiord.

"This here is just a bunch of useless herbs," Flynt says. "We advertise it in *Hustler* and people buy the crap. It's unbelievable. I guess they put it in with their grass, or maybe the dealers cut their grass with it. I don't know."

I look the stuff over: ginseng herb, which can be bought at any health food store, and a couple of other herbs, probably oregano. Price: $4.95.

"Don't you advertise that people can get high smoking this stuff?" I ask.

"Not exactly," says Flynt. He gets a copy of *Hustler* and shows me the ad. It reads: "2 Brand New Ancient Ideas For Lovers. Sensuous Exciting herbal blends that you smoke like marijuana, or mix with your stash. Volupte is a secret mixture of herbs used as aphrodisiacs for centuries, including ginseng root from China, plus damiana, verbascum, flowers and more. Fiord contains African yohimbe bark, one of the most powerful sex herbs ever discovered, said to even have caused spontaneous erections. Fiord sells for $4.95. Volupte sells for $5.95."

"You wouldn't kid folks, Larry, would you?" I say. Flynt smiles and looks in the cabinet for some other goodies. "No, sir," he says. "I wouldn't want to lie to Archie Bunker. See, I know what he wants. He likes this stuff because it's exotic. Here is something you might like to take back to your girl." Flynt hands me a huge rubber penis with a giant head at either end.

"That's the Double Dong." Flynt says. "You get two lesbians hanging on that thing . . . it's wild."

"You're kidding," I say.

"No. You mean you never seen that? You ought to come to one of our orgies. I was going to try and throw one for you, but it being Thanksgiving, I didn't know if we can get many of the girls together. You ought to come out to our big Christmas orgy though. We get about thirty girls together and about fifteen guys. It's wild. Of course, you got to have 'screamers.'"

"Screamers?"

"You know, chicks that start screaming as soon as you put it in 'em. That's what gets everybody else turned on. Here's something else." Flynt hands me a rubber, flesh-tone object with hideous lips and ugly-looking hair. He also hands me a catalog describing what is in my hands. "ARTIFICIAL VAGINA FOR YOUR LOVE! (rubber type with hair implanted on the outside) will provide hours of stimulating pleasure. These artificial vaginas can be of aid when normal penetration is not possible. Two models: personal size, Pocket Pal, #73 for home use, and family size, #41, for couples."

I stare down at the artificial vagina. Behind it is a long plastic sack, presumably for one's penis. I feel a vague wave of nausea wash over me, and Flynt begins to laugh.

"Something for everyone," he says. He is enjoying my reaction. Suddenly, without warning, his mood changes and he chews out a boy who has failed to properly paste on labels.

I put down the Pocket Pal, and we make our way out of the Fulfillment Room.

Hometown Girls

Upstairs, Larry introduces me to an attractive girl named Chris Zwilling, who answers the phones for *Hustler*'s mail order service. I ask her what kind of phone calls she gets.

"Weird ones. I'm used to it now. But the first few really shocked me. A lot of people call up and want you to describe the stuff to them and how to use it. Soon you realize that they are using you to get off sexually. Either that or they just start saying what they'd like to do with you."

"Does that bother you?"

"Not really, not anymore. I just tell them politely that I have work to do and hang up."

The red button on the mail order phone lights up and Chris answers the phone. After she has taken the order, I ask her if Flynt has approached her about appearing in the magazine. "Oh yes," she says. "I'm probably going to do it soon."

"Don't you feel any reservations about appearing in *Hustler*?"

"No. Why should I? Everyone around here has done it: Marie and Vicki and Cindy Spain—they've all appeared in it. And Jocelyn, down in the mail room. You get a nice trip—like Jocelyn just got back from Jamaica—and you get paid pretty well now, $750."

"But what about the women's liberation arguments? You know, that you're being exploited, that it's degrading."

Chris Zwilling shrugs her shoulders and smiles vacantly. "I just don't see it that way," she says.

Nor does Jocelyn of the mail room, who tells me that everyone treated her with great courtesy on her Jamaican trip, that she got to work with James Baes, one of the leading European photographers, and that she was put up at the home of Lyle Stuart, the New York publisher who made his millions with *The Sensuous Woman* and other sex fantasies.

"How about feeling exploited?" I ask her.

"No," she says. "I had a great trip. I wouldn't want to do it for anyone else though. I mean I like it here."

There is a simplicity about the women who work at *Hustler*; they are hometown girls, naive and provincial. One has the sense that for them, at this stage in their lives, the whole *Hustler* world seems romantic and exciting. What could be simpler? Just spread your legs and lie about and you are paid $750. It seems easy, harmless—after all, everyone else does it.

When I ask another girl if she has taken part in Flynt's orgies, she sheepishly admits she has. "But only once," she adds. "I was surprised that I wasn't uptigtht. It was a very exciting experience. And next time I go I'll get paid."

"Paid? How much?"

"Fifteen or twenty dollars. Whatever I want."

She stops, her face reddens and she looks nervous, even a bit fearful, "Maybe I shouldn't have said that," she says.

"He pays you to go? Does he pay everybody?"

"I don't know," the girl says. She rubs her face nervously and swallows hard.

The Kahiki Room

Columbus's three best restaurants are all owned by Lee Henry, the man who had attended the lunchtime sexual confessions of Althea and Larry two days before. Flynt, Althea, and I are eating a delicious Polynesian dinner and sipping something called a mystery drink from stone goblets. Around my neck is a pink plastic lei, and all around us fake lightning flashes and a sprinkler system shoots out a booming mechanical downpour.

"What about this payment thing?" I ask Flynt. "Do you have to pay everyone to go to these things?"

Flynt blinks his eyes and smiles a big, innocent smile. "I don't know what she could have meant," Flynt replies. "We pay the girls to deliver drinks or be waitresses but not to go to the orgies. I never tell people who to fuck."

Althea smiles, shakes her head, and opens her Orphan Annie eyes. The pair are the absolute apogee of small-town innocence.

"Look, I'll tell you honest," Larry continues. "I don't have to pay people. Once they get into the spirit of things, they just want to screw. I recently went to a retailers' convention in Las Vegas. Now I took a whole bunch of girls with me. I never said to them, 'Screw so-and-so because he helps sell *Hustler*.' I didn't have to. I mean, I didn't take no squares with me, if you understand what I mean—but that's all part of good business. And like I say, the girls I take like to have fun."

"You don't think you are repressing them or exploiting them?"

"Repression?" Flynt looks aghast. "That's what I'm against! *Hustler* isn't like the repressive magazines. We'll print anything. We believe in getting hang-ups right out front."

"Well how about your Butch and Peaches spread?" I say. "Now a lot of people would say by publishing a black man with a huge cock like that you're merely trading on the oldest racist tale known. And by having him making it with a white woman you are appealing to the fears of white men. Not to mention the fact that the whole thing would be denounced as the fantasy of a male chauvinist pig."

Flynt smiles and sips his drink.

"Well, first of all, I knew that. I mean I figured it would be funny, and I figured it would outrage everybody. The whites, the blacks, the women—everybody. But that's why *Hustler* is so successful. We're irreverent and that's why people love us. As for the male chauvinist stuff, I am a male chauvinist; women are here to serve men. Look at them, they got to squat to piss. Hell, that proves it."

Althea laughs proudly. "Larry got the award as Male Chauvinist Pig of the Year at one place he worked," she says.

Larry squeezes Althea, and she puts her head on his big stomach.

"We been together four years and never even have arguments," Larry says.

Althea

In her office, Althea Leasure details her favorite jobs at *Hustler*.

"I came up with the idea for the Bits N Pieces part of the magazine," she says. "I came up with the 'Man Eating Shit' feature. I also came up with the 'Guillotined Cock' feature, also the 'Bit Off Nipple,' and stuff like that. Weird stuff. I get my ideas by going across the street to a novelty store and looking around. Like I'll see a little guillotine and I'll think. 'What if it was a guillotine for cocks. Hustler readers would like that.' People go for the shocking and the weird and the strange. You ever seen the 'Man Eating Shit'?"

"No," I say, "I don't believe I have."

Althea smiles and yells out, "Eric. Eric."

From next-door, a small, gnomelike-looking man comes meekly into the room.

"Eric," says Althea, "go get the slides of the 'Man Eating Shit' and the 'Guillotined Cock' and the 'Girl Catching the Man with the

Fishing Line Up His Ass' and 'Bit Off Nipple.' Bring them in here please."

"Yes," says Eric. "Let's see . . . that's the 'Man Eating Shit' and the 'Bit Off Nipple' and what else?"

"'The Fishing Rod Up the Guy's Ass,'" says Althea, getting a little cross.

Eric smiles weakly at me and disappears down the hall.

"You see," says Althea, "I know what turns men on. I know what turns women on. Women like the big stud and the 'force-fuck.' I think that's a big turn on for women. I mean not rape, but the 'force-fuck.' A woman likes to know that a man is willing to take the pussy no matter whether she's going to give it or not."

She stops and gets a glazed look in her eyes. "You know what would turn me on, what I would really like and I plan on having? Two female slaves. I want them to dress in old Roman gowns, and I want to have their hair piled up on their heads like Greeks, and I want them to be my ladies-in-waiting. I mean my slaves. I'd treat them good. They could go shopping with me, and they could take baths with me, and they would be there to serve my guests and to take care of them sexually, but only if I told them so. And I wouldn't want them to sit around chewing gum and gossiping and watching television and that kind of stuff while I was gone. They would have to act like that all the time. I mean if they didn't, it would ruin the whole fantasy, wouldn't it?"

"Yes," I say, "I suppose it would. Tell me, what did you do before you got into this line?"

"Well, I was an orphan," she says. "I lived in a lot of orphanages all over Ohio. I ran away from most of them, they were so repressive. I was at the Soldiers and Navy Orphanage and I lived with my aunts. Say, what do you want to know stuff like that for anyway?" She is getting nervous, fidgeting with her T square.

Tony's Mistake

It is the day before Thanksgiving and Larry Flynt is looking over some new girlie photos that have been taken by a very hip-looking black photographer from New York named Tony. In the past, when Hustler was still struggling and Flynt was using freelancers a lot, he depended on Tony's work. In the December issue of *Hustler* alone, Tony shot the cover, the centerfold, and another girlie spread called Donna Sea Nymph. Now, however, though Tony doesn't yet know it, things have changed. *Hustler* is doing well, and Flynt is planning on using fewer American photographers. Instead, Larry wants to pick up on people like James Baes, the cameraman who is famous for his pictures in the French magazine *Lui*. For the past two days, Flynt has raved about what good artists the Europeans are. It's as though he has discovered the Cubists or the Surrealists. But these great artists have vastly different aims, such as shooting "great genital shots," getting "good color textures to the skin" and using "exciting, exotic backgrounds" and "original layouts." like those found in *French Schoolgirls Meet Dracula*.

While Tony, in a leather leisure suit, smokes a cigarette and paces the floor, Flynt is hunched over the light table.

"You're gonna love these girls, Larry," says Tony. "These are Grade A girls."

I watch Tony prance about. Though he has been exuding confidence, personality, and hipness ("Like I have put together this really totally unbelievable package, which I knew Larry and Althea would be stunned by"), it's obvious the man is very nervous.

"You get rejections on these from *Oui* and from *Playboy* before I see 'em, Tony?" Larry says.

Tony feigns horror and passes his long artistic fingers across his face.

"That's absolutely ridiculous," he says. "These are pictures taken strictly for *Hustler* magazine, Larry. I want you to know that."

Larry begins to shake his head. He sucks in his breath and gives out a little sigh.

"Tony, you take great ass shots. You know I love your ass shots. But this chick's ass is ugly. Bob," he says to me, "I want you to look at this chick's ass. Look closely and tell me what you see."

I lean over the loop, squint my eye, and look down at a perfectly normal ass. (Having seen several thousand asses this week, I have come to look at the human body as a mere piece of meat, and not a particularly interesting one at that.)

"Looks like a normal ass to me, Larry," I say.

"Look again, Bob. Look right in the ass."

I squint and look right in the ass. I see nothing unusual. "I see nothing unusual about this ass," I say.

"For Christ's sake," Larry says, grabbing the loop out of my hand. "Look again. This chick has got the hemmies. Tony, I can't believe you'd try and sell me a goddamned group of pictures with an ugly-looking whore like this whose hemmies are hanging out!"

Tony is sweating and looking like he'd like to crawl out of his leathers and fade away.

"Hemmies," he says. "I didn't notice any hemmies!"

Larry is pounding his hands on the counter.

"Not only does this whore have the hemmies," he says, "but her pussy isn't even opened up. You've got to get that pussy open, you hear, Tony? I mean you make it with these broads. Do it yourself."

"Honest to God," says Tony. "I never laid a hand on her. . . ."

"Well maybe," says Larry, "maybe you should have. She's got to have an open pussy, Tony. I want that pussy opened up like a beautiful flower, you understand? The way it looks now is like a pile of cow shit a wagon wheel has rutted through!"

Tony is sweating. All his New York City hip, hustling Superfly cool is fast fading away.

"Take a look at the other ones, Larry," Tony says. "I'm sorry about those. I didn't mean to break your chops, heh heh. . . ."

Larry looks at another group of photos.

"Not bad. This is a good-looking girl with a nice ass. How much you want for these?"

Tony manages to recoup a bit.

"For you, Larry, $1,500 for the whole package, and I'll pay the girl."

"I'll tell you what," says Larry. "I'll give you a thousand dollars for these pictures, Tony. I'll pay the girl myself. She gets $350 and another $400 if she doesn't appear in another magazine for six months."

Tony gulps and shakes his head.

"Larry," he says. "I mean, you're paying her a total of $750. I've already got expenses of $400. Which means I clear only $600. She makes more than me . . . and I worked and broke my chops to put this package together. That's not right, Larry."

Larry gets up from the viewing table and walks over to Althea's desk. He picks up a copy of *Lui*, and opens to the centerfold.

"You see this?" he says. "You see this? Can you take pictures like this, with these colors that just jump off the page? Can you get locations like this? Can you make the water on the broad's stomach stand out like that?"

Tony is shell-shocked. Here he is, the leading man for *Hustler* magazine, a man with three covers and even Donna Sea Nymph to his credit, and he is being treated like a swine.

"I could, Larry," he murmurs, "if I had the money."

"Tony," Larry says, "I'm using Michelle Moreau and Dominique from Switzerland and James Baes. All these people are bankrolled. They go wherever they want, and if I ask them to shoot something again, they do it forty times until we both got what I want. You take your pictures in some broad's apartment on her couch, Tony. *Hustler* is going first-class now. That stuff was all right before, Tony, but it's out now, over and out!"

Tony starts to speak, but words fail him and he slumps down on the table.

At the door, a little photographer's agent named Nat shows up. He has an overbite that makes him look like a ferret.

"Hello, Larry," he says. "Wait till you see what I brought you from France."

Tony looks as though he wants to leap out of the window. Larry spreads out Nat's hundreds of girlie slides on the viewing table. In a few minutes Larry is whistling and commenting on the "great pink" shots. Nat is smiling and shaking his head, and Tony is standing around, all loose, uncoiled, as if a tense wire spring inside him has snapped, leaving him a formless mass of bad nerves.

"Man," he says. "Everywhere I go I get my head beat in."

Larry's Big Problem

Larry Flynt and I are sitting in the basement of the Wine Cellar, a classy backdrop that conflicts with Larry's crude, hilljack persona. Right now Larry is a bit down in the dumps.

"I know *Hustler*'s writing stinks," he says. "I wish I personally knew more about writers. Say, you're a writer, Bob. Who's the greatest writer of the century?"

"James Joyce," I say. "But you can't buy him for *Hustler*. He's dead."

"Hmm," Larry says. "Did he ever win a Pulitzer Prize?"

"No," I say, oddly touched by his massive ignorance. "He was too good to get a Pulitzer."

"Well, hell, did he ever have a bestseller?"

"Not exactly."

Larry shakes his head and shoves his fork in the air.

"Well, I don't get it! I mean why even write a book if it ain't going to be a bestseller? I wish I had some good writers," he says. "I'd like to have writers for *Hustler* as good as . . . as . . . Hemingway."

"But then your readers might be turned off," I suggest.

Larry nods. "Yeah, that is a problem. What I need are some writers as good as Hemingway who specialize in pornography. That's it. I need some pornographic Hemingways!"

Thanksgiving Day

Althea and Larry and I are driving out of Columbus on the Interstate to Althea's sister's house for the Thanksgiving feast. Larry is telling me about his marriages.

"I've had four wives and five kids," he says, "I really miss those kids. Next year I'm going to buy the old governor's mansion and move in there and get the kids. Then Althea will gradually leave the magazine and take care of the kids. I really want the kids now. I don't approve of the way their mothers are raising them."

"Won't the judge hit you with some kind of rap like 'A smut king shouldn't be allowed to raise kids'?" I ask.

Larry laughs and shakes his head. "No, you don't understand. I'm not going through the courts. I'm just going to each of the mothers and making them an offer."

"You're going to *buy* your kids from their mothers?"

"Well, I'm not going to put it that way," Larry Flynt says, "but that's what it comes down to. Every woman has her price."

"How much do you think it will cost you?" I ask.

"Oh, maybe continued support payments for the rest of their lives."

"That will be astronomical, won't it?"

Flynt again shakes his head.

"No. I only give about twenty-five dollars a kid now. Of course I spend a lot more. I buy all their clothes and stuff like that. But I only have to legally pay twenty-five dollars a week per kid."

"How can that be?" I ask, astonished. "I mean you say you are going to make six million dollars on *Hustler* this year, and you've projected your profits for next year at twenty million dollars, so how come you pay so little child support?"

Flynt pulls the car into a working-class neighborhood, turns a corner, and stops in front of an old white, wood-frame house.

"Well," he says, "it works like this. In Ohio there is this wonderful law which bases a man's support payments on his salary, not his holdings. Now, as it says right in *Hustler*'s publisher's statement, I draw a salary of only two hundred dollars a week, so I pay support based on that and not on all my holdings."

"I see," I say. "And you also tell the working people who buy *Hustler* that you have a two-hundred-dollar-a-week salary just like them. So that makes them identify with you."

Flynt chuckles, and we get out of the car and walk up to the house. Althea's brother-in-law and sister answer the door. They are sitting in their living room, watching a football game.

"Welcome, Larry," says the man. "You all want a beer?"

We say we do and sit down on the couch. It's a small place, and the dinner is going to be served in the kitchen.

"You know," Larry says to me, "Althea was raised in a Soldiers Orphanage. She never had nothing as a kid, I mean. I really want to get my kids so they can have all the advantages. I want to take them to ball games, let them be kids. I don't think kids should be punished for what adults do, which is fuck up the world.

"I like you," he says. "You're a hip guy. I'm kind of hippie myself, you know. Half hippie and half hick. I call myself a hickey."

I smile and shake my head. It's a corny term but somehow adequate. Some more relatives show up, good old boys who work at a construction site. One of them starts telling Larry how he "took a couple copies of *Hustler* up to the site, and you shoulda seen the guys."

"Yeah, well, wait till you see what's coming up," Larry says. "We're offering Jackie Onassis a million dollars to appear on *The Tonight Show* with me."

The relative doesn't seem astonished.

"Think she'll take it?" he says.

"I don't know," Larry says. "She might not, but then again, you can never tell. She's just like everybody else. There ain't much people won't do for money."

"That's true, for sure," the man says.

"Amen," says Althea, winking and laughing. "Now let's all get out here at the table. You men can eat first, but make it quick 'cause I'm hungry."

We trudge through the house and sit at the table. Larry looks at me and smiles, then glares around the table and starts laughing. "Althea," he says, "you say grace."

Althea smiles and winks again and makes her hands into a little chapel: "God is great/God is good/Let us thank Him/For this food/Now let's eat!"

Her voice is little, childlike, and sends a chill down my back.

"Great job, baby," Larry Flynt says. "We all got a lot to be thankful for. Now let's dig into this good country cooking!"

He gives a big down-home grin to his relatives, who stare at him with open awe. These are his people, the poor, the wiped out, the hopeless, the ones he knows so very well. Without another word, he grabs the plate of sweet potatoes and starts helping himself.

On December 18, the day after this story went to the typesetter, Larry Flynt was indicted in Cincinnati on charges of bribery and sodomy. Along with Flynt, Cincinnati Police Chief Carl Goodin and six vice-squad officers were indicted on charges that included bribery, extortion, and perjury. Ward spoke with Flynt by phone the next day. His comment: "It's just harassment. They probably are gonna say I was giving presents and money to the police. Which is, of course, not true. You know I'm not the kinda guy who would do anything like that."

Postscript

When I got back from Columbus I slept for two days solid. Being around Larry and Althea was exhausting. The entire time I was out there I had affected an Arkansas accent. I had gone to school in Fayetteville, Arkansas, and picked it up easily. It wasn't as pronounced as a true Arkansas or Mississippi accent but sounded both Southern and Southwestern. I was a natural mimic and found myself using that talent to good effect with Larry. I also made a number of cornball jokes and basically established myself as a good old boy.

When Flynt had asked me whether the piece was going to be positive or negative, I came up with an answer that even surprised me. I said, with a big, wide, Andy Griffith smile, "Larry, I am here to set the record straight!" He smiled and shook his head.

I could hardly believe he had gone for that, but I found out that that fame was a heady drug. People wanted to believe that their side of the story was the only side and since you were there to talk to them, then, of course, you would be exclusively giving their side.

After that day I used the "I'm here to set the record straight" line every time I met with a subject, and not once did anyone ever question what it meant. It was a great answer, because it was the truth. The record was the truth and I was there to get it. If they couldn't figure that out, that was their tough luck.

Though it had only been a few months I was already taking Tom Wolfe's advice and becoming much tougher regarding my work. This wasn't a joke or an experiment anymore. I wanted to do it, and I had to take it seriously.

I was dead tired and I was counting on a whole week to write the piece but another editor, Marty Bell called me one day after I got back.

"Got some tough news for you," he said. "One of our lead articles for the new issue didn't work. You have two days to write it and get it here. I know you can do it."

With that he hung up.

I felt my heart racing, my mouth getting dry. Two days. Jesus, I had like a book of notes. Five or six notebooks chock full of outrageous stuff. I could spend a month on this piece. Easily.

But that was the business.

I put on some coffee and started reading my notes.

I worked nonstop for thirteen hours, collapsed, slept maybe three hours, got up again, and started writing again.

By the end of the weekend I had the piece you've just read. Ten thousand words!

The article was a huge success. A few people called *New Times* and cancelled their subscriptions, but I was on the radio all over the United States. I got phone calls from other magazines, including *Rolling Stone*, and I was thrilled. The guys at *New Times* loved it and found themselves getting more newsstand sales than ever. The PR more than made up for the cancellations.

I still wondered, however, what Larry Flynt felt about it all.

About a week after the piece came out I found out.

I was sitting in my Geneva apartment having a drink with Robin when the phone rang. I picked it up. It was Larry. He spoke in a high-pitched Southern drawl.

"This here Bobby Ward?"

"Yep. Hi, Larry."

"I just want to say one thing to you. I ain't mad. That was one hell of a job you done on me but I ain't mad. But Jimmy, my brother, is furious."

"Jimmy," I said. "But he's barely in the article."

"Yeah, but you said his new shoes made him look like a Puerto Rican hustler on Forty-second Street. He wants to hit you in the hade with a ballbat!"

"Holy shit," I said.

"Yeah, I'm trying to talk him out of it but no telling what ol' Jimmy might do."

I couldn't help it. I started laughing.

"Well, I'm glad you aren't too mad, Lar," I said. "I thought it was a pretty good likeness."

"Yeah, well, live and learn," Larry said. "You one of them truth-tellers. You fucking guys. . . . I'll be seeing you, Bobby."

He hung up the phone and so did I.

A chill went down my back. Man, I had only done two or three pieces and two of my subjects, the Geneva cops and Larry Flynt, wanted to kill me.

This gig was even more exciting than I had thought. But nothing could have prepared me for what happened next.

About a week after Larry had called me to tell me how Jimmy wanted to beat up my head with a ballbat, the phone rang again. This time Robin answered it.

"Yes, yes. Oh, hi, Larry."

She looked at me and started laughing.

"It's Larry Flynt again."

"Yeah, yeah," I said. I was already immune to being threatened.

"Listen, Larry," I said, taking the phone. "Let's cut the shit. I don't want to hear any more of your threats, okay?"

"Wait, wait, wait," he said. "You got me all wrong. I ain't gonna threaten you. No, sir. I been thinking about it and I come to the conclusion that anyone who could fool me as good as you did should be on my side. I need a new editor for *Hustler* magazine and I want him to be Bob Ward!"

To say I was surprised by this offer would be the greatest understatement of my life. I almost fell over from the shock.

"I'll start you off at fifty thousand a year but you'll make a lot more than that in year two."

I was making eleven thousand teaching. Fifty thousand a year sounded like BIG money. But *Hustler*?

"Larry, thanks, but. . . ."

"I knew you was going to say that, but at least think about it for a day or two, Bob. We would have a hell of a lot of fun and all the pussy you could ever want!"

I was in shock. I mumbled goodbye and hung up.

Needless to say I didn't take the job. I didn't lose any sleep over it, but for a guy with about five hundred bucks in his pocket it was tempting. Still, living out there with Flynt and those other characters? I knew I could never look at myself or any of my family again.

Two months after I turned him down Larry Flynt got his man, Paul Krassner, of *Realist* fame. Paul, who is now a friend of mine and a brilliant guy, went to Columbus and lasted about one year.

I thought that was the last time I would ever hear from Larry, but he called me a year later and asked me if I wanted to get my friends Alan King and Rupert Hitzig (who were producing my feature movie *Cattle Annie and Little Britches*) involved with a documentary on his life.

This I was interested in but only if it was going to be as real as my article had been.

We had a meeting in New York but Larry had already learned his lesson. He wanted control over the content of the film. And final cut.

So no deal.

But Flynt isn't a man who gives up. He eventually got the movie he wanted made: *The People vs. Larry Flynt*, which made him look like a First Amendment Hero.

I once asked the movie's screenwriter, Larry Karaszewski, if he knew of my piece. He said, "Oh, yeah, we read that. That was a great piece. You told the truth. We took the . . . uh, more mythic approach."

The Playboy of the Western Art World

LeRoy Neiman may be the third-highest-paid artist in the world.
So how come only he takes himself seriously?

LeRoy Neiman is resplendent in white! He is wearing a white cardigan sweater, a pair of white white flaring pants, pointy-toed white high-heeled loafers—Wonder Bread clothes—and it's all set off by a creamy delicious pink shirt and a groovy metal bird pendant (symbolizing peace and love) that dangles from his neck. Next to LeRoy, draped on his arm, a trophy, is his woman friend . . . Lucette. Dig it. You got a girl named Lucette? Not a chance. But then you ain't LeRoy Neiman, America's favorite painter. Lucette is perfection itself . . . beautiful. . . . LeRoy met her in Cannes, and she came to the United States to be with him. Like in *The Other Side of Midnight* . . . she just met LeRoy and realized he had "vibrations," that he was "magic," and so here she is at Shea Stadium, walking around with him, a triumph of color coordination. . . . Oh, yes! She, too, is dressed in white. Lord, they look like two lanky snowbirds out there on the green green grass of Shea Stadium, with the gigantic football players loping around them. ("It's Frankenstein Land out here," says Lucette to LeRoy, but he says nothing back to her . . . he's busy swiveling around, looking for Richard Todd, the Jets quarterback, whom he is going to sketch.) LeRoy and Lucette walk past the Oakland Raiders bench, and the fans start a little chant—"Hey Lee-Roy . . . Lee-Roy . . . Lee-Roy"—so Lee-Roy puts his fist in the air and winks at the fans. Then he smiles and rubs his mustache, and smiles some more and says, "See, they all love me. It's like I told you the other night. . . . There is no artist in America who is as loved by the people. No one. Hey, I'm not bragging, you know? I've got the magic." He wiggles his fingers like a hula dancer's *tuchus.* "There," he says. "I'm a wizard!" He waves to his fans again, carefully keeping his sprayed hair in perfect elegance. Lucette smiles, too. "Lee-Roy ees wonderful," she says.

Well, God knows it's true. People *love* LeRoy Neiman. They buy his paintings, his prints, his silk-screens, his etchings by the busload. The man can't turn out enough. In 1977, he made over four million dollars, and that was only the beginning. Since his appearance on television during the 1976 Montreal Olympics, painting his famous Wall of Fame mural (for my money, one of the great moments in TV history), LeRoy has become, arguably, America's best-known artist. I don't mean in the Art World, which doesn't exist outside of New York, anyway, but in Kansas. Call up someone in Kansas and ask him what painters he knows, he's going to say LeRoy Neiman. After all, they eat at Burger King out there, and last summer the deal was you bought a double burger and you got a LeRoy Neiman, because Burger King recognized the mass appeal of LeRoy's genius. But LeRoy sells in the Big Apple, too. According to his dealer, Maury Leibovitz, president of Knoedler Publishing Inc., LeRoy's serigraphs are tremendously hot.

"He's done 145 limited editions of 350 serigraphs each. If you multiply the 145 times the 350, you come up with 51,000 serigraphs. That's 51,000 serigraphs in American homes—although it may not be actually 51,000 *different* homes, because some people have two or three Neimans. Anyway, the average serigraph goes for fifteen hundred dollars, although some have exceeded four thousand. It's simple arithmetic. If you multiply fifteen hundred dollars times 51,000, you come up with a market value in excess of seventy-five million dollars. Then you've got to consider LeRoy's oils, which sell from twenty to fifty thousand dollars, and he's done several hundred of those. He's not as prolific as he once was, but he still does fifteen to twenty paintings a year." Leibovitz admits that some of LeRoy's earlier paintings don't go for quite as much—"Most of his early '50s and '60s paintings only sell for eight to fifteen thousand"—but Leibovitz attributes this to the fact that Neiman's style has changed. Then there are Neiman's drawings, which he dashes off at an astonishing rate, and for which he gets one or two thousand dollars, though "some have gone as high as five thousand." And Leibovitz and Neiman both think that the market can only get bigger, for LeRoy is going to do more TV (a top-secret project with one of the networks that he just can't divulge), plus he is a constant talk-show guest. He's also seen at every major fight and most recently made a guest shot at the Super Bowl. Leibovitz's conclusion that "no other artist in the world has LeRoy Neiman's exposure" seems just.

There is a general debate about whether Neiman is the richest artist in the world: Marc Chagall, at ninety-one, might be richer; Andrew Wyeth is right up there; but it's safe to say that LeRoy Neiman makes Big Boy Bucks. Yet, for all his fame and dough, little is known about him, and serious art critics have their, er, reservations about his work. Many of them actually think LeRoy Neiman is not an artist at all, but the living embodiment of what's wrong with the art world . . . or even America. On the other hand, Americans don't give a damn about art critics. They liked Norman Rockwell in his day, they liked Peter Max in the '60s, and they like LeRoy Neiman now. The question is, what do they respond to? How has a man who started as an illustrator for *Playboy* magazine become America's best-loved artist? And what does he think about as he prances in the limelight, surrounded by beautiful women, Hugh Hefner, and the hundreds of jocks who have become his models?

The Artist lives in the fashionable co-op, Des Artistes, at Sixty-seventh Street and Central Park West (home of the chichi Cafe Des Artistes), and to get to his studio I ascend in a walnut-paneled elevator that smells like money. Oh, deeply burnished wood . . . oh, blue-uniformed elevator man, with his hand on the controls (in New York, the older an elevator, the more status accorded the occupants of a building). I alight on the third floor and am immediately besieged by riots of reds, blues, blacks, and greens, the primary colors, as it were—LeRoy Neiman posters, which show Olympic runners, football players, Frank Sinatra starring in *The Detective*—and I feel suddenly that I am actually in a movie . . . a 1940s movie, where the young reporter comes to the home of the suave artist, smirkingly played by George Sanders, replete with silken gown and polka-dot ascot. LeRoy Neiman greets me dressed in an all-white robe, open at the chest so his manly hairs stick out. His hair is perfectly coiffed, his mustache is gallantly clipped: He looks like one of those old RAF flying aces in *Dawn Patrol*. Indeed, the initial impression LeRoy Neiman gives is, well, multifarious . . . it's as if he has invented himself from old movie ideas. He warmly shakes my hand, smiles, and says, "Come on over to the couch and we'll talk." On the back of his white robe are the black, bold words: MUHAMMAD ALI.

"Is that actually Muhammad Ali's robe?" I ask.

"Sure," LeRoy says, in his high, rather nasal voice with a trace of a lisp. "He gave me this. He gave me his gloves, too."

LeRoy points to his genuine Moroccan leather bag with silver coins sewn into it.

"That's my pencil and colors bag," he says, slinging it over his shoulder. "I carry it with me everywhere . . . Muhammad Ali has carried that bag. Sinatra, Dean Martin . . . they've all carried that bag."

"All of them?" I say.

"Sure," LeRoy lisps, sitting down in his chair. "I've got to go downtown soon, but we can talk for a while here. . . . Get to know one another."

Neiman's smile now seems genuine. He is even likable. After I get past his braggadocio, I see that he is scared, that he is shy, wants very much to be liked. Looking harder at the face, I see things not easily noticed on television: a thin, weak jawline, a kind of mistrust and unhappiness in the eyes, vulnerability. Neiman talks of his past:

"I started off in St. Paul, Minnesota. . . . I was always a hotshot with the pencil. I could draw anything. We were a poor family, I had a lot of street fights . . . nothing big, I don't want to sound like a tough guy, but later I went into the war . . . and I fought in England, Germany, and Normandy. . . . I've got five battle scars . . . that's something people don't know about me. I'm fifty years old now, even though I don't look it. Anyway, after the war I went to the University of Chicago on the GI Bill. I was such a hotshot in my art classes they had me teaching courses as an undergraduate. Of course, I was influenced by the abstract expressionist movement; you can see that in my work today. It was a tremendously exciting time. The abstract expressionists were doing things that no one else had ever thought about with paint. . . . There was something a little strange about it, though."

"What's that?" I say.

"Well, it was primarily a Jewish movement . . . ninety percent of the theoreticians were Jewish. . . . At the University of Chicago, for example, I didn't have one Gentile teacher. . . . A lot of people think I'm Jewish, but I'm not."

I wait for Neiman to expand on his Jewish theory, but he suddenly shifts gears.

"Anyway, the abstract expressionists believed in performance . . . they believed in getting to a deep, subjective response. It was a really new and valid way of looking at painting. Before the army, my favorite school had always been impressionism, but when this came along, it was so powerful. There was a man named Max Beckmann in St. Louis and there was Clement Greenberg . . . and these people had a tremendous continuity of thought. All the people I went to school with became abstract expressionists and most of them still are."

This last is delivered in a kind of smug tone.

"Well, you can certainly see the influence of both impressionism and abstract expressionism in your work," I say, pointing at a mural depicting Olympic runners racing around the track. "But your work is still representational, too."

"That's right," says Neiman. "I've got a little of everything in my work, but it adds up to something unique. No one else can paint the way I do."

Suddenly, his mood changes. He's on the defensive.

"But they don't treat me seriously," he says. "Look at how they write about me." He gets up, goes to his big table and pulls out a huge pile of press clippings. Most of them are newspaper personality profiles. He shows me one from the *San Francisco Chronicle* and sighs with distaste.

"First, they have this lousy artist draw this dopey picture, then they spend the entire time talking about how much money I make. Then, they say I'm the world's ultimate pleasure seeker. They treat me like I'm some kind of Keane painter—you know, the guy who paints the little kids with the big watery eyes? Well, I'm no hack like Keane. I'm a real artist.

"Look at this," he says furiously, handing me a strange announcement for a unique show.

I look. It's an announcement from a Palm Beach gallery. On the front is a picture of E. Howard Hunt, convicted Watergate conspirator:

Hunt having a one-man show in West Palm Beach. LeRoy Neiman is positively puffing with rage.

"You see that?" he says. "Now look."

He opens the gallery's brochure and inside is an announcement for LeRoy Neiman's show.

"Putting me on a brochure with that . . . *criminal*!" he says. "Can you believe the things they do to me?"

LeRoy Neiman and I are hustling downtown in a cab. He is in a better mood now; indeed, when he is on the move, heading from one place to another, he is at his best.

"I know you are tremendously successful," I begin, "but this summer I was reading a history of contemporary art and . . . well, frankly, your name wasn't even mentioned."

"I know," says LeRoy. "You want to know why?"

"Yeah."

"Well, you may not know too much about the art world. You've got to have a kind of lobbyist group. You remember what I was telling you before about the Jews? Well, the Jewish critics support their own . . . you know . . . they don't like me. Of course, it's not completely because I'm not Jewish. A lot of it has to do with my deals with television, with my *Playboy* image. I started out with Hefner in 1954, when I was still at the University of Chicago, and Hef was just getting *Playboy* started. . . . I did my first illustrations for *Playboy*: a Charles Beaumont story, a Jack Kerouac, and a Budd Schulberg. . . . Lenny Bruce was always around, and Mort Sahl and Buddy Hackett. . . . We had fifteen great years there. . . . Later I moved into sports. It wasn't a calculated move. . . . I just moved to sports because I liked sports and always covered them. I used to go to ringside at the Garden, and the cameras used to catch snatches of me, and maybe there would be a little comment. Then I went along on the second Liston-Ali fight. I was at Ali's training camp in Lewiston, Maine, and there was nothing to do, so the sportswriters started writing pieces about me, and the whole thing began to snowball. Well, you see, all this makes the critics hate me, because in the art world you are supposed to make all your money within the prescribed limits the critics set up . . . and I didn't. And they resented it. The same thing when I went on television. They hated me for it. . . ."

"I see," I say. "So it's merely a matter of snobbishness. . . ."

"Of course it is," LeRoy says. "I mean, you can see from my work. I can paint as well as anybody in the world."

"Well, if it's just a matter of going outside the traditional modes, how do you account for the fact that a guy like Andy Warhol has gone outside the established pathways and yet is the darling of the critics?"

"That's easy," Leroy says. "He has the homosexual mafia behind him. You see, they are another big taste-making clique, but if you quote me on this, please don't make it sound as if I'm anti-gay, because I'm not . . . but ask around . . . any honest person will tell you that there are a large number of gay critics and painters who support one another. I don't fit into any of these molds."

"You go your own way."

LeRoy nods seriously. "I have always gone my own way. That's what people respond to. Wait till you hang out with me. . . . Forget the critics . . . look at how people respond to me. I can't pay for a suit of clothes. I can't pay for a drink in any restaurant. People want to buy for me. . . . I don't want to sound like a braggart, but there's never been anything like me."

I am on the phone with David Bourdon, art critic for the *Village Voice*. I ask him about LeRoy Neiman's painting.

"Oh, come on," he says. "This is a witty idea . . . but what can I say? He's a schlocky artist. He produces a stylistic mishmash, a kind of warmed-over impressionism. People with untrained eyes find it pleasing. . . . His art is a pleasant nothing."

"Who would you compare Mr. Neiman to?" I ask. "Peter Max?"

"Sure," says Bourdon. "They're both merely decorative. Except Peter Max is a better painter."

I try art critic Lawrence Alloway, a Brit. When I tell him about the piece, he begins to laugh.

"LeRoy Neiman! Let me just say there is a confusion between artists and commercial artists. Neiman is a commercial artist who has made inroads into the serious art world."

"Well," I venture. "What of his technique?"

"Really!" says Alloway, sounding like a duke.

"Hmmm. Thanks."

Well, let's see . . . How about a more traditional critic? I call the *New York Times* and ask for Hilton Kramer. A rather cool, detached voice comes across the phone. I tell him my mission and ask for a few thoughts on LeRoy Neiman's work.

"That might be difficult," says Kramer. "I never think of him."

LeRoy and I are at Toots Shor's to do a pregame hockey tape. We sit at the table with a PR man and an interviewer named Chip Cipolla. Chip is asking questions before a Rangers game. The questions are routine: Why does Montreal want to get rid of its star? "They can't pay his salary," says LeRoy condescendingly. LeRoy has a million answers. He's done his homework. I think of what a friend told me about Warhol: "Warhol was the first artist to realize the process of fame itself was an art form. He made it acceptable to be a celebrity." The difference is, of course, that Warhol has it both ways. He is regarded as excellent by nearly all the critics and he is a real wit. Neiman is a poor man's Warhol, incapable of wit or irony. After two days, I've grown to feel protective of him. He is at once intelligent and witless: "I usually bring a good-looking chick with me. It's all part of the act. I don't *really* dig the [sports] scene, but if you're with the guys, you have to answer questions about sports. So if you have a chick with you, you can just draw. You don't have to talk."

He delivers this bit of chauvinism with an earnestness beyond ridicule.

Meanwhile, the PR man for Toots Shor's grabs my copy of Neiman's book, *LeRoy Neiman: Art and Life Style*, and smiles at me.

"There is this one picture in here of Joe [Namath] . . . here it is. . . ."

He points to a picture of "Joe" going down the runway at Shea Stadium during the '68 season. The guy shakes his head, looking deeply moved.

"That's how it really is," he says. "I've been on that runway a million times and that's how it is."

I stare at a lot of blotchy grey strokes and a recognizable Namath head, but the PR guy is deeply moved. He beams at Neiman, and LeRoy seems happy.

LeRoy fields a few more questions and then accepts a big steak and home fries on the house. He has a sip of white wine, then goes to work.

"He just captures it," the PR guy says, shaking his head. "LeRoy's a genius."

A few days later Barbara Zabel, an art historian at Connecticut College, visits me. Barbara is no snob. Her tastes in music run to Willie Nelson. Her taste in movies runs from *The French Connection* to Louis Malle. She digs Marvel Comics. I pick up LeRoy's book, point to a portrait of Satchmo, and raise my eyebrows.

"Come on," she says. "Over here on the right we have some puddling effect. Probably something he got from Hans Hofmann—it's a genuine technique, and Neiman knows how to use it, but to what effect? In Hofmann it had to do with the seasons, the way he saw nature, abstracted what he saw, then found a form for it. Content and form were wedded to make a personal, original statement. Here it's just done for the hell of it, because right over here we have a purely representational effect—Louis Armstrong's head, easily recognizable. And to make matters worse, the representational detail is sloppy. Looks like it was done in a hurry. The only part done carefully is these giant teeth, and the reason he does that is that the public already *knows* about Armstrong's giant teeth. He gives them the one detail every hack artist has emphasized again and again—Armstrong's smile. So what sells is just prepackaged personality. Neiman takes a high-art form, like abstract expressionism, and tosses a little of it around in a hack painting like this, so that it looks 'modern,' but people aren't challenged at all. They can easily recognize what's there. The kindest thing you could say about it is that it's okay as a magazine illustration, but it's absurd."

The next night LeRoy, Lucette, and I go to the Cookery, a jazz joint in the Village, to hear a wonderful piano player, Jimmy Rowles, and a terrific eighty-two-year-old black jazz singer named Alberta Hunter. Our table is right next to Rowles's piano, and the owner comes over with drinks, once more on the house. LeRoy is in a good mood.

"Look at this," he says, as Rowles begins a set.

Quickly, with real flair, Neiman draws a sketch of Rowles that is, to my untrained eye, remarkably good. It catches every bit of strain and joy in Rowles's sophisticated but funky face. I think of what the critics have said and wonder if it matters that LeRoy Neiman isn't Picasso. He does have a real flair for performing, and during the next hour he captures both Rowles and the wonderful Hunter, to both their delights. In fact, the simple pen drawings seem to be his real *métier.* . . . Unlike the hodgepodge of styles in his paintings, Neiman's drawings show an economy of line, and for once he really does seem to be a wizard. . . . Hunter is quite obviously thrilled by his gift of a drawing. But Neiman keeps turning and saying, "Nobody can do things like this."

I try to bring the talk around to his "exposure."

"Look," I say, "These drawings are good, but don't you worry that *too much* celebrity can ruin your talent?"

Neiman scoffs at the suggestion. "No, my *performance* is part of my success. You should have seen the animals I painted at the San Diego Zoo on the *Dinah!* show. People loved them. Come around and I'll show them to you."

It's almost as if he hasn't heard me. But Lucette has.

"It ees true," she says. "LeRoy has a very beeg talent, but he ees self-destructive. The celebrity thing could be very harmful to heem, if he is not careful. Since he got on TV he thinks he has a self-image to protect."

But Neiman isn't having any. He begins a bullish argument. "I can draw," he says. "There's no one in the world like me. . . . You talk about great painters. . . . Name a painter who is better than me."

I mention Jackson Pollock.

"Nah," says Neiman. "He couldn't draw. I'm telling you."

He holds up his portrait of Rowles. "Look at this," he says. "You ever see anything like that?"

Lucette holds his hand. Neiman's eyes are blazing in a mixture of arrogance, pride, and petulance. Behind us, Hunter begins a song, and Neiman settles back, but he can't drop it.

"It's bull that you should have to suffer, that being a celebrity can get in your way. Look at Pete Hamill. He was married to Jose Torres's sister, a Puerto Rican, and he had a bunch of kids. He was a good writer then. Now he's divorced her and he might marry Jackie Onassis, but his writing never suffered."

LeRoy wants to go uptown to another jazz club to paint drummer Max Roach, and so we are off. A while later we are in Storyville, a crowded cellar-joint in the '50s, and LeRoy glides by the paying customers and gets good seats up front. Then he is given a special chair, right next to Max's band, which is wailing away, and he has out his pens and pad and is doing his thing, just sketching away like crazy, and people are saying, "That's LeRoy Neiman . . . the artist." The artist has become his own art form, and then LeRoy motions to me and whoosh, like magic, a chair appears and I am up there, and people are looking at me, and some good-looking blonde hangs her Veronica Lake haircut over my shoulder and says, "Are you famous?" and I say, "Hell, yes . . . I'm Hunter Thompson," and she laughs and LeRoy laughs, and she hands me a drink. Goddamn, it *is* intoxicating. I don't give a shit if I ever write again, just let me be on that stage with that blonde hanging over me. . . .

The next morning I am nursing a terrible hangover when LeRoy calls. He sounds panicky.

"Bobby," he says, "Bobby . . . I just don't think we are really getting at the core of me."

"The what?" His voice is like the E train in my ear.

"What I'm really about. You know?"

"The real you?" I say.

"Right," LeRoy says. "We're just not getting at it."

"Let's get at it," I say. "How about lunch? Then we'll get to the real you."

"Great," says LeRoy. "See you then, Bobby."

I hang up and go back to bed.

When I arrive at LeRoy's studio he has gotten out a few certificates for my edification. One is an Official Proclamation from the Mayor's Office of the City of San Francisco.

"Read this," says LeRoy, thrusting it forward.

I read it:

Office of the Mayor
Proclamation
City of San Francisco

Whereas LeRoy Neiman is an internationally renowned artist who has captured the drama and rhythm of world-wide athletics with his vivid style of painting and been appreciative of the electric excitement of sporting events;
Now Therefore Be It Resolved that I, George R. Moscone, do hereby salute the artistic achievements of LeRoy Neiman, and call upon all San Franciscans to experience and enjoy the exciting, dynamic artwork that he has created over the years. . . .

"That's a hell of a scroll," I say.
LeRoy shrugs. "I'm a Kentucky Colonel, too," he says.
"Wow," I say.

Later we go downstairs to the Café Des Artistes to get to the real LeRoy.
"You see, I spent fifteen years at *Playboy* . . . traveling . . . going to first-class hotels. Victor Hammer of Hammer Galleries kept saying I shouldn't do sports. He didn't like my sports image, or my leisure image. But I did it anyway. You see, it's like I said the other day. The 'official' gang decides what 'elegant' is. But I never wanted to hang out with them. I'm part of a new American phenomenon. The American art market, which only got big and powerful after the war. I'm not a real rebel, but I am alone. There is only one other American artist who is associated with an American magazine, and that's Rockwell."
"Yeah," I say, "but Rockwell never considered himself an artist. He always referred to himself as an illustrator."
"So what?" says LeRoy. "I consider him an artist, but he came out of a different America—the small-town America. I came out of

America as a world power. The fun and games America, where sports and recreation are an industry. I paint the bright, glossy exterior of things and I myself identify with the world I paint. It wasn't like I lived in a hut and just went and visited Vegas. I was into it. People are charmed when they think the artist who painted the whorehouse really got laid in it. I mean, what I do is valid. Listen, there were these sociologists when I was at the University of Chicago, and they were investigating the world of play. I went to them and became intrigued. It's a legitimate field to study or paint. I always remember Dr. Johnson's quote: 'You can tell a man's problems by the pleasures he seeks.' I care about what people buy. I always understood that we are judged by our labels. So sport is part of that, too. I paint sport as spectacle. . . . Listen, sports is a maiming thing. When I started painting sport there were three heroes in New York—Mickey Mantle, who could barely walk; Willis Reed, he'd go down on the floor, they'd have to drag him off, but he'd come out and win the game in the last second; and Joe Namath, the biggest of them all. And I paint them at their best. . . ."

LeRoy stops for breath, and I try to digest what he is saying. He seems to see himself as, simultaneously, a social satirist, a pop artist, and a commercial artist.

"Take Reggie Jackson," LeRoy says. "I know he makes errors in the field. I know he falls down sometimes, but he is a great hitter. He is the guy who hits the big ones. That's his essence. That's why he's special. That's why I paint him hitting a home run. I paint the most important part of him.

"Before me," LeRoy continues, "sports art was not even considered art. Believe me, it won't be that way anymore. Everyone's into it now. It's going to be a movement, a movement like the . . . pornography movement."

I look hard at him, but he is smiling. So I switch to television. How did he get started?

"Through Roone Arledge. But it wasn't a pushy thing. It happened naturally. In 1971, the TV guys had a strike, so they couldn't film the Ali fight. I stepped in and did drawings and the next day I was on with Cosell and Ali, and they used my drawings as a point of reference. The next big one was Bobby Fischer against Spassky in Iceland. They had a stage there, and Bobby Fischer kicked the cameras off because they were distracting him. Roone called me and asked me to go. They put me on the stage, but Fischer was going to have me thrown off because he could smell my felt-tipped pen. He kept sniffing the air. So I switched to an ink pen. But the strokes of the pen, scratching, that got him upset, too. So I switched to pencil. Then in 1972, I was on the Olympics. I was on every night for a couple of minutes. I did a drawing of Mark Spitz under a hair dryer, and it was a far-out revelation. I did a 360-pound wrestler reclining in a cheesecake pose. That was a gas. Between the Olympics I did a lot of TV . . . the World Series. . . ."

"Would you consider the last Olympics the height of your artistic career?"

"The height of exposure. Not the height of my painting. My best paintings are social paintings, but I never forget the little guy. If I'm going to a super party the elevator operator takes me down, the limo driver takes me to the party, I walk in and a man takes my coat, I get into the room and another man hands me a drink. So you mustn't ever forget the working man: At these super parties, everyone is working. There are gossip columnists, and deals are being made. Then the poor slob watches the party in the *News* or the *Post* and they see Mick Jagger and Bianca, and the artist Leroy Neiman, and they want to be there. They dress like us. We're the news for the poor working guy."

"Do you feel guilt for living well, while the poor guy can only watch?"

Neiman looks shocked at the question. "No, I'm not guilty at all. I'm working *for them*! It's not easy to be in attendance at these things all the time. When I go to a snob occasion, the working-class slob is there, too, because I take my background with me. I never put down a waiter . . . of course, I won't put up with any shit if he's rude.

"It's not easy at all," LeRoy says. "I have rules I live by. I am very wary of yachts. I don't go on weekends on great estates. I don't go to parties around acquisitions of one of my paintings. I stay away from condominiums and ski resorts. It's not easy having these things. People who own them have a hard time assembling the right cast. I never go to Westchester. I never go to the Hamptons in a host's car. In any of these situations, you can't get away. If a personality clash comes into existence, there might be an effort to prove to you that you aren't as great as you think you are. Say you're in a car, they insult you, and there's another hour on the road . . . they may even branch off into another language or something for a whole hour."

"Tell me about your wife," I say. "Janet seems nice, but you have all these other girls?"

"Yes," says LeRoy. "I met Janet twenty years ago, when she was a young, beautiful art student. Now she's in her late forties. But we keep it together. She isn't jealous of my girlfriends. But *they are* of her. A lot of these girls think they can reform me, get the *decent* side to be the main side. But a guy who has lived like I have . . . it's like a girl trying to reform a fag. . . ."

"I see," I say. "Well, you have all these women friends . . . is it okay for Lucette to have male friends?"

"No," says LeRoy Neiman. "I demand devotion. But I don't cry."

I ponder that non sequitur for a moment, then say, "Well, LeRoy, I think we've gotten into the real you."

He looks hopeful.

"Hello?" I say. "Andy?"

"Yes," says Andy Warhol.

"I'm doing a piece on LeRoy Neiman. I wonder if you have any comments on him."

"I think he's wonderful," says Andy Warhol. "I watched him on the Olympics . . . every night from start to finish. . . . He was terrific. I'm doing sports figures myself now."

"You really like him, huh?"

"Oh, yes," says Andy. "I think he's very *sweet*."

It's half time at the Jets game. LeRoy, Lucette, and I are in the owners' special club eating their buffet. It's been a good first half for the Jets against Oakland. Richard Todd has thrown four touchdown passes, and his team has a big lead.

"How about that Todd?" I say to LeRoy. "He's really looking sensational."

"Yeah," says LeRoy. "He sure is. You know I talked to him before the game. You saw me. I told you, when I talk to them, it makes a difference."

"You know," says Lucette, looking like a Dresden doll. "You know that LeRoy has ESP. . . . He feels vibrations."

"It's true," says LeRoy. "You know Todd wanted me to paint him. I told him five thousand dollars. He said the price was too high . . . but if he keeps having great days like this, he'll be able to afford it. Then he'll be worthy of me painting him."

"Right," I say.

"You should have been at the Series the other night," LeRoy says. "I got some great sketches of Reggie hitting home runs."

He opens his bags and shows me some rather good drawings of Jackson.

"You know I was with Reggie right before the start of the last game and I said, 'I'm going to draw you.' And then he did it. . . . Of course, I'm not saying *I* did it. . . .

"You know, Reggie is coming in on Monday to see the drawings I did of him. He wanted me to paint him earlier this year, but I refused."

"How come?" I ask.

"Well," says LeRoy, "he just wouldn't sell."

"What?" I say. "Reggie Jackson? Come on. I have to disagree with you."

"It's true. Look, at the time he was only hitting about .250 and he was making a lot of errors. . . . I didn't want to do it.

"Besides," LeRoy says, "Black athletes don't sell well."

"No?"

"No. I did Lenny Randle, the Mets' best player, and we were walking away from the ballpark, and not one person recognized him. Of course, they would recognize Reggie . . . but I wouldn't want to make a deal with him now."

"Why not?"

"Because of the World Series. He'd want an impossible amount. I could make a poster of him from the drawings I have here. But there's one condition."

"What's that?"

"I always have to get the most money. The athlete has to get less."

"What kind of split would you make with Reggie now, sixty-forty?"

LeRoy nods. "Yeah, I'd take that now . . . not later, but now. Sometimes, though, I only give the athlete ten percent."

Lucette smiles and says nothing. We have a few more glasses of wine, and LeRoy greets George Steinbrenner and some other people who, he tells me, own the Jets. They look like the kind of people you see at horse shows. I wonder what kind of painting George Grosz might do of them.

"Well," I say, "I'm going down to my seat to watch the second half. This is a hell of a game."

"Not me," says LeRoy. "I'm going home. I can always watch the game on TV . . . but I probably won't. I've had years of this stuff."

He snorts a laugh, takes Lucette's arm, and they stride away through the crowd.

Part Two

Sports

As a kid in Baltimore I was a massive reader. I read from the first time I picked up a book. I loved reading just as much as I loved playing sports. My neighborhood in Baltimore was called Northwood, and consisted of three streets: Winston Road, Stonewood Avenue, and Pentwood Road. Kids in the '50s didn't have play dates, and most of our mothers didn't drive. That was fine because we didn't need to go anywhere but out the door, and down the street. All my friends lived within those three blocks. I would run down Winston, and knock on my friends' doors, Johnny Brandau and next to him John Littman. Then the three of us, bats and gloves in hand, would run around the corner to Stonewood where we would pick up Mike Thomas, Spencer Rowe, Craig Gill and a little further up the street, Denny Smith. We'd then run over to Pentwood and pick up Don Hoffman, John Boring, and Jack Wills. All of us were baseball crazy, and we had the perfect place to play, Tom Mullan Little League Field, which was just beyond Pentwood. Every day of every summer we were there to play baseball. And in the fall we'd go a little further, cross Hillen Road, and use the fields of Morgan College to play tackle football. We got along great with the black students there, and never once was there a racial incident.

No one ever got hurt very badly; no one ever got picked up by a pervert. No one had ever even heard the term "serial killer."

When I wasn't playing with my pals, I was reading book after book. I knew I wanted to be a writer by age six. One day around that time my mother asked me what I wanted to be when I grew up and I said: "I am going to write books." She said, "Well, isn't that cute." I was enraged by her attitude. I didn't know the word "patronize" yet but I knew that she was "talking down" to me and I screamed at her: "I am going to be a writer and there's nothing cute about it." Then I stalked off down the cellar to read some more.

When I wasn't reading the Hardy Boys, Jules Verne, or my father's ghost stories, I was deep into my favorite magazine *Sport*. There were always in-depth pieces about my favorite ballplayers, and I got to know the names of the writers too. Like Ed Linn, Al Zuckerman, and Ed Fitzgerald. I loved reading *Sport*, and had all my magazines carefully stacked together in my room. It never occurred to me back then that one day I would write for *Sport* magazine, but reading all those pieces was my own feature writer education.

Finally, in 1976, Robin and I left Geneva and made the big move to New York City. We got an apartment on West Twenty-first Street, in a carriage house with two rooms on top of one another. A short but slippery spiral staircase connected the pint-sized rooms. The place was so cramped I felt like I was starring in "The Premature Burial." But we survived.

I had saved about three thousand bucks. Meanwhile, by reading the original *Citizen Kane* script, I had taught myself how to write screenplays and had written both a screenplay and a novel called *Cattle Annie and Little Britches*. Right after I moved to New York, a friend, Marty Bell, an editor from *New Times*, hooked me up with an agent, Karen Hitzig, whose husband was just starting to produce movies. That's the way things happened in New York. You could live in a town like Baltimore for fifty years and never meet anyone in show business. One week in New York and Karen had given my screenplay to her husband, who optioned it for fifteen thousand dollars. So three weeks after getting to New York City my bank account had gone up from three grand to eighteen thousand. With one hundred and fifty thousand promised if the movie got made.

Meanwhile, I sold the novel to William Morrow for ten thousand, so three months after getting there I had almost thirty grand.

Coming from a teaching gig where I made twelve thousand a year, I felt like Rockefeller.

But I knew I couldn't miss any months doing pieces or I'd run out of dough quick. New York was ridiculously expensive. Cabs cost a fortune, dinner and drinks were outrageous . . . I couldn't believe my bills.

I already had become a regular contributor to *New Times* magazine but I needed more than that. What if they could only give me a couple of articles a year? I'd be broke in no time.

Fortunately, *Sport* magazine seemed to be interested. I'd done a couple of pieces for them and they wanted to talk to me about more work. I thought I'd be meeting with the legendary Dick Schaap, who had hired me in the first place, but Dick was away a lot of the time, as he broke into television.

That left editor Berry Stainback to meet with me.

Our first "editorial meeting" was held at Rocky Graziano's restaurant in the mid-'50s. As I walked inside the place I saw Rocky himself slapping people on the back. I remembered seeing *Somebody Up There Likes Me* with Paul Newman, when I was just a kid. It never occurred to me that I would someday be talking with Rocky himself.

That first day I was a nervous wreck. What if this Stainback guy didn't want me to write pieces for them? Maybe he didn't like my work as much as Dick had. I had myself tied up in knots with worry.

But not for long. At Graziano's I asked Rocky where the *Sport* table was and he pointed to Berry in the back booth. Stainback was with a couple of other *Sport* people, Kevin Fitzgerald and Dorothy Afta, the magazine's adorable photographer. Berry looked as disheveled as I did. His hair was thick and sort of hung down over his eyes. Indeed, he looked—was this possible?—very stoned.

As I approached the table I smelled the weed. Jesus, the three of them were drinking martinis and smoking pot right in the restaurant. Berry got up, smiled, and hugged me.

"Bobby Ward," he said. "Man, are we going to have fun! Here smoke this shit and order a martini and we'll get right down to work!"

"Yeah, okay," I said. "I think I can handle that."

That first lunch lasted three and a half hours. I told stories, Berry told stories, Dorothy took our pictures, Kevin went out to make a phone call to his bookie and came back. We celebrated his return by ordering another round of drinks.

I was so wrecked after two hours that I could barely sit up.

But we still hadn't talked about who I was going to interview.

Finally, feeling a little worried, I brought it up.

Berry cracked up: "Oh, yeah, right. I knew there was something we should discuss. Okay, who do you want to do?"

"In which sport?"

"Any of them, though we need basketball right now."

"How about Pete Maravich?" I said. "He's the greatest player I've ever seen but he's never been on a winner. Now he's back in his home-town, New Orleans."

"Yeah, New Orleans," Berry said. "You and Pete in New Orleans. That sounds like a piece to me."

"I've always wanted to do a piece on Earl Weaver too," I said.

"Great. We love Earl. That crazy little bastard. Here, smoke some more of this and let's think this thing through."

"Right," I said. "This shit will probably make us come up with a lot of great ideas."

"Undoubtedly," Berry said. "There's no question about it. I knew I was going to like you, Bobby."

We smoked and drank for another hour. By the time I left the place I had three or four new assignments and felt as though I was floating a few feet above Fifty-first Street.

I hugged Berry and the whacked-out staff goodbye, and somehow found a cab. This is New York, I thought, as I waved my new employers goodbye, and Holy Christ, do I love it.

That was it, my first . . . uh, editorial meeting. I staggered home and fell into bed. It was mad, wild. . . . Only a few months ago I had been in Geneva, New York, where the biggest thing that happened every year was snow.

Now, I was hanging out with big city editors and having the most fun of my life. And on top of it all, they treated me like an adult. Get stoned, get drunk, do whatever the fuck you want, just make sure you get the good stuff.

Not once in all the years I wrote for magazines in New York did anyone ever tell me how to write a piece. They assumed I was a pro and that come hell or high water I'd get the piece right.

Man, I thought, why hadn't I come to New York years and years ago? I thought of John Lennon, who was then very much alive. He had been quoted as saying, "Why wasn't I born in New York, instead of Liverpool?" I completely understood that feeling. In towns like Baltimore or Liverpool, the answer to anything you wanted to do was "No, hon, you can't do that. That'll never work." "You want to be a writer? That's ridiculous. You're a small-town guy, that's never going to happen. I mean look at you, putting on airs." My own father used to laugh at me as I toiled away writing my first stories: "Oh, look at Mr. Hemingway. Oh, yeah, you're going to set the world on fire, Hemingway. Well, you'll see. You'll see. Nobody cares. Nobody is going to help you. You'll find out, pal." God, how I hated him when he screamed that stuff at me. I wanted to rip his head off. But, somehow, hearing his spiel didn't stop me. It just made me write more. I remember lying in bed at night, thinking, "I'll show him. I'll show all these fuckers."

Now I was in the big city where anything you could think of could happen, as long as you worked for it and you had the drive and talent.

So coming to The City was so much more than just making money. I found a whole new spirit inside. I could fucking do anything. My girlfriend, Robin, felt the same way, and soon she was writing for *Sport* too. We ended up breaking up (but remained friends) and she went from New York to Minnesota, where she worked on the *Star*

Tribune, then came back to New York and has had a long and successful career on the *New York Times*.

I was glad to help her get her first gigs, and she came through like the brilliant person she was and still is.

But that, I found, is New York. Tough, sometimes impersonal, competitive, but if you're good at what you do, it's the place that gives people with talent a real shot.

Without New York and the incredible people I met there I would have gotten precisely nowhere. People can put down the Big Apple but not around me. I really do LOVE New York.

The Bird Is the Word

Halfway through his first season as a major leaguer, Mark ("The Bird") Fidrych has returned innocence to the summer game, and pure joy to Detroit.

"Go Bird. Gooooooo Bird! Go Birrrrrrrrrrd!"

The four men in the yellow Big Bird costumes are leaping up and down along the first base box seats, leading cheers in the $4.50 section. Down behind home plate, a woman is holding her hand over her mouth, as if she is witnessing The True Life Second Coming. Around in the left field stands, the entire gallery is on its feet hooting and hollering; out in dead center field a giant cloud of marijuana blows lazily up into the big lights and a fifteen-foot sign appears, looking as if it's been scrawled by an idiot. It reads THE BIRD IS THE WORD.

Out on the mound here at Detroit's Tiger Stadium, a twenty-one-year-old pitcher, Mark "The Bird" Fidrych, goes through his warm-up tosses before facing the Baltimore Orioles. Obscure as you and me just a few months ago, The Bird is now a bona fide phenomenon. Here in the Motor City, he has been a hometown favorite since his first victory, but it was only in late June that he became a national hero by whipping the league-leading Yankees on national TV. Twenty-eight million people saw his now highly publicized antics, and since then he has wormed his way into the national heart like no one in recent sports history. This evening, as the Orioles game is about to begin, The Bird goes through a few of his colorful routines.

He gets down on his hands and knees and smoothes out the pitcher's mound. The woman sitting next to me behind home plate sighs, "He looks jes like a little boy out there making sand castles." Her girlfriend, Agnes, who works for Ford Motors, shakes her head, gnaws on a hot dog, suddenly leaps up, spreads her legs, cups her mustard-covered fingers over her mouth and bellows: "Go get 'em, Bird!" Then she sits down and smiles sweetly. The Bird is through working on the mound, and one might think his warm-up tosses would begin in earnest. But instead he begins doing a few deep knee bends, then jumps up and down a few times—jumping jacks, by God. The lad is working out, doing calisthenics! A couple of seats to my left, Hugh Dugan, a steel salesman, his wife and their two sons are enjoying The Bird's pregame antics.

"What's going on here?" I ask Hugh, while sighting The Bird through my binoculars. "I mean, what's happening?" The fans have just given Fidrych a standing ovation simply for running out on the field.

Hugh, a big man with a likable warm face, smiles: "You gotta understand Detroit," he says. "This town is a great sports place. We go see anybody. We go see the Lions and they always lose. We go see the Pistons and they stink. We go see the Tigers and they haven't had anything exciting since 1968 when we won it. You don't have a lot of Broadway shows in Detroit. You don't have much to do. Now this kid comes, and he's a winner. What's more, he's a natural. I mean, he's such a likable kid. I don't know how to put it, but he's got two things going for him. One, he's a hell of a pitcher. Everybody saw the Yankee game on television and how he talks to the baseball and congratulates his teammates after good plays, and everybody is writing about that. But I've been following baseball a long time, and this kid has got the goods. He keeps the ball low and away, and he gets tougher when men are on base."

Hugh's wife, a dark-haired version of Loretta Haggers from *Mary Hartman, Mary Hartman,* adds, "And he's so cute. Will you meet him?"

"Sure."

"Well, you tell him the Dugan family loves him."

After The Bird has finished his pregame antics, the first batter for the Baltimore Orioles steps in. The Bird is hunched over already, double pumping, talking to the baseball. Using high-powered binoculars, it's fairly easy to read his lips. The Bird is saying, "Get your ass in gear. Get it over there now. Get it on." There's a rhythm to his words, as if the point of his talk is to put himself into a kind of trance. Unfortunately, Orioles leftfielder Al Bumbry seems not to have been drawn into The Bird's Baseball Bardo. On the first pitch, Bumbry cracks a line single to left field, and the fifty-one thousand fans at Tiger Stadium give out a huge groan. Now Bumbry, a fast man on the bases, inches toward second and the fans start in with that chant again. "Go Bird. Go Bird. Go Bird." Orioles centerfielder Paul Blair lays down a perfect bunt and nearly beats it out, but he is caught by a quarter step on a beautiful scoop throw from the third baseman, Aurelio Rodriguez. The swiftness of Rodriguez's throw seems to get The Bird hyped. He turns toward third, nods, and then throws a ball outside to the Orioles' leading hitter and the All-Star second baseman, Bobby Grich. Annoyed at himself for missing the corner, The Bird takes the ball and motions toward the plate with it, as if he's reminding himself where he wants to place it. The fans adore it. "Talk to him, Bird. Talk to him, baby. Show him now, Bird!" And The Bird does. His next three pitches to Grich are knee high and hit the outside corner. On pitch number three, Grich swings from the heels, misses by a good foot, and leaves Bumbry an easy target at third for catcher Bruce Kimm. When Rodriguez applies the tag to Bumbry, the fans are on their feet. Another standing ovation, and The Bird is leaping, gawky and stork like, off the mound, raising his right fist to Kimm and leading the team off the field to the dugout. I look over at Hugh Dugan, who smiles.

"This kid will last forever if he doesn't break his leg on the dugout steps," Dugan says. "Have you ever seen anyone come off the mound like that?"

When it is all over, Fidrych has posted his ninth win, a 4–0 shutout. After the last out, The Bird stops at third base and shakes hands with his entire team, pounding them on the back, hugging Ron LeFlore, slapping hands with Bruce Kimm, pummeling Rodriguez, Rusty Staub, and Alex Johnson. I start to leave, but there's no way out. The fans have started to scream again. "We want The Bird! We want The Bird! We want The Bird!" A huge armed phalanx of security guards rims the dugout. Kids are scrambling over the roof. The Big Birds are leaping up and down, flapping their arms. Finally, after two minutes, The Bird appears, waving from the dugout, and there is a cheer that rocks the pillars of the old ball park.

The Road to Detroit

For a young man only two years out of high school, Mark Fidrych's unlikely rise from class C in the minors to the major league sensation of 1976 sounds something like a 1940s Jimmy Stewart baseball scenario.

The irony is that Mark Fidrych was not even a great high school pitcher. "He won a few and lost a few," as Tiger public relations man Hal Middlesworth puts it. At age nineteen, Fidrych was still in Northboro High School. When the school wouldn't let him play any more baseball there because of his advanced age, he transferred to nearby Worcester Academy. The school didn't have much of an athletic program, but Tiger scout Joe Cusick was impressed with what he saw of Fidrych. "First of all, there was his body," Cusick remembers. "He had a lean, string-bean body and that's a good sign. We don't like to get pitchers who have too many muscles in their upper arms, shoulders, and chest. It makes them muscle-bound. The other factor was that Fidrych got the ball over the plate. He had unusual control for a high school kid."

On June 9, 1974, Fidrych was signed and sent, at semester's end, to the Tigers' rookie team in Bristol, Virginia. There he pitched in the shadow of Bob Sykes, a fellow rookie who went 10 and 0 (and today remains in the minors). Nonetheless, Fidrych performed well enough to be sent on to Lakeland, Florida, the Tigers' class C club. In two and a half months, he posted an uninspiring 5–9 record and 3.77 ERA, but the Detroit management's enthusiasm was undeterred. "He was a lot better than his record indicated," says Tiger manager Ralph Houk. "He kept the ball low and away." By mid-July of the following summer, Fidrych was promoted again, this time to double-A ball in Montgomery, Alabama. He pitched exactly fourteen innings and was promoted after a month to the Evansville, Indiana, triple-A ball club, the last stop before the major leagues. This time Fidrych finally began to fulfill the Tigers' expectations. He posted a 4–1 record and, even more impressively, gave up only 1.59 runs per game over forty innings.

Encouraged, the Tigers invited Fidrych to spring training this year, where his ERA immediately bloated to 4.66 in a handful of outings. What saved Fidrych were the other Tiger pitchers, who performed with equal lack of distinction. Manager Houk took a flyer and decided to bring Fidrych along after spring training as a nonroster player (meaning that he was officially still on the Evansville roster).

Fidrych first pitched in relief against the Oakland A's on April 20, gave up a hit to the first batter, and was promptly taken out. Three weeks later, he pitched a scoreless inning against Minnesota in relief. Finally, ten days later, he got his first start against the Cleveland Indians.

The rest is instant history. He went the route in that start, giving up only two hits, winning a 2–1 decision. After a 2–0 loss to Boston, The Bird suddenly began to fly. In rapid succession, he won eight straight games, compiled a 9–2 record by midseason and was named the American League's starting pitcher for the All-Star Game. His record is now 11–4 and he also has the lowest earned run average in the major leagues—1.97 at the beginning of August.

Everyone seems to love The Bird now (he was so nicknamed for his remarkable resemblance to Big Bird of *Sesame Street*). Wherever he ventures he is surrounded by great, teeming hordes of reporters; teenage girls, who swoon in his presence; middle-aged mothers, who seem to feel some uncommon bond with him; and even middle-aged men, who find in The Bird's youthful exuberance something they themselves have lost. Yet, for all of the national Birdmania, it is merely the thinnest imitation of what is going on locally in Birdland—formerly known as Detroit. Here, The Bird has become a cause célèbre. Daily, he receives over a hundred letters and presents from fans—homemade cakes, bird dolls, flowers. The Ford Motor Company recently loaned him a new Thunderbird so he could travel in style (he had been driving a Dodge Colt). Breakthrough, a Detroit right-wing group, has been trying to cash in on The Bird's instant fame by distributing banners of Fidrych with the logo "The Bird Came Like A Breath of Fresh Air. The Bird For Mayor. Recall Young" (Detroit Mayor Coleman Young). The Bird hardly takes the posters seriously, though he seems to enjoy them: "That's life," he says amiably. "A bunch a nuts, right?" For all his fame, however, Mark Fidrych still makes a humble $23,500 a year—a base pay of $16,000, plus the standard rookie's bonus for sticking with the team. Indeed, his salary has become almost as legendary as his pitching skill. Michigan State Representative Dan Angel introduced a bill into the state legislature that would mandate Tiger general manager Jim Campbell to tear up The Bird's old contract in midseason and issue him a better one. Though the Tigers refused—Campbell said he'll take care of The Bird next year—there does seems to be a case for special pleading here. According to the Tigers' public relations department, the average attendance for a home game in which Fidrych does not pitch is a mere 20,594. On The Bird's second home start, the attendance at Tiger Stadium was 17,894. Since then, the young pitcher has regularly drawn sellout crowds of fifty thousand for his home starts. By figuring the average Tiger ticket at three dollars, which local columnist Joe Falls did, and multiplying that by the twenty-seven thousand extra fans The Bird brings in, he represents an eighty-one-thousand-dollar bonus for the Tigers each time he pitches. Adding concessions, which Falls figured at slightly less than a dollar a head, The Bird's last four home starts alone have been worth an added half-million-dollar gross. Of course, the visiting team gets 20 percent of the gate and the American League takes a 4 percent cut, but the Tigers make up for that on the road, where The Bird has drawn 32,678 to Texas, 30,425 to Minnesota, and 37,504 to Cleveland in recent starts. Not bad for a team that is mired hopelessly in fourth place, still playing under .500 ball.

In the Locker Room

In the Detroit Tigers' locker room after the Oriole game, The Bird is standing bare-assed, sipping a Stroh's, the local beer, and surrounded by twelve reporters, many of whom are sticking microphones in his affable, smiling face. And what a face. It is long and loose-lipped like Mick Jagger's, his curly blond hair falling over his ears like an untrimmed plant. The Bird is the picture of sensual, all-American innocence. Lanky, wiry, and muscular, his whiplash body is deceptively strong. At first glance, one's impression is that The Bird looks quite a bit like a rock star, most especially like Roger Daltrey of the

Who. All resemblance to the articulate, intelligent, and very British Daltrey, however, is shattered when The Bird speaks. Here is a language that is pure baseball Americanese, as much a surprise at first hearing as his antics are at first sight.

Example: an overweight local sportswriter, wearing blue-and-white checkered pants and a blue Alligator shirt, approaches The Bird with a tape recorder and summons up his interviewer's deeply resonant voice: "Well, another victory for Mark Fidrych. Yessir, this has been quite a year for the young man from Northboro, Mass. Tell me, Mark, what *are* your feelings as you stand here on the eve of your ninth victory?"

The Bird waves his gawky muscular arm through his mass of yellow ringlets and shakes his head: "Well, to tell you the truth, I, ah . . . see up dere onna clock, it's ten-thirty, and I'd like to go out and get laid!"

The sportscaster is agog and it's clear from the guy's scrunched-up look of pain that he's wishing there was some way he could get this comment past the station manager and on the air. But no way. Perhaps a technical question.

"Mark, this was your first shutout of the year."

Fidrych: "It was? Boy, that's good, isn't it?"

"Ah, yes," says the announcer. "That's *very* good! But what I wanted to know, Mark, is just what was it you were throwing out there? Was it a slider? A fastball? Does your pitch sink?"

Fidrych takes another slurp of beer and tries to swallow it without smashing his face into the half dozen mikes that are perilously close to his nose.

"Well," he replies in a voice so soft it can barely be heard, "I jes throw it . . . and it goes somewhere." Fidrych sits down on a stool with his back to his locker. Behind him, clipped onto the gray metal, is a picture of an eighty-one-year-old Japanese shot-putter. Beneath the picture is the caption "One of a kind." I look at the photo and try to figure out why it's there. A local reporter tells me that Mark's mother sent it.

"Mark, Mark," says an eager reporter. "Do you think the media will have any effect on your game?"

Mark looks around at the ten microphones threatening him and the notebook pads being scribbled upon.

"No," he says. "I'm the same kid now I was when I got into this game. And I want to get out of it the same way."

The reporter is persistent: "Come on, Mark. Isn't there *some* difference in the way you are working? I mean all these interviews, all these people hassling you and following you around and shoving microphones in your face. Well, isn't that getting to you a little bit?"

Fidrych shakes his head and for the first time looks a little weary. "I leave my phone off the hook," he says. "Then I can get some sleep. I mean I can't even go out and get a bite to eat. It's ungodly."

Jerry Green of the *Detroit News* nods and gets a look of intense seriousness in his little wolf eyes. "Mark," he says, in a quietly melodramatic voice. "I've got one question for you."

"What's that?" Fidrych says softly.

"What's my name?"

Fidrych smiles and waves his arms around like a kid who is splashing water in his backyard rubber pool.

"Gee, I don't know," he says affably.

"You don't know who I am, Mark?" says Jerry Green, getting a little put out and tugging on the lapel of his herringbone jacket. "I'm the sports editor of the *News,* and I write for *SI!*"

"Gee," says Fidrych, "what's *SI?*"

Jerry Green looks up at the rest of the reporters as if he has just been stoned. "*Sports Illustrated,* Mark! I mean, I put your picture on the front page of the *News* and you don't know *my name?*"

"Well, gee, I'm sorry," says Fidrych. "I mean, I don't read the papers. Maybe I should, huh? People say that the papers are important. I should read them. I should know your name. I should. But so many people come around here. It's hard to remember everyone. I should, though, huh?"

"How about the money, Mark?" says another reporter. "Do you think the Tigers should give you more dough?"

"Heck no," says Fidrych. "I'm already making more than my old man ever made. Hey, what if they tore up my contract, gave me a lot of money and it all went to my head? What would happen then?"

Earl Weaver

Earl Weaver, the manager of the Baltimore Orioles, is sitting in the dugout with his aging superstar third baseman, Brooks Robinson, and third base coach Billy Hunter. They are talking about The Bird:

"I'll tell you one thing," says Weaver. "Bobby Grich says he doesn't have overpowering stuff. He's not a Nolan Ryan or a Jim Palmer. But he has that natural ability to change speeds. He's like Catfish Hunter that way. And that's something you can't learn. I mean, Hunter will throw about ninety different speeds at you. The Bird does the same thing. He got Paul Blair on a fast slider last night, so Paul comes back and tells Lee May about it. May gets up, gets behind two strikes, and is waiting for that fast slider. He's all set. The Bird gives him a slider all right, but he takes just a little bit off of it. We all saw it coming in and, well, that was all she wrote. You can't teach that kind of stuff. It's the one facet of the game you can't teach. That kid's got it. I'll tell you one thing more. I wish to hell he was on our side!"

Rusty Staub and Bill Freehan

I am sitting in the locker room with Rusty Staub, the Tigers' best hitter, and Bill Freehan, their aging but still powerful catcher. Fidrych had agreed to meet with me the next morning, but he is now out on the outfield grass, shagging flies. Staub, a big happy-looking man in his early thirties, is pulling on his sweat socks and shaking his head: "Whatever you see is for real. There's nothing fake about Mark. But I just hope they don't spoil him. People like Bill and I are doing our best to help him. We've been around a while, and we know how heavy it can all get. I mean we don't run his life for him, but if he asks us then we will try to help."

"We don't want anybody screwing him," Freehan says.

"All in all, he's handling it pretty well," Staub says. "Still, it could all change just like that. I know. I've been around both ends of it."

I watch Staub and Freehan go out on the field, and Ron LeFlore, the Tigers' All-Star center fielder comes in. Behind him is The Bird. "Sheeet, Bird," LeFlore says in a joshing voice and pointing at The Bird's scraped-up old tennis shoes and battered torn Levi jacket. "Look at these old shoes and this jacket. You are making money now, man. You've got to get some *real* clothes."

"I like my tennis shoes," says The Bird. "Heck, they've already stopped me from wearing cutoffs. They want me to wear leisure suits. I'm not gonna wear that stuff. That's ungodly." He halts and suddenly turns away: "Oh, my gosh!"

Before I can ask him what's wrong, The Bird is running through the locker room into the training room. A few minutes later he comes back. "My daisies," he says. "Jesus. Jack forgot to water my flowers, and now they are gonna die. I hate it when things die."

LeFlore looks up at him and shakes his head. "He ain't nothing but a baby. You just can't help but love The Bird. Let me tell you one thing. We all love playing behind The Bird. He is the realest thing that's ever hit this team and we don't want anybody fooling with him, on the field or off."

The Autograph Session

Cookie Baker is the wife of Art Baker, who owns Auburn Discount Drugs. Cookie is an attractive middle-aged mother who is now waiting patiently in line along with about four hundred other people for The Bird's autograph. The Bird himself is seated at a makeshift desk that is roped off to give him a little breathing space. Cookie is ecstatic: "What do I think of The Bird?" she says. "I think he's the greatest thing for Bicentennial America. The Bird is gonna lead us back to the top. The Tigers, Detroit, the whole country."

A second later, a woman describing herself as the cheerleader for a team of Little Leaguers called the Sterling Heights Giants pulls three kids up to me. "Are you a writer?" she asks, introducing herself as Mrs. Poplawski.

"Yes," I say.

"Well, the Sterling Heights Giants are behind The Bird 100 percent. I just wanted you to know that. Since The Bird started talking to the baseball, all my kids talk to their baseballs now. They also talk to their gloves, their bats, and their hats."

Mrs. Poplawski looks at me with a very serious expression. Then she breaks into a grin. "I'd like you to see Sean talk to a baseball," she says.

Behind her, a miserable-looking kid is staring down at his feet, which point in opposite directions.

"C'mon, Sean." says Mrs. Poplawski. "Talk to the ball."

Sean looks down at his ball and starts to talk but no words come out. "Ah ah ah," he says.

"Well, he does it every day," says Mrs. Poplawski. "He usually talks to the ball just fine. I don't know what's come over him."

Mr. and Mrs. Bird

Mr. and Mrs. Paul Fidrych (Mrs. F. is known as Mother Fidrych to her son, Markie) and their two daughters, Carol Ann and Laurie, are sitting in the third floor of the Pontchartrain Hotel. This is the Fidryches' first trip to Detroit to see their son pitch. The game is on Friday night, and they are calming their nerves with a few beers.

Mrs. Fidrych is a small woman with a pixie haircut and shy, frightened eyes. She is also quite a talker. Like Mark, she seems to say anything on her mind: "They gave my Markie a new car today. The Ford people. They gave it to him. A Thunderbird. Isn't that wonderful? Markie gave us his old Dodge Colt. He's at a team barbecue at Rusty Staub's house now."

"This must be pretty much for you," I say. "I mean all this attention."

"It's very exciting," says Mr. Fidrych, a heavyset man with sideburns, a mustache, and a large friendly face.

"That was so nice of them, the Ford people," says Mrs. Fidrych. "Markie is having a dream come true. I just hope nothing happens."

"Oh, Mother," says Carol Ann, Mark's teenage sister, "what could happen?"

"They could hurt Markie. I mean the crowd. I hear that they don't let him get any sleep. You know that. He's an excitable boy, anyway. He doesn't get much rest. The reporters are always asking things. A lady called me up from the *New York Times* and wanted to know what kind of things I have on my walls. I had to describe my whole house to her. But it's all wonderful, too. The neighbors just cry when Markie pitches."

"They cry?" I said.

"Yes, they do," says Mrs. Fidrych. "The next-door neighbor cries and the lady at the filling station cries when she puts in my gas. She says Markie brings tears to her eyes. I mean he's such an honest boy.

So good. Do you know he went to Holland just to see the tulips? He brought me back some, too, and a clock."

Carol Ann pouts and shakes her head. "If I know Mark, he went over for the girls!" she says.

"No," says Mother Fidrych, shaking her head. "The tulips. He brought them back. He's a very affectionate boy. I don't see him so much now. I get phone calls but I would rather get letters. I guess I've got to stop treating him like a baby. He's a major leaguer now. A man. But I worry. Still it's all so wonderful."

"Oh, shut up, Mother," says Carol Ann.

"Don't talk like that to your mother," says Mr. Fidrych. He turns to me. "This is all a little exciting for us, you know. I mean, it's wonderful."

"Did you ever think Mark was going to make it?"

"Sure," says Mr. Fidrych. "He was always a good athlete. He won in high school, he won in the American Legion, and he did well in the minors."

"Did you encourage him in his style?" I ask.

"No," says Mr. Fidrych. "That's just his way of loosening up. He's always been a hyper kid. I went to see him when he pitched in Boston, and when I got into the locker room he couldn't stop moving. He was doing chin-ups the whole time he was talking to me."

"This is all so wonderful," Mrs. Fidrych adds. "People give us free meals and drinks because I tell them I'm The Bird's mother."

"Really, Mother," says Carol Ann, squirming on the bed.

"Did you see the Big Birds over at the stadium?" I ask. "People dress up like giant birds . . . and jump up and down and flap their wings."

"Really!" says Mrs. Fidrych. "Isn't that wonderful. They make special birds all for Markie."

"Not *special* birds, Mother," says Carol Ann. "Those are the Big Birds from *Sesame Street*. You can buy them in any department store."

This piece of news does not faze Mother Fidrych. "Oh, isn't that nice," she says. "Markie has helped bring back *Sesame Street*." She sips her drink and smiles affably out at the world.

Game Time

The Bird is on the mound again. There are fifty-one thousand fans in the stands. It could be a repeat of the TV game against the Yankees, or of the recent shutout against the Orioles. But tonight things are just a little off. The ball is coming in low and away, but a bit *too much* away. The Royals, whose whole hitting philosophy is to hit the ball where you can (if the ball is low and away, don't try to pull it, but instead hit it to the opposite field), are waiting a little longer and getting their quick bats around in time to poke line drives to right and left. Still, the only run they are able to score is on an infield hit. Unfortunately for the fans and The Bird, Dennis Leonard, the Royals' fastballing stopper, is at the peak of his form. Perhaps miffed that neither he nor any of the Royals pitching staff was picked for the All-Star Game, Leonard is popping in his fastball. Leonard fans eight, and The Bird goes down to defeat, 1–0. (It will become a Bird trademark: Fidrych's three other defeats have been either by one run (4–3) or by shutout (2–0 and 1–0).)

In the locker room immediately after the game, The Bird is sitting at his locker, drinking beer. Even here, we can hear the screams of the Tiger fans, "We Want Bird! We Want Bird! We Want Bird!" The Bird blinks, confused. "I lost it," he says. "I just didn't feel mean out there tonight, you know. I was getting behind the hitters, 2 and 0, 2 and 1. I just didn't have it. I didn't challenge them."

The reporters are surrounding The Bird, thrusting mikes into his face. "Do you think the media had any effect on your lack of meanness?"

"No," says The Bird. "I could say that, but it would be a cop-out. I mean, I just didn't have it."

He gulps and what looks like a tear starts to come to his eye, and suddenly you realize that this is really the *youngest* of kids. Suddenly, from the doorway, a man with graying hair and a worried look rushes into the crowd.

"Mark, you gotta go back out there. They won't leave."

The Bird looks down. "I lost," he says. "What do they want me for?"

"They love you, Mark," a reporter says. "Losing 1–0 is no crime."

"It's not that I lost," The Bird says. "It's that I didn't challenge them."

"Talk later," says the stadium man. "Please! They'll tear the place apart."

Mark Fidrych agrees to get on his old sweatpants and shirt, and go out. He is barefooted as he runs down the runway, the whole great gaggle of scribes behind him. Out on the field the cops are holding arms. The Bird waves to his fans. "BIRD BIRD BIRD," they scream.

Back in the dressing room, after the place clears out a bit, LeFlore looks at me and smiles. "We hate to lose behind The Bird. He's such a nice kid. Really, he ain't nothing but a baby."

The Baby and the Nest

The Bird is relaxing with his family at their room in the Pontchartrain. He is wearing his Muhammad Ali T-shirt, old Levis, and tennis shoes, and he is drinking a Stroh's. Cuddled up on the bed next to him is his little sister, Laurie. Carol Ann is curled at the end of the bed; his parents are sitting in chairs.

"You don't look too sad now," I say to Fidrych.

"Nah," he says. "I'm with my family now. I don't want to take the game home to them. But I'll worry about it all night. Beat my pillow and beat a few beers."

Mother Fidrych looks concerned: "Markie, Markie, listen. I got a book for you to read. It's 'How to Hang Loose.'"

Fidrych opens his rubber lips and shakes his head: "Yeah, you drop your pants. That's how you hang loose."

"Now, Markie," says Mrs. Fidrych.

"Don't tell me what to say, Mother," The Bird says. He looks over at me and opens his hands. "She's always telling me what to say."

"When did you start this talking to the ball?" I ask, breaking the silence.

"Markie talks to cars, too," says Mother Fidrych. "When they don't work, he just talks to them, and then they do."

"Yeah. I talk to 'em all right. With a monkey wrench. If they don't work, I beat the hell out of 'em. Then they work!"

"What did you think of the fans giving you a standing ovation even though you lost?"

"That was great. It's life, isn't it! I mean, losing and all. But the fans have been great."

Father Fidrych shakes his head. "I'm glad you came back out," he says. "The people who stay to see you are the people who have the seats out in the bleachers and way up in the upper deck. They are the real fans. The rich guys who have the good seats along the baselines aren't really the real fans."

"That's right," Mark says. "I love the kids in the bleachers. Hey, there was a cop up there in the bleachers who gave a kid hell. Started beating on him for no reason, and the kids out there just did a job on that dude. That cop was *history*, man. I don't like to see the police hassling kids. I don't like poor people not being able to have good seats. It's not right. I mean *I'm one* of those kids."

"I met a Puerto Rican lady today," says Mother Fidrych, "and she even liked you."

"Hey, Ma," says Mark. "Really. 'Even.' Hey listen, I'm Puerto Rican myself. I feel that way. I hate it when they scalp tickets and some rich guy can get a better seat. It's not right." .

"Yeah," says Father Fidrych. "And they are selling pictures of you on T-shirts and you aren't getting a cent. We ought to see about that!"

"No," says Mark. "That's life. They gotta make money, too. If some guy wants to make money selling my picture, then let him. That's life isn't it?"

"But, Mark," says Mr. Fidrych. "They're taking advantage of you."

"So what? It doesn't hurt me. I'm happy this way. I don't want to get involved in lawsuits and things. I just wanna play ball. I don't ever wanna change."

Fidrych points to the man on his T-shirt, Muhammad Ali. "Here's a champ. Here's a man who is himself. You gotta hand it to him."

Suddenly, Mother Fidrych is up out of her chair, rushing over to her son.

"Joe Louis," she says. "I never knew you liked Joe Louis, Markie!"

"Oh, Ma," says Mark. He hugs her and tells her that she is staring at Muhammad Ali. "I love you, Ma," he says. "But sometimes. . . ."

Postscript to The Bird Is the Word:

Unfortunately Mark Fydrich's mother wasn't worried in vain. He finished his rookie year (1976) with a 19–3 record, and was runner up to Jim Palmer for the Cy Young Award. He was given a $225,000 contract by the Tigers and things looked bright indeed. But the very next season he tore his rotator cuff while pitching in Baltimore and he was never the same pitcher after that. His natural sinker was gone and he was hit hard. By 1980 he was out of baseball. The Bird went back to Massachusetts where he bought and drove his own dump truck. Eventually he bought a farm, but at the age of fifty-four he suffered a strange accident. A friend found him under one of his trucks, dead. It was ruled that he'd had a heart attack. Thus ended the life of one of the most beloved players in sports. Even though he was really only a star for one year, it was his eccentricity and sweetness which won over the entire nation. In the year of the bicentennial he and his family seemed to embody the very best in America. Talent, kindness, and an innocence that I doubt anyone will see again.

Reggie Jackson in No-Man's Land

One day I was hanging out at *Sport*'s offices getting ready for another nine-hour drinking bout . . . I mean "editorial meeting," when editor Berry Stainback said to me: "You, sir, Bob, have you read all that guff Reginald Martinez Jackson is laying down at the Yankees spring training camp?"

"No, sir, I have not," said I, "In point of fact, I just read, in that highly regarded intellectual journal, the *New York Post*, that Sir Reg is being very humble at said camp, telling the world how he's a team player, just one of the guys, the saintliest among a team of saints."

"Precisely what I'm talking about," Berry said. "Everybody knows he has the biggest ego in world history. Eventually it has to all spill out. Why don't you fly down there and see if you can use your finesse and deadly charm to get him to speak words unfettered by the bounds of false humility!"

"So be it, fair prince," said I, picking up on the Arthurian cadence of our speeches. "But now that we have discussed this matter have we not need for both solid food and liquid repast?"

This quiz threw Sir Berry for a loop. But only for a second. "Ahhhh, well, indeed there is much we have to discuss as to the shaping and tone of the piece, the tongue and groove, the warp and the woof."

"And this cannot be done without food, liquor, and tawdry women," said assistant editor Roger "The Dodger" Director.

"'Tis true, gentle knight," I said. "You are well spoken, sirrah!"

So saying, the humble scribe and their brave editors descended to the streets and the rabble therewith. And over a feast at the round table of Sir Rocky Graziano's they laughed, and drank and worked ever so hard until darkness fell upon the land.

Knightly posturing aside, I was somewhat confused how I would play it with Reginald Jackson. Should I act in awe of his mighty prowess with the bat? Nah, he must get that every day. Should I say how excited I was as a New Yorker to have him here in my adopted city? Nah, he wouldn't go for that. Too corny.

I tossed and turned the night before I left, trying to figure an angle to get close to the great man.

As usual, I couldn't think of anything and decided the best thing to do was to play it by ear. So much for preparation.

The Yanks were in Fort Lauderdale and the very first thing that happened when I walked into the locker room was key.

To wit, I saw a bunch of little sportswriter guys colliding around Reggie's locker, hanging on his every word. They looked and sounded like freaking munchkins:

"Hey, Reg, how's the toe?"

"Yeah, Reg, the toe okay?'

"Hope that toe is ready to go."

Okay, it wasn't quite that bad, but that's the general idea. "Fawning" is not too strong a word. I decided, at that second, I would go in the exact opposite direction. First of all, I wouldn't even approach him for a while. I knew he'd already seen me so I barely made eye contact with him. Instead, I walked around asking some of the other players about him. I talked to Chris Chambliss, who was having a discussion with Willie Randolph about DNA. Honest! Neither of them had much to say. I talked to Ken Holtzman, and later, Sparky Lyle. Neither of them seemed too thrilled about dealing with Reggie, and Lyle said so.

When I finally did get around to talking to the Great Man, Jackson started stonewalling me.

"I don't know if I want to talk to *Sport*. They screwed me one time."

"But that wasn't me," I said, my second-best noncommittal answer.

"Is this going to be a positive or negative piece?"

You know what my answer was: "Reg, I am here to set the record straight!"

Reggie smiled. "Well, I'm not sure if I want to talk, man."

"Fine," I said, smiling like an insurance man. "I'll just go back and talk to the other guys again. I can come back in a little while and ask you again. If you don't want to talk I can write the piece without you."

For those of you who might want to be journalists, remember tone is all. I didn't act like I wanted to suck his big toe and I didn't slobber over him. What I did was act brisk, businesslike, and above all, capable.

My tone was "Listen Big Guy, the piece is going to get written whether you participate or not." And by going around talking to the other guys on the team while he watched me, I knew it would drive him crazy not to know what they were saying.

Having said my piece in no uncertain terms—like I could give a fuck whether he lived or died—I proceeded to walk around the room and gather more material.

By the time I got back again, Reggie was dying to know what his teammates said.

I said, "Well, maybe I could tell you some of it, if I could have some time with you, alone."

He then suggested we meet at the Banana Boat Bar, the place where the real interview went down.

Trust me, dear and gentle reader, by the time I left the locker room that day I already knew I was going to get some good quotes. The Great One was chomping at the bit. But I had no idea how good they would be and what craziness would ensue.

I met him at the Banana Boat in the afternoon. The place had a horseshoe bar, with seats and banquettes in the front, where Billy Martin and Mickey Mantle were playing backgammon with an Aussie dressed all in white. He was somewhat overweight, and had a mustache. He looked like a backgammon player from an F. Scott Fitzgerald book. Martin was killing him in the game.

Everything Reggie said of any real interest is in the piece, but I left out a few of my own statements. I was there to get his ideas and not tell the reader how I got them.

But here—FOR THE FIRST TIME—is the unvarnished truth.

As we sat feeling each other out, I thought of what one of the other sports guys had said, and that was: "He's like a torrent of material." Then I noticed that Mantle, Martin, and Whitey Ford were all sort of goofing on him down at the other end of the bar. They were calling out "Hey, it's a Superstar," and making lame high school kind of jokes like "Is that really Reggie?" etc. All harmless stuff, but I could see that Reggie was sensitive to it. So, off of the top of my head, I said: "Maybe those guys don't like you because you are really smart. Is that possible?" That's when the torrent really began. Reggie nodded his head and said, "Yes . . . that's right. . . ."

It was then that he started in with the bit about developing his intellect. I had no idea that he would respond so vehemently, but there it was. He saw me as a person who understood him, and in fact,

I was. A few minutes later, Whitey Ford came down and gave him his pink cashmere sweater for Reggie's SUPERSTAR T-shirt as old buds Mantle and Martin mocked him again. Reggie played along with the gag but it was obvious he was hurt. I played right into his pain, suggested that they maybe didn't understand how smart he was and he was off again, talking about how he was a person of substance. I mentioned Cosell, who I had always thought patronized him, and he went on another tear.

In short, all one had to do to get him going was to suggest that someone didn't really understand him and he was off like a horse spiked with methedrine.

Eventually, we got to the leadership of the Yankees. I mentioned how Munson was the captain of the team and I made it sound like nothing could change it. He was so anxious to correct me that he went on his endless rap about being "the straw that stirs the drink." Truthfully, it was like shooting ducks in a pond. Anything you mentioned regarding other people belittling him or not understanding his greatness was met with a torrent of defensive commentary.

For all his money and fame, the Big Guy was the most insecure person I'd ever met. After a while, I even began to feel kind of sorry for him. He had said so many harmful things that I actually wanted to give him a chance to take some of them back. So I asked him: "You sure you want *all* this printed?" He slammed his fist down on the Banana Boat bar and said, "Print it."

So I did.

And so did Reggie Jackson's words condemn him to a very trying year.

And yet one which ended in his triumph. Ironically, he led the Yankees over the Dodgers in the World Series in 1977, and ended up winning the *Sport* magazine Corvette as Player of the Year. I even went to the big event but Reggie and I weren't speaking.

I've heard for years that he hates me to this day, but all I did was ask him some questions. He didn't have to say a word. For what it's worth, my own theory concerning Reggie is that he's the kind of guy who has to put himself in a deep pit. He has to see enemies all around him, and then he can be the hero, and show the freaking world. Working in Hollywood as I have for years, I've met many of these kinds of people. They don't work *with* people. Instead, they have to create a legend that they are the only ones who know how to write a script (direct a movie, act a part, etc.) in the right way. If they just weren't surrounded by all these fools and incompetents they could shine. Well, they'll show them all, the moronic idiots . . . etc., ad nauseam.

Reg seems like that kind of guy to me. It makes for big heroic moments, but it's kind of a lonely way to go through life. Guys like Reg don't have too many friends. But, then again, with an ego big enough to fill up Yankee Stadium, maybe he doesn't have room for anyone else.

From the moment Reggie reached spring training, there were fire-works on the Yankees. Before season's end, the Bronx Bombers could explode.

Oh, golden, yellow light shimmering on Reggie Jackson's chest! Yes, that's he, the latest member of the American League Champion New York Yankees, and he is standing by his locker, bare-chested, million-dollar sweat dripping from his brow, golden pendants dangling from his neck. God, he looks like some big baseball Othello as he smiles at the gaggle of reporters who rush toward him, their microphones thrust out, their little ninety-eight-cent pens poised, ready to take down his every word. But somehow, it's hard to ask the man questions . . . certainly not such standard ballplayer questions as "How's the arm?" or "Toe hurt?" . . . for not all ballplayers are Reggie Jackson, whose golden pendants catch the sunlight filtering through the steamy Fort Lauderdale clubhouse windows and reflect dazzlingly into your eyes. What are these priceless reflectors? Well, first, there is a small golden bar with the word "Inseparable" on it, a gift from Reggie's Norwegian girlfriend, and gyrating next to that memento is a dog tag—the inscrutable Zen koan (though slightly reminiscent of the Kiwanis Club), "Good Luck Is When Hard Work Meets Opportunity." And, finally, there is the most important bauble of all, an Italian horn that Reggie tells a reporter is supposed to keep the evil spirits away!

Evil spirits? Egads. What evil spirits can be following Reggie Jackson? The man has been on three World Series Championship teams (Oakland A's 1972–1974), has led the league in RBIs (1973: 117), home runs (1973: thirty-two, 1975: thirty-six) and was the American League's MVP in 1973. Since then he has topped his on-the-field-feats by playing out his option under Charles O. Finley, and refusing to sign with his new club, the Baltimore Orioles, until they gave him a gigantic raise. Finally came the *coup de grace*: signing with the New

York Yankees for three million big ones. Reggie is expected to be the biggest thing to hit New York since King Kong. So where are the evil spirits?

"No evil spirits, actually," Reg says, answering a newsman's question. "Just in case, you know? Hey, could you move that mike out of the way? Shoving it up my nose like that is *sooooo* uncomfortable. . . ."

The little man yanks his mike back.

"I am not merely a baseball player," Reggie says to another reporter, who nods gravely. "I am a black man who has done what he wants, gotten what he wanted and will continue to get it.

"Now what I want to do," he adds, "is develop my intellect. You see, on the field I am a surgeon. I put on my glove and this hat. . . ."

He picks up the New York Yankee baseball hat. Itself a legend. Legendary hat meet legendary head!

"And I put on these shoes. . . ." Reggie points down to his shoes. "And I go out on the field, and I cut up the other team. I am a surgeon. No one can quite do it the way I do. But off the field . . . I try to forget all about it. You know, you can get very narrow being a superstar."

Reggie removes his cap. "I mean, being a superstar . . . can make life very difficult, difficult to grow. So I like to visit with my friends, listen to some *fine* music, drink some *good* wine, perhaps take a ride in the country in a *fine* car, or . . . just walk along the beach. Nature is extremely important to me. Which may be just about the only trouble I'll have in New York. I'll miss the trees!"

Then, in his quiet, throaty voice, Reg politely says he must be off to the training room.

"Terrific," a jaunty reporter says as Reggie leaves. "He's so terrific. He's the kinda guy you don't want to talk to every day . . . because he gives you so much. It's like a torrent of material. He overwhelms you!"

"Yes," I say. "But how do the other guys on the Yankees feel about having a tornado in their presence? I heard Thurman Munson and some of the others gave him a chilly reception."

"No problem," says the reporter. "All that stuff about problems on the team is just something somebody wrote to sell papers. Hell, Reggie hasn't even been here for a week. There hasn't been time for resentment yet!"

The next day after practice, Reggie Jackson is once again standing by his locker, once again surrounded by reporters, who ask him to reveal his "personal philosophy of life."

I look down the seats before lockers and see last year's Yankee stars sitting like dukes around the king. Next to Jackson is Chris Chambliss. Remember him? He hit the home run that won the pennant for the Yanks. But no one seems much interested in this instant (though brief) hero's developing intellect or his reflections on recombinant DNA, which happens to be the subject Chambliss is discussing with Willie Randolph. And down the line a little farther is old gruff and grumble himself, Thurman Munson. Today he rubs his mustache, and stares at the floor, looking like Bert Lahr in the Wizard of Oz. Folks aren't rushing to ask him about the philosophical questions that are addressed to Jackson, yet Munson is the acknowledged "team leader."

And across the room is Catfish Hunter, the wise old Cat, and businesslike Ken Holtzman. Their combined salaries are enough to send up a space shot to Pluto, but no one is asking them if they like to recite Kahlil Gibran. It's strange, a little dreamlike. There is the Super-team, but if this first week is any example, Reggie Jackson has taken over so totally that it's almost as if the other players were rookies who had yet to prove themselves to the press.

Now, Jackson says goodbye to the reporters, and tells me he is going outside to sign a few late-afternoon autographs. Would I like to come? Certainly.

And so we stand out by the first baseline while the fans crowd around, pushing and shoving and holding up their cameras.

"Smile, Reggie," says a woman with a scarf on her head, tied up so she looks like she has two green rabbit ears.

Reggie produces a semi-smile.

"You have such white teeth," she says.

Jackson turns to me and raises his eyebrows, then moves along signing scraps of paper and baseballs when a man on crutches is pushed precariously close to the edge of the stands. Jackson stops signing and demands that the other fans help the crippled man. The fans do what he says.

Finally, after Reggie has signed endless signatures, a young boy says, "Thank you, Mr. Jackson."

Reggie stops, looks up at me, and says: "You sign a million before anyone ever says thank you."

On that perfect exit line, Reggie does a perfect exit. He picks up a loose ball and flips it to the crowd, who cheer and applaud. Waiting for Jackson to get his rubdown, I ask Sparky Lyle, who is seated in front of his locker: "How's it going?"

"Great,'" says Lyle. "I may be leaving tomorrow. We are only about two hundred and fifty thousand dollars away from one another."

Perhaps not the best time to ask him about the new three-million-dollar superstar. But duty must be done.

"I don't think we need him," Lyle says. "Not to take anything away from his talents, but what we really needed was a good right-handed hitter. A right-handed superstar."

Jackson comes strutting into the room. Not a self-conscious strut. Just his natural superstar strut. He can't help it if he is bigger than all indoors.

Lou Piniella strides across the room and says, "Hey, Reg, How you doing?"

"How you doing, hoss?" Reggie says affably.

"I'm not the horse, Reg," Piniella says, with a good deal of uncertainty in his voice. "You're the hoss. . . . I'm just the cart."

Jackson smiles, trying to pass the remark off as a joke.

Jackson and I enter the Banana Boat Bar, and he undoes his windbreaker just enough to reveal the huge yellow star on his blue T-shirt. Around the star are the silver letters that spell out SUPERSTAR! At the bar, he discards the jacket. All around us people start staring and the waitresses start twitching in their green Tinkerbell costumes.

We order Lite beers, and Reggie gives me a pregnant stare and says, "If I seem a little distant, it's because I got burned once by *Sport* magazine. They wrote a piece which said I caused trouble on the team. That I have a huge ego. That I only hit for a .258 average. That I wasn't a complete ballplayer. They only say that kind of stuff about black men. If a white man happens to be colorful, then it's fine. If he's black, then they say he's a troublemaker."

I tell him that I have no intention of showing him as a troublemaker. As far as I'm concerned the league could use fifty more Reggies, and fifty fewer baseball players who sound like shoe salesmen.

But almost before I'm finished, Reggie has forgotten his fears.

"You see," he says, "I've got problems other guys don't have. I've got this big image that comes before me, and I've got to adjust to it. Or what it has been projected to be. That's not 'me' really, but I've got to deal with it. Also, I used to just be known as a black athlete, now I'm respected as a tremendous intellect."

"A tremendous intellect?" I say.

"What?" says Jackson, waving to someone.

"You were talking about your tremendous intellect."

"Oh, was I?" Jackson says. "No, I meant . . . that now people talk to me as if I were a person of substance. That's important to me."

I mention Jackson's reportage on the Royals-Yankees pennant playoffs last year for ABC, saying that most of my friends felt that

Reggie had done a much better job of analyzing the motivation of the players than Howard Cosell. What's more, he did it in the most hostile atmosphere imaginable, with Cosell constantly hassling him and chiding him for defending Royals' centerfielder Al Cowens on a controversial call.

"Well, that is part of my problem," says Reggie. "I do everything as honestly as I can. I give all I have to give. But I don't let people get in my way. Cosell was insecure. He thought I was trying to put him down, make him look bad by correcting him. He made quite a stink about me to the big people at ABC, but they took up for me. I really wasn't trying to compete with him. I was just being myself. And it got me in trouble."

Jackson smiles, sits back, and folds his arms over his SUPERSTAR chest. A second later we are joined by Jim Wynn, who at thirty-five is trying to make a comeback with the Yankees. Once a tremendous long-ball hitter known as "The Toy Cannon," Wynn has been faltering, and certainly he can't have more than a year or so left. He orders a drink, and then Reggie and he begin to talk about hitting in Boston's Fenway Park.

"You are gonna love the left-field fence," Reggie says.

"I know I will," Wynn says. "If they play me, you know I'll hit some out."

But he doesn't sound convinced. There is a lull in the conversation and then Wynn looks over at Reggie, and says, "You know, Reggie, I hope my son grows up to be like you. Not like me. Like you."

Wynn smiles in awe at Jackson, and I realize that for all their professionalism, the Yankees are just as subject to the mythology of the press as any fan. Just by showing up, Jackson has changed the ambiance of the locker room. And no one yet knows if it's for good or ill.

As I ponder, two of the original mythmakers appear at the Banana Boat—Mickey Mantle, now a spring batting coach, and his old crony, manager Billy Martin. Soon they are settled into drinking and playing backgammon, and when they are joined by Whitey Ford, Jackson hails a waitress and sends them complimentary drinks. The waitress comes back to Reggie and says, "Whitey Ford appreciates your offer of a drink, but says he would rather have your SUPERSTAR T-shirt."

Jackson breaks into a huge smile, peels off his shirt, and runs bare-chested across the room. He hands the shirt to Ford, and then Ford, in great hilarity, takes off his pink cashmere sweater and gives it to Jackson. A few minutes later Reggie is back at the bar, the sweater folded in his lap.

"That's really something, isn't it!" Jackson says. "Whitey Ford giving me his sweater. A Hall-of-Famer. I'm keeping this."

He smiles, looking down lovingly at the sweater.

On the Yankees the old-timers still retain their magic, even to the younger stars like Jackson. In a way it is easier for him to relate to them than his own teammates. For they were mythic, legends, as he is. . . . In fact, their legends are still stronger than Reggie's, coming as they did back when ugly salary disputes didn't tarnish both players and managers.

This becomes even more apparent when Jackson moves to the backgammon table to join the crowd watching Mantle and Martin play one of the most ludicrously bad, but hilarious, games in recent history. Both of them beginners and slightly loaded, the two men resort to several rather questionable devices. The object of the game is to get your men, or chips, around the board, and into your opponent's home, then "bear them off the board." The man who gets all his men out first wins. (You throw a pair of dice to decide how many spaces you can move.) Martin rolls a seven and quickly moves nine spaces. Jackson and Ford laugh hysterically. Mantle rolls his dice, moves the properly allotted amount, and then simply slips three of his men off the board and into his pants pocket. Martin, busy ordering drinks and taking advice from Reggie, misses Mantle's burglary, which gives Mickey a tremendous advantage in the game. Martin's next roll lands him on two of Mantle's men and sends them back to the center bar. Mantle rolls the dice, orders another round of drinks and, while Martin chats with the waiter, takes four more of his chips off the table and puts them under his chair. Mantle chuckles as Martin, unaware of what has happened, rolls the dice. Reggie tries to control his laughter—unsuccessfully—the mirth bursting out of him. And now everyone is laughing, Mantle so hard that tears are streaming down his face. Martin suddenly notices that Mantle, despite weaker rolls of the dice, already has fewer men on the board.

"You bastard!" Martin shouts. "Where are all your chips?"

Mantle protests his innocence with great vigor but Martin reaches down and pulls out the evidence from under Mantle's chair. Mantle screams in mock surprise, and then throws up his hands. "Hell, Billy," he says, "you were beating me even though I was cheating."

"You bum," says Martin, "You bum. I'm just too good. I'm a winner."

"Nobody can beat Billy," Mantle says as he beams at his old buddy.

Reggie is still laughing, shaking his head, and I can't help but feel that he has missed something. Mantle, Ford, and Martin have a kind of loyalty and street-gang friendship that today's transient players don't have time to develop. Soon Mantle and Martin are involved in another humorous game, and Reggie goes back to the bar. Alone.

Minutes later I join him and try to gauge his mood. What did he feel watching Mantle and Martin? In a second I have my answer, for Reggie starts talking and now he is less the showman. He seems to be talking directly from his bones:

"You know," he says, "this team . . . it all flows from me. I've got to keep it all going. I'm the straw that stirs the drink. It all comes back to me. Maybe I should say me and Munson . . . but really he doesn't enter into it. He's being so damned insecure about the whole thing. I've overheard him talking about me."

"You mean he talks loud to make sure you can hear him?"

"Yeah. Like that. I'll hear him telling some other writer that he wants it to be known that he's the captain of the team, that he knows what's best. Stuff like that. And when anybody knocks me, he'll laugh real loud so I can hear it. . . ."

Reggie looks down at Ford's sweater. Perhaps he is wishing the present Yankees could have something like Ford and Martin and Mantle had. Community. Brotherhood. Real friendship.

"Maybe you ought to just go to Munson," I suggest. "Talk it out right up front."

But Reggie shakes his head:

"No," he says. "He's not ready for it yet. He doesn't even know he feels like he does. He isn't aware of it yet."

"You mean if you went and tried to be open and honest about it, he'd deny it?"

Jackson nods his head. "Yeah. He'd say, 'What? I'm not jealous. There aren't any problems.' He'd try to cover up, but he ought to know he can't cover up anything from me. Man, there is no way. . . . I can read these guys. No, I'll wait, and eventually he'll be whipped. There will come that moment when he really knows I've won . . . and he'll want to hear everything is all right . . . and *then* I'll go to him, and we will get it right."

Reggie makes a fist, and clutches Ford's sweater: "You see, that is the way I am. I'm a leader, and I can't lie down . . . but 'leader' isn't the right word . . . it's a matter of PRESENCE. . . . Let me put it this way: no team I am on will ever be humiliated the way the Yankees were by the Reds in the World Series! That's why Munson can't intimidate me. Nobody can. You can't psych me. You take me one-on-one in the pit, and I'll whip you. . . . It's an attitude, really. . . . It's the way the manager looks at you when you come into the room. . . . It's the way the coaches and the batboy look at you. . . . The way your name trickles through the crowd when you wait in the batter's box. . . . It's all that. . . . The way the Yankees were humiliated by the Reds? You think that doesn't bother Billy Martin? He's no fool. He's smart. Very smart. And he's a winner. Munson's tough, too. He is a winner, but there is just nobody who can do for a club what I can do. . . . There is nobody who can put meat in the seats [fans in the stands] the way I can. That's just the way it is. . . . Munson thinks he can be the straw that stirs the drink, but he can only stir it bad."

"You were doing it just a few minutes ago over there with Martin, weren't you?" I say. "Stirring a little."

"Sure," says Jackson, "but he has presence too. He's no dummy. I can feel him letting me do what I want, then roping me in whenever he needs to . . . but I'll make it easy for him. He won't have to be 'bad' Billy Martin fighting people anymore. He can move up a notch 'cause I'll open the road. I'll open the road, and I'll let the others come thundering down the path!"

Jackson sits back, staring fiercely at the bar. A man in love with words, with power, a man engaged in a battle. Jim Wynn resumes his seat next to Reggie and watches him with respect. An ally.

But, I wonder—are there any others?

Billy Martin is sitting in his office at Yankee Stadium South. He is half dressed and his hair is messed, but for all that he still has what Jackson called PRESENCE. Now he runs his hand through his hair and laughs: "I couldn't lose to Mantle, could I?" he says.

"You had him psyched."

Martin laughs again and nods. "And he was trying to act like he wasn't mad."

Mantle comes in the door sipping coffee and looking about two years older than the night before. "You know," he says, "I woke up this morning, and I had me a whole pocket full of them white things!"

After we finish laughing, I ask Martin if he thinks there will be any problems having Reggie Jackson on the team.

Martin, who as Reggie himself said is "no dummy," smiles and asks, "What kind?"

"Like team leader problems?"

Martin shakes his head: "Not a chance. We already have a team leader. Thurman Munson."

I walk into the locker room and sit with Catfish Hunter in front of his locker and talk about Reggie. Catfish shoots a stream of tobacco juice on the floor, and shakes his head slowly, philosophically. "Reggie is a team leader," he says. "The thing you have to understand about Reggie is he wants everyone to love him."

For a second I think Cat is going to elaborate on this theme, but he holds back, chooses a new path—a safer one. "I mean," he says, "he can get hot with his bat and carry a team for three weeks. He's always ready to go all the time."

Hunter squints at me as if to say, *"That's all, my friend. I'm staying out of this one."*

Chris Chambliss's locker is right next door to Reggie Jackson's. The men literally rub elbows when they dress. Yet when I ask Chambliss how he feels about Reggie, he says, "I haven't had a chance to talk to him yet. I think he'll help the ball club. Most of the rumors you have heard are untrue. Still, we do have a lot of personalities on this team . . . things could happen. I doubt it. But they could."

I catch Thurman Munson as he comes in to practice. An hour late. I wonder if he isn't having some kind of psych battle with Jackson. Which star arrives on the field the latest? Gruffly, he declines to talk to me until after practice, and then he declines again for some thirty minutes. Finally, he nods me over and I ask him about Jackson.

"What are you asking me for?" he says. "Why does everybody ask me?"

"I'm not singling you out," I say. "I've asked quite a few others. But there has been talk that you two will have problems competing as team leader."

Munson shakes his head, makes a face. "No. No way. And what difference does it make if I'm not 'team leader'? There are a lot of leaders on this team. We've got a lot of stars. They are all leaders. As far as Reggie goes, he's a good player. He'll help the club. Has a lot of power."

"How about jealousy over his salary?"

"No," Munson says, "I don't care about that. He signed as a free agent. I hope he makes ten million dollars. Is that all?"

Munson turns away and begins to talk to a businessman about a shopping center they hope to build in Florida.

It's late in the afternoon and Reggie Jackson is taking extra batting practice. The only people left on the field are Thurman Munson and Chris Chambliss. And a young pitcher, a rookie who is new to me.

Jackson fouls off a couple of pitches, and Chambliss looks at Munson and says, "Show time!" There is a real bite in his kidding.

"Hey," says Munson, "are we out here to see this?"

Jackson digs in and fouls off a few more.

"Some show!" says Munson. "Real power!"

Jackson tries to laugh it off, and finally connects on a pitch. It falls short of the fence, and Munson and Chambliss smile at one another. Munson steps into the cage, but Jackson hurries into the locker room.

I am about ready to leave, and I thank Reggie for his cooperation, but he seems disturbed by my going. "Listen," he says, "I'd like to know what the guys thought of me. You talked to them. How about telling me?"

"Okay," I say. "I'll meet you back at the Banana Boat."

An hour later, at the Banana Boat, I tell Jackson that Lyle had said the team didn't need him, that Lyle said it was nothing personal, but the Yankees needed a right-handed hitter more. Then I tell him that Munson had denied there was any problem, and I mention that Chambliss had said, "I haven't had a chance to talk to him yet."

"Yeah," says Jackson. "You see it's a pattern. The guys who are giants like Catfish, the guys who are really secure . . . they don't worry about me. But guys like Munson. . . . It's really a comedy, isn't it. I mean, it's hilarious. . . . Did you see him in the batting cage? He is really acting childish. Like the first day of practice he comes up to me and says, 'Hey, you have to run now . . . before you hit.' You know he's playing the team captain trying to tell me what to do. But I play it very low key. I say, 'Yeah, but if I run now I'll be too tired to hit later,' and Munson says, 'Yeah, but if you don't run now, it'll make a bad impression on the other guys.' So I say, 'Let me ask the coach,' and I yelled over to Dick Howser, 'Should I run now or hit?' and Howser yelled, 'Aw, the hell with running. Get in there and hit.' So that's what I did. It really made Munson furious. But I did it so he couldn't complain. Listen, I always treat him right. I talk to him all the time, but he is so jealous and nervous and resentful that he can't stand it. If I wanted to I could snap him. Just wait until I get hot and hit a few out, and the reporters start coming around and I have New York eating out of the palm of my hand . . . he won't be able to stand it."

Jackson delivers all this with a kind of healthy, competitive, and slightly maniacal glee. It's as if he has said to himself, "Okay, they aren't going to love me. So I'll break 'em down. I'll show them who's boss." And he might. I can't help but think that the situation would be a lot healthier if the other Yankees had come to him.

"How has Chambliss been treating you?" I ask.

"Standoffish. They all have. You see Piniella in there yesterday? He said that stuff about me being the horse and him being the cart. That's how they feel. But at least he talked to me. That was a kind of a breakthrough. That and the thing with Whitey, with the sweater. That was good, too."

"Maybe you are overreacting," I say. "It is a new year, and everyone has heard about your legend, and they feel like they can't be the ones to come up to you and try to break the ice because then it will look like they are trying to kiss your ass, and they'll feel embarrassed and self-conscious."

Jackson nods hopefully. "Yeah, it could be that. I know it could be. Say, did you talk to Billy Martin about me?"

"Yeah," I say. "He told me that the Yankees had a team leader."

"Yeah? Who?"

"Munson."

Reggie laughs ruefully.

"But maybe he's gotta say that," I say. "It wouldn't look good to say you are the team leader this early. It would hurt Munson's pride."

"That's right," Jackson says. "I just want you to know that [coach] Elston Howard came up to me today and said, 'No matter what anybody says, you are the team leader.' So I think there is some real heavy stuff going on. But it is weird. You know, up until yesterday Martin had hardly said two words to me. But he has made me feel I'm all right. Still, I don't understand it."

"It could go back to your verbal ability," I suggest. "I mean, a lot of athletes are suspicious of people who can talk well. It makes them feel dull and stupid, so they resent the other guy and get hostile toward him."

"Right," says Jackson. "That's true. I've been through that one before. But you know . . . the rest of the guys should know that I don't feel that far above them. . . . I mean, nobody can turn people on like I can, or do for a club the things I can do, but we are all still athletes, we're all still ballplayers. We should be able to get along. We've got a strong common ground, common wants. . . . I'm not going to allow the team to get divided. I'll do my job, give it all I got, talk to anybody. I think Billy will appreciate that. . . . I'm not going to let the small stuff get in the way. . . . But if that's not enough . . . then I'll be gone. A friend of mine has already told me: 'You or Munson will be gone in two years.' I really don't want that to be the case . . . because, after all is said and done, Munson is a winner, he's a fighter, a hell of ballplayer . . . but don't you see. . . ."

Reggie pauses, and opens his hands in a gesture that seems to imply, *"It's so apparent, why can't Munson and Chambliss and all the rest of them understand the sheer simplicity . . . the cold logic?"*

"Don't you see, that there is just no way I can play second fiddle to *anybody*. Hah! That's just not in the cards. . . . There ain't no way!"

Postscript

It was a hot summer day in June 1977, and I was on the Long Island Railway coming in from my house in the Hamptons. For the past month I had holed up in this old red-shingled house on the bayside just a few miles south of Montauk. Jann Wenner had come over one night to tease me about not having a house, or a compound, like he did on the ocean side. But the truth was I loved it where I was. Tall grass, swans that swam up to the beach every night, and plenty of room for my dog, Byron, to run around chasing rabbits. My girlfriend, Robin, loved it too and it had been a wonderful month, writing my screenplay, *Cattle Annie and Little Britches*. I wanted and received no phone calls. This was, of course, before the days of the computer so there were no e-mails, no phone machine, and no one had my number. I didn't want to be bugged by my magazine editors. The truth was I was kind of burned out interviewing endless people and now that I was making money writing scripts that seemed a better way to go. (Little did I know I would have another eight years of struggling before I cracked Hollywood. It's a good thing we don't know what lies before us because if someone had told me I would be looking forward to eight more years of living hand to mouth I might have turned to a life of crime instead.)

So there I was with my typewriter, perfect sunsets, swans, Byron, and on weekends gorgeous Robin, who had a job at Ballantine publishing. Everything was fine and dandy.

I never once gave a thought to Reggie Jackson.

Why? Because in those days magazines, like *Sport*, had a three-month lead period. That meant you handed the piece in three months before it was going to be published. In fact, I had done three or four other pieces after it for other magazines, plus my screenplay, and some short fiction. Reggie Jackson was the last thing on my mind.

One day, however, I wanted to go into the city to see some of my friends. I was getting a little cabin fever writing all day and night, and I wanted a little city-action. So I took the train into town and got off at Penn Station. I was headed to a cab on Eighth Avenue when I happened to see the sports page of the *New York Post* on the magazine rack. The headline was in big bold letters.

It read: "FUROR ON THE YANKEES!!"

I walked over to the magazine stand and picked it up. As I read, my heart beat faster and faster. I don't recall the exact words but the gist of it was: "A bomb exploded in the Yankee clubhouse today due to an article on Reggie Jackson written by Robert Ward of *Sport* magazine. . . ."

"Holy shit," I said, and ran for a payphone. I called Berry Stainback; he wasn't in. But Dick Schaap was.

"Robert," he said. "Where the hell have you been? The whole goddamned world wants to talk to you!"

"They do?" I said. I'd had some violent reactions to my writing before but nothing like this. Dick then listed five radio shows and three TV shows that wanted me on. Not to mention every newspaper in the country.

"It's great," Dick said. "We haven't had a story like this in a long time!"

"Right!" I said. "Great!"

"Why don't you come up here now and we'll plan on what we're going to do first!"

"Is it okay if I get to my apartment and change clothes first?"

"Yeah, sure," Dick said. "But get over here. The Yankees are going nuts. I talked to Phil Rizzuto about twenty minutes ago."

The thing was, even though I was a tough guy reporter, who really would print anything no matter what the fuck anyone said to me (and especially if they threatened me), I was still an All American kid, who had always loved Phil "Scooter" Rizzuto. The idea that I had done something that would make him hate me really bothered me. I mean, hell, I had his baseball card!

"So what did Phil say?" I said, buffering myself for the shock.

"He loved it," Dick said. "Phil's just like all the old Yanks. They can't stand Reggie."

That was only a partial relief. I didn't want people to hate Reggie. The truth was, I kind of felt sorry for him. And did the old Yanks hate him because he was black and smart? Or was it because they couldn't take his big ego, his fur coats, and all the rest? Or were they just jealous of him because it was his time in the sun and theirs was over?

That was one problem with journalism that I never got over. You stirred up a hornet's nest, but then left to do other pieces and never really knew what the real answers were.

Ah, well, I told myself, you should feel good about it. You've only done one piece on the New York Yankees and it's become world famous.

Such are the small victories of freelance writers.

I am writing this little postscript to my most famous piece in 2010. Another world. A million other stories have taken place in sports and maybe half a million on the Yankees since the Reggie story of 1977. I thought the world had long forgotten what I'd written.

Then one day in 2005 I got a call from ESPN Sports. They were doing a piece on Reggie for their Top 100 Athletes of the Twentieth Century series and they wanted me to be interviewed for it. I said sure, and soon I was on an hour-long documentary about Reggie. But what made it really sweet was they let me tell my side of the story. For years Reggie had been lying about how I made up all the quotes I attributed to him. But on the documentary I got to tell my own side of the story, the true side. I heard from mutual pals that Reggie was furious.

Well, that had to be the end, I thought. No more of the Reggie Jackson story.

Wrong again. In 2006, Jonathan Mahler, a brilliant New York journalist, called me and said he wanted to get my quotes for his new nonfiction book, *Ladies and Gentleman, the Bronx Is Burning*. Mahler's idea was to take all the major stories of 1977 in New York—the Son of Sam terrorizing the streets, the blackout and subsequent riots, and the Yankees winning the World Series—and tie them together in one great book. I was happy to be part of it. And this time I was able to cite the first interview Reggie gave after the piece came out. He told the late Pete Axthelm in *Newsweek* that he didn't deny saying any of it. He said, "He (meaning me) caught me off guard." Which was true, except that a mouth like Reggie's doesn't seem to have a guard on it.

Only later when teammates had ostracized him, and basically hated his guts did he start saying that I made it all up.

No one on the Yankees believed him then and I doubt any of them do now.

I told all of this to Mahler, who to his credit used it in his excellent book. He was the first guy to get it a hundred percent right.

That was fun. All those years later to have the truth written by a first-rate writer.

Well, I thought, that must truly be the end. I had been on Reggie's own documentary and I had been in Mahler's brilliant book.

But even more fun was to come.

One day in 2007 the phone rang again. It was a casting director who said she was looking for Robert Ward, the author of the Reggie Jackson piece.

"That's me," I said.

"Well, ESPN is doing a docudrama-miniseries of Jon Mahler's book and we need someone to play you."

"Who are you thinking about?" I said. I thought they were asking me my opinion of who would be best. After all I had been a writer/producer on *Hill Street Blues* and the exec co-producer on *Miami Vice*. I knew many younger actors. I tried to think of someone who could play me in the '70s. Had to be someone in their mid-thirties, brilliant, handsome, witty, etc.

"We were thinking you could play it," the casting woman said.

"What?"

"The director Jeremiah Chechik saw you in the doc about Reggie's life and he thought you would make a good Robert Ward."

"Yeah, but I'm thirty years older than I was then!"

"That doesn't matter," she said. "You're a print person, and a producer. No one knows what you look like."

"Yeah," I said. "I guess you're right."

"You interested?"

"Why not?"

"There's only one thing," she said.

"What's that?"

"You have to read for it."

A long pause as I considered the philosophical and Sartreian ramifications of this.

"What? I have to audition to play myself?"

"That's right," she said. "How do we know you will be any good at playing you?"

"Good point," I said. "I might be a lousy me."

A day later I found myself at the casting offices, sitting in a room with a couple of character actors, who were auditioning to play ME!

For the first time I began to feel a little worried. What if one of these jokers was more like me than I was? That would be a fine thing.

A few minutes later I was sitting in a room across from the two casting directors. They handed me a script. The scene I had to play had two people in it, myself and Reggie Jackson. The speeches were written by a screenwriter, but the lines the two men were saying were directly out of my article written thirty-one years earlier.

The whole thing had a surreal feel to it. But it was also as easy as falling off a log. I just acted like myself, sitting at the bar all those years ago. I was tense and excited just like I was back then. Of course, for different reasons: My motivation in the old days was "I have to get this goddamned story or I can't pay the rent!" Now my motivation was, "I have to get this part or I'll look like a bleeding fool. No freaking actor is going to play me better than I do!"

So, in each case, I had to tamp down my feelings and play it cool. I read the scene with one of the casting directors. When I was done they looked at one another, shook their heads. Then they asked me to do it again, which I did.

Halfway through the second time the senior casting person stopped me. Christ, I thought, she doesn't think I can do it. I've failed to be me. I'm not me at all. Holy Christ, who am I?

But she looked at me and smiled. "You know what?"

"What?"

"You're really *good* at playing you. You've got the job."

"For real?"

"For real. Not everybody can play themselves. They get uptight but you're a natural. You fly out to Connecticut day after tomorrow for your first scene. Congratulations."

I hugged them both and headed out to my car. It was unbelievable. The Reggie Jackson piece had been written about in thirteen books, including *The Top of the Heap*, a book with the best pieces ever written about the Yankees since their inception; it was still constantly quoted on television during games; it had gotten me into Reggie's ESPN documentary; and now I was playing myself in the docudrama. I sat in my car and shook my head.

Mickey Mantle and Billy Martin were gone. Reggie couldn't play himself because he was too famous, and too old. The Son of Sam, David Berkowitz, was in prison. I would be the only original person in the entire miniseries who was actually there when it all went down in 1977.

It was amazing. "Reggie Jackson in No-Man's Land" was the piece that wouldn't die.

I ended up going back and forth from LA to Connecticut three times. They flew me to Hartford, then drove me down to the set in Mystic. A young actor named Daniel Sunjata was playing Reggie, and he did a remarkable job. When we were sitting at the Banana Boat Bar set, I kept feeling like Rod Serling was going to show up.

Most of my lines were in the first episode, and it was a gas meeting John Turturro, who played Billy Martin, and Oliver Platt, who played George Steinbrenner. The few times I've acted (I've been in three movies, one documentary, and two TV shows) I've always been stunned by what royalty even the lowest actor is on the set. I've been the executive producer on *Miami Vice* and *Hill Street Blues* and no one pampered me, or worried whether I was hungry or would like to meet a fan. No one cared about the executive producer, even though he and the other writers are the guys who write the entire script, work with the directors, hire the actors, and so on. Writers and producers are treated like peasants compared to the actors who the average lighting person thinks of as the "real talents." It was great being taken care of by the makeup and hair people. "Can we get you another cup of coffee, Robert?" Damn if anyone ever got me coffee on *Miami Vice*.

Though people who work in the business know better, they get carried away by the idea of the noble artist actor as much as any TV fan. What's odd is that I've seen producers have the same worshipful attitude toward the actors they created.

If an actor is famous he eclipses everyone around him. On the set, that is. But off the set, unless he's a superstar, he has very little power.

I knew all this but enjoyed being thought one of the stars of the show while I was there. The third night there, the great Yankee third baseman, Craig Nettles, paid us a visit. He took one look at me and said: "I'm the straw who stirs the drink." We all laughed and had a ball together.

I heard rumors that Reggie was coming but he never showed up.

Well, now that my piece has been in every conceivable form, except a feature movie or Broadway play, I guess the furor is finally over. But then again I thought that twenty years ago and look what's happened.

Who knows where and when "Reggie Jackson in No-Man's Land" will strike again? If there are any Broadway producers out there who want me to sing my part in the musical version, check out my website. I stand ready.

Pete Maravich Is Still Magic

Ron Behagen and Jim McElroy are back-pedaling as fast as their legs will carry them, windmilling to guard their basket. But the lads might as well stay down the other end and pray for snow in August in New Orleans, because all the racing and windmilling and yelling ("I got him!" "Check him now!") isn't about to stop Pistol Pete Maravich.

Standing on the track in the gym above the court, I wait with anticipation for Pistol to put on a little move . . . maybe throw his wrist pass to Louie Nelson, who is fast-breaking under the boards . . . or perhaps take Behagen in low, and put in one of those impossible twisting shots that defy anatomy and gravity. But, lo and behold, Pete simply stops at the key, and tosses up the shot lazily, softly . . . the ball, like a small cotton cloud, trails through the dank air of the Metairie YMCA, and glides through the hoop. Though Louie Nelson raises his fist to Pete to indicate "Nice shot," I feel a trifle disappointed. For I've been standing here watching this preseason three-on-three game for about a half hour now, and during that time, the Pistol hasn't put on one of his extraordinary moves.

Certainly, he has played well, yet when one comes to see the former Great White Hope of the South, one cannot help but be mesmerized by the legend . . . the stories one hears! How when he was eight and living in Clemson, South Carolina, he challenged the Clemson Tiger players in Horse (shot for shot), and won half of his games. How when he was a high school freshman he was able to beat college players one-on-one. How Pete scored sixty-six points in one game for LSU against Tulane and won another contest with a forty-foot hook shot at the buzzer (a shot he has practiced since he was eight) . . . how he averaged 44.2 points for three varsity years at LSU . . . became the all-time scoring champ, but beyond his scoring were the tales of assists he made . . . passing the ball behind his back, through both his and his opponents' legs to hit a man underneath the basket for the winning field goal . . . his famous wrist pass, which looks for all the world as though it's going right, but miraculously ends up left, and his full-court behind-the-back pass, which has left lesser players crying.

But the word has gone around the league that there is a new Pete Maravich. No longer does lanky Pete slap his head in the Good Grief sign when one of the lesser mortals on the Jazz catches one of his blindside, behind-the-back bounce passes in his chops, instead of in his mitts. The Pistol has changed his game . . . become the Great Pro everyone knew he could become. "A leader," says Bud Johnson, director of public relations for the Jazz, who has known Pistol since the boy was an LSU freshman. "I always knew he had leadership ability, but he never was mature enough to exercise it. Now that's changed. Pistol is a solid guy now. He's grown up, and is the leader this team needs so badly."

When Maravich came out of LSU they said he would revolutionize basketball. Yet Maravich's pro debut at Atlanta was anything but spectacular, with everyone on the team despising the aloof kid with the floppy socks, the floppy hair, and the Big Bucks in the Bank. Things were so bad with the Hawks that they once held a team meeting and told Pete not to shoot jumpers! Pistol Pete grounded? Exactly! Like a junkie hanging around Times Square, Maravich was to wait under the basket hoping someone would fix him up with a shot. Soon coach Richie Guerin departed and Cotton Fitzsimmons came in, but the damage had been done. The pressure for an instant winner, for Maravich to transcend mortality every time he received the ball, made both Pete and Cotton more than a little crazy. And so, Maravich was dealt off to the brand new Jazz. The year Maravich joined the Jazz (1974–75), he averaged 21.5 points per game and delighted the hometown fans, most of whom remembered his days at LSU. By the second year, last season, he averaged 25.9 per game and, for the first time in his five-year pro career, was named to the first-string All-NBA team.

Pete Maravich, the magician, has matured, and so has his game, and I meet him at the Metairie YMCA to talk about the new Pete and other things. Because I've been through the third ring of Hell to get the interview (Pete doesn't answer my phone calls, Pete doesn't answer Bud Johnson's phone calls, Pete races off to Florida to hole up in his new condominium), I'm a little concerned that Pete won't have much to say. But once Pistol P starts talking, his language has the same free-wheeling, improvisatory flavor of his basketball. . . . The man loves to talk! True, not everything he says seems to touch down on old terra firma, but then again, what would you expect of a magician?

"Yeah, well, right now," Pete says in his new mature voice, lean-ing up against the wall, and shaking his head, "right now I am really ticked off at the NBA draft system. The whole thing is just a general reflection of how basketball is being ruined by turning it into more and more of a business. I'm talking about the merger. The Jazz has to keep the nucleus we had. Without the merger, we might have made the playoffs. But now we've got to put up with the Nets, who are going to be very tough, and we are going to have to play Chicago with Gilmore, and Atlanta got real good player . . . and the Jazz weren't allowed to get anyone in the draft. I mean, everyone says we've got Sidney Wicks, but I don't see him here yet . . . we may never get him [they never did] . . . and the reason all those teams like Chicago, New York, Boston get all the good players is because they are in the major TV markets.

"You don't see the Jazz on TV anywhere except New Orleans, right? And another thing, Boston and New York and teams like that, they don't have to take very long road trips. The Jazz have to take three-week-long road trips. Those are very exhausting trips."

Pete looks out at the gym and shakes his head sadly, as if deeply into the injustice of the world.

"Well, you do have Gail Goodrich," I say, trying to cheer him up.

"Sure . . . but I'll bet you've already heard how we aren't going to be able to play together. . . . That's what idiots say, man. People that don't know anything about basketball. That's another thing we have to put up with all the time. Did it ever occur to the average fan that most guys who write about sports are just little overweight creeps who never touched a basketball in their lives? These guys couldn't make a goddamned foul shot, you see, and yet they have the right to write just about anything about us. For example, this Goodrich crap. Gail has played with Jerry West. He's able to move with or without the ball . . . and as for me, I hate having the ball. Let me move without the ball, get a good shot, and score. It's teamwork that counts. That's what you have in Boston, Robert, teamwork, and conditioning."

Now Pete's words are flying out like buckshot.

"I mean, in basketball you don't necessarily have to have the greatest players. Look at the Celtics. They take an average player like Don Nelson, see, and they have him come off the bench, and he knows exactly what he has to do. And he does it!"

Pete's handsome dark eyes are now flashing, and his hands are whipping around. I am amazed at how large his hands are, how long his legs are.

"What was I talking about?" says Pete. "Oh, yeah, sportswriters. . . . Most of them are just know-nothing creeps. I've had about everything said about me anyone can ever have said. If I make a great play, they say I'm not a team player. If I miss a shot, then I'm a ball hog. But the truth is, I always play pretty much the same game."

"Didn't you just say that you hated to have the ball?" I say. "That seems a curious thing for Pete Maravich to say. Your ball handling is legendary."

Pete shakes his head. "No . . . I mean I don't think that way. I do whatever I have to do to win. Believe me, Robert, I'm a team player. I'll be glad to have a guy like Gail Goodrich on the team. I wish I had had good players all my life. Can you imagine if I had been on Washington or Boston or Los Angeles? I'd already have two championships under my belt, and they'd be saying I was the greatest player of all time. But when you are on a losing team . . . well, then everyone says you didn't live up to your potential. Oh, I hate the way they write things like that. Sportswriters are always looking for some little sensational piece of crap to hang a story on. I'm telling you, man. . . . Hey, look, what if you had a choice, a choice, see, of reading about the stars, astronomy and astrology and the planets, something really good, or if you had the choice of reading some kind of crap about an auto accident, where a bunch of people were decapitated. Which one would you read?"

"Ah, well," I say.

"Right," says Pistol P. "You'd honestly answer that you'd read about the stars. Man, I have always been into the stars. Do you know what I think? I think someday a spaceship is going to come down and take me away from all this . . . stuff. My idea of heaven is a place just beyond space. I mean, the heavens are going to open up, like this—"

Pistol Pete puts his hands out in front of him like he is getting ready to do the breast stroke. Then he moves them outward and he smiles widely, his eyes twirling in his head like basketballs.

"You see, the space will open up, and then beyond that will be heaven, and when you go inside, then the space closes again, and you are there . . . definitely a wonderful place . . . everyone you ever knew will be there. Great!"

"Yeah," I sigh. "Let's go today."

Pete smiles. "It wouldn't be such a bad idea. But where was I? Yeah, well, a sportswriter could give people good news about sports, or he could print bad news. . . . Not that all sportswriters are bad guys . . . but most of them are just headhunters."

"Personally, I always thought the Atlanta thing was blown up out of proportion," I say. "Before I came down here, I looked through some old clippings from Atlanta, and seems to me that you were given a pretty bad going over by the press."

Pete smiles and shakes his handsome head again. He looks very much like a giant little boy.

"Listen, the pressure there was terrific. I mean, the resentment on that team. I don't even like to think about it. They all said I'd lost confidence, but I hadn't at all. The real problem was the resentment and the superhuman expectations people had. But it wasn't only at Atlanta. No, sir, all along success has caused envy and resentment. You have to realize I've been a star since I was about eight years old. I've lived with envy and stuff all my life. If you want to know the truth, there are about four or five people I feel I could call real friends. Everyone else is just out to get some piece of me."

"Does that bother you?"

"No, not really . . . nah, it makes me want to keep to myself, that's all. It makes me want to just do my job, and live my life. The only time I have control over what happens to me is during the off season. Do you know that when I come up to a stoplight in my car, I mean . . . I stop eight feet behind the man in front of me?"

"Isn't that a little bit odd?" I say, smiling like a shoe salesman. "Stopping eight feet behind the other guy?"

Pistol Pete shakes his head. "No, sir . . ." he says. "Hey, listen, what if I were mobbed, and I was right up behind the other guy bumper to bumper—then what would happen? This way I've got some space, I can get away."

Pete smiles affably, with no trace of self-consciousness.

As we close the interview for this day, I wonder about Pete Maravich. There is something terribly likable about his nonstop rap, as if he communicates without a filter. The man would have been happy among the Surrealist poets. But where they had to unlearn self-consciousness, Maravich in his own way seems to be a natural surrealist. Which may explain a little bit his magic on the basketball court. For what he does with a ball is always spontaneous, yet that spontaneity is the product of countless hours of very conscious application. As a result of that dedication, his whole psyche is geared to a finer pitch than most people's. Yet there is a darker side to all this. Dreams of escape, dreams of perhaps leaping up, up over the basket, without ever having to come down . . . the heavens shall part and I will escape the sportswriters, the fans, the autograph nuts, and float FREE.

That night I go to the rookie camp and talk to Gail Goodrich and assistant coach Elgin Baylor. Goodrich is shorter than I imagined, and his California tan is still with him. He moves with short, quick steps, and he is a very tough and tricky player. Still, if my eyes don't deceive me, he doesn't look quite as quick as he used to. Baylor, though years retired, is only a little out of shape, sitting over on the bench, watching the doomed rookies go through their paces.

"Pete," says Elgin Baylor, "is a different guy than he used to be. I mean on the court. I don't know him that well off the court, but on the court, he has learned to throw the right pass, he has learned to keep his emotions under control. You have to understand that about Pete. He's an almost totally emotional individual on the court. It used to be that every little thing bothered him, and then he would get upset and his game would suffer. In college he had to be the whole team. His father, Press, was the coach at LSU, and I can't say for sure, but I know all that one-on-one stuff in college had to hurt him when he got with Atlanta . . . plus, he was weak on defense, and that hurt him, too. Now he's a much better defensive player. He's been working with weights every day this summer. You ever see pictures of him as a kid? He was skinny. But now he's 215 pounds, and very strong. That means a lot."

Goodrich comes over and I say, "A lot of people are already saying that you two guys won't be able to play together."

Goodrich shakes his head. "That's so stupid. I play well without the ball. That's a large part of my game. After all, I played with Jerry West, and Jerry needed the ball to be effective."

"Pete's the same way," says Baylor. "We want him to have the ball. He's not nearly as effective without it."

"How would you rate Maravich?" I ask Baylor.

"I don't rate players. But I'll say this. Oscar Robertson was the best guard I ever played against; Jerry West the best I ever played with . . . and Pete the best I've ever seen."

This mysterious answer sounds like some kind of Zen koan. Does Baylor the Elder mean "seen" as in the all-encompassing sense of "ever played" or does he merely mean, best since West and Robertson?

Baylor won't go any further, but soon he and Goodrich are involved in an interesting debate.

"Robertson didn't have the great eye Pete has," Baylor says. "There is nobody who is more of a natural shooter than Pete. But Oscar had that fantastic court sense . . . leadership . . . the discipline. . . . He wasn't as good a passer as Guy Rodgers, who in my opinion was the greatest passer of all time . . . but Oscar had the fundamentals down to perfection . . . the discipline. He was in control of himself, and when he ran the team . . . it all seemed to flow right from him."

"I'd disagree with you a little on some of that," says Goodrich. "I think Oscar *did* have the natural abilities . . . equal to Jerry and Pete . . . but you're right about that one thing. When he ran the game, the whole thing was completely under his pace. No one ever did that better than Oscar."

I leave the gym thinking, that kind of control is what Maravich wants now. Maravich is sacrificing a little style to be a general. One might even say that the new Maravich will finally become the Great Maravich, if he can marshal all his talents, and become the team leader the Jazz needs. As for his tricks, I could see a little more clearly now how he would be willing to part with some of them. They are beautiful, transcendental, but they finally are the product of a kind of out-of-control dervish, who might forget the larger picture. What Maravich wants now is complete Mastery of the Game . . . every aspect of it. Mastery is the difference between the spectacular and the Truly Great.

But there is some nagging doubt that bothers me here, for Maravich seems to me to still be growing . . . and his paradoxical answers to my questions ("I hate to have the ball" is certainly a case of him stating his case a little too strongly, as if to convince himself) suggest that he certainly hasn't yet gained complete control over himself. Finally, one thinks that he may still be a couple of years away from that ultimate mastery.

This impression is buttressed the following afternoon when I meet Pete and his father. Press Maravich looks a lot older than the pictures I had seen of him, and it is clear that the scar of his wife's suicide two years ago continues to hang over him.

As I watch Pete play another three-on-three game, I tell Press some of my impressions of his son, and he says, "I'd say you are right. The truth is there is nothing more that can be done with a basketball beyond what Pete can do. So now he wants to get a kind of mastery . . . but he's still growing . . . he's still a kid in a lot of ways. I've told the Jazz that Pete will have his greatest days when he's between thirty and thirty-six. He has a great body, so he'll be able to play that long, barring injury, and I expect by then, he'll have the total maturity to really be able to become one of the greatest players of all time. He knows this, and can sense it coming in himself, and he wants to make it happen, so he's been working on his weight lifting, and practicing every day for hours. If anyone realized the kind of sacrifices he makes for the game. . . . It's been his whole life. But things still get to him. He still can't take a loss well. He replays the game again and again, and he falls into very dark moods . . . I mean they are terrible. You can't talk to him at all. I just stay away from him after a loss."

"I heard about the death of your wife," I say softly. "I'm sorry about it, and I wondered how Pete took that."

Press looks a little glassy-eyed, and stares out at the court. "For the longest time he just couldn't get over it," Press says. "It hurt him deeply. Deeply. You see Pete is a tremendously loyal person, and those close to him have all his love, and he is a deeply emotional person, too. We are Serbian and we have very violent emotions . . . which are hard, very hard to contain. But Pete's over it now . . . and he's progressing."

As we are talking I watch Pete lead a fast break, and make a pass that is purely impossible. The ball caroms off his wrist, bounces under the defender's hand, and hits Aaron Jones for an easy layup.

Press smiles, and pats me on the shoulder. "Nice huh?" he says.

A few minutes after his game, Maravich and I are standing on the gym floor at the Metairie Y, while Pete graciously does a few "ball tricks" for me. The words "ball tricks" and "trick dribbles" fail to convey the grace and ease and sheer magic of Pete Maravich.

"Here's a little one I developed when I was eight," he says, and then casually does his "Knee drop" trick.

Pete smiles and explains: "This particular trick involves taking the ball, putting it behind your knees, like this." Maravich stoops a bit, and places the ball behind his knee, wedged in by his calf.

"Now what you are trying to develop here is hand quickness," Pete says. "You've got to drop the ball, clap your hands, and catch the ball before it hits the floor. It's pretty tough, and I haven't done it since I worked on it for Red Auerbach's *Roundball* TV show. Let's see."

Maravich claps his hands a couple of times, then drops the wedged ball, claps his hands so fast you see only a blur—and grabs the ball.

He then does the trick seven times in succession. An unbelievable exhibition. Bud Johnson and I exchange looks.

Pete's smile broadens, and you can see him warming up. I am reminded of what Elgin Baylor told me about his "emotions," and this afternoon, what guard McElroy said, "Every once in a while Pete goes nuts and just has to take off. He's got all this energy, and if the game is dragging, he'll just start firing up things that are unbelievable." Which, in spite of everything I've heard about becoming the Ultimate All Around Player, is somehow good to know. One would hate to see the flashy little boy in Maravich lost no matter what the prize.

"Here's a good one," says Pete. He stands up, and spins the ball on his fingers. First the index, then the third finger, and then all the others. Finally he flips the ball up in the air, and catches it on his little finger. Watching the old schoolboy trick, one realizes one has never before seen it done with such ease. Like Mosconi and his cue, the basketball seems to be merely an extension of Pete's arm. I comment on that, and he nods.

"Yeah," he says. "That's a good observation. That's what you want it to be. That's how it was when I was a kid, you know. The things I'd do then. I'd play twelve hours a day out on the playground. I just couldn't stop. When I got home, I'd have my TV dribble . . . learn to dribble the ball as low as I could, while still watching the television set. See, it goes like this:"

He gets down on one knee, and starts a fairly high dribble, then makes it lower, and lower, still amazingly keeping the same time signature.

"Important to keep the same rhythm. It's got to be as steady as a metronome. . . . Make it perfect . . . like so . . . then keep it as close to the floor as you can, without losing the dribble or breaking rhythm. Like this. It's only about an eighth of an inch off the floor now."

I bend down and, though I can hear the ball pumping against the wood, I can't see any space at all between the ball and the floor.

"You see Robert, I've worked. I guess some kids thought I was nuts. But I knew already. . . . At twelve I remember saying in the paper that I could make a million dollars playing in the NBA. I always knew how good I was. . . . But I had to work to get it. . . . That's why it's painful to read that you don't care about the sport. My father and I, we both love the sport. Ah, the days we had then. . . . I mean we'd go to a game, and then we'd come home, and the other coaches would all be hanging around. We'd talk with Joe Lapchick, and Fuzzy Levane, Doody Wooden—it was a great way to spend a childhood."

Pete shows me his high dribble, and his low dribble, running across the gym, dribbling in and out of his legs.

He comes back across the gym, and looks far away, as if he is trying to regain something forever lost:

"There was a real love of the game. There was a mutual respect, and a kind of. . . ."

"Community?"

"Yeah," Maravich says. "It was like that. A kind of community. I don't guess I'll ever be as happy as I was those nights, listening and talking about the game. . . . There was a love. Now it's dog eat dog. I've seen guys traded in the airplane on the way to a game. I've seen a guy come into his locker, look in and see the opponent's uniform sitting in there. Can you imagine the way the guy felt? The owners don't care about basketball. Most of the new coaches, they don't know what it really means. They have no love for it. The existing philosophy these days is: 'Go out and buy the five best guys you can, stick 'em on the floor, and get your championship, and your money, and forget the whole thing.' But my dad, and the old timers, they didn't make a lot of money, but they cared about the game. I can't get that across to many people, because they think, 'Well, he's making a million bucks.' But that's just the point—I've got so much money, I could quit now, and live off my investments and never have to lower my standard of living at all, you see? So what I'm saying is the truth. The truth is I'd have played basketball no matter what it paid. I'll always play it . . . but I can't tell you how much those days as a kid meant to me. . . ."

Maravich breaks off his reverie and asks Bud Johnson to come over and assist him in a trick.

"I called this my Homework Basketball Game. My dad and I invented all these. In this one, Bud, you hold the ball behind my neck, at the back of my neck, and let it go. I'll try to clap my hands and catch the ball behind my back before it hits. Don't tell me when you're going to drop it."

Johnson puts the ball on the back of Pete's neck, and Maravich starts clapping. Johnson waits until Pete is in the middle of a clap, and lets the ball go, but somehow Maravich manages to snap his arms behind his back, swing them back out in front of himself again, clap, swing them back a second time, and catch the ball before it gets past his waist. He does this particularly difficult trick five times in a row.

"I don't know what's in the future. I want to play now . . . to really play at the top of my capacity. I want to play on a championship team just once. Can you imagine me on the Celtics, or the Lakers? But I love New Orleans. My roots are here, and my friends. . . . I love the food in this city, the style of living . . . the only way I'd leave the Jazz is if I didn't think there was any chance we could really improve.

"Here's another little trick," he says. He spins the ball on the end of his finger, flips it up in the air and catches it with the middle finger of his other hand, where it continues to spin.

"Hey, not bad huh, Robert?" Pete says, smiling.

I stand there watching him and feeling a real affection for the man. In an era of basketball players—and athletes in general—where concerns about contracts and individual success overshadow interest in their team, Pete Maravich is a throwback. Childlike and likable, the man has not yet ousted the boy in him. For the world that Pete Maravich would like to escape to is not outer space or "heaven," but childhood. The world where one is forever young and life is reduced to the good struggle on a sunbaked court. And no matter what changes the Pistol introduces in his game—you can bet that whenever he gets the ball there will continue to be much to cheer about.

The art director of *Sport*, Al Braverman, comes in and asks Pete to dress up like a magician to illustrate this story. "Sure," Pete says, putting on a large feathered turban and a black cape. "Let me have the cane," he says.

He flips the basketball into the air and catches the spinning sphere on top of the cane. Then he starts walking around the gym with the ball whirling atop the cane and intones like a magician: "The Grrreat Maravich weeeeel enter-tain YOU—ahahahahaha!"

He never looked more like himself, and as he approaches a basket he says, "Watch this one, Robert," and canes the ball into the air, then, as it descends, leaps and heads the ball toward the rim. It sails up and falls through the net. "I don't do that one every day!" he shouts ecstatically.

But you know he could.

Postscript

If you got the idea that I liked Pete Maravich, you're right. He was not only charming, friendly, and kind, but a born teacher. He absolutely loved showing me the tricks and letting me try them. Needless to say, I couldn't do any of them, but he encouraged me the entire day.

"That's good. You almost got it. Robert, if you went home and worked on that every day for an hour by next week you could do it."

Later that afternoon when the gym was empty I said to him:

"Okay, I know you are a great behind-the-back passer, but how far could you throw one accurately?"

Pete smiled and said: "The whole length of the court."

I was stunned. Frankly, even though I had seen him do all these other remarkable tricks, I couldn't fathom it. It wasn't like I thought he was lying. It just didn't seem possible. So I kind of laughed like, "Yeah, right!"

Pete smiled, took the basketball, and ran down to the far end of the court.

"Okay, Robert," he said. "You run over to the sidelines . . . near half court. Good. Now run diagonally to the basket."

I shook my head in disbelief, and on his head nod, I ran toward the basket at the other end of the court.

Pete watched me go and when I was about halfway there he flicked me a behind-the-back pass. The ball came at me chest high the whole way. It looked like the massive boulder speeding after Indiana Jones. It was just totally unbelievable. The usual sports writing line would be "Pete threw it effortlessly," but that doesn't begin to make it.

I saw his arm and hand with the ball in it go behind his back and then the ball seemed to appear out of his body like it had been shot out of a cannon. I mean this was not some bloop pass that finally bounced to me. It was . . . (I can't help it) faster than a speeding bullet, more powerful than a locomotive, etc.

Really, a missile of a pass. Belt high and sizzling as it sped toward me.

The ball hit my hands about two steps from the basket, the perfect layup lead. I caught it and banked it home.

I knew that as a reporter I was supposed to look cool, objective, nod, and say something like "Good pass, old chap!"

Instead, I stood there like any teenage boy who is playing ball with his idol. My mouth dropped open, and I shook my head and just started laughing like an imbecile. Pete ran up the court, laughing himself.

"Believe me now?" he said.

I couldn't answer. I was too stunned. So, mouth hanging open like a yahoo, I made some stuttering noise like, "Uh-huh. Yea . . . Uh."

"Nice shot, Robert," Pete said.

I remember what I said then. Very unprofessional. "Holy fucking shit!"

We both cracked up and Pete began to spin the ball on all five of his fingers, then up his arm and on his head.

That day was the greatest display of pure basketball genius I have ever seen.

But Pete's display of ball-handling skills and his stories of how much he had practiced as a kid (every waking hour after school, and on weekends) has, over the years, had a weird effect on me. At the time I wrote the piece, I was just so stunned by his talent that I only wanted to convey how awesome he was.

But now that I am older and Pete is gone I feel a deep sadness when I think of him. He was the only real genius I have ever met. As his dad, Press, said, "When it comes to ball handling (after Pete) there is nothing more to learn." But for all his greatness, Pete never got to play on a good team, except the '79–'80 season when he was traded by the Jazz to the Celtics. By then his career was over, due to injuries. Pete was deeply disturbed by the fact that he never could win a championship. The truth was, on his other teams, Pete wasn't selfish with the ball. The fact is, he had few other players to go to. He had to be the whole team. And that was true of high school, at LSU (where he led the NCAA in scoring with 44.7 points a game average), and in the NBA.

Pete was like Mozart without the orchestra. Or Miles Davis minus his quartet.

He was a genius, but basketball is the ultimate team sport. Nobody can do it alone, no matter how great.

The oddest turn of all in Pete's story came at his death. He was forty-one years old and playing three-on-three ball on an outdoor court in Pasadena. He went up for a jumper but never got it off. He fell to the blacktop and was dead within seconds. After his death, the coroner made a remarkable finding. All of us have two arterial systems that feed the heart. But Pete Maravich had only one. Most people with this condition die at a very young age. No one can understand how a person with one main arterial system missing could become a basketball player, much less be the greatest of his generation, and in some people's eyes—mine among them—the greatest player ever.

And when you think of the things that Pete told me about spirits coming from the stars to take him away . . . well, I know better than to believe in miracles or angels but there is definitely something otherworldly about Maravich's life.

As a fiction writer I can easily see Pete's life turned into a sci-fi drama.

You can go to YouTube right now and look up Pete Maravich. You'll see ball handling, shooting, and passing that is indeed from outer space. Having watched his "Greatest Plays" video many times, I am still not sure how he made the plays he did.

The term "genius" is thrown around about anyone now. But Pete Maravich was a genius, and a terrific guy to boot.

Zombies Every Sunday

The following piece was written for *The Village Voice*. Those of you who aren't hip to the *Voice* should be. It's still available in hard copy and online and it's still a gas to read. What was great about writing sports for the *Voice* was that there were no guidelines on how to write the piece. This piece is part opinion piece, part rave, and all satirical. I had spent a miserable 1980 watching the Giants and the Jets, and just wanted to blow it out, riff like a jazz musician on the theme of "Ultimate Hideousness." The *Voice* was the place to do it. As long as you were funny and had a hip attitude they let you write anything you wanted. My editor, Rudy Langlais, encouraged me to just go for it. . . .

I remember walking from my apartment down Barrow toward Eighth Avenue, thinking, "Gotta get this piece in by tomorrow. Should be at typewriter hammering away. Why are my feet taking me toward the Lion's Head? This is all wrong!" The Lion's Head, as anyone of my generation knows, was *the* literary bar in the Village. Anytime night or day you could stop in and find just about any of your literary heroes, heroically sitting at the bar. They were, of course, looking for inspiration, in need of just the right magical amount of booze, dope, cigarettes, and flirtation with the few women who came into the joint. Then, said inspiration found, they would rush back to their nearby Village apartments and turn out masterly poems, novels, or pieces for the New York mags. Sometimes, alas, the perfect combination of booze, drugs, talk, and sexual longing wouldn't present itself for one or even two days.

Or even longer.

The joke was that these were "drinkers with writing problems."

The night in question, for example, when I should have been home knocking out my *Voice* piece, I sort of ended up at the Head around seven thirty at night, and there was my friend James Baldwin there, with our mutual agent, Jay Acton. Jimmy was his usual nervous self, smoking obsessively, and talking a blue streak, all of it brilliant and fantastic. He had just come in from the south of France, where he lived most of the time in the picture-perfect town of Saint-Paul-De-Vence. He and Acton were reliving some obscenely drunken party they had just survived. I had little choice but to have a few drinks with them. After all, James Baldwin was one of the greatest writers in America, and he and I got on extremely well. He was incredibly kind, and every time he saw me he told me how much he had loved my first two novels. He was a wonderful storyteller and soon we were talking about his old friends Billie Holliday, Lester Young, and Bud Powell. He knew literally everyone worth knowing and was welcome anywhere but always took time out to have lunch or dinner with me when he came back to America.

I was worried about him though. Jimmy had this terrible cough, which sometimes went on for a full minute. Frankly, it scared the shit out of me, and I was half ready to drag him around to Saint Vincent's. But he always stopped coughing just short of me putting him on a gurney.

"Fucking cough, Robert," he said, as he took another long drag on his cigarette.

"Jimmy, maybe if you stopped smoking for a while."

He would pop open his already huge eyes and say, "I can't do that, man."

"Why not?"

"'Cause without smoking what would I do with my hands, baby?"

We all laughed. Jimmy moved his hands nervously as he spoke, drawing invisible formations in the air. The cigarettes steadied his nerves a little, let him relax as he talked. But at such a terrible cost. His health was always a wreck.

Anyway, it grew darker and we all decided to eat dinner at Head, which had recently hired a new chef. The food was actually pretty good and the crowd was amazing. I looked around that night and saw Dermot McEvoy, a journalist talking with Joe Flaherty, the great Irish novelist and journalist; John Cusack talking to Sigourney Weaver; the great character actor Jack Warden drinking and talking to Big Tommy the bartender; and Val Avery, another wonderful character actor. Later that night, Richard Price came in and drank with Baldwin, Acton, and myself. I drop these names not to impress you, Dear Reader, but to show you the type of place the old Head was. There was always a lot of action there, and even on slow nights you could talk to the great raconteur owner, Wes, and his wife, Judy. Or the brilliant painter/waitress Jennifer. I wrote much of my novel *Red Baker* at a table in the corner, and ate a thousand good meals there. I met just about everybody I ever wanted to meet in the Head, except one. Before my time, there was this super-gorgeous blonde who was a waitress there. Everyone thought she might become an actress. Her name was Jessica Lange, and the word is she did pretty well in Hollywood.

Anyway . . . with all these interesting folks around and the sheer number of drinks Baldwin and I drank, I sort of forgot my piece. I was having too much fun.

Eventually, around three A.M., when we all took off, and I hugged Jimmy goodbye, I staggered back to my apartment at 72 Barrow

Street, and it wasn't until I stepped over two gay guys making love on my doorstep ("Sorry, guys. No, don't move, I can jump over you.") that I remembered, "Oh shit . . . the *Voice* piece." Then it all came back to me. I had gone to the Head looking for a little excitement to give me a psychic leap into the piece . . . and now I was coming home wasted, talked out, and exhausted.

And the piece was due tomorrow.

Christ, I had to sleep. There was nothing else a man could do.

I went upstairs to my apartment 5-J, opened the door and fell inside. Minutes later, still dressed, I collapsed on my bed and went into more of a coma than sleep. I remember thinking: At least I can sleep until ten. Then I'll get up and bash this baby out.

I felt myself sinking down down down . . . the sky was dark, only an occasional truck smashed over the hump at Barrow and Hudson . . . everything was fine . . . sleep till ten.

I slept beautifully. No terrible nightmares, no weird dreams of my crazy childhood in Baltimore . . . everything cool. Until the dream was interrupted by this horrible sound . . . *Neeeek. Neeeeek. Neeeeek.*

What the fuck was that?

I woke up startled, freaked out. Was the fucking place burning down? Had Flaherty gone nuts? Was he acting out some terrifying bit of Irish history and starting a conflagration? Had my next door neighbor, Wilfred Sheed, gotten fucked up and locked himself in the elevator? Or maybe Billy Powers, the photographer downstairs, lit some of his developing fluid. . . .

I looked at my clock, which sat upside down on the floor, next to my mattress. It said 5:04 A.M. What the fuck? I had gone to sleep at 3:37.

I hadn't even been asleep for two goddamn hours. Termites ate through my brain. Jimmy Baldwin's smoke-wreathed hands were still winding around in my head.

What the fuck was that terrible sound?

Then I realized it was my horrible doorbell. *Neeeek. Neeeeek. Neeeeek.*

Shit, maybe it was that girl who had been stalking me for three weeks. I'm serious. I had gone to the Head one night and flirted with this sick woman with sexy eyes. She had started ringing my doorbell about two weeks ago. Friends had seen her following me around. Holy shit, the Stalker.

I ran into the kitchen in my underwear, buzzed down and screamed: "Listen, you fucking lunatic. Don't buzz my house anymore. I'm going to have you gutted and thrown into the East River."

It was a line I'd heard in some old Richard Conte movie. I figured it would scare her off. I doubted she'd even respond, but held the button down anyway, in case she wanted to bark back at me.

I got a bark all right, but it wasn't a female voice. It was the gruffest voice I had ever heard and one I knew all too well: "Bobby, you sick fuck, let me in before I have to climb up your fucking fire escape and cut your heart out!"

Oh no! Not now. It wasn't possible. No no no. . . . It couldn't be. Not with this hangover. Christ help me!

But it was.

Shit, yes. It was Jim Crumley. The greatest detective writer in America on the strength of one awesome novel, *The Last Good Kiss.* He'd written other good ones too but *The Last Good Kiss* was the fucking *Great Gatsby* of crime. The perfect hard-boiled thriller. Crumley was one of my best friends. I loved him like a brother. He'd been my thesis advisor at the University of Arkansas Creative Writing program. This meant that he had to meet with me twice a week to smoke huge amounts of dope, drink beer, and listen to Lightning Hopkins records. Sometimes, though, we varied the routine by listening to John Lee Hooker and taking speed as well as smoking pot. Once or twice he asked me a few literary questions. Like, "Sir, would you say that Lionel Trilling is a flaming asshole?" My answer was, "Yes, My

Lord, of course he is." "Right," Crumley said. "You know this shit, Ward. You're going to do fine."

Anyway, here he was now. All two hundred and fifty pounds of him, pressing on my buzzer.

Ohhhh, fuck!

"Jim," I said, laughing like Don Knotts. "Ah, what are you doing here?"

"I'm staying with you for three days. Don't you remember, Bobby? Now open the fucking door before I tear it down."

He could have too.

"Oh, sure. Come on up."

I hit the buzzer and let him in.

Jim Crumley, who did more dope, drank more booze, and got into more trouble than any ten other men, was going to be sleeping on my fold-out couch for a week.

Oh, the horror, the horror.

Seconds later, he was there, actually there in my living room, hugging me and saying, "This is great. In New York, with you. We may top our time in Juarez together."

"Right," I said. But I was thinking, "Jesus God, no. . . ."

We'd gone to Juarez after a reading I'd done, when Jim was teaching at the University of Texas, El Paso. We'd had a good Mexican dinner, then Crumley had taken me to the Mexican Pharmacia where you could still buy Robitussin AC cough syrup, one of my favorite Baltimore teenage highs. As a gag we'd gone in and ordered a half gallon of the monstrous syrup, knowing full well that we would never get said stuff.

Surprise! Seconds later the Mexican pharmacist came out with what looked like a liter bottle of coke, only it was actually the syrup of wild dreams.

We walked outside on the street in a daze, whereupon Crum put the massive bottle to his lips and drank half of it.

"Jesus Christ," I said, "You could die from that shit."

"Yes," Crumley said. "This is true."

He then handed the bottle to me. I took a good swig before I felt like vomiting, but it was naught compared to Jim's Big Gulp.

The rest of the night was a film noir blur. Nightclubs, hookers, pool games, men with knives. At one point Crumley began screaming, "We are playing pool with Mexican teenagers. How great is that?"

"Pretty fucking great," I said, lying in the Juarez gutter. "Pretty fucking great, indeed, sir. But where are the tables?"

And here now . . . at my apartment was my dear old pal, the person I could least afford to see. I had a piece to get in. I was "cleaning up my act." Meanwhile, I was overwhelmed with a need for sleep. I felt like I would die if I just didn't nod off. There seemed to be a hand squeezing my heart. Oh God, sleeeeeeeep.

"You see," I told Jim as we opened his bed in the living room. "I have this piece to get in to the *Voice* and well . . . I sort of stayed up all night with Jimmy Baldwin, and myriad others, and . . . well, I am too tired to write. Actually, I think, like, I'm dying, man."

Jim nodded, stroked his Yosemite Sam moustache and said, "No problem. I have just the thing for you, Bobby. Just the thing."

He took out an envelope. Inside was some tissue paper, and inside the tissue was this white powder.

"You just need to snort this," he said. "Then all will be well."

"Coke?" I said. "Is it any good?"

"Oh, yeah. This stuff is amazing. Christ, Bobby, you'll write the story in no time."

"Well, . . . gee, okay," I said.

We rolled up a twenty and made some lines and snorted the stuff up in about fifty seconds.

I waited for that clear crystal rush of coke, but it never came. Instead, there was this monstrous whipsnapping rush in my head, legs, and heart. In fact, my heart seemed to have stopped beating in a regular manner, but was all one big . . . BEEEEEEATTTTTTTTT!

"Holy shit," I said, unable to breathe. "Fuck, Jimmy, this ain't coke."

He smiled in a shy way, and his eyes twinkled like jolly old Saint Nick.

"Gosh," he said. "You caught me. It's crystal meth. Ain't it fine?"

"Ahhhhhhhhhhh fuck," I said. "Oh, my God. I can't freaking breathe. Oh Jesus. . . ."

"It's just the first rush," Jim said. "Start writing Bobby. You'll never get greater inspiration than this!"

I ran into my little study and slipped a piece of typewriting paper into the old electric Remington. And started typing.

Exactly thirty-two minutes later I produced the piece you are about to read.

As for Jimmy and myself: That week and all its tattered glories will be in my next book, my memoirs, but for here suffice it to say, by week's end of it I prayed to God that He (She or It) would make Jimmy C. leave.

I remember the exact words of my prayer: "Dear God Almighty, I love Jim Crumley like the brother I never had but please make him leave because I still have a lot of good writing to get done and if he stays one more day I know I am going to die an agonizing death and go straight to hell."

God took pity on me. Crumley moved on, and I survived.

Read and, I hope, enjoy.

Of Zen Football, "Donovan's Brain," the Rayatollah, and other New York pigskin follies and farces.

Wait a minutes, wait. There, that's better. Let me breathe in and out a little. AHAHAHAHAH. . . . Okay, okay, just a little anxiety attack. My kids are responsible, Shannon and Kevin, they're getting to be teenagers now, feeling a little weird about the old man. They tied me up with some old Colts sweatshirts last weekend and made me watch the Jets-Dolphins game without any sound. Can you believe how horrible they are without sound? I mean they won, and they were still terrible. The hideous green jerseys, that porkball coach, Terrible Todd, running backs with names like Scott Dierking. What kinda name is that for a back? Sounds like a CPA hanging out at Maxwell's Plum. You ever see the guy make a move? He stops, makes the move, then inches ahead. By that time it's Avalanche City.

And Terrible Todd. Third-and-eight, he snorts some Drano in the huddle, foams at the mouth, and throws the ball downfield for Wesley Walker of Gaffney or Laugh Jones. Just tosses the son of a bitch up like he's throwing a Frisbee to a pack of dogs in the Sheep Meadow. Meanwhile, Miami has four guys fighting each other for the interception. The guy throws three interceptions against a team with so many injuries they got fans in the defensive backfield.

Oh, hell, it's starting again. The pains in the chest. The bad spells. I can't help it. Watching so many bad games weakens the moral fiber. They're driving me crazy. Where was I . . . the Jets . . . not the Giants . . . the *Giants* they got backs worse than Scott Dierking. Guys like Heater, and Matthews. Third-and-fourteen against the Redskins and they try an end-fucking-run. Watching Matthews on an end run is like watching time lapse of a flower opening in a Disney flick. He takes one mincing step, like he's Esther Williams testing the water. Ohhh, cold. Takes another. And another. Finally, he's rumbling along. But not around the end. He's headed the other way, trying to elude a wall of ancient Redskin defenders. How fast do you have to be to get away from the Redskins? These guys are so old that even the Indian on their helmet has age spots.

Don't tell me about the youth movement. Don't tell me Walt Michaels is building, that Ray Perkins will get his team turned around. I don't buy it anymore. All I know is this: I watch these teams all year because I am trapped in New York, and I didn't have any fun. DIDN'T HAVE ONE SINGLE DAY OF FUN. I sit here in my room, gags stuffed in my mouth, and recall the Jets' year like it was some fever dream. Five straight losses to start it off, including giving up thirty-seven points to San Francisco. Then, after a win over at Atlanta, and a slight ray of hope, the hideous game against Seattle, where they blow a 14–3 lead. Pure horror. And endless losses . . . to Buffalo, on the last play of the game, with Dykes giving Frank Lewis the outside of the end zone; the stompings from Los Angeles, the Browns, the Saints. The ultimate insult. There doesn't seem to be any real hope for improvement. The Jets are simply *not* in the same class as their opponents.

Nor are the Giants. They toyed with us by coming out and whipping the Cards, 41–35. My pals at the Lion's Head were strutting around saying things like This Is the Year and Team of Destiny and Phil Simms Has Come of Age. Well, surprise. Things could have scarcely turned out worse. They lose to the Redskins. Personally, I began to feel the knells of doom at that moment. The Skins are hideous, and hopelessly lame. If the hometown boys couldn't beat them, what might that augur, hey? And alas it be so. . . . Everybody kicked the Giants' ass: Philly, Dallas, San Diego (a memorable 44–7 loss in which Ray had to be restrained from calling up Andy Robustelli, Rosey Grier, and other heroes of yore for help), Denver, even Tampa Bay (30–13). Finally, the team rallied for its one season highlight, beating Dallas at home, 38–35—and I missed it. They managed just two more wins: Green Bay (yawn), and Seattle, which play at home like they've all done cough syrup. The season ended with a 33–17 embalming by Oakland, a game that made me so wild with anguish that I had to call Dr. Ronald Fieve for heavy lithium therapy. But not even miracle-mood elevators will wipe out memories of the Giants' onside kick, picked up by a hysterical Oakland player and waltzed into the end zone. Even now, trying to retain some semblance of journalistic objectivity, I begin to get the pins and needles. I mean, is this right? Is this any way to treat me?

I feel so nervous. All charged up. My friend Billy C tried to help me. Billy C who steals Volkswagen tires for a living, he don't blame Walt. He blames the Zen Temple. According to Billy, who is seldom wrong, Walt's troubles began when he read this book called *Orientalism* by Edward Said. It got him interested in Zen, and pretty soon he was hanging out at the Zen Temple, and letting foreign influences mess up his football strategy. Like the other teams in the league, they got a Western slant to their offenses. Like complexity. Multiple pass-and-run options, stuff of that stripe. But Walt began to get brainwashed with bliss, and pretty soon he was spending more time at the Zen Temple than he does at Kmart (where he buys his husky checkered Zen pants). Soon he's espousing the so-called Oriental Simple Shafted Arrow Approach to football, namely, a one-play offense. A few other plays are perfunctorily tried (like a Scott Dierking run) and then Walt has Terrible Todd go back to the Famous Swing-Pass-to-Bruce-Harper, the smallest man in football. Smallness and simplicity being a Hallmark of Zen. The play is a kind of Zen Parable: One Small and Noble Peasant Running Amidst a Sea of Warriors. Billy C says the guys at the Zen Temple frolic about when Walt calls the play. Which is fine and dandy for a bunch of foreigners but what about us 100 percent Americans? We watch this stuff not for esoteric enjoyment but for FUN. You try working down a Point all day, pal, and come home to a Jets No Play. No goddamned fun, I'll tell you. So I don't call for Walt's head so much as I call for him to get the hell out of the Zen Center, and do it now, Walt. Football isn't a gentle and restive sport like flower arranging. Get some goddamned big guys on steroids and let them get out there and kick hell out of people. Either that or move your ass to Japan. And I mean it!

But Walt, for all his sloppiness, for all his puffball Patton-ness, at least the guy's human. This guy Perkins? Is he for real? I personally think so, but Lenny G, a pal of mine who boosts Pep Boys Auto Parts to fight inflation, he says different. He has this theory that Perksie is really a living sequel to this horror movie *Donovan's Brain*. This movie starred Lew Ayres, and it was about a mean millionaire's brain that unfortunate Lew takes out of a light plane wreck. Soon he's got the brain set up in a lab, and then that gray matter goes to work telling him what to do in this heavy-metal voice. Stuff like, "You've got to eat Cheese-O's. You've got to eat Cheese-O's." Some crazy stuff. Anyway, by flick's end, the brain is in a fire, and it looks like it's going to go bodiless forever, but according to Lenny G it escaped, and found this stiff from Alabama, moved inside his head, and convinced him to become the coach of the Giants. To prove his point, Lenny came over the other night with some hot socket wrenches, and we watched *The Ray Perkins Show* on the tube. Well, I'll be damned if he didn't almost make a believer out of me, because Perksie definitely looked possessed. I mean this guy needs help fast. He doesn't move anything when he talks. His mouth don't move, his eyes don't shine, his hair don't toss, his ears don't wiggle, and he definitely don't dance. I tried like hell to work up a little compassion for him; after all, I figure he don't mean to make me feel this bad on purpose, but he is not the kind of guy you feel like feeling sorry for. He's sitting there with this other guy who can barely talk, in this futuristic set, overtop a football stadium, and I thought, well, there's a dead giveaway, because if he's human, where the hell is he sitting? I mean, the way they got it set up, it looks like he and the announcer, Dick Lynch, are hovering in the sky! Well, Lenny gets all riled up. Says the Rayatollah is so tough, so mean that his players are too scared to play ball. Maybe Ray knows it, too, because at the end of the show he says, *The best chance we have of beating Oakland is to get out there and play a wild, wacky football game.*

Wild? Wacky? Like what? Come out dressed like a chick? Yell hike when you're centering the ball? Count Three-Mississippi? Play three complete? Any of those would have been preferable to what happened. A fumble on the first possession, and the Raiders walked in. More fumbles later leading to more gift points. Absurd interceptions, lame tackling, and the onside kick, which capped the year with an irony so sophomoric and bald that it would have been too obvious for a TV sitcom. But that in itself is the only way I can recall the Giants' season without breaking out into Giant Hives. You see, they weren't really playing at all. The two o'clock broadcasts were really only TV movies . . . a riotous wacko series called *The Worst Team in the World.*

I could go on. I'd like to talk to Mr. George Young, general manager of the Giants. George used to teach me history in high school in Baltimore, and one of the things he used to stress was George Santayana's saying, Those Who Don't Learn from History Are Doomed to Repeat It. There is a hell of an irony in there somewhere, George, but I don't want to push it. I just want a couple of big guys breaking into the clear, zigzagging their way through the defenders who clutch at them, like trying to grab oil in a tube. Just a quarterback who throws some good twenty-yard passes, sets up the defense, and then tosses the big bomb. Just some pounding linemen who look like they're thinking about kicking ass rather than the future of the country. Maybe the Jets and the Giants have been influenced by a bunch of assholes who tried to humanize the game, made her hometown boys think they had to learn to speak, be a credit to their race, and even read *Dune.* Don't listen to 'em, Walt. Pay no attention to Big Ray. Hire big dumb fast mean guys! Make 'em run around and hit people. Yell stuff like Hubba Hubba. Ring the old Bell. What are you, some kinda pussy?

The old-fashioned All-American Way. If you gotta be modern, let 'em snort coke, crystal meth, anything. Just make the bastards mean!

I can't wait much longer. I can't stand anymore of this garbage. Neither can Lenny or Billy C. You don't come out the gate like a werewolf next year, we're gonna start watching (I never thought I'd say this) soccer. That's right. Little guys in short pants with names like Ergflugle Gerhardt. We don't want to, boys. But we will. I mean it. I can't stand no more. I'm getting all sweaty thinking about it. Makes me have a sick headache. You do something . . . nowwwwwww.

The Oakland Raiders' Charming Assassin

George Atkinson is the nicest fellow you'd ever want to meet—unless you're an opposing receiver and you think you want to catch a pass.

Lynn Swann is floating across the field. His long legs are rippling through the air, his arms are pumping, evenly, smoothly, slowly. Behind him, is another man, also moving in slow motion. Not quite so fluid a runner as Swann, the second man is dressed in a black jersey with a silver helmet. He seems to be measuring his steps, carefully trailing Swann. Then it happens: We see the second man's arm jut out in front of him, lock into place, then swing toward Swann's neck. Slowly, slowly, the arm whips through the air, so stiff that it scarcely seems a human arm anymore, rather a board, or the limb of a tree, or perhaps the locked arm of a Frankenstein, wildly sweeping away medicine bottles and tables. Yet, there is a difference: Frankenstein was a brute out of control, terrified, unable to comprehend the world he was thrust into. But the man smashing Lynn Swann seems cool, seems to know exactly what he is doing and why. His arm crashes into Lynn Swann's head, and as we watch Swann go down, we see the arm fall back to the side of the attacker. Once again, the arm seems human, relaxed, at rest. It has ceased to be a club. Swann, of course, is unaware of all this, because he has been knocked momentarily unconscious. When he comes to, he feels as though he is in a tunnel, a great roaring place where everything is very far away, and there is a terrible pain in his head. When he tries to get up, his balance is gone, and he wishes somebody would get him out of the tunnel, pull him to his feet, get him moving again. . . .

Of course, you have seen this tableau on TV several times by now. It happened in the Oakland Raiders' first game of the 1976 season, against the Pittsburgh Steelers, a match between the once and future Super Bowl champions. The arm-club involved belonged to George Atkinson, the veteran Oakland safety who, after eight years of relative obscurity, emerged suddenly as the embodiment of football evil, surpassing such prototypical villains as Mean Joe Greene and Dick Butkus and even Atkinson's teammate, Jack Tatum. Atkinson's assault was one of the highlights of the first Monday Night Game last season, and it was rerun in slow motion, again and again, on Monday nights and on local sports shows and as a prelude to the playoff games that carried Oakland, and George Atkinson, to the peak of pro football.

As soon as Lynn Swann's head cleared, Pittsburgh coach Chuck Noll said, "Apparently, there's a criminal element in the National Football League." Ed Levitt, a columnist for the *Oakland Tribune,* stopped rooting for the Raiders long enough to write that George Atkinson "could have killed Swann, instead of giving him a concussion." Atkinson responded by filing three million dollars' worth of lawsuits against Noll, the Steelers, and Ed Levitt. And as the 1976 season roared toward its Super Bowl anticlimax, George Atkinson inspired the same sort of bloodthirsty prose on the sports pages that a fellow named Gary Gilmore was stirring up on page one: Was Atkinson a cold-blooded killer? Or did he wake up at night sweating with remorse? Did he really—as Pittsburgh fans suggested—deserve to be shot at dawn? In search of answers, I went to Oakland to see Atkinson.

Outside the Oakland Coliseum before the last regular-season game, a well-dressed man with silver-grey hair parked his Lincoln Continental, swept out of the car and slammed the door as if he were testing the metal. From the other side of the car, a small boy emerged. The boy was also dressed in a suit, and his shoes were so polished you could see the clouds in them. Smiling affably, I approached the man and his double, and explained to them that I was a reporter from New York working on the Atkinson-Swann affair.

"How do you feel about the fact," I asked, "that Chuck Noll called Atkinson one of the 'criminal element' in the National Football League?"

"Well," the man said in a deep baronial voice, "some people called it a 'cheap shot,' too. And it was a 'cheap shot'—a 'cheap shot' by the media. They took one play a guy made . . . one that he is not particularly proud of . . . and they pick it out and call him a 'criminal.' George Atkinson has been around nine years, young man. . . . Isn't that right, Little Don?"

Don, who looked about twelve going on forty, nodded confidently.

"As I was saying," the man said as he took blankets out of his car, "George Atkinson has played for nine years. He used to run back punts for the Raiders, and in one of those years he was the AFL Defensive Rookie of the Year. Isn't that right, Little Don?"

"In 1968," said the boy. "Atkinson graduated from Morris-Brown College in Atlanta. He holds all the Raider punt-return records and he's played one hundred twenty five consecutive games. A great player. Let's go, Pops."

"Don hates to miss the players warming up," the man said, looking down at his son. "You write in your magazine that Don and Little

Don Burns of Oakland love George Atkinson, and are damned proud of him."

Five minutes after the Raiders had wiped out the Chargers, 24–0, I nervously made my way through the Oakland dressing room in search of the man who had been labeled a killer. Squeezing by monstrous Otis Sistrunk, and coolheaded Ken Stabler (who hadn't even played), I expected the worst. As I approached George Atkinson, I pictured him to be a tough, slightly crazed guy with blood coming off his teeth, and a hard dumb look around the eyes. Instead, sitting stripped by his locker, was a muscular black man with a neatly trimmed mustache and goatee, and a pair of very luminous eyes. Still nervous, I introduced myself, expecting him to mumble something about "not wanting to talk," but he smiled and said he had looked forward to meeting me. "Be right back, as soon as I shower," he said. "Meanwhile, why don't you meet my son, Craig?" Sitting next to the locker was a handsome child, well-groomed and polite. I said hello to the boy, then went over to ask wide receiver Cliff Branch what kind of guy George was.

"A serious guy," Branch said, "a really dedicated guy. He's very talkative and likable. The minute you meet him you establish a real relationship with him. Actually, I can't say nothing but good things about him."

In minutes George was back, and getting dressed in a very flashy continental suit. He smiled again, and offered his hand to his son, pulling him up. There was a look of obvious pride on his face, and one had a tough time recalling that the hand was on the end of the same arm that had clubbed Lynn Swann unconscious two months before. That was the second time Atkinson had knocked out the Steelers' best receiver. In the third quarter of the 1975 AFC Championship game between Pittsburgh and Oakland, Swann caught a pass slicing across the middle, and Atkinson almost sliced his head off with that scythe-like right arm of his. The ball fell loose and was recovered by Oakland, and Mean Joe Greene ran out and recovered the comatose body of

Lynn Swann, carrying him off the field in his arms, as a father might carry a stricken child.

Swann was asked at the time if Atkinson's blow had been a cheap shot, and Lynn said through a sardonic smile: "I had the ball and nobody blew the whistle. I was an open target, head to toe. He clubbed his arm and caught me in the head, and if you'll notice, Oakland is a team that goes after the head more than any other part of the body."

Atkinson was fully dressed now and talking in his very soft, melodious voice, interspersing his words with an infectious, easy laugh that tended to blur the memories of his terrible swift arm.

"No," Atkinson said, "I don't consider myself a dirty player. And no one else did for the last nine years. But football is about hitting. That's what it is. I weigh 185, and I go up against tight ends: 220, 230, 240. You take a guy like Russ Francis. He's 245 pounds. You aren't going to do a lot of intimidation on a guy like him. But you got to have tactics all the same."

"Tactics?" I said. "What do you mean by tactics?"

Atkinson's smile revealed a charming army of teeth. "Well, for example, a guy is coming off the line. Now he's going to be thinking about his pattern, about catching the ball. That is, unless you use some tactics on him. Suppose I give him a shot around in here—?"

George made a motion with The Arm in the general area of his own neck. "You see," he said. "That's going to slow him down. He's going to be coming off the line like this—"

Atkinson hunched over like Quasimodo, and put his hand over his face, as if to fend off an attacker. "See?" he said, laughing. "Now he's got to run the pattern like that. Hell, he ain't gonna catch no ball running like that, is he?"

"Heck no," I said. "But isn't there something we are overlooking here? What about the morality of your 'tactics'?" I mean, what you did with Swann, wasn't that a little . . . a bit much!"

Atkinson smiled and shook his head. "I don't think so. First of all I was caught at a bad camera angle. It looks like I just came up and hit him in the back of the head. But if you had seen the play from my point of view . . . it looked like Bradshaw was throwing to Swann. . . . So I was just trying to stop the play. Besides, as far as Lynn Swann goes, I don't have much respect for him anyway. He's got good hands, great speed, and he runs his patterns well, but he doesn't have any guts. Not like Cliff Branch or Fred Biletnikoff. I've seen Biletnikoff play with a broken nose. Or Lance Alworth. Now *he* was a great player. He was the kind of guy you just can't intimidate. He took his shots and he didn't bitch.

"I mean, football ain't no pussy sport . . . they haven't put any dresses on us yet, as far as I can see . . . but Lynn Swann . . . hell, I hit him a good clean shot in the playoffs, and even that wasn't right . . . he was bitching about that. Him and that Chuck Noll. That's why I've got my three million dollar lawsuit out there. Noll said Jack Tatum and I were a 'criminal element' in the game. Well, that's ridiculous. I've played this game nine years. I've been hit lots of times by guys. . . . You know that the backs and the linemen aren't supposed to clip you or hit you below the knees, but they do it all the time . . . but Howard Cosell doesn't mention *that.* I been hit below the knees so many times I've lost count. . . . Man, I have played hurt, but I didn't go running to the commissioner. I'll tell you, Pete Rozelle or nobody else is gonna alter my style of play one bit."

"I take it you are not an undying fan of Howard Cosell?"

"Him? All he knows about football could be shoved up a gnat's body. How could he know anything about it? He doesn't hang out with the players. He doesn't come down and prepare for a game with the team . . . he doesn't even know anything about strong-side rotation or keying on players . . . I mean, all he can do is come down on somebody. I can't remember the guy . . . but a couple of weeks ago on the Monday night game a player was smiling on the sidelines, and Cosell says, 'He shouldn't be smiling when his team is losing so badly. If Vince Lombardi was out there he wouldn't be smiling.' Well, hell, maybe the guy was smiling at the craziness of it all. Or maybe he wasn't even smiling. Maybe he was grimacing in pain. Cosell doesn't know what the guy was thinking . . . and he doesn't care. Just like the Swann thing. He brings on Lynn Swann to talk, and tell his side, but he doesn't have me on. He wanted to have me and Jack Tatum on afterward. I said, 'Let's have us all on together, and talk about it.' But Cosell figured he'd get me on, and say Lynn Swann said this and that . . . he could throw his big vocabulary at me. So I said forget it, we either go on together or not at all. Cosell, whew . . . I'll tell you what he does best. 'I remember on such and such a day that this great man . . .' That kinda crap. . . . Talk about cheap shots. I have no respect for his knowledge of the game at all. . . ."

Atkinson had been talking for a half hour and Craig was getting jumpy so George and I decided to call it a day.

"I'll walk out with you," I said, and moments later Atkinson, his son, and I stood at the wire gate that marks the Players' Entrance. A group of teenage kids started cheering, and yelling Atkinson's name. Charming, and dashing as ever, Atkinson smiled, and signed his name in their autograph books. He signed an Oakland Raider pennant for one young boy with light hair and perfectly bronzed California skin.

"Thanks, George," the kid said. "You guys gonna play the Steelers again soon?"

"I hope so," George said.

"Me, too," the kid said. "Then you can get that crybaby Lynn Swann again. Oh, I loved the way you took him out. That was some hit. It was almost as good as the time you guys got Boobie Clark. Ooooh . . . was that great!"

"See you tomorrow, Bob," George said to me.

George Atkinson lives in a beautiful A-frame house high atop the Oakland Hills. He paid sixty thousand dollars for the place but it's probably worth twice that much now. Divorced, Atkinson and Craig live alone (Atkinson's wife and their fourteen-year-old daughter, Michelle, moved to Atlanta) and Atkinson claims he doesn't have much of a social life.

"I like to go to a club once in a while. Jack Tatum is very close to me, and some of my friends are in show biz. Smokey Robinson is a pal. But really I just like to stay here."

It's easy to see why. His house is extremely comfortable, tastefully furnished. There is a stone fireplace, and the photos above it are Atkinson's special passion . . . horses. He's started racing them, and wishes he had more time for it.

"It's not a hobby," Atkinson said, as he got me a beer. "It's more like an addiction."

After a few beers, and some small talk, our conversation returned to the Swann affair, and the Commissioner's attitude:

"Rozelle had us in his office. Me and Jack Tatum. He showed us some rolls of film. They had four shots of me hitting people, and one of Jack. . . . It was a joke, really. You could do the same thing to any player in the league. But they were picking on me because it got on the tube. They fined each of us fifteen hundred dollars, and warned us. . . . I think it's all over but it might not be. But it's crazy. Then this writer Ed Levitt from the *Oakland Trib* writes that I could have 'murdered' Lynn Swann. That's why I'm suing him, too. Hey, he writes that I'm a murderer and I've never even *met* the man."

While I pondered this non sequitur, Atkinson went on: "It's like I was telling you yesterday. Football is about hitting. I play strong safety. That means I am the last line of defense. I can't afford to let anybody get by me. . . . You let a few guys beat you and the next thing you know you are out of a job. So I have my tactics."

"Yes," I said, "but Swann had a concussion. He couldn't see. Doesn't that bother you?"

"No. First of all, I had strong doubts that he even had a concussion. With a concussion, you usually regurgitate; he never did. But he was walking off and talking to his teammates."

"George," I said, "I've got to admit that you seem like a good guy. But I can't believe that blow doesn't bother you. Don't you ever wake up late at night and think that was a cheap shot? . . ."

"No; I don't. . . . Look, I know the theories. . . . There is one guy who did a study of defensive backs . . . a doctor. He said that defensive backs were under the most pressure of anyone in the game, and that for anyone to be a good defensive back, he had to love to hit people. He quoted Dick Night Train Lane who said, 'I wasn't a nice guy.' Well, that's how I feel. . . . We have to be able to read a play in a second . . . we have to know whether to come up fast and stop a run, or watch for a deep pass. . . .

"Man, you sweat out there. . . . It's tough. . . . So you don't have time to sit back and think, 'Oh, I'll get this guy. . . .' You just react. If someone comes in your area, you have got to make him pay. Swann came in my area once and I kind of hit him with my knee on the way up; and he said, 'What the hell you do that for?' I said, 'What the hell you come in here for, muther?' I mean, it might sound cold, man—but that's the way it is. I don't think I have to make any excuse for it. It's the law of the jungle. You know, it's exactly like nature, the survival of the fittest. But I will say this: I don't try to intimidate the really quality players . . . like Riley Odoms, or Charley Joiner, or Otis Taylor . . . or Russ Francis . . . you only do it to the ones you know will be affected by it."

"You sound like the former Baltimore Colt and New York Jet villain, Johnny Sample," I suggested.

Atkinson laughed appreciatively. "Now there," he said with more than a trace of nostalgia, "was one of the really *great* dirty players. He wasn't really much of a defensive back, you know? Hell, he'd trip a guy as he went by him, hold, do anything he could. . . . He was a real dirty player. Pat Fischer of the Redskins is another one. He'll do *anything*. But the problem isn't dirty players so much. I think it's the way the American people see football. . . . They think it's an All-American game and all that. What it is is a jungle . . . where the guy that hits the most, who intimidates the most . . . *he* is the *winner*. You take the new offensive players. They are physically better than the older players, but they don't have the same spirit, the guts. Older players like Pete Lammons, Hewritt Dixon, they were tough, man. They didn't whine or bellyache. They played the game the way it's supposed to be played."

"I'm familiar with the theories that shrink mentioned," I said. "He contends that defensive backs are the most insecure people, that they have to get by with a superhuman macho quality. He says the great ones have that kind of superman complex to fend off huge anxiety, and fear . . . and the other ones crack up and quit."

Atkinson shrugged. "If you want to know if I am a psycho, the answer is no. I'm very solid. I have a business in town. Own a bar and restaurant. I did come from a very competitive background. I grew up in Savannah and went to Morris-Brown College, where we had a very competitive situation. A lot of great players come from my school: Tommy Hart, Alfred Jenkins, a whole lot. My father worked at the Union Bag and Paper Plant . . . my mother was a registered nurse. Now they live here and run my liquor store. I had my share of fights as a kid, but nothing unusual. . . . Really you know, all this is comical to me. If they want to make me out a bad guy, it's okay with me. I've been around a long time, and nobody said nothing much, but now . . . I'm the villain of the year."

I couldn't help but laugh with him. Atkinson seemed to be a living embodiment of an old line I remember from T. S. Eliot. "It is better to be evil than mediocre." And then a line from Reggie Jackson came to mind: "Before Atkinson, the Raiders were faceless, bland. They didn't have an identity. Now they have it. He gave it to them. A kind of team image to live up to."

I left George Atkinson thinking: He's one tough, mean dude on a football field, but he is also one of the nicest guys I have met since I started covering sports.

Cut to the New England game and Patriot tight end Russ Francis, one of the "quality players I don't try to intimidate," Atkinson had said. Francis came off the line to the inside and a linebacker shadowed him. Francis turned to his right to lose the linebacker. At that moment, in front of a national television audience, George Atkinson struck again. Leaping up, Atkinson sent The Arm through Francis's facemask, and broke his nose in three places. As I sat watching the replay in total disbelief, I wondered if Atkinson had consciously chosen to be the Bad Boy simply because it gets him more ink. After all, no one wanted to do feature stories on him in his pre-"tactics" incarnation.

Whatever, a day after the Super Bowl I discussed my confusion with Lynn Swann himself.

"So George thinks I'm not a man because I griped about that?" Swann said over the phone. "Well, first of all I don't play football to prove my manhood. George is a headhunter. Watching a film of him before the playoffs, we all noticed that he hardly ever makes a tackle. Practically every play he is involved in he goes for the guy's head. It looked like he was just trying to take the shot where it would do the most damage. I don't think this is football at all. There have always been cheap-shot artists. They hit a guy in the head because they can't take him down head on."

"How serious was the hit on you?"

"I had tunnel vision for quite some time. I had bad headaches. What was worse, a lot of other defensive backs began to think they could take cheap shots at me. In Cincy, Lemar Parrish, who is a small back, he thought he could hit me and I had to go after him. I had to say, 'This is enough!' I'll tell you, the joy of playing football is just about gone from me. People think I'm just saying this stuff about the violence in football because I'm trying to get my salary up . . . but that's not true. I'm serious. The penalties aren't strong enough. If a team can take out a Kenny Anderson, or an Isaac Curtis, do you think a mere fifteen-yard penalty is going to stop them?"

"The whole thing reminds me of the movie *Rollerball*," I said. "More and more escalating violence."

"That's right," said Swann. "And you know what is really the scariest thing about it? George Atkinson really believes that what he is doing is right. He believes it a hundred percent. And he is absolutely wrong. Sure, intimidation is part of the game . . . you can hit a guy once before he gets off the line . . . but you don't go for his head and try to injure him. How can anybody call that 'sport'? It's a sad thing. And the fans love it . . . or seem to. They look forward to their team putting out the other quarterback. I'll tell you, it's very demoralizing to me. . . . I'm thinking seriously of finding a new way to make a living."

Russ Francis echoed Swann's sentiments, but he added a few thoughts of his own: "So Atkinson thinks that he is a real man?" Francis said in a conversation I had with him just before the Pro Bowl game. "Well, if that's the case . . . if that's what it comes to in football, then I'll make sure my son never plays the game. But I don't think it will come to that."

"Why not?" I said. "From every indication football is getting more savage every year."

"I know that," Francis said. "But there is one group of people who can really stop it, and that's the players themselves. And, believe me, there has been an awful lot of talk about these guys like Atkinson in the past few months. I personally don't believe in revenge. I'd rather go out and catch a touchdown pass like I did off Atkinson, than come at him. But I thought about it hard. It took every bit of restraint I had in me not to simply come off that bench and kill him. And there are a lot of other players in the league who are talking quite openly about getting rid of players like George. George says that Lynn Swann isn't a man for complaining to the commissioner? Well, I hope George remembers that next year or the year after when he's not making his big salary, when he's sitting in a wheelchair without the use of his legs, I hope he reacts like a 'real man.' And doesn't say anything at all."

Postscript

This piece on George Atkinson seems to me to be prophetic. Back in his day little was done to deal with concussions. They weren't even really considered injuries. But these days everyone in football (and for that matter, baseball, as well) knows just how deadly they can be. A few "harmless concussions" and soon a world-class athlete can't remember his car keys or what day it is. Full-on memory loss and early Alzheimer's disease are so common now among football players that the league has had to step in and stop the antics of players like Atkinson and Tatum. But think how long it took them. What Swann said was right. The fans do love violence, and there is a *Rollerball*-like mentality when it comes to football. Francis was right as well. The players have stepped in, and hopefully football is headed for a more sportsmanlike future.

The Night the Lights
Went Out in Baltimore

I loved the Colts for reasons that transcended football. They enabled me to see life's larger possibilities.

The night the Baltimore Colts left town under cover of darkness for Indianapolis, I phoned Ned Myers, my oldest friend in Baltimore. As teenagers we had lived and died a thousand times on the passes of quarterback Johnny Unitas, the diving fingertip catches of receiver Raymond Berry, and the graceful feints of one of the most underrated running backs in football history, Lenny Moore. We had sat in the stadium screaming "Gino! Gino! Gino!" as the great Marchetti smashed through triple-team blocking to bring down that old nemesis, Bobby Layne.

We sang, "So drive on you Baltimore Colts/Go in and strike like lightning bolts." One season the Colts needed to win only one of their last two games—both on the road—to sew up the division title. They managed to lose those two. Ned locked himself in his room and refused to eat. I almost kicked in my grandfather's television set. But in 1958 the Colts beat the New York Giants for the world championship in The Greatest Game Ever Played; Ned, I, and every other kid we knew in town replayed that game over and over for years. For that matter, people in Baltimore bars still relive the game as though it had happened yesterday.

When they lost the 1969 Super Bowl to the New York Jets, I was shocked at how badly it hurt; I wanted to cry, to smash something. And two years later, when they beat the Dallas Cowboys on Jim O'Brien's last-second kick, I was ecstatic. Even when the team lost Unitas, and the other old Colts retired or were traded, Ned and I continued to love the team. And we didn't give up on the Colts when they started to slip. Bert Jones, we always figured, had more talent than any other quarterback in the National Football League. As a New York sportswriter I once went down to Baltimore to watch training camp and saw Jones flick—and I do mean flick—the ball on a straight line fifty-five yards in the air to Roger Carr. Jones was brash and hot-tempered, as opposed to the quiet Unitas, but he was also a leader who, like Unitas, could change the direction of a game with one rifle-like long pass.

But Jones was a man caught in the whirlpool of sports history. Gone were the days when the quarterback called all his own plays. The Colts under head coach Ted Marchibroda played some exciting football, all right, but for the most part they had succumbed to a dull and predictable offense featuring routine play calling. It worked just well enough to get them into the playoffs for three consecutive years, only to be eliminated in the first round. Jones showed flashes of the greatness I expected of him, but only when the Colts had fallen behind by a couple of touchdowns and the game plan had to be scrapped. Then Jones would limber up his arm, go to work, and fire strike after strike.

Against the Jets in 1974, he completed seventeen straight passes, then a record. He managed to keep all of Baltimore excited, but even then we could see the end coming. Except for Jones, the Colts were just another dull, modern football team without a soul. And when Robert Irsay bought the team and got into his notorious feud with Jones, culminating in the quarterback's being shipped to the Los

Angeles Rams, the Colts that my buddies and I had worshiped from childhood were close to dead.

Now they are gone, probably for good. As a Baltimorean, I find it a hard fact to face. I know that sounds melodramatic, but understand that in '50s Baltimore, the Colts were the city's only claim to national pride. Winning the 1958 showdown with the New York Giants told all of us in the hometown that we counted. Alan "The Horse" Ameche barreling into the end zone to win that game in sudden-death overtime is the single greatest moment I've ever witnessed in sports.

We loved the Colts in Baltimore as we loved family, as we loved best friends in the neighborhood, with a kind of fierce, provincial love that scarcely exists anymore. But what made our relationship with the team so special? It had to do, for myself, with being twelve years old and living three blocks away from a rookie quarterback named Johnny Unitas. I lived on Winston Road, and he, for the time being, was living just beyond the Tom Mullen Little League Field on Cold Spring Lane. One hot summer afternoon, my best pal Johnny Brandau and I went around to the red brick row houses on Cold Spring. We had heard that the Colts' starting quarterback, George Shaw, lived there, and we had our autograph books and pens ready. But when we shyly knocked on a door, a grizzled man in his underwear answered it. I recognized him immediately as Carl Taseff, the Colts' defensive halfback and expert punt returner. He looked exhausted and grouchy, and I stammered, "Uh . . . you're Mr. Taseff, aren't you?" He looked at us hard for a second, and then said, "Sure, kids. Come on in."

Johnny and I wandered into his furnished room. He offered us both Cokes, which we accepted, smiling and winking at each other over our extraordinary good fortune. Soon we were talking to him about an interception he had made in last week's game. He smiled, said it was luck. Our courage bolstered by his good mood, we asked if any other Colts lived in the neighborhood.

"Sure," he said, yawning. "We got a quarterback right next door."

We were positive it was George Shaw, and both of us felt our hearts racing. Taseff threw on some shorts with the words PROPERTY OF BALTIMORE COLTS on them (and what crime would I not have committed to have those shorts?) and took us next door to introduce us to the quarterback.

But when we got outside, the quarterback was already there. He was throwing passes to another player we didn't know. The passer sure as hell wasn't George Shaw. He was a funny-looking guy with a crew cut and a kind of twisted grin.

"Think fast, kid," he said to me, and that was how I caught a pass thrown by Johnny Unitas.

I threw it back to him, and he sent a soft floater to Johnny Brandau, who was much the better athlete of the two of us. Johnny threw him a bullet back, and the three Colts laughed and said, "Hey! Good arm!" We were then introduced to this strange, skinny-looking guy, and even his name sounded funny. He signed our autograph books, and after a little more awkward chat, Johnny and I went back across the sunbaked Little League field to Winston Road.

"What was that guy's name?" I asked.

"Johnny Un-a-tiss or something," Johnny Brandau said.

"Well, he sure isn't George Shaw."

"Yeah, but at least he was a quarterback."

"Right," I said. "And we got to meet Carl Taseff!"

We ran the rest of the way home, knocking on Mike Thomas's door, and Spence's door, and later that night I called up Ned.

"The Colts, they live right around the corner. And they're real good guys."

Three weeks later Shaw was injured and never regained his starting job. The clumsy-looking kid from around the corner took over; late in the season he saved coach Weeb Ewbank's job by beating the Washington Redskins with a fifty-two-yard pass in the game's final seconds.

To say that my friends and I loved Unitas merely shows the inadequacy of words. In my early teens I dreamed I was Johnny Unitas. I practiced his little shuffle as he went back into the pocket. I read every single scrap of paper on him and could recite to you the minutest trivia regarding his passing percentages. But there was more to it than that. When he and the Colts won, they proved to all of us that Baltimore could succeed in the larger world. You see, as much as we loved our close-knit neighborhoods, the conventional wisdom was that Baltimoreans were losers. Worse, we were told, one shouldn't try for anything more. "Grow up!" was the catchphrase of the '50s; it meant, "Go to high school, get a job downa' plant, marry, eat crabs, and live out your life like Mom and Dad." For a person of talent and ambition, there was nothing that could smother you so fast as this strange, twisted code of love.

The Colts' winning changed all that for me in a way no teacher or parent ever could. It made me understand that the world was bigger than Northwood and bigger than even Baltimore itself.

And so, at least in part, I loved the Baltimore Colts for reasons that transcended football. They enabled me to see life's larger possibilities.

But there is one more reason that we loved them. A crucial one. The players on the old Colts played football with a crude, old-fashioned spirit, like a legendary band of brothers. The Johnny Unitas who lived around the corner didn't mouth off like Joe Theismann. He didn't advertise hair spray or pose in underwear ads, nor did any of his teammates. They were nice to the neighborhood kids, but nice like real neighbors, not as if they had some media consultant telling them how to go over with the plain folks. (And they are still that way today. Catch Art Donovan on the David Letterman show sometime. He's still as vulgar, crude, and lovable—like Baltimore—as he was in the '50s.)

The old Colts played before slickness replaced honesty. All they were was great.

Most of them made a lot more a year than my own father. But they played with passion. I remember Unitas's being knocked silly by Bears' defensive end Ed Meadows in a fierce, close game televised from Chicago. Unitas was dazed and bleeding. The team called a time-out; the trainer iced down the quarterback's nose and taped up his head. Then Unitas trotted slowly back to the huddle.

With nineteen seconds showing on the clock, he called the exact same play that had just gotten him creamed, dodged the charging Meadows, and threw the ball thirty-nine yards downfield toward Lenny Moore. Moore waited at the goal line along with Bears' ace defensive back J. C. Caroline. Both of them went up, but Moore came down with the ball for the game-winning score.

Moore didn't go into a dance. He didn't shove the ball in Caroline's face. He merely handed it to the official and walked toward the dressing room. Unitas didn't point his finger at Meadows or run around hugging people. He held some more ice to his nose and stalked off silently while the crowd stared at him as though they'd seen a miracle.

There were no postgame interviews.

There was no personal philosophy espoused.

Even when he was there, right in the neighborhood, Johnny Unitas always kept his distance.

But Unitas, and Alan Ameche, and Art Donovan, and Lenny Moore, and Gino Marchetti, and all the great old Colts knew a camaraderie over the years that today's players will never experience.

Like us people in Baltimore who grew up in one neighborhood, they were virtually a family and, without saying so, shared a species of love almost extinct in the modem world of pro sports. They were working-class guys in the perfect working-class town. They played on real grass, under the real sun. And they didn't quit, ever.

Today the NFL is filled with artificial turf, domed stadiums, and overmuscled studs who run fast—but only for themselves. They are too hip to believe in teamwork or even sport. Turkeys like Theismann and the Jets' Mark Gastineau perfectly embody a corporate game that is pantomimed for big-moneyed lawyers sipping martinis in their glassed-in private stadium boxes. SELF and only SELF is the narcissistic goal of every game.

Last year, during one of those endless interviews by a sports-media moron, I listened to Gastineau saying he would continue to dance over sacked quarterbacks because he really believed in what he was doing. The saddest part of the interview was, he sounded as if he really *did* believe in it. But in what? Humiliating your opponent? Or making an ass out of yourself? Try to imagine Gino Marchetti (who was ten times the player Gastineau is) dancing over a fallen quarterback.

No, it's not only the Baltimore Colts who are gone. Pro football itself has disappeared. It's not much more of a sport nowadays than pro wrestling. Camaraderie, sportsmanship, identifying with a team over a number of years, love of the game for the game itself—all of these values have been obliterated. Which brings us back to my phone call to my old friend Ned Myers. The night the Colts skipped town, I half expected him to be glumly sipping a whiskey, cursing owner Robert Irsay, football's answer to George Steinbrenner. I even thought he might be hurt by the team's defection, like a man losing a lover.

"Hey," I said when he picked up the phone. "You hear about the Colts? I can hardly believe it."

"Believe what, Ward?" he said.

"You know, that they're gone."

"Hey, man," he replied wearily. "Let's face it. The Baltimore Colts have been gone for a long, long time."

Postscript

Rereading this story, I'm struck with how dark it is. When my old team left town I was turned off for years to pro football. I really didn't get back into it until the Ravens came to Baltimore. Like every other

Colts fan I was struck with sadness when the team left. Remembering how my friend Johnny Brandau and I had gone around to Cold Spring Lane and met Unitas only made them leaving that much more painful.

Like everyone else in Baltimore, I worshipped Johnny U. He was our first real star, and his weekly miracles at Memorial Stadium have never been surpassed anywhere. The piece was my last gasp of sentiment for the team I'd loved as a kid.

The response to the piece was gratifying. Friends from Baltimore called me up and said that I had put into words their own feelings. I even got a few letters thanking me for writing the piece.

Then one afternoon the telephone rang, and there was a strange southern voice on the line:

"Hi, is this Robert Ward?"

"It is. Who's this?"

"Well," the voice said. "You might remember me as a player on the Colts. My name is Alex Hawkins."

I laughed. Hawkins was a player who had no specific role. He ran at halfback, played on special teams, and even played flanker. He was a kind of super-sub and one of the most popular guys on the team. In fact, they had made him captain of the team for several years. The joke was that when he went out pregame for the coin flip, the referees would introduce the captains of each team, but after they said: "This is Captain Hawkins," the other team captain would often say, "Captain Who?" Nobody but Colts fans knew his name and not even all of them. But he was a valuable role player, nonetheless.

"I just called to tell you I loved your piece in *GQ*, Bob," he said.

"Wow. Thanks. How did you get my number?"

"From our mutual agent Esther Newburg. She's selling my new book of memoirs. It's called *That's My Story and I'm Sticking With It.*"

We chatted for a little longer. I was really touched that he would call me personally to tell me. Then Hawkins pulled a real fast one on me.

"There's somebody else here who liked your article and wants to thank you too," he said.

"Hi, Bob," a voice said. "That was really a great piece."

I almost collapsed. It was a voice I'd heard on a million interviews. The same crewcutted guy who had once thrown me a pass.

"Johnny Unitas?" I said. I must have sounded like a twelve-year-old kid.

"Yep," he said, laughing. "That was one hell of a piece. You got it dead right. Especially the part about how much the guys loved each other. That was exactly how it was."

Hawkins agreed with him.

Anyone who knows me personally knows I've never been at a loss for words. But that moment I was speechless. There was a long silence. Finally, I said:

"Do you still have your restaurant, The Golden Arm, John?"

"Sure do. You oughta come over one night and have a drink with us."

"Absolutely," I said. "I will do that."

"Well call ahead and I'll meet you there," Unitas said. "And again, Bob, thanks. That piece really was terrific."

I said goodbye and hung up the phone.

I'm not ashamed to say I felt a kind of golden glow all over my body. My childhood hero had called me up to thank me for a piece I wrote. Frankly, it was inconceivable. I could barely believe it even after it happened.

And the really great thing about it was that Unitas was as nice and humble and kind as he had been when Johnny B. and I bothered him that hot summer night after practice.

A few years ago I picked up the *Los Angeles Times* and read that Johnny Unitas had died at the age of sixty-nine. I knew he had heart problems but it still came as a shock. I went to my computer to look up what the Baltimore *Sun* had on him. But before I could even get through the first article I was weeping like a bloody baby. It was like losing a family member, someone you loved so much that no words could really capture the emotion. I scrolled down the comments people wrote about him and found that the kindness he showed me was typical of his life. He was no saint, of course. His first marriage blew up and he was lousy with money, but no big star was so kind to his fans. One fan after another wrote of the little kindnesses he showed them. Many of the remembrances started, "I am sitting here weeping as I write this." Indeed, it's impossible for me to think of any current figure in sports who could engender such emotions.

Now reading back on my piece I think it could have been better, maybe not so judgmental about Joe Theismann, who I've learned to like as a very knowledgeable and bright announcer. But I am glad I wrote the piece and that my idol and boyhood hero liked it well enough to call me and tell me so. That day stands out as one of the most thrilling in my journalistic life.

R.I.P. Johnny U. The greatest quarterback and one of the finest guys I've ever known.

Part Three

Entertainment

Redneck Rock

The vanguard of country music is flourishing in Austin, Texas. But behind the studied "outlaw" images, singers such as Jerry Jeff Walker, Waylon Jennings, and Willie Nelson often ply the safe, commercial ground they once sought to escape.

The out-of-work mechanic with the beer gut, and the four turquoise rings, and the Gene Autry (pink and lime green) cowboy shirt with real pearl buttons, and the mutton chops, and the straight-back greased-down hair, and the big rhinestone belt, is stomping his heels and pounding his motor-oiled ham hock on the bench. "Bring on Jerry Jeff. Jerry Jeff. Jerry Jeff. Play 'Redneck Mother,' Jerry Jeff!"

The object of all this frenzy is Jerry Jeff Walker, a late-thirties, ex-folkie artist turned progressive country rocker. Up on the big stage here at Armadillo World Headquarters in Austin, Texas, Walker is twice as drunk, twice as wild, and twice as "cowboy" as his audience. He has a dark beard, a cowboy shirt that hangs out to conceal his growing beer gut, a big ten-gallon hat, and National Saddlery boots (hand-stitched by Charley Dunn). In his hands he holds a guitar. He stands perfectly still, raises his arm and smiles like a goofy, tranquilized cow, and the 4,800 people at Armadillo World Headquarters go wild.

"'Redneck Mother,' Jerry Jeff."

"Hi ho, buckaroos," Jerry Jeff says, and the show is on.

He is weaving and bobbing and staggering about, stoned on coke, grass, and uppers, but he's still sober enough to belt out Ray Wylie Hubbard's country-rocker classic "Up Against the Wall Redneck," popularly known as "Redneck Mother."

So it's up against the wall redneck mother
Mother who has raised her son so well
He's thirty-four and drinking in a honky-tonk
Just kicking hippies' asses and raising hell.

On the word "hell," the whole crazy audience of Austin shit-kickers, bikers, farmers, and graduate students throw off their cowboy hats, shriek and hoot, kick up their heels, and start in buck-dancing.

Jerry Jeff Walker smiles his happy puppy grin again, takes another hit of Johnnie Walker, trips on the mike chord and falls backward over the cables. Oh, Christ, he's out of it again. He's going to fall through the drums like he did a couple of months ago at Castle Creek.

But not tonight. Not at the Armadillo! In the nick of time, Jerry Jeff rights himself and staggers, laughing, back to the mike.

"I'm rallying and fading, buckaroos," he says, laughing.

The audience cheers wildly. They love him here in Texas. In Houston, Jerry Jeff and singer/songwriter Willie Nelson easily outdraw the Who. In Dallas, at Nelson's Whiskey River Club, Nelson, David Allan Coe, or a visiting outlaw-country rocker like Tompall Glaser can sell out the house every night of the month.

But it's Austin that all the new progressive country musicians really love. There are over four hundred bands in Austin right now, and the level of musicianship is both lyrically and musically sophisticated. The new country-rock may occasionally deal with the old country staples—divorce, the bottle, bad luck, and hard women—but it also confronts less provincial American themes, like the closing of the frontier and the coming of the machine age to a small Texas town.

All of this good news on the Austin scene started in the late '60s when a number of singer/songwriters, mostly Texans who had moved to the big urban music centers like LA and Nashville, decided that they needed to get off of the commercial songwriting treadmill and go back to their own roots. So around 1968, many of these folks found their way back to Austin. And back to country.

In the early '60s, these same musicians had scorned country music as ignorant and silly and hideous. If you were a young hip Texan, country was music for rednecks, something you wanted to get away from. It took the Byrds' *Sweetheart of the Rodeo* and a little-known album by former Kingston Trio member John Stewart (*California Bloodlines*) to give ideas to the prodigal sons of Austin. Soon, musicians like Michael Murphey (best known for his songs "Geronimo's Cadillac" and "Backsliders Wine"), wild folkie Jerry Jeff Walker, esoteric mountain musician Bobby Bridger, talking jive artist Steve Fromholz, and a host of others were experimenting with traditional country music tunes, but writing lyrics that expressed their own visions of things. The visions were more complex, ironic, and articulate than those of the older, uneducated country musicians. These talented singer/songwriters then joined forces with local rock 'n' roll musicians, fiddlers, and banjo pickers to start a new hybrid form. It was at once lyrical, topical, and personal, while retaining the hard-thumping, hard edge of rock 'n' roll. During a typical performance of the Lost Gonzos, Jerry Jeff Walker's current backup band, you could expect to hear a country beat, a jazz break, a tasty rock lick or two, some down-home fiddling, and all of it played faster and harder than mere country.

For several years Austin became a place where musicians could gather, learn, and cooperate. The scene was one in which, according to Austin musician Bobby Bridger, "personal growth and the music always took precedence over cash and success."

Perhaps the best example of a musician who found himself in Austin is that of middle-aged Nashville songwriter Willie Nelson. Nelson had been pumping out songs for other people for fifteen years and had made a pile of loot. Everyone from Johnny Cash to Perry Como had cut Nelson's songs. Yet Nelson was a frustrated man. His own singing career had never progressed beyond a cult following, and he was sick to death of the business parties, the back-stabbing, and the hypocrisy of Nashville. So in the late '60s, Nelson moved to Austin. That may not sound like much, but in Nashville music circles it was considered tantamount to slitting your wrists and locking the bathroom door. Nelson's friends besieged him. He was making money. He was popular. Why had he grown his hair long? Why did he hang around with hippies and Commies? What would happen to him in Austin? Nelson, as uncertain as anyone, simply knew he could stand no more. "Nashville almost broke me," he says now. "I had to go. No matter what."

To his surprise, Nelson met scads of talented musicians in Austin who felt as he did. It wasn't long before he had given up his Nashville-Bible salesman look for good and was seen smoking joints, wearing a red bandana around his forehead, drinking Lone Star beer, and eating nachos with the local crazies. Instead of fading away, his career boomed. He came out with new songs, new records. This past year he had his greatest hit ever, "Blue Eyes Crying in the Rain," and when Bob Dylan brought his Rolling Thunder Revue to Houston recently, Nelson played with them for a night. His subsequent album, *Red Headed Stranger*, has won all sorts of awards, including Best Country Album of the Year.

Nelson and the other Austin singers have become so popular that their very success has threatened the purity they sought. Music leader and Austin idol Michael Murphey recently left town, complaining that the scene had been taken over, like Nashville before it, by business freaks, record wheeler-dealers, and hustling managers. Sure enough, calls flood into Moonhill Productions, Austin's top booking agency, every day. But even though Moonhill handles some of Austin's most popular artists (Rusty Wier, B. W. Stevenson, Denim, Asleep At The Wheel), there is a great deal of bitterness between the company and some of the Austin musicians who haven't forgotten why they came back to Austin in the first place. "I don't want to live in Music City, U.S.A.," says Bobby Bridger. Moonhill is certainly not the only business enterprise to see dollar signs. Nashville singer Waylon Jennings, whose career was finally launched by picking up on the cowboy, Rough Rider image, wants to open a recording studio in Austin, and there are a dozen other people with similar ideas. (Right now, Austin has only one recording studio, Odyssey Studios.) And, of course, the media have not been slow to pick up on Austin either. *Rolling Stone* and *Crawdaddy* have been paying close attention, and just last month *Qui* magazine featured a rave article about the town.

The Austin pictured in the media, however, is one that many Austinites abhor. They feel that the "cosmic cowboy-outlaw" image that Walker, Nelson, Jennings, Murphey, David Allan Coe, and endless hordes of imitators are spreading is exactly what the town and its music don't need.

"I can't stand that stuff," says Austin artist Jim Franklin. "I remember when Rusty Wier was a hippie who laughed at country music. Now he wears a cowboy hat, and in between his songs he tells stories about being out on the range or down in the barn. It's embarrassing."

Other critics of the scene see more serious implications. "It's a bunch of crap, this cosmic cowboy bullshit," says ex-Austinite country music singer/critic Dave Hickey. "They get up on the stage and come on like bad-asses. Most of these guys like Jerry Jeff Walker have never been near any real violence."

Delbert McClinton, a terrifically talented rhythm and blues singer/piano player who has spent a lot of time in Austin, agrees. "You see all these cowboys singing about kicking hippies' asses, and people like Edgar Allan Coe [McClinton's name for David Allan Coe], who jumps off the stage screaming, 'I can kick the shit out of any man in the bar,' and it makes you want to get sick. I mean, I been playing honky-tonks all my life, and I've seen real violence, and there ain't nothing cool about it. I saw one man rip another man's stomach out with a beer bottle, and lemme tell you . . . it was about as far from cool as you can get. I don't relate to this cowboy ass-kicking stuff. It's cheap and it's dangerous."

Austin Comes to Nashville

If critics were becoming disillusioned by the pyrotechnics, the performers themselves were becoming disenchanted with the music environment in Austin. Even a diehard like Jerry Jeff Walker went back to Nashville to record his latest album.

A doper and rambler from Oneonta, New York, Walker had come to Austin in the late '60s and found the perfect backup in the Lost Gonzo Band, a group of Texas rock musicians who were experimenting in the new country rock mode. In 1970 the group holed up in a little barn in Luckenbach, Texas, put up bales of hay for baffling, and spontaneously cut what many people still think is the best album to come out of progressive country: *Viva Terlingua*.

The album, fine as it was, promised even greater things for the Gonzos, and Jerry Jeff. It sold well over three hundred thousand copies, and it looked as though Redneck Rock was on its way to national launching. The next album, however, *Walker's Collectibles*, was a major disappointment. The tunes were half done, and only a few, such as "The Last Showboat," were really distinguished. Worse, the record sounded as though it had been produced in a wind tunnel.

In fact, it was this thicket of problems that brought Walker up from Austin to record his newest record with the expertise and consistency that only the studio musicians of Nashville can provide. Thus, it was in a darkened control room in Quadrophonic Studios in Nashville that I found the best-known Austin musicians. What's more, they weren't playing but sitting around in the booth and hallways, while the Nashville professional studio men did the larger burden of the work. The irony of all this was not lost on the Gonzos' keyboard player, Kelly Dunn, who explained to me how Austin had come back to Nashville: "The first album, *Viva*, was just the perfect combination of all the right forces. Jerry Jeff was *up*. We had a casual outlook. It all happened by accident. On 'London Homesick Blues,' that crowd reaction you heard was all spontaneous. But on *Collectibles . . .* things fell apart. Jerry Jeff was out of it, got pissed off at himself and was like a bear . . . he drinks a bit, you know. He came into the studio shaky and stoned, and with the songs half learned, and in some cases half written. Oh, it was the worst!"

"Is that why *Ridin' High* (Walker's last album) was cut here at Nashville with studio musicians instead of Austin?"

Dunn nodded and looked downcast.

"Yeah, to be frank, it was sheer panic time. So he didn't want to give Odyssey another chance. When you come up here and use the studio session men, you know exactly what kind of product you are going to get. Kenny Buttrey, Wendall Miner, Bobby Thompson, David Briggs, Johnny Gimble, and Norbert Putman have been playing together on so many sessions so long they have it down to a science."

"How does it make you and the other boys feel to be shoved aside?"

Dunn shrugged, and sucked in on his joint. "How do you suppose it makes us feel? Kind of useless."

Through the glass window I could see Jerry Jeff sitting on a stool, strumming his guitar. Around him were the Nashville Pros, the studio men who make over a hundred thousand dollars a year playing sessions. All of them are virtuoso performers, and the work they were doing this night was nothing short of superb. Walker had just finished cutting a tune called "Some Day I'll Get Out of These Bars," a sad, beautiful song about an old honk performer who knows he'll never be a star. His pathetic refrain, "Some day I'll get out/Some day I'll get out," had been handled with remarkable sensitivity by both Jerry Jeff and his sidemen. Yet, there *was* something missing. The song sounded almost too produced, the steel guitar seemed too prominent, too whiny in the grand old soap opera tradition of steel bathos. It was good, but it wasn't the Austin sound at all. The energy and enthusiasm of the early records were missing.

During the break I walked out of the studio and into the crowded little dimly lit foyer, where the studio men refreshed themselves with Coke, cigarettes, and coffee. Kenny Buttrey, Nashville's leading session drummer, was curled up in a chair:

"Same old thing," he said glumly. "One, two, three, four. It gets dull as hell sometimes. I don't know why they call this stuff progressive country. There's nothing progressive about the beat. I was in a real progressive country band with David and Norbert, and some other people. We were called Area Code 615, and we mixed jazz with rock and bluegrass. We were really good but we were before our time, I guess. The country deejays wouldn't play us because we were too funky, and the funky rock deejays wouldn't play us because they said we were too country. Wheww!"

Buttrey shook his head and tapped lightly on the chair's arm.

"I been playing sessions since I was fourteen. I've played with everybody, including Dylan. I played on *Blonde on Blonde* and *Nashville Skyline*."

"How do you like playing this session?"

Buttrey shrugged his shoulders.

"One, two, three, four," he said.

The Outlaw's Roost

The image Jerry Jeff Walker, The Lost Gonzo Band, Waylon Jennings, Willie Nelson, David Allan Coe, and countless other would-be stars from Austin (and Nashville) like to promote is that of the hard-riding, fun-loving, vaguely tragic, two-fisted cowboy. Jerry Jeff is a perennial good-time boy with flashes of sensitivity, while Waylon Jennings is a rugged but aging buckaroo who is often heartbroken but still fights the good fight. (If that sounds vague, it's because it is. Pop images are carefully chosen to look like anything one wants them to be. Thus Jennings could either be a drunken sot who has lately cleaned up, a good man who has been wronged, or a tough-assed hillbilly with a heart of gold. Choose whichever cliché gets you through the night.) Willie Nelson is a late-blooming fatherly sort of hippie-cowboy with a beatific smile. David Allan Coe, with his rhinestone earrings on the one hand, and his ultimate machismo on the other, is an extreme example of both sides of the "sensitive ass-kicker" that all these "outlaws" romanticize and exploit.

For it is the Desperado, the Bandito, the Outlaw that is the common denominator for all the new cowboy-country singers. Not only do they dress like cowboys, but some of their most memorable work deals with the same timeless, romantic myths. Walker sings Guy Clark's "Desperados," which equates the love of a young boy for his father figure with the love of "two desperados waiting for a train." Jennings sings "Slow Movin' Outlaw," a tune that tells us about an old cowboy who is being shut out of the Wild West ("Where does a slow movin'/Quick drawin' outlaw/Have to go?").

And David Allan Coe simply sings of himself: "People all say that I'm an outlaw. . . ."

It is the stuff that has made legends of the James Gang and the Daltons. It is the myth that made Sam Peckinpah a rich man. Though it's corny and hokey, it's also irresistibly American. Still, there is a dark side to all this posturing.

One young Austin singer had this to say about the outlaw image: "It's just a lot of crummy jive. As people feel more and more trapped in their lives in this country, with their dull lifeless jobs, boring family lives, and hopeless inflation, the music industry tantalizes them with these images of fake rebels to look at."

Similar sentiments were expressed to me by Neil Reshen. Known as "Mad Dog" for his negotiating toughness, Reshen manages Willie Nelson and Waylon Jennings. In a telephone conversation I had with him, Reshen was quite candid about the "outlaw" bit:

"Shit," he said. "You couldn't find two guys who are less like outlaws than Waylon Jennings and Willie Nelson. They are such homebodies that they will travel only on weekends. The rest of the time they like to be in their swimming pools with their families. It's all a bunch of horseshit really. But if the public wants outlaws, we'll give them outlaws."

Sure enough, the new cowboy singers live in the plushest, tackiest bourgeois luxury. Jerry Jeff Walker, for example, lives in a beautiful sixty-five-thousand-dollar suburban-styled home outside of Austin, complete with modern kitchen, fireplace, sliding paneled doors, swimming pool, and basketball court.

In between takes at the studio, I asked Walker about his house.

"Yeah, I got all that, but I threw my color television set in the swimming pool."

That one incident is reported again and again in article after article on Walker. The disparity between myth and reality was brought thumpingly home when I visited Walker and his friends at his suite in the Spence Manor, Nashville's plushest hotel. Catering especially to rich country music stars and record company executives, the Spence Manor is very expensive; there are no "Rooms To Let, fifty cents" at the Spence, only exclusive three-room suites. Bums, transients, and desperados need not apply.

The night I joined a party in progress at the Walker suite, Jerry Jeff himself was still at the studio, but his friends, Texan Guy Clark ("Desperados," "L.A. Freeway," and now his first album, *Old No. 1*); his wife, Susannah Clark, also a budding songwriter; Dick Feller ("The Coin Machine"); Nashville songwriter Dave Loggins (who scored big last year with his hit record "Please Come to Boston") and his wife; and TV and record star Jim Stafford ("Spiders and Snakes," "Bill") and his girlfriend, Debbie, were enjoying themselves snorting cocaine, smoking pot, taking speed, and drinking Jack Daniels.

"Let's call room service and order a whole bunch of hors d'oeuvres," Susan Walker said.

"Is M.C.A. paying for it?" Guy Clark asked.

"Right!" Susan said. "Of course." She declined the cocaine but accepted a joint.

Guy Clark picked up the guitar and began to strum. Deborah looked over and stared at Clark sitting there half-poised to play.

"Oh . . . play 'Desperados' . . . please play 'Desperados'. . . ."

Dick Feller, a short pudgy man, nodded seriously.

"Guy's version is great," he said. He then started to sweat a little and looked over at Susan Walker. "I mean . . . I like Guy's and Jerry Jeff's, of course . . . they're different."

Like everyone else, Feller cannot afford to alienate Walker, on whose albums he often plays. The session money is too good.

Susan Walker gave her Pepsodent uptown-Dallas smile and nodded her head. "Guy's version is a monster," she said.

"A monster," said Dave Loggins.

Guy went into a rather ragged, coked-out version of the song, and in the chorus everyone joined in: "Like desperados waiting for a train."

Even in the Spence Manor under the influence of booze, coke and dope, Clark made the song come alive.

At the song's conclusion, everyone fell silent for a moment.

After the pause, Jim Stafford began explaining his musical aesthetic to me.

"Think Pop," he said. "I have a sign that says 'Think Pop' on my office door."

"Money, money, money," Susan Walker said. "That's the name of the game!"

"Makes the world go round," David Loggins said.

"Think Pop," Jim Stafford said. "Say, who's got the coke?"

David Allan Coe

Of all the new cowboy rockers to hit the scene, the fastest-rising and most infamous is David Allan Coe. His press release makes him sound like the Definitive Outlaw, and Coe himself has gone to pains to establish his identity as authentic. According to Coe himself, he "spent most of [his] life in institutions, orphanages, reform schools, and jails." This career grande reached its zenith in the early '60s, when Coe was supposedly arrested for burglary, put in Ohio State Prison, and there murdered a man. According to the legend, Coe then got out, receiving a pardon because no one knew he had committed the prison crime and because Johnny Cash heard his songs and intervened on his behalf.

Coe came to Nashville in the late '60s, bummed around the streets, hanging out with the Outlaws, a band of motorcyclists not unlike the Hell's Angels. His first hit record was a single written for Tanya Tucker, the teenage recording star. The song was called "Would You Lay with Me in a Field of Stone," and it proved that beneath the wild, ambitious, and unpredictable presence there was a real talent—sensitive, intelligent, even lyrical.

Coe, however, chose not to go the straight and narrow path—firmly establishing oneself as a songwriter, then cutting an album. He figured he could cut years off his apprenticeship by becoming the baddest, the meanest, the most dangerous outlaw of them all. Where Jerry Jeff was boyish, and Waylon and Willie Nelson were older and obviously playacting, Coe would be the real McCoy, a murderer! Soon he had a new act. David Allan Coe—The Mysterious Rhinestone Cowboy. He took to wearing rhinestone suits and black masks, which made him look like Zorro. Huge, ugly rhinestone earrings hung from his right ear. He'd show all those shit-kickers and Austin creeps who was a bad-ass! In gig after gig, Coe won publicity by challenging the audience to fight him, by mocking Waylon Jennings ("He's just a greaser") and by doing devastating imitations of Jerry Jeff's goofy, friendly smile. Though traditional country fans despised him, Coe got his share of the young, hip audience who loved the new rock sound in country. And he also got another type of fan, the kind who cares nothing for the music but gets faint with excitement at the possibility of spilled blood.

I was sitting in the Exit Inn watching the last set of the David Allan Coe show. Tonight Coe was dressed relatively conservatively in a denim jacket, Levis, cowboy boots, and a big black hat. The rhinestone in his ear shimmered in the night lights. Behind him his band of young Austin-Houston-Tennessee rockers were pouring out the hard-pounding, driving new country sound, while Coe sang his newest hit, "Long Haired Redneck."

"People all say that I'm an outlaw," he wailed.

On the word "outlaw" the entire front rows of people stood up at their tables, raised their glasses and bottles and screamed!

"You tell 'em, David. Outlaws, you tell 'em!!"

These enthusiastic fans were the Outlaws, Coe's old motorcycle gang, and they were a terrifying if predictable sight. Leather jackets, beards, goggles, iron crosses . . . they stamped and screamed and pounded one another on the back.

Coe's voice, hoarse and rather puny to begin with, could barely be heard over the incredible wailing of the guitars, the pounding of feet on the floor.

After his last song, Coe went through a side exit to the outside. He was staggering wildly, and the Outlaws all got on their head gear and trailed after him. I put on my jacket and walked out among the crowd of screeching bikes and screaming, drunken men.

"Gonna ride my hog over the hill. Gonna ride all the way to the mo-tel," Coe shouted.

"You can't ride, David," a short Outlaw said, holding Coe around the middle to keep him from jumping on his big Harley.

"TAKE THE BUS TO THE MOTEL," a fat, powerful-looking Outlaw yelled, his little red eyes burning like a mad razorback's.

"Gonna ride my hog," screamed Coe.

But he didn't get on his bike. Instead, he half fell up the steps of his big bus, which had his name in foot-long black letters on the side.

I followed him on the bus and met a man who claimed to be a childhood friend of Coe's. "David's real drunk," the man said. "But he's not that drunk!"

"What do you mean?"

"Oh, he's just putting on an act. He won't really ride the hog to the motel. He just wants to let them talk him out of it."

"I see. And did he really kill anyone?"

"Hey," the guy said. "You're a writer, aren't you?"

"Yeah."

"Are you the guy who wrote the expose in *Rolling Stone*, the one that said David Allan wasn't a murderer?"

"I never heard of that."

"Good. I think a cunt wrote it, anyway. She said David Allan wasn't a murderer at all, that he was only in on possession of burglary tools."

Suddenly, the little Outlaw with the set jaw of a frothing dog sat down beside me.

"David's a real outlaw," he said, smacking his fist into his palm. "You a writer? You ought to come with us to the motel. You can ask him all about it."

"Okay. Is he driving his hog?"

"No," the little man said, hitting his fist into his palm again. "He's going in his limo."

The bus floated through the Nashville streets and stopped at the James Thompson Motor Inn. I got out and walked with Tommy (the Outlaw) and Coe's old friend, Bobby.

"It's on the fourth floor."

We climbed the steps and walked down a long motel corridor. Looking over, I noticed it was a good seventy-five feet to the parking lot. At the door, Tommy waited for me.

"Come on in, writer."

"Sure."

I felt frightened by his tone—soft, but mocking. I had assumed that there would be women, other musicians, and whiskey. But there was none of that. Instead, there were Outlaws, about fifteen of them, sprawled around the room. I looked at their eyes, which were all trained right on my own. In the exact center of the group, like some ancient fertility god, David Allan Coe sprawled on a bed. On his lap was an ugly, trashed-out looking woman, who was laughing insanely.

Behind me the door snapped shut. "This here is the writer," someone said in a steel-wire voice.

Everyone was totally silent.

"The writer who wrote that shit about David Allan *not* being an outlaw!" someone else said.

I felt my breath leaving me and tried to laugh it off.

"Hey, c'mon, you guys. I didn't write that stuff."

A short, squat, powerful man, the same Outlaw I'd seen screaming at the Exit Inn, came toward me. "You wrote that shit, did you?"

He reached in his back pocket and pulled out a five-inch hunting knife.

"Hey, wait now," I said.

He started flicking the blade at my jacket, my arms and my jaw.

"Stick him and throw him over," someone yelled.

"Got to stick the writer," said a long, bony-looking man with a broken nose and space goggles.

I looked at Coe for assistance. A dull, cruel smile passed across his face. He said nothing.

"Put the knife down," a voice said.

I turned and saw a big, bearded man coming out of the adjoining room. "Everyone cool it," he said.

The man took my arm and guided me into the back room.

"I'm David Allan's brother," he said. "I jes want you to know that it ain't like this most of the time. It's jes that the boys are a little sticky about the *Rolling Stone* article. If you're gonna write something, you be sure and correct that shit now, heh? David Allan has been in institutions all his life. He's an ex-murderer and a real outlaw. He ain't like a lot of these phonies, ya know?"

"Yeah," I said. "I got the picture."

Waylon Jennings

Of all the singers in the new country scene, Waylon Jennings easily has the best voice. For years he had recorded at RCA under Chet Atkins's supervision, and for years everyone in Nashville thought he would be the star to make the big crossover into the all-important Pop Market. It never happened. Instead, Jennings's albums (seven of them) were marred by the very thing that had sent so many excellent singer/songwriters packing off to Austin. Instead of emphasizing Jennings' rich Texas voice, his incredible phrasing and texture, the albums were strictly one-shot, treadmill productions. No matter that a song would be better with a lone steel guitar or a simple rock lead. At Nashville RCA, everything was turned out in the same dull fashion.

It wasn't until Jennings left Nashville RCA and cut *Honky Tonk Heroes*, an album entirely written by Texan Billy Joe Shaver, that he finally really made use of his greatest asset: his voice. Stark, simple, and full of longing for the past, the album is a classic of progressive country. Songs like "Honky Tonk Heroes," "Slow Movin' Outlaw," and "Rose of a Different Name" come at the listener unencumbered with girl choruses, violins, and foul-sounding Al Caiola Romantic Guitars. Interestingly enough, it was on *Honky Tonk Heroes* that Jennings changed his image. Up till then he had been a slick-backed, clean-cut country boy who posed staring off moodily into the sun. On *Honky Tonk Heroes* a new Jennings emerged—The "Outlaw" Waylon Jennings. Complete with beard and black shirt with white pearl buttons, he posed at a glass-strewn table with his band and the three-fingered Billy Joe Shaver. Since that time Jennings has become one of the most popular acts in the country. Right now, his new anthology album, *Outlaws*, is riding high on the country and pop charts. The album features a wanted poster on the front and pictures of Jennings; his wife, singer Jessi Colter; Willie Nelson; and Tompall Glaser, whose own band is called . . . *The Outlaws!*

I met Waylon Jennings at his huge, walnut-paneled office at Glaser Brothers Studios in Nashville. A large, powerful man with deep creases in his face and wide, sensitive eyes, he exudes old-fashioned John Wayne–variety manliness.

As we began to talk, Jennings's secretary came in and gave him a plaque. He had won yet another award as Best Male Singer of the Year.

"Put it somewhere," Jennings laughed. He sat down behind his walnut desk. There were three phones on it, and every couple of minutes they lit up. I couldn't help but think of the incongruity of a man who sings of the last trains and the last gun fights, sitting behind a desk with three white phones and ten red hold buttons on them.

"How do you feel being a cowboy on the one hand and a businessman on the other?"

Jennings shook his head.

"I used ta not like it, but hell, Hoss, if I don't take care of business I'd still be out making those turkeys for Chet. You see, I had to become a businessman or I wouldn't have survived. I been on the road since Kitty Wells was a Girl Scout! I did three hundred days a year on the road for eleven years. On pills . . . I was being destroyed."

"What's all this outlaw stuff now? Isn't it being overkilled?"

Jennings struck a thoughtful pose.

"Yeah, I suppose it is. I don't know where it comes from. I think the fans gave it to me. I was the first outlaw, you know."

"I thought Jerry Jeff Walker was."

"Hell no," Jennings said. "I was the first to buck Nashville . . . not that I have anything against those boys. They just don't ask the artist what he thinks. No, Walker picked up on it after me . . . but you know what?"

Jennings leaned across his desk and peered at me with hugely earnest eyes.

"He never has made it. You know that, doncha?"

"What of David Allan Coe?" I related my story of the knife threats.

"Well, that beats all," Jennings said. "He's crazy. He thinks he's bucking the system, but the test is whether you can play what you want or what they tell you to play. I have control over my life."

Suddenly Jennings looked startled and asked what day it was.

I told him the date.

"Oh, God. I missed Valentine's Day. I got to call Jessi and get her some flowers and candy." A second later Jennings was on the phone with his wife.

"Hello, darling. . . . Yes, I love you and I'm sorry I missed Valentine's Day. . . ."

The Promised Land

"The thing is we might have reached a saturation point with the cowboy-outlaw bit around here, but nationally it's still an open ball park."

The speaker is Tom White, a pale-faced, balding young man who introduced himself as the publisher for many of the best new Austin groups and single acts—acts like Steve Fromholz, Rusty Wier, B. W. Stevenson, Denim, and Asleep At The Wheel. The location is Moonhill Productions, Austin's only major booking agency.

"Do you think of the music as an art form?"

White smiled and shook his head. "No. I tell all my people to think hits."

He got up from his office desk and walked over to a tape machine.

"Music is capitalism," he said. "When I was in college and all this outlaw rock scene was just starting around here, it was true that people wanted to get away from it all. And it was also true that people felt that country-rock was maybe gonna be the next art form. I used to think that Jerry Jeff Walker and Michael Murphey and Willie Nelson might be the Hemingways and Faulkners of our generation. But it's not true. The form is too limited. It's something like a commercial. You can get startling effects, but they don't last . . . they can't be built on, only repeated, with minor variations . . . so, practically, I think that it's a shit heap. Right now, Moonhill Productions is on top of the heap, but basically it's all still shit."

"But some people, like Walker and Nelson, really have done remarkable things with the music."

Tom White shook his head. "Yeah, that's what amazes you. As crummy and corny as it all is . . . all this outlaw business . . . there still is good work being done in the form."

I said goodbye to Tom White and made my way out through the office. On the wall were pictures of Rusty Wier in a cowboy hat and beard, Steve Fromholz in a cowboy hat and beard, B. W. Stevenson in a cowboy hat and beard.

"The second generation of Redneck Rock?"

"Yeah," Tom White said.

Bobby Bridger

Bobby Bridger is a thirty-two-year-old Austinite who left Nashville in 1968. He came to Austin because of the dream, that it was a place where a man's talents wouldn't be wasted, where he wouldn't be run to death.

At El Rancho Restaurant, he drank a Carta Blanca and shook his head.

"Tom White . . . Moonhill . . . they say the forms are no good, but the forms are fine . . . fine . . . if they would just leave them alone! Let them be. But the worst thing is what the musicians themselves have done. The term 'outlaw' is now anathema to me. At first, it was fun, maybe it even meant something, but now it's become a completely synthetic term. You're an outlaw if you wear a cowboy hat and a couple of turquoise rings. I don't call those creeps 'outlaws,' I call them Cowboy Babbitts."

"Aren't you tempted to make it yourself?"

"No! I was doing well at Nashville in the '60s for Monument Records, but I came here to be somebody different . . . we all did. But in seven years, I've seen most people bitten with the success bug. It's not just a few people . . . it's most of them. A few aren't. Willis Ramsey and Townes Van . . . Waylon Jennings and Willie Nelson . . . they are both good musicians, but instead of finding their own way, too many of the younger kids are jumping on their bandwagon."

"What should they be doing?"

"Finding their own voice," Bridger said, shaking his head. "I don't like Jerry Jeff personally, but I'll say this. He is his own man. His songs reflect his personality. Now people like Rusty Wier and the younger crowd . . . their music reflects a commercial myth. . . . I mean originally country-rock united the two cultures, hillbillies and hippies. That was when it was good. Now they are trying to turn it into this big macho American John Wayne trip. It's Nashville all over again. Real talent gets devoured, reshaped, remolded . . . all for the sake of money."

As we finished eating, Bridger told me how he was still hanging on, living cheaply out in the woods in a place called Comanche Trail. Later, we sat in my hotel room and listened to a tape Bridger had brought with him. A startling original work called *Jim Bridger and the Seekers of the Fleece*, the form is a country-epic. Chapters of spoken rhymed couplets are alternated with songs about a real mountain man, Jim Bridger (Bobby Bridger researched his life for three years). The actor Slim Pickens, a close friend of Bridger's and an amateur historian, reads the oral poetry. Bridger himself sings and he is backed up by the Lost Gonzos. The tape lasts for an hour. The story, though familiar, is compelling. Jim Bridger, a tough mountain man, a pioneer, goes west to find the new good place. He finds his Eden in the mountains, marries an Indian girl, but gets sucked into expansionist business schemes. In an attempt to "expand," he loses his world. I listened and was deeply moved. Bobby Bridger picked up the tape and smiled.

"Well," he said. "I guess you can see why I wanted you to hear that!"

"Yeah."

"That's what's happening now with the country-rock scene and to Austin. It's new, brand new, and there's a lot of energy. So much talent. But everything is moving too fast . . . people aren't thinking."

He put on his coat, and we shook hands.

"I love Austin," he said. "And I would hate to see the day when they come in here and do a movie about the place."

"You mean like *Nashville?*"

"Yeah," he said. "Like that."

Postscript

Not counting Larry Flynt, the first piece I ever wrote on entertainers was "Redneck Rock," and as you have now seen, it was an assignment which nearly got me killed. Not for the first time, either, but this time was very "hands-on," trust me. The Geneva police had scared me and then humiliated me, Larry Flynt's brother Jimmy threatened to kill me with a ballbat, and even LeRoy Neiman came up to the *New Times*' offices in search of me, when my less-than-polite piece on him came out. Needless to say I am pretty sure Reggie would like to punch me out, as well.

But up until the time I went down to do my piece on the phenomenon of redneck rock no one had actually pulled a hunting knife on me before.

That, Dear Reader, was some scary shit. And here's what happened after the knife almost pierced my ribs.

After I survived the unpleasant little scene with David Allan Coe and his pals, I made it back to my room at the Spence Motel and called my editor at *New Times*, Jon Larsen. I was wired up to my teeth by almost being stabbed and thrown off the motel roof and I guess I was pretty wound up on the phone:

"Jon," I said, breathlessly. "You can't fucking believe what just happened on this story."

I then riffed through the whole crazy experience, all the while fingering my leather jacket where the hunting knife had sliced it into frazzled tassels.

"Man," I said, winding up my tale of heroic survival against an outlaw gang, "those fuckers almost killed me!"

There was a long silence on Larsen's end. I waited, thinking he was probably feeling pretty bad that he had sent me down here, where I had almost bought the farm. I half expected him to say, "Man, that is really too bad, Bobby. I am so glad you made it, buddy."

But he had other things on his mind:

"Let me ask you this, Bob," he said in a kind of reflective and slightly quizzical voice: "Did the Outlaw's knife actually cut through your leather jacket and into your flesh?"

"Huh?" I said. I was stunned.

"I mean were you actually stabbed? Any blood, Bob?"

"No," I finally said. "But it reduced the arm of my jacket to tattered strips of leather."

Another long silence. Then in a really irritable voice:

"Yeah, I know that, Bob, but if the knife had actually *cut* you we could have had a much more promotable story. We might even make the network news. As it is . . . with just the jacket sliced . . . well, you see my problem. We can't really promote that."

As the old saying goes down on the docks in Baltimore, when I heard that I didn't know whether to shit or go blind. The whole scene had been surreal anyway, but Larsen's reaction was the coup de grace. I couldn't believe it. I started yelling in the phone:

"Well, gee, Jon, I am really fucking sorry, okay? I mean really, man, if I had thought this thing through a little better when the fucking guy took the knife out I would have OFFERED HIM MY FUCKING ARM TO SLICE AND DICE LIKE THE RON POPEIL MAGIC SLICER. I MEAN, IF I HAD ONLY THOUGHT OF MAKING IT ON THE NETWORK FUCKING NEWS INSTEAD OF MY OWN SURVIVAL I GUESS I'D BE A REAL JOURNALIST. SERIOUSLY, LARSEN, I WAS SO SELFISH. LET ME GO BACK TO THE JAMES THOMPSON MOTOR INN AND SEE IF I CAN GET THOSE GUYS TO FINISH THE JOB, FER CHRISSAKES!"

On the other end of the line Larsen was chuckling in his well-bred Harvard way.

"Hahaha. Love working with you, Robert, but next time make sure you take the wound for the team, okay?"

"Holy shit! Fuck you, Jon," I said and hung up.

I walked over to the mini-bar, got out two bottles of Scotch and downed them both in five minutes.

Then I fell into a deep, nightmarish sleep.

I woke up in the middle of the night, and thought, "Well, in a world of pretend outlaws, I finally met some real ones, and Delbert McClinton was dead-on. It wasn't cool, not at all."

On the other hand, I have to admit, having survived it, it makes for one hell of a good story. And that's what being a journalist is all about.

Down at the End of Lonely Street

It is Saturday morning, 1956. I'm twelve years old, sitting in the basement of my Baltimore row house home. I am miserable because I am in love with a girl named Kathy Martin, a girl I have absolutely no chance of speaking to, much less taking out. She is dark, beautiful, and though I don't know it at the time, she is from a rather well-to-do family. This accounts for her social polish, her style, her ineffable grace. My family's lack of money, our stone Baltimore provinciality, our very real working-class fears combined with our very loony super-stitions, sense of doom . . . all of these have conspired to make me play the fool. When I see Kathy in the hall at school I stammer, attempt hopeless jokes, and suddenly see myself as Ralph Kramden. Over-weight, sickly, too damned sensitive for my own good, and unable to tell anyone about it for fear of seeming unmanly. In short, there seems no release, except in movies, books, and this brand new thing on the radio called rock 'n' roll.

Every Saturday morning I trek down to the half club cellar (we don't have enough money to have a full Club Cellar, which is my mother's small dream) and I sit in the cool shadows and turn on the Buddy Deane Radio Show: Buddy Deane is a Southerner, from Pine

Bluff, Arkansas. He has made it big in Baltimore with both a radio show and a weekday TV dance program à la Dick Clark. Buddy, however, will never be as successful as Dick Clark, because Buddy is a hick. His mouth is too wide, his teeth are too big, his hair too long and greasy. He is too obviously a Baltimore local, destined for the small time. There is on Buddy Deane, in spite of his local success, the stamp of failure. Like myself, he is too eager to please, too vulnerable, too obviously ready for a rebuke.

In many ways Buddy Deane seems the embodiment of the Baltimore Myth. "Do your job, but don't shoot too high, don't try for too much." Or as my father always said, 'The bastards will get you in the end. The smart boys in New York . . . they know how to get it, and they grab it all. . . ." Best, under such imposing restrictions, to finish high school, marry a nice girl from around the neighborhood, buy a row house, have a coupla kids, eat a few hard crabs, drink a little National Bohemian Beer, watch the Birds and Colts; and . . . well, that's it. Already I have seen the older boys in our neighborhood doing just these things and I have no reasonable doubt that someday (if anyone will have me) I will do likewise.

Yet there is something else in me, something gleaned from movies, from books and from the radio—something so small that almost any put-down could make it seem ridiculous, foolish, absurd. But then it blossoms forth again, in a random act of violence like smashing Northwood Elementary School's windows, or ramming a shopping cart into the side of a car—stupid acts, and ones I pay heavily for in guilty, sleepless nights.

But all the same, it is *there*, not only in me but on the radio— barely conscious, like an itch. Buddy Deane is part of it too. And on this particular morning, as I sit in an old lawn chair, a John R. Tunis book in my hand, listening half-heartedly to Buddy's Top Ten, he becomes crucial. The Number One record is something called "Dog-faced Soldier" by the Russ Morgan Band, and I listen groggily, aware of the mounting heat, of the sound of my father getting out the old hand mower. I know he will come in soon to get me to help him. I dread it. Another day on the damned lawn: bugs, sun, nothing. . . .

Deane does a shill for some acne medicine, and then his voice breaks out of its customary slick patter and takes on a quizzical tone. He says, "Now I've got something, well, *strange* here. It's a new record, and I'm going to be honest with you: I don't know if you are going to like it or not." There's a pause, dead air, as if Buddy Deane is stumbling to express himself. "This is the craziest record I've ever heard. I don't even know how I feel about it. But I do know one thing—I've never heard anything like it."

I can feel myself growing tense. My hands grip my book, while outside I see my father's feet shuffle by the basement window, the mower chopping away the crabgrass. "This record is called 'Heartbreak Hotel,'" Deane says. "It's by a new young singer named Elvis Presley. Whether you like it or not, call in, and let me know what you think." He gives the number of the station, then he spins the disc.

Years later, in college, I will learn Edmund Wilson's term, "the shock of recognition." It describes that transcendent moment when you lose yourself entirely in a book, because the author is expressing perfectly all the longings that lay buried nameless within you. You become conscious of yourself and the great shared human spirit. On this day, sitting in my cellar, I have no words to describe what is happening to me. I only know pure, perfect physical and mental bliss. Every syllable of this Elvis Presley's voice speaks urgently, directly, powerfully to me: "Down at the end of Lonely Street at Heartbreak Hotel."

Instantly I can see it, feel it, touch it all . . . I'm there . . . I've always been there . . . on the blackest of streets . . . and I can see the bellhop, his face in his hands, and the desk clerk, sitting behind a worm-eaten desk with his black shirt, black face. Behind him are the letter slots, but they are empty today, tomorrow, forever—it's the saddest, loneliest tableau in the world, and the singer's voice, expertly complemented by the raw blues guitar (and I have never heard the word "blues"), makes this world seem an ideal. It's not like my sadness over Kathy Martin, over the dull brute facts of my life—instead it's a *perfect* loneliness, a perfect dream space where all the pain is around me and yet I'm magically protected from it by the tough, vulnerable, infinitely sensual voice.

Nothing in my entire life has hit me with the force of the first moment I hear Elvis Presley sing "Heartbreak Hotel." I literally cannot bear for the song to end, and when it does I race upstairs and call the station (something I had previously considered infinitely "uncool," the kind of thing stupid girls do). I have been transformed, overwhelmed, and I don't care who knows it. Apparently, however, other kids in our great sluggard of a city have been sitting right next to their phones, for the line is busy—and keeps being busy for half an hour. (Meanwhile, I race back down to the cellar and turn the radio up, just in case the song is played again.) After forty minutes I give up and go downstairs to stay, while Buddy Deane begins to tally the results.

Again he sounds altered, stunned. "We've never had a response like this," he says. "Already there have been hundreds of calls—and so far almost all of them have said the song is going to be a big hit." He stumbles again. "And what's more, most of the callers have asked us to play the song again, and, so here we go, Elvis Presley singing, 'Heartbreak Hotel.'"

The song starts again, and instantly I am transported as I had been the first time. The exquisite pleasure I get from Presley's voice—the way it seems to put me in touch with something infinite and magical—is so baffling to me, so wonderful, that after the song finishes for the second time, I'm so dazed I can't remember his *name*. I know it is something weird, wild and lovely and sweet all at once. I have to own the record, without delay. . . . Even at age twelve I am self-conscious enough to wonder, "Why am I acting like this?" But the answer doesn't seem to matter.

Upstairs, I riffle through my top drawer (knocking my tube of Butch Wax on the floor), find about eighty-nine cents (the price of a 45), race down the steps and get on my old rusted-up American Flyer named "Betsy" (after Davy Crockett's rifle). Waving goodbye to my father, I open the gate to the backyard and start pedaling the two miles through our row house neighborhood toward recently opened Northwood Shopping Center (the city's second shopping center, and to our eyes a wonder to shame Frank Lloyd Wright).

My bike is three years old, a wreck; the pedaling is hard, across a parched Little League diamond and up a good long hill. Finally I get to the turnoff at Hillen Road and make my way up the huge new macadam parking lot to the Music Mart. Leaning my bike on the red brick wall outside Food Fair, I race inside and stare at the record racks.

The display is a Top 40 singles board, with each hit record stacked on a thick peg that resembles the spindle of my plastic pink-and-black record player. I look at the records quickly, trying to get Pat's attention. Pat is a red-haired, freckled woman with a ponytail. She and her husband run the store, but he is rarely around. Or if he is, we boys don't notice—for Pat is lithe and sexy, and we are all secretly in love with her.

She's busy, so I look at the part of the board where she keeps new releases. No luck. I begin to feel a pang of disappointment. . . . The record isn't there, and I can't remember the singer's name. Eventually, Pat turns, smiles at me, and says, "Hi, Bobby, can I help you?"

"Well," I stammer, "there was this record on the radio, on Buddy Deane, you know? It was called 'Heartbreak Hotel' and it was by a guy called . . . Melvis Peasley, I think." She looks at me as if I'm a seed pod from *Invasion of the Body Snatchers*.

"It's by who?" she says.

"Melvis Persley . . . or Gelvis Pesley . . . I can't remember the guy's name." I suddenly feel like the biggest fool in the history of the world. Christ, I've pedaled like a maniac through the hundred-degree Baltimore heat, and 103 percent humidity, my shirt is soaking wet, I can hardly stand up . . . and I can't get the guy's name right. Then I remember the effect the song had on me, and I almost yell at her, "Listen, I know I sound like a nut, but Pat, I'm telling you this guy Belvis . . . Pesley is going to be the greatest singer of all time!"

Pat shakes her ponytail, gives me a "Yeah, yeah" shrug, then turns away.

"If it comes in," I say, "call me." She turns back around and stares at me curiously. "You ought to go get a Coke and get out of the sun," she says, smiling.

Then she takes my number and I leave. I grab Betsy and drift on down to the Arundel Ice Cream Parlor, get myself a root beer float and sit outside, sipping and staring at the half-built department store. The Hecht Company—the last and greatest building in the shopping center.

I'm disappointed, but something new and warm and good seems to be born inside me. It is almost a physical presence, a kind of tough warmth. It is as though I have found a secret friend—a great, wonderful, tough but sensitive older brother who has been through all I have been through and a lot more. And as I sit there in the killer heat, I begin to feel strangely good about everything. Real fine. Solid. Not so lonely anymore. Not so worried about Kathy Martin. I have never felt anything like it before and I don't bother to analyze it. It just seems that somehow, in the most unlikely way, something really wonderful has happened to me, at long last. And I reason, as I start the long, sweaty bike trip home, that something else might happen again. And it too might be good.

All the way down steaming Hillen Road, I sing part of that song by what the hell was his name? "The bell hop's always crying, the desk clerk's dressed in black. They been so long down on Lonely Street, they'll never oh never get back. It's been so lonely, baby, so lonely, baby. Baby, so lonely . . . I could die."

God, I feel good singing those sad words. Pedaling and sweating and singing, I have never felt so goddamned good in my whole life. Whatever his name is, I love him. His great, distant/near, tender/rough voice lifts me up, gives me strength, courage, and above all, ecstasy. He is mine, all mine. . . .

Now it is August 1977, and I am thirty-three years old. I have abandoned the city of my youth (and feel strangely guilty about it, as though I have carelessly sliced away a piece of my soul) and am living in New York. There is no lawn to be cut where I now live, and the local "shopping center" is midtown Manhattan. My life lacks no novelty. If I am bored, I can take a six-minute walk and be in the theatre district for a play or a movie. If I am hungry, I am two minutes away from several of the best French restaurants in the United States. I am writing a commissioned screenplay on this particular evening, and outside of a recurring ulcer problem I'm feeling pretty good.

Still, there are always things to be traded away for success. Without sentimentalizing it, I miss the sense of neighborhood that Baltimore offered. I miss the fierce, close friendships that I grew up taking for granted. And, of all things, I miss a sense of continuity.

Often while walking my dog at night I think of how few things I have carried over with me. Practically nothing material . . . a few old records . . . a black-and-white television set that I no longer use . . . a few old books, and nothing else. During these moments I will be hit with a sense of panic, a terrible feeling that I must be drawn back, back to Baltimore, to streets that have my own signature on them. Yet, I don't go. The action is here, and I am a man who thrives on it now. Or at least that's what I tell myself. Still, the feeling remains constant, ghostlike, always ready to surface at some hint of the past . . . like a desperate call from an old friend. . . .

I sit at my desk, trying to figure out the logistics of a scene, when the phone rings. Automatically I pick it up, and automatically I assume my professional voice of authority. (One wants to be ready to face failure of friends with a mask of tough courtesy.) I can tell immediately from the tone of the static on the wire that the call is long distance, and I feel a certain tension . . . long distance might mean California . . . might mean career. . . .

But it's not the present or future calling at all . . . it's the past. My father is on the line and he sounds tired, older than usual.

"Hello, Bobby?"

"Yeah. Hi, Dad."

"Listen . . . how you doing?"

"Okay. . . . Good. . . ."

"That's great, son. I got to thinking of you tonight, you know, when I heard that Elvis Presley died. You know how much you used to like his records."

Instantly, all my professional cool—all the defenses that I have proudly erected—are obliterated. I almost start to laugh. It's too damned much . . . like a cheap novel. Your old man . . . the one person you can't bullshit . . . your old man calling you . . . to tell you that a rock singer—he was just a goddamned rock singer, fer Chrissakes, and it's not like you were buying his records anymore . . . but Elvis Presley dying.

"How can he be dead, Dad?" I'm numb, unable to talk.

"They found him on the floor. You didn't know? God, I thought you'd hear sooner in New York."

"No, Dad, I didn't know. Christ, I can't believe it, but I feel like I could start crying. That's ridiculous, isn't it. Jesus."

There is a long pause, and then my dad sighs deeply: "I remember the Christmas we gave you that record with 'Jailhouse Rock' on it," he says. "You played that damned record until I thought I would go nuts."

"Yeah," I say, so ridiculously shaky. It's like your own past coming to bury you. . . . I think of a couple of years ago, when I had forgotten all about Elvis. My girl and I were driving in upstate New York when "Suspicious Minds" came on the radio, and I had to stop the car, I was so moved. Moved that he could still do it, that he was still *great* . . . when I had almost consigned him to my great submerged past. (One I wanted to forget in a lot of ways. Best to live now. Travel light. Reflect little. Keep moving. *Score*.)

"Well, I don't want to bother you if you're working," my father says. "I just miss you. You ought to come down to Baltimore soon."

"Yeah," I say, suddenly feeling dizzy, sick. "Yeah . . . in two weeks. Yeah." I tell him I love him, and hang up, and sit there remembering 1956, how far I've come, how much I've left behind, and how he was one of the things you took for granted that you'd always have around. And now . . . Christ . . . he's gone. You were sitting with Denny Blake and Ned Myers at the Boulevard Movie, flipping out over *Jailhouse Rock*, and he is dead.

During the next few days, "Elvis" is all you hear. THE KING IS DEAD screams every paper, every TV show. You are told by Walter Cronkite, you watch a sixty-minute assessment of Elvis's career by noted social philosopher Charles Kuralt, during which Kuralt attempts to "put Elvis into the perspective of the '50s." You retch a bit as you watch one of the brilliant devices used in this instant documentary: They juxtapose Elvis with other "things that made it big in the '50s," among them "instant coffee and power lawnmowers." You stare like a tranquilized goon as they carry his body down Elvis Presley Boulevard, and you hear amiable newsmen fake sympathy so they can elicit a little grief from the thousands of mourners outside Graceland.

Yet the TV flacks seem befuddled when the grief is real. Usually their patter assumes a Ted Baxter solemnity: "They came thousands of miles in pickups, in beaten Chevys, in Greyhound buses. Mostly they were white, middle-aged, Southern, and poor." The operative word is "they." Oh, yes, "they." The "*they*" of the world being your old man, your mother down in funky, mill-town Baltimore. The "*theys*" who never even heard of the Hamptons, or could imagine a "private screening," and thought backgammon might be some faggot version of dominoes. And suddenly as I watch, all the old redneck in me comes out and I want to call the stupid bastards and say . . . say . . . what? What could I say? Unlike Elvis, I had left my home. I wasn't New York, but I wasn't Baltimore either. Not anymore.

But I could still grieve. I could remember. I could be a little proud that a few months back I had been offered a job to coauthor a book with three of Elvis's bodyguards, and I had instantly turned it down because it smelled of shit. Now that book, *Elvis: What Happened?*, had hit the stands, had a five-million printing, and its author, Steve Dunleavy, would become rich. Dancing on the grave. A true Heartbreak Hotel. I could sit and wait for the call from my mother, who secretly loved Elvis, and I could hear her say "Do you know this Steve Dunleavy character? No? Well, if you ever see him, tell him I think he is a creep. I saw him on Geraldo Rivera and I wanted to kick in the TV set. Elvis was a good boy."

I sit around my sweltering apartment feeling dazed, trying to sort it out. . . . Elvis's huge talent, the rich mystery of his voice, which like Garbo's face was always just beyond reach of exposition. How many times had I heard people do Elvis imitations (or done them myself) to the amusement and knowing smiles of our friends? Yet we knew that we had missed it. The voice was his signature. His genius. Not ours. The true magic was that Elvis's voice spoke to us so naturally that we assumed ownership.

Indeed, another call comes from my oldest Baltimore pal, Richard Moss, now working for the government in D.C. He tells me that he has just come from the Egyptian Embassy where young Egyptian bureaucrats sat humming "Love Me Tender," drinking wine, and feeling as blue as the housewives who waited up all night outside of Graceland.

The shock of losing him . . . for me the shock of the shock, as well . . . is not unlike the trauma of losing JFK or Martin Luther King. In spite of all the smears written about all three of them, they seemed an extension of what we believed best in ourselves.

So why the meanness in the press coverage? Perhaps there is a deeper sadness here. A sadness which transcends one great American's death. It is the sadness of my generation, many of whom (perhaps myself included) cannot get used to the idea that we are mortal. Of course, Elvis was our symbolic Never-Aging Rebel. And, of course, he manipulated the image, and grew rich and famous off of it.

And we went for it. We went for it in the '50s, when we needed it. When we needed—oh, how we needed—to cut out; hit the road, Jack; ride the mystery train.

And we went for it again, in a bigger way, in the '60s . . . when most of us literally did the things we dreamed of doing (and that we though Elvis *was* doing) in the '50s. We headed down the American Highway never thinking that the last exit could be Heartbreak Hotel.

Which brings us to now . . . now that we are having trouble with *our* weight, have been through one or two marriages, have seen ourselves easy prey to the petty careerist jealousies and all the other human frailties we so loudly proclaimed abolished. It's as though we are unleashing our own sense of failure, of bitterness, on our first love:

"We loved you. You were our Youthful God, and when we believed in you, you made us believe we too were gods. And then you went and did it, man. You got old, you got fat, you grew lazy, confused. And then you went down the crapper. You flunked, baby. You weren't a legend at all. You were only a mortal, and a Southern shitkicker to boot, like your shitkicker fans. And you left us all alone."

And so some of us feel he failed us in some essential way. That, or he cheated us. He was romantic in the '50s, that most existential of ages. And we loved him for ushering in our own Romance. Which is, of course, what I felt that day in my cellar . . . the Call . . . the First Stirrings of the Call. . . . Not merely sex, but Art, Beauty, Perfection, Idealism . . . and we lived it to the hilt in the '60s. But now we've become older, more tired, cynical, and, quite frankly, afraid. His death is too much for us, because he represented too much to us . . . all our love, and good bodies, but also all our own terrible, sensational, and grotesque waste.

Yet, like our hometowns, like our parents whom we once rejected—like our own pasts—finally we are powerless to reject Elvis without severing the vital connections that keep us alive. His life was a triumph over low birth, lack of education, and a deadening conformist era that broke many a more advantaged man's heart. He taught us how to begin to feel, what it meant to turn yourself loose. He seized his time, and he gave it back to us—recharged, renewed, filled with all the courage, tension, and sweetness that made up his own complex and lonely heart. In short, he was simply one of us—and for a very long time, one of the best. As Auden wrote on the death of W. B. Yeats, "He became his admirers." It is Elvis's legacy, and his challenge to us, that we do as well for those other children of the dead '70s, sitting alone in their dark cellars, waiting for the Word.

A Fistful of Critics

Paco is in a world of trouble. He has this noose around his neck, see, and he is balanced ever so precariously on this tombstone, which is just about to tip over on the godforsaken plain. Miles and miles of sagebrush. Not a human being in sight. Check that. There is one, well, semi-human nearby. Only a couple of hundred yards away, really. The problem is, Paco's lone potential savior is the very man who strung him over the hanging tree to begin with. Paw's last best hope lives with this squinting, poncho-clad, cigarillo-smoking, black-hat-wearing, lean, long drink o' water who likes killing better than breath itself. Oh, things do look grim for the sleazy little Mexican hustler. Any second that marker is going to tip over and it'll be snaperoo city. So Paco—tough, wily Paco—is reduced to pleading, belly-screeching for help.

"Come back. . . . Come back. . . . Don't leave me here!"

But The Man With No Name is just ambling onward, receding into the purple-speckled sky. The son of a bitch has done that the entire time the two of them have been hustling for gold, just ambling about, squinting and smoking, and every so often drawing crossed guns from underneath his serape and blowing big holes in

*twenty, thirty, forty guys at a time. And it doesn't look like he's about
to change now. There he goes, as pleasant and casual as you like,
riding slowly, slowly away. His horse's tail brushes away the annoy-
ing desert mosquitoes and you know The Man With No Name is
enjoying every second Paco is twisting, sweating, pissing himself as
his sweaty, scumbag life drips away. Oh, Lord, the Man is cool.*

*Now Paco is reduced to twittering birdcalls—"Don't leave
Paco . . . don't leave him. . . . Hey. . . . Hey . . ."—talking about
himself in the third person. He's already cashing it in. The Man
With No Name is just at the crest of an impossibly barren hill.
Around him is something that looks like burning driftwood. He
turns slowly, ever so slowly, squints into the camera and takes out
his rifle. With one hand he brings the sight up to eye-slit level
and fires. Paco's rope snaps, the mangy greaseball crumbles to the
ground. He gets up, starts to run for the hill. The Man With No
Name has a heart after all. He hasn't let old Paco hang. Now he'll
get him out of this hellhole of a desert. He runs, runs. . . .*

*But, oh, Sweet Virgeeen, The Man With No Name is turning
around again. Receding into the mirages at that slow, sadistic sidle,
just fast enough to stay out of Paco's reach. And Paco is running,
screaming. "Wait! Wait, you devil. Wait for Paco!" And he keeps
running, as the eerie conch shell music crescendos and The Man
With No Name ambles toward the setting sun.*

It is 1969 and I am just emerging from *The Good, the Bad, and
the Ugly*, starring this actor I vaguely remember from the TV show
Rawhide, a guy named Clint Eastwood. Truth be told, I went to the
theater for laughs, because my liberal literary friends across the country had been telling me that the ultimate in moronic mindlessness had
been born, the dumbest actor of all time, starring in the most ridiculous movie since *Teenagers from Outer Space*. So I had gone, stoned on
uppers, grass, and Romilar, ready for an experience in High Camp,

like seeing *The Son of Flubber* or the Three Stooges in Spanish (for my money, still one of the primo experiences to be had on TV). What I had in mind was ecstasy; I would get stoned on the purity of the lameness.

But I had been surprised, shocked, stunned. Even through the haze of my chemical aids I had seen something in this discarded TV actor that I hadn't expected. To put it bluntly, I had been thrilled by the damned movie, and this embarrassed me. I strolled out and tossed off the usual liberal folderol—"He sure does squint good"—but I felt like a coward. For what my frontal brain was telling me and what my visceral reactions truly were . . . well, Jack, they was at definite odds. There was something about him—that poncho, that cigar, that black hat . . . the way he held the gun. Goddamn. Though I wouldn't have the courage to say it, I knew right then that here was the heir to John Wayne.

But more than that, he was also the Rolling Stones; there was a wonderful sadistic/good-guy edge going on there, everything done so damned stylishly that he just had to know that he was overdoing it. (Or did he? No, he couldn't.) His movies were "spaghetti Westerns," and it was important not to like anything D-U-M-B, wasn't it? And whatever else, even the movie crit crowd had to admit that the picture was "visually rich."

But to hell with that stuff: What had gotten to me was Clint Eastwood. The guy was the Ultimate Legendary Mythic Cowboy, the Stranger from Nowhere. There was a little of Richard Widmark's Tommy Udo in him, the thrill of the sensual sadist, like Jagger singing "Paint It Black." Hey, this here Clint Eastwood was one mean motherfucker. (But I'd never tell a soul.)

Well, those days are long gone. Clint Eastwood—that maligned, critic-punished, low-graded, scoffed-at, cast-off, spaghetti Western–making, *Dirty Harry* "fascist" (critic Pauline Kael's term), male-chauvinist, robot-faced, talentless apex of nadir—has only gone on to become the biggest superstar in the film world. He has been the top box-office draw, or close to it, in nine out of the last ten years. And now even such highbrows as John Simon and Andrew Sarris are grudgingly giving ground. These days it's a basic tenet of all those with literary pretensions that a "sense of irony" is the common denominator of heightened sensibility. So now critic Molly Haskell is commenting on Clint Eastwood's "ironic stance." Just like they used to with Henry "Hank" James and other American Real Honest-To-God Artists. So the worm has turned indeed. No longer do I have to defend seeing *Dirty Harry* or *Magnum Force* forty times. Clint Eastwood is okay to like.

ABSOLUTELY NO PARKING—RESERVED FOR CLINT EASTWOOD says the sign in front of Big Clint's *Big Sleep*–style Mexican hacienda on the Warner Brothers lot in Burbank. God knows I'm not going to try and cross him. He could hop out of his car and, seeing me in his office, string me up to the chandelier. Little reptilian eyes glowering at me, he tips the chair under my feet. . . . Hellfire, let me park in Santa Monica and bus back out here rather than risk that!

Once inside, I don't feel any more secure. Everywhere are posters of Big C. Here, he's hanging from a mountain in *The Eiger Sanction;* there, tracking you with the infamous .44 Magnum from a *Dirty Harry* world he never made (but is sure as hell going to clean up); over there he's holding a killer cannon in *Thunderbolt and Lightfoot.*

Suddenly (could Clint appear in any other way?) he is ambling across the room, smiling a cascade of white teeth, looking down at me from six-foot-six of pure sinew and grit. And it's not the Man With No Name squint, or *Dirty Harry*'s killer smile; he seems actually friendly, all genial Californian charm. And definitely the most handsome person of either sex I've ever met. Christ, at forty-seven, the way he is poured into his Levis, leather boots, and powder-blue T-shirt with a sunburst of Aztec god on the front . . . the sun god comes off a poor second.

"Good to see you," he says. "Come on into the office."

Aha, I think, the office. Gun racks, victims' shrunken heads, gorgeous dames whom he never kisses. But alas, it's anybody's comfortable California exec office, with a big mahogany desk, Mexican couch, some homey table lamps. Nothing faintly evil, macho, or even tacky-dumb. The only sign that it's Eastwood's lair at all is the weight machine in the corner and some sporting trophies on top of a big Spanish cabinet. Golf, tennis—civilized sports.

It's too normal. Eastwood is offering me a beer, sitting down on the couch, stretching out his long, lean body, getting down-home cozy and running through his early years, when his family drifted around California, finally settling in Oakland. It says here he went to trade school.

"I took aircraft," he says casually. "I rebuilt one plane engine, and a car engine too. I never had any dough so I could never afford anything very nice. I think kids go through certain times, in certain towns, where cars are their whole life. Cars first, chicks second."

"Yeah," I say, "that's how it was in Baltimore. Baltimore and Oakland are a lot alike . . . working-class towns. We used to go down to junkyards and buy engines, bring them back and open them up, just to see how they worked."

Eastwood smiles. "I used to buy engines. I used to go to junkyards and buy engines on spec. I remember once I bought a '39 Ford, a modified T-Roadster, and the damn thing ran like a charm. I was really surprised."

He seems to have been more interested in cars than in acting. His film bio says he never acted in a school play.

"No," he says. "Once, when I was in junior high school, I did a one-act play. It was part of an English class, an assignment, and the teacher gave me the lead. I guess to help me, because I was an introverted kid."

For a second I'm surprised, but then it seems natural. Though Eastwood's heroes are all men of action, they are also painfully shy. They look as though they want to speak but aren't sure enough of their words. They seem afraid to appear foolish. Obviously, then, Eastwood draws on his own introversion, gets an aesthetic distance from it and creates that sense of menace that lurks just beneath the surface of all his best and most violent creations.

"We had to put it on for the senior high school, and I was so scared I almost cut school that day. But I finally did it—it was a comedy—and it went over fairly well. So I thought, 'I managed to do that.'"

His first comedy. Eastwood's movies are *all* comedies. His natural flair for hyperbole creates a wild, black humor and it seems important that his first role, the one in which the introverted grease monkey first realized he had some sort of artistic sensitivity, was a laugher. Yet, one can't be sure. The word on the street is that Clint is perhaps not so . . . bright. Maybe he just doesn't know his movies are a riot. I am still more than a little jumpy about asking him; what if he doesn't find it so funny and pulls his .44?

"So it was a comedy?" I venture timidly.

"Yeah," says Eastwood, leaning back in the perfect California mellow slouch. He seems so damned relaxed. Maybe I can risk it.

"One of the, ah, things that makes your movies different from say, Charles Bronson's, is the humor . . . wouldn't you say?"

"Yeah," he squints. "I like action adventure movies, but there is a humor aspect. I love to laugh, and I enjoy it when other people laugh, and I hope other people do."

Dirty Harry is walking headfirst into a trap. Some psycho is hellbent on chopping off his hands and gouging out his eyes. Harry is walking down a dark alley. The killer waits. It looks like the Big

Casino for our man. I am on the edge of my chair, terrified. Behind me, a black guy can no longer stand the angst. He stands up in his seat and begins to scream:

"Ceee Eeeeeeee!" he yells. "C.E. won't fall for that shit. No. Way. That's my main man, C.E."

"'C.E.,'" Eastwood laughs. "'C.E. won't fall for that shit!' I'll have to remember that one. I like that. That guy has paid his dough and he just wants to be taken on a trip. Now, there's all kinds of levels. Hopefully, you can move people on other levels too. But that's great, when he's talking with you. I've been in movies where the guy was talking against you. That's not so great."

"Yeah," I laugh. "I couldn't believe you were in *Francis the Talking Mule*."

Eastwood chuckles. "I've been in some of the worst films ever made. I started out at Universal with one- or two-liners. Sometimes, if you were lucky, you had three or four lines. Say, are you all right?"

Eastwood has noticed that I am filling up scores of handkerchiefs with nasal New York venom. "You ought to have some tea and an oatmeal cookie," he says.

Not me. Nobody ever took an oatmeal cookie from Dirty Harry. It's probably got tiny projectile "oats" which spring out and perforate your jaw.

"No," I say. "I'm not allowed anything with caffeine in it."

"But this is herb tea," Clint assures me. "No caffeine. And these oatmeal cookies are out of sight. Wait, I'll get them for you."

He returns a few seconds later with a steaming mug and the largest oatmeal cookie in the Western Hemisphere. He waits for my judgment.

"Delicious," I say.

"See," says Clint. 'That's just what you need."

"Right." I take another bite. Not bad. "I understand you did a lot of tough gigs before you became an actor," I say through the crumbs.

"I was a firefighter, a lumberjack, I was in the army and I dug swimming pools," he offers, "but I never knew what I wanted to do. A lot of people have long-range ambition, but I never had that. I thought I might be a musician for a while, but every time I'd get going there'd be an interruption."

He stops, stares at the ceiling.

I wonder why he was aimless for so long. "What did your parents do?"

"Well, later in life, when we lived in Oakland, my dad worked for a container corporation. Before that he worked as a pipe fitter for Bethlehem [Steel] and in gas stations."

"So, like your characters, you kind of wandered."

"Sure," Eastwood says. "And I use that. My dad finally started doing well about the time I was out of high school, but by that time I was pretty much on my own anyway . . . drifting around."

There is a hint of loneliness in Eastwood's voice. Not self-pity, but something lost, something he missed in childhood: security, closeness. Clearly, he has fed off that loss.

"You had no intention of being an actor in those days?"

"Jesus, no," Eastwood smiles. "I always felt the same thing that everybody felt about actors, that they were extroverted types who like to get up in front of two thousand people and make an ass out of themselves. I still don't like to get up in front of two thousand people, unless I have some lines to read. But to stand up there just as Joe Clyde . . . whew."

"Joe Clyde" . . . a curious phrase from the '50s I used to hear in Baltimore. Meaning, of course, Joe Nobody. Indeed, Joe Clyde could be the collective self-image of the working class, the same class that scarfs up Eastwood's pictures.

He smiles and explains how he made the transition from Joe Clyde to bit actor.

"I got drafted into the army. I was a swimming instructor at Fort Ord, California. It was a pretty good job, as far as keeping me off the front line, anyway. After I got out I came down here and went to Los Angeles City College on the GI Bill. I was twenty-three. This friend of mine was an editor, and he introduced me to a cinematographer, who made a film test of me just standing there—a shot here, a shot there—and Universal put me under contract at seventy-five dollars a week. I thought that was great stuff, but I was a little apprehensive. I mean, I didn't know what it was going to be like when I had to start playing scenes *in front of people*. But I thought, what the hell, as long as they are paying . . . it was a hell of a lot more money than I would be making on the GI Bill. So I thought, 'Well, I'll just give it a good try. I'll give it six months.' But you can't give it six months, 'cause nothing works out that quick. So what you do is you give it six, and then six more, and pretty soon it gets in your blood and you really want it.

"I kicked around there for a year and a half, but then they dropped their program and kicked me out, dropped my option. So then I did a lot of TV, both in New York and LA, and bounced around there. I was actually getting better parts in television than I was at Universal. But then I had a real slack period for a year or two."

"When you were bouncing around, was there ever a sense of desperation? You know, 'Christ, I'm not getting anywhere' . . . ?"

"I'll never forget," Eastwood says with that *Dirty Harry* smirk. "I did a whole mess of shows for a year or so, then all of a sudden not much was happening around town, a lot of strikes and stuff, and I started collecting unemployment. But I couldn't just do that, so I'd go and get jobs. I got a job digging swimming pools, and I'd be running back at my lunch hour and call my agent and ask, 'What's happening?' And he'd say, 'Nothing.'

"I finally got to a state where I was really depressed and I was going to quit. You know, I was married, no kids. But I got to do this one picture, a B movie, a little cheapo—did it in nine days, really a grindout. It was called *Ambush at Cimarron Pass* and I did it and forgot it. And then another slack period, no jobs, nothing, I hadn't been employed for months. The movie finally came out and I went with my wife down to the little neighborhood theater, and it was *soooo* bad. . . . I just kept sinking lower and lower in my seat. I said to my wife, 'I'm going to quit, I'm really going to quit. I gotta go back to school, I got to start doing something with my life.' I was twenty-seven."

"That's the age you start to question yourself . . . moving toward thirty. . . ."

"Yeah," Clint says. "I was saying, 'What am I doing here . . . spinning my wheels?' and thinking this is the only profession in the world where there are three or four jobs and seven million people all want 'em, you know? The competition is really intense. You go into a producer's office to audition for a part, and there are ten guys all sitting around, your size and your color. And you look at them like this . . ." Eastwood stares out of the side of his eyes, scared, flipped out, ". . . and you think, 'There's another one that's going to go into the toilet.'" He stops and lets out a sigh.

"After a while you start thinking, 'Well, I wonder if I'll blow this one on the handshake.' I started thinking I must be really bad because *Wagon Train* and all these other series were coming up, and I wouldn't even be able to get in the front door. If I did get to meet the producer, the guy would give me a handshake, the dead stare, put the cigar out in the ashtray, and say, 'Sure, we'll get in touch with you, we'll call your agent.'"

"That must have done a job on your spirits."

"Oh . . ." Eastwood moans. "You have absolutely no control. It's not like any other profession. If you're a physician or something you can set up practice and work. It got so bad, I said, 'I just can't stand this anymore,' knocking your head against the wall, coming up empty. I was never a particularly good salesman, either. I couldn't go in and . . . like some other guys give the producer some good gags and a lot of hotshot stuff, and they'd get the parts. So I started thinking, 'I've got to go back to school.' I was thinking of all kinds of alternatives."

"What *were* your alternatives?"

'That was the problem, I had never really figured any out. So I was visiting this friend of mine, she was a story reader for Studio One, Climax. And I was talking to her, just having a coffee or tea or something, and a guy walks over and says, 'How tall are you?' And I thought, why does he care how tall I am? But I said, 'Well, six-six and I'm an actor,' but I wasn't very enthusiastic because I figured screw it, I'd had it. The guy says, 'Well, could you come into my office for a second?' and meanwhile my friend is behind me motioning, 'Go, go!'

"It turns out he develops all the new shows for CBS. So I say, 'Would you mind telling me what this is all about?' and he says, 'Well, this is a new, hour-long Western series' . . . because *Wagon Train* was a hit and they were all getting on the bandwagon I thought, 'This could be something . . . but I was dressed about like this." Eastwood points to his jeans, his two-hundred-dollar boots, and his blue Aztec T-shirt, ". . . a slob."

"All of a sudden I realize, 'Hey, I'm playing this like it's zero, I better sit up straight.' So the guy says, 'We'd like to talk to you and your agent.' So I give him the number and I leave and the agent calls me when I get home and tells me to make a test tomorrow. I say, 'Can I get to the scene ahead of time?' and they say, 'No scene, we're just going to ask you questions.' I thought, oh, hell, that's the worst kind of test you can have. I never could read that well, I couldn't read scripts out loud. If I knew the lines, I was fine, but I wasn't a great reader.

"So I go down to make this test and the guy who interviewed me the day before is there and it turns out he's the actor, the producer, everything. He says he *has* a scene for me to do. And there's these other guys there, about four of them, and I'm thinking 'One more cattle call, but maybe I can beat a few of these guys out.' Anyway, this guy makes this huge speech to the camera, and I think, 'Holy shit, there is no way I am going to learn this, no way in the world I am going to learn this dialogue.' But there were three transitions in it, so I just picked out the three points I wanted to make and took out everything else.

"So I got up and came in, and I started going . . . and the guy is looking at me really strange. I was playing it rather well, at least I felt like I was . . . I was believing it, I thought. I did it again twice, and then I finished and he looked at me coldly and said, 'Okay, we'll call you.' (I found out later he was a writer and he didn't want the words tampered with.) So I go into the dressing room and take off this western costume, and as I'm leaving I hear this other guy doing it word-for-word, letter-for-letter, and I said, 'Well, that's the end of that.' So I walked out and I wrote that one off.

"Then about a week later my agent called up and said, 'Yeah, they want to use you!' Well, ironically, the guy who projected all the tests for the wheels who came in from New York and LA was an old army buddy, and he told me that the wheels didn't know what the dialogue was, and didn't care. They were just looking at all of us, and what happened was that one of the wheels pointed at me and said, *That guy*: and all the other little wheels said, 'Yeah, that guy, that guy. I agree, J. R. He's absolutely perfect.' So I had a job. It was incredible.

"But there were a lot of stumbling blocks before it happened. We started making them, and it was really great—for ten straight weeks I had work. Then, after ten episodes, the word came down that we're way over budget and behind schedule and we're stopping it here at ten and 'reevaluating our position.'"

Again the *Dirty Harry* snicker. The notorious, fictional hatred of red tape comes into clearer focus.

"Then they said that hour shows aren't going anymore, only half-hour shows. So they put all the shows on the shelf and they sat there for weeks. It was supposed to go on for the fall and it was cancelled for the fall, and I thought, 'Oh, my God, my career is going to sit there on the shelf.' I remember I was up for a part at Fox after that and I asked them if I could show one of the episodes I had the lead in, and they said, 'No, we don't want to show it to anybody,' and I thought, 'My career is going to sit in the basement in tin cans at CBS.'

"Finally I got on a train, just to go visit my parents, and I got a telegram on the train that it was going to replace some other show. And I didn't know, we had so many false starts. . . . But the show jumped right into the top ten. It was a hit, and it was the first steady job I ever had."

Eastwood smiles and sinks back into the couch. There has been a curious gentility to his recollections, as if he were retelling another life. The palpable silence behind his words, his laconic delivery, reveals a profound patience also visible in his film characterizations. We begin to discuss his step from TV to the movies.

"I had seen *Yojimbo* [a Japanese Samurai film] with a buddy of mine who was also a Western freak, and we both thought what a great Western it would make, but nobody would ever have the nerve, so we promptly forgot it. A few years later my agency calls up and says, 'Would you like to go to Europe and make an Italian/Spanish/German coproduction, a Western version of a Japanese samurai story?' and I said, 'No, I've been doing a Western every week for six years, I'd love to hold out and get something else.' And he said, 'Would you read it anyway?' so I read it and recognized it right away as *Yojimbo*. And it was good! The way the guy converted it had a tremendous amount of humor in it. So I thought, this looks like fun, it'll probably go in the tank but at least it'll be fun to do. The Italian producer thought it was going to be a nice little B programmer, but of course it went through the roof."

"In Europe?"

"Yeah, they couldn't release it in this country for a while because of a threatened injunction by the Japanese."

"Because they thought it was a rip-off?"

"Well, it *was* a rip-off. The Italian producer had gone over to Japan to make negotiations, and when the fee the Japanese asked was too high, he just withdrew negotiations and went ahead and made it anyway."

Eastwood laughs and shakes his head like a man who has early on learned to live with the absurd. His Man With No Name was called nonacting. In fact, his entire career has been called nonacting.

"They called me everything," he says. "One critic wrote that I did nothing better than anyone who ever was on the screen, and there was a lot of name calling. It was that way with *Dirty Harry* too."

Critic Pauline Kael called him a fascist. "That was just the style of the times," he says deliberately. "People liked to throw around the term 'fascist.' It didn't bother me because I knew she was full of shit the whole time. She was writing to be controversial because people expect it of her, that's how she made her name. If *Harry* came out now, Kael would be onto something else. But the public liked the picture, and they realized it was just about a guy who was tired of the bureaucratic crap."

"I get the impression you are more or less apolitical."

"I don't have any political thoughts. I feel like an individualist."

"Your movies have been criticized as being anti-progressive," I remind him, "or as advocating a kind of police state."

"That isn't the case," Eastwood says firmly. "Anybody could see what the problems would be if the law enforcement agencies of any state were allowed to do anything they want. It would be dangerous. But the opposite is true: If you stifle the law, you invite getting bad people and corruption. It's the opposite extreme."

"But in the films themselves," I continue, "like *Dirty Harry*. . . He says, 'Screw all the red tape, I'm going to get the job done, bring these guys in'. . . ."

"Yes, that was true in the first film. He wanted to get the job done. [Director Don] Siegel and I put ourselves in the victim's standpoint; if I was a victim of a bizarre crime, I'd like to have someone with that kind of inspiration and imagination trying to solve the case. Sure it was an extreme case, but that doesn't mean that Don Siegel or myself adhere to any kind of ultra-rightwing organization. In *Magnum Force*, we talked about just the opposite: If a rightwing group becomes the underground of the police force. . . ."

Josey Wales lines up the Gatling gun. Below him are a hundred men, the scum responsible for the death of his wife. He squints, sets up the sight and begins to grind away. The men panic, scream, fall. Blood is gushing from their chests, arms, eyes. When he has run out of ammunition, Wales lopes away alone. He vows never again to become involved with any species of love. But there is this dog . . . a gangly, ugly, yellow dog . . . and it just won't leave. Wales watches as the mongrel nears him. He waits until it is within range, then spits, Whack—a stream of tobacco juice slaps the mutt on the head. The dog whimpers, then disappears.

It is night now. Wales beds down in the brush and waits for what is left of the gang he has ambushed to come after him. There is a noise, Wales jumps, whips out his gun. Something is moving toward him. He tenses, chews his tobacco, waits.

There is more movement. Then, around the bend, the dog is staring at him, unabashedly in love. Wales looks at it. His face softens. He grits his teeth. The dog comes toward him. Wales waits, then spits. Again, right on the head. The dog whimpers, moves away, but will not leave. Smoke rises from the fire, Wales watches the dog, stares at it, then shakes his head and goes to sleep.

Dogs and women. Eastwood, as prototype for monosyllabic movie machismo, has taken some vehement abuse for sexism in his films. It is a subject which he has obviously given some thought.

"When I did *Play Misty for Me*," Eastwood says, "I took it to Universal, and the first thing they said to me was, 'Why do you want to do a movie where the woman has the best part?' Before that I had done *The Beguiled*, with six major parts for gals. I did *Two Mules for Sister Sarah* . . . a lot of movies with good women's parts. I don't consider myself sexist at all. I dig chicks probably as much as, if not more than, the next guy."

There is an awkward pause.

"And you can probably call *that* sexist because I said 'chicks,' but I grew up where the guys in my neighborhood said that. The other day a female journalist asked me if I was intimidated by women, and I said, 'No, I had a great relationship with my mother . . . I think she's marvelous.'"

"I've even heard that your movies are really gay fantasies," I say.

Eastwood roars.

"People do put you down for macho quality," I add.

"That's getting back to those words again," says Eastwood. "'Fascist' was the word before. Now it's liable to be 'macho.' I never thought about being macho. I remember when I first came to Hollywood a director told me, 'Play this scene real ballsy,' and I said to him, 'I don't know what you're talking about. I wouldn't know how to do that.'

"I never thought about being anything other than what I am. I put myself in a situation, learn the motivations of the character, and just go. If you started thinking about it, tried to play something like that, you'd come off like an idiot. It would be caricature. If you think too much you can shut out things that work for you. So I really don't think I'm sexist. Jessica Walters was very happy to have that role in *Play Misty*, and there was the *The Beguiled*, and in *The Gauntlet* Sondra

Locke has, if not a better role, at least as good a role as me. I mean, she *is* the brains behind the whole thing."

"But isn't there a danger there? Your audience comes to Clint Eastwood films with certain expectations. The Man With No Name and Harry were both men in total control. Shockley, in *The Gauntlet,* is much more vulnerable. He's an alcoholic, and not so smart. What's more, he falls for the girl! I should think you're treading on slippery ground here. The fans rebel, think you're getting soft."

Eastwood nods but doesn't really address the problem:

"I guess there is a dyed-in-the-wool *Dirty Harry* fan who will be disappointed because I don't grab a cannon and mow down everything in sight, but I think we can expand on the women's parts. And in *The Gauntlet* there's still enough action to also satisfy the audience. It's so hard to find really good stories and scripts. It's amazing we could find three *Dirty Harry*s. I'd do another one, maybe, if we got a good script."

Eastwood seems tentative here, and perhaps he should be. Though *The Gauntlet* started out well, its receipts are reportedly slipping. Certainly it will not go in the tank, but it could turn out to be a financial disappointment.

"Don't forget *Josey Wales,*" says Eastwood. "It was different, warmer, and it was a box-office success."

"And easily your best picture," I agree.

"I'd never done that type of Western," he says. "I'd always done allegorical things and I wanted to do a saga. And the humor in that wasn't like in some of the others—total camp—it was warmer. Like with the dog—he spits on the dog, but he really wants him . . . yet he feels he brings bad luck on everybody."

Eastwood seems anxious to establish himself as the intelligent, civilized man he is. And although he is among the biggest stars in the world, he does seem to feel somewhat tarnished by the constant criticism. The increasing humanity in his films, and his vigorous, polite defense of himself, would seem to indicate he is trying gingerly to establish his full humanity, as an actor and a man.

"Many people who love your movies think they are either unintentional comedy or that the director makes them funny," I say. "Many people assume you're like Charles Bronson."

"They should analyze Bronson's movies," Eastwood says curtly. "Are *they* funny?"

"No."

"Well, then, how come my movies have that humor and his don't?"

"Well, people assume that the director puts in the humor."

"I've been the director on six of them," Eastwood says. "Do you think it's just by accident?"

"All right," I say, "The Man With No Name in the Italian westerns. How did he happen?"

"Okay," he begins, "I invented the costume, for example. I took it over with me, they just said, 'Come on over.' I went down to a costume store. I had one hat, three shirts, a sheepskin vest. I bought myself these black Levis, two sizes too big, and washed them. I wanted them to be kind of baggy. I didn't want them to fit too well, I wanted everything to be just a little off. Only the shoes fit right. I had the boots, so I took those . . . took the boots and spurs. . . ."

"Did you and [director] Sergio Leone create the character together?"

"Well, he couldn't speak English, and I couldn't speak Italian, so we had an interpreter. But I could see he was a jovial guy with good feeling for black humor, so I figured it was going to be fun. The script had a lot more dialogue, I cut a lot of it out. To keep the mystique of the character it was very important not to have the guy say too much. Very important not to know his past. And the less you knew about him, the better. If you stop and give a big expository scene to explain everything that's going on, audiences resent that. I think what you have to do is internalize the imagination of the audience, and then they'll be right with you."

"So you were aware then that the movie had a camp quality all the way through it."

"Oh, yeah . . . it was a *slight* parody."

"It was, and it wasn't."

"Yeah, but you still do it serious, you don't wink. You see guys who do that, they're winking at the camera all the time they're up there, then the audience doesn't believe that. They sit back and say, 'Oh, yeah, we're going to see Joe Slapstick here.' Even Chaplin and the Tramp, he played those scenes very serious. Or Gleason and Carney in *The Honeymooners*, they weren't sitting there talking to the audience, or the crew, or the backstage or anything. You gotta play the part and the camp will come out of it. And it took a lot . . . It *takes* a lot," he emphasizes. "You light cigars, you spit on the dog's head—it's easy to crack, to do takes on it. But I don't. It's played absolutely serious. You've got to believe it, and the audience wants you to believe it. It's not stand-up comedy."

Frankly, I'm happy to hear this. And yet I wonder, "Why do people think you're dumb?"

Eastwood sighs, shakes his head. "Because in an age of cynicism it's easier to believe he's just a big stupid guy standing there, doing these tricks and just accidentally pulling it off. I'm not the smartest guy in the world from a classic point of view, or an educational point of view—I don't pretend to be any Rhodes scholar—but I do have animal instincts about things and I rely on them. Nobody, I don't care who it is, is anywhere just being stupid."

It's been a rough day for Dirty Harry Callahan. He's taken shit from just about everybody on the police force and on his beat. Finally it's lunch hour. Harry collapses at an outdoor chili parlor and orders up a hot dog and a Coke. He has just taken a bite and wiped the mustard from his mouth when he hears a commotion across the street. Slowly, like a wounded reptile, he turns. A bank is being robbed. Harry watches with supreme disinterest, his eyes and facial muscles registering not a whit of disturbance. Around him, people are screaming as the armed robber makes his way out the door. Harry studies him. What's all the commotion, ain't no real problem here. Slowly, almost like a zombie, Harry finishes his hot dog, carefully wiping his mouth. Then, still chewing, he strolls across the street, knocks the thief's gun to the street and places his own .44 Magnum at the base of the man's skull.

"I've had a couple of fights already today, punk." says Harry. "I've shot most of my bullets . . . maybe. Maybe I've got one left. You want to try your luck?"

The punk collapses on the ground. He looks longingly at his own gun, only a foot away. All he has to do is reach for it. But there are these snake's eyes staring at him, and this huge barrel. Saliva forms on the edge of his mouth. He starts to reach out, then looks again at that death-mask face. You can see the life going out of him. Harry finishes chewing his hot dog and slowly, sadistically, licks his lips.

"I thought it would be interesting to have Harry not quite able to digest the hot dog, to keep right on eating it. Now, I don't believe there's a law officer in the world who would do that. It's dumb, ridiculous. But I liked it, and I knew the audiences would like it. I mean, it's funny!"

"It's hilarious."

"But it wasn't in the script at the end, and I thought it would be great to have it come back in like an epilogue. Only that time *there's* no hot dog. He plays it utterly straight. He's getting this guy he's gone out of his way to find, and he's broken every rule, political and judicial, and it's a sad moment, almost. Pauline Kael calls it a moment of glee when he shoots the guy, but there is no moment of glee. If she looked at it again I think she'd realize there's actually a *sadness* about it. And when he drills the guy there's no happiness, no smile."

"She obviously wasn't looking at the movie. She was looking at the last Robert Altman movie."

Eastwood laughs and stretches out his frame. "There's *sadness* in all of them," he continues. "In *The Enforcer*, the girl is killed and he goes off alone. There's a certain loneliness in all of them."

"In the new one, though, he finds a girlfriend."

"That's right," he says, "and not only a girlfriend, but one he wouldn't respect. She's a hooker and he's a cop—two different kinds who would never respect one another but who can learn to. It's more of an *African Queen* situation. It's more of an old-fashioned movie. Look at *It Happened One Night*, how much reality is in that? But you enjoy the people—you enjoy the guy, you enjoy the gal. It's entertainment."

"But your movies are incredibly violent," I say. "Do you worry about a carryover from screen violence to crime in the streets?"

"If that were the case," Eastwood says, "then every guy on Death Row would have reason to be released because Tom Mix or James Cagney or Hoot Gibson shot guys on the screen. Or go back before movies to literature—Shakespeare, Greek tragedy—everybody can find some fall guy for why they commit some act of violence. You can say 'My family insisted I learn about the Crucifixion of Jesus Christ.' That's a violent act where somebody is impaled on a cross."

"Besides," I agree, "there is a distinct difference between the violence in your movies and, say, *Taxi Driver* or *The Texas Chainsaw Massacre*, where you literally want to throw up."

"Well, yeah," he says, "except I wasn't appalled by the violence in *Taxi Driver* because they went so overboard. Like, the guy holding his hand out so he could wait for his fingers to get shot off—I found myself laughing at that."

Harry Callahan is standing in front of the mayor of San Francisco, a slick, beaver-faced man with grey ringlets drooping off his head. The Mayor looks faintly like Nero. Harry looks like a slob. His

herringbone tweed jacket is too small for him, his shirt is unbut-
toned at the top, he has a big mouse under his eye where a psycho-
pathic killer clipped him. Now, after almost being killed five times,
Harry is being rewarded for his dedication by being taken off the
case.

"I'm sorry, Callahan," the Mayor says, "but you've broken the
law. That's what keeps the fabric of society together, you under-
stand? No, you wouldn't understand. Not your kind."

"Somebody has to get him," Harry spits.

"Not you, Callahan. You're through. Now, get out."

Harry looks around for support. From his chief, from the May-
or's flunkies. Forget it. Slowly, with a profound torpor, he turns and
moves toward the door.

"Asshole," he mutters under his breath. "Assssshole."

"Asshole" is to a Clint Eastwood film as "Rosebud" is to *Citizen
Kane*. A signature, a recurrent coda. He always mutters it with a distinct nasal vehemence. I mention it and Eastwood roars.

"That's my South Oakland background. I have college kids come
up to me on the street and say, 'Hey, man, say *asshole* the way you say
it in the movies.'"

"Kind of a working-class talisman. . . ."

Clint is really laughing and nodding now. "Oh, yeah. No matter
how high you go, it's something you never lose. I use it, because it was
from my background, a certain way I got pissed. If Laurence Olivier
tried that, it wouldn't work at all."

"No," I laugh. "Perhaps 'ass-hole: High Tea version.'"

Clint smiles again. "You don't leave your background behind," he
says. "I'm the first in my family to ever make it. That's one more reason I don't play down to them; I came from that place. People know
when you're talking down to them. They instinctively know what's

going on. . . . All the good actors know this. Cagney, John Wayne, Gary Cooper. . . ."

"Were they your influences?"

"Cagney, especially. I loved that stuff."

"Yet he was outgoing. With you there's a kind of silence at the core of your characters. They're slightly removed."

"Well," says Eastwood, "I think if you analyze all the great actors of the past, it's not what they did so much as what they might do, what they were about to do. It wasn't what they said—a lot of guys can do dialogue better than those guys. Charles Laughton was a great character actor and he had all sorts of tricks, but if he was on the screen with Gable, your attention was on Gable, even if Laughton was doing the talking.

"There's a famous story. I can't remember the character actor's name, but he was talking about being onstage with Gary Cooper where he had this tremendous big monologue and Cooper didn't say a word. And the character actor said he went to see the thing and he thought he had really wrapped the scene up, and he said when he got into the theater he noticed that during his big monologue, everyone in the theater was staring at Cooper. And then he realized the worst part of all: *He* was staring at Cooper. That's what real acting is all about."

We both laugh and it's time to go. Eastwood sees me to the door.

"Where will you go from here?" he says.

"Baltimore," I say, grimacing a little.

"Yeah?" he says. "Do you get back to your old hometown often?"

"Not that often. And every time I do, my love-hate affair with the place surfaces and I end up kind of upset."

Eastwood smiles and pats me on the back. "I know what you mean," he says. "I feel that too. But you never want to lose contact with it altogether."

"I guess not," I say, not quite sure.

"Nah," says Eastwood. "You got to go back every now and then so you don't forget how to say it."

"Say what?" I ask.

With his best *Dirty Harry* smirk, Eastwood sneers: *"Asshole."*

Postscript

Clint Eastwood is now such an icon, and so beloved, that hardly anyone remembers the days when he was considered a handsome stud-muffin with no brains. But as late as 1978 that's exactly how most of the public and all the movie critics viewed him. Pauline Kael was the main culprit. She considered *Dirty Harry* a fascist picture. She thought Eastwood was nothing more than a John Wayne, without talent.

It was very fashionable in those days to put Clint down, to laugh at his movies, his squint, and grimace. I laughed at him myself and made fun of his lack of acting chops with my cool, sophisticated friends.

The only thing wrong with my attitude was I'd never seen any of his pictures.

Finally, while visiting home in Baltimore, I went with a friend, the artist Scott McKenna, to the Towson Theatre to see *The Good, The Bad and The Ugly*. I expected nothing more than a campfest. We'd laugh at the horrible actor, make fun of the rotten Italian western, and go home feeling smug and superior.

Instead, Scott and I sat in our seats without so much as going to get popcorn or even take a piss for nearly three hours.

As we walked out in that special daze great movies put you in, I looked at Scott and said: "I think we've just seen one of the best movies of all time."

Scott nodded, and we spent the rest of the night in a Towson lacrosse bar called the Crease, going over the many great parts of the film.

What we both agreed on was that: TGTBATU was one of the great movies, just a little behind *The Wild Bunch* in both our estimations. And that Clint Eastwood was a great actor. Pauline Kael didn't know jackshit about acting or movies. Because Clint played the piece straight, which made the movie work. Any hint of winking at the audience, or playing it for laughs would have ruined the whole delicate deal.

The movie was an epic western and an epic comedy, and an epic drama, and it all worked. Sergio Leone, whoever he was, was a genius. The guy who did the music—we didn't know that his name was Ennio Morricone—was also amazing.

When I told my friends how much I loved Clint they laughed at me, and shook their heads. But I found, very quickly, that none of them had seen it.

It was sort of like discussing *Moby Dick* with writers. Everyone says it's a masterpiece, no doubt. But when you try and discuss individual scenes with them they sort of change the subject. Why? Because no one ever finished it.

All I knew is that I felt Clint Eastwood was a great actor, and he deserved a serious interview. One in which he could answer his critics. So when editors Mitch Glazier and Tim White called me from *Crawdaddy*, and asked me to interview Clint, I was more than ready.

I flew to Hollywood, and met Eastwood at his bungalow at Warner Brothers, and he couldn't have been kinder and more open. I was told he never liked to talk and would only give people, at most, a half hour.

Instead, he gave me two hours.

I shook hands with him and left. I felt really excited. I had a great interview with the Man With No Name. I was so happy I decided to hear a little of it on my way to my rental car.

Then the worst happened, the reporter's nightmare.

I had always hated tape recorders but more and more people told me they were invaluable, so I used a mini-tape recorder for the East-wood interview.

I hit rewind, then play, and I heard . . . ZERO.

Nothing, nada, blip. . . .

I felt my blood freeze. The guy who never gave interviews had liked me and given me two hours. Two hours to *Crawdaddy*, not exactly the *New York Times* or *Rolling Stone*. And now I was faced with going back to his bungalow and prostrating myself, begging him to do it all over again!

I tried to figure ways around it. Maybe I could remember every-thing he said. But for two hours? No way. I had no choice. I retraced my steps and went back to his office. I told his assistant what had happened. She looked at me like "Are you kidding me?" I wanted to crawl under her desk. I waited as she went into his office and told him.

Two minutes later he came out and looked at me, grimly.

I totally forgot that this was a professional situation and fully expected him to kill me.

That was fine. I wanted to die anyway. Just shoot me in the head so it's quick, okay?

"Heard you had a little problem," he said. In his low *Dirty Harry* voice.

"Uh, ah well you see I uh . . . hahaha. . . ."

Clint smiled and opened the door into his office, the same office we'd just sat in for two hours.

"You have a cold," he said. "You need another cookie and tea."

And he did the whole interview, all two hours of it, over again.

To put it very simply, after that I loved the guy. I didn't change one thing in the interview but as far as I'm concerned of all the giants I've met Clint stands out as one of the kindest.

I think too, that this interview was very brave. I asked him tough questions and often not flattering ones, like "Why do people think you're stupid?" He answered them all reasonably and with a deep understanding of his craft.

I think that maybe this interview is the first time anyone saw how smart he really is, and how he might morph into the great actor/ director he is today.

Drinks with Liberty Valance: Lee Marvin Shoots from the Hip

Ransom Stoddard, attorney at law, is doing his best to cover up, but the hell-forged maniac above him just keeps grunting and drooling and lashing him with a bullwhip. Stoddard is backed up as far as he can get against a stagecoach wheel, has his hands covering his face, but the whip is getting through. You can tell from the look on the Eastern dude's face that he knows the whipping isn't the worst of it. It's the fact that this guy above him, this Liberty Valance feller, doesn't look human. And the other guys in the gang aren't exactly preppies themselves. Just behind Valance is Lee Van Cleef, with those little ferret's eyes that are so narrow they look like cracks in old leather, and to the side, clapping his retarded hands together and giving this high-pitched, near-falsetto psycho laugh is Strother Martin. "Ah hah hah hah . . . you show him, Liberty . . . hah hah hah. . . ." But as bad as those two are, the leader of the gang makes them look positively social. He's got his feet spread and his head cocked to his shoulder, and this drooling, hanging lower lip that looks like it's covered with swamp moss . . . the son of a bitch just hangs to his right shoulder, quivering, and spit flying with stone-cold hatred as he brings the whip down again.

Finally, Van Cleef and Martin realize Liberty is going too far. Hell, they just wanted to rob the stage. Van Cleef snakes forward and grabs Liberty by the arms.

"Come on, Liberty. The law might come."

But Liberty is pulling out of Van Cleef's grasp.

"You want to know about the law, dude?" he says to the terrified, dazed, and badly beaten Stoddard. "Well, let me show you law [*whip*] . . . Western law. . . ."

Suddenly, without warning, the whole feeling of the scene changes. At just the right moment, the camera closes in on Liberty Valance and you feel his torture as well as Stoddard's. He not only gives out pain—he is in constant, unrelenting pain. He's in some kind of private, soul-killing hell.

But it's only a second or two. Then, as before, the whip comes down.

"Jesus," I say, holding on to the edge of my seat as Lee Marvin clicks off the videotape of John Ford's *The Man Who Shot Liberty Valance* (1962). "You looked like the devil himself in that scene, Marvin. How the hell did you pull that off?"

A few feet away in his comfortable, hacienda-style home in Tucson, Arizona, an urbane and congenial Lee Marvin reaches for the bottle of wine.

"I'll answer that question, Ward," he says, "right after we have this one final drink. If you know what I mean?"

"Now, Lee," says Marvin's wife, Pam. "Haven't you had enough? You might not feel . . . well tomorrow."

Lee Marvin cocks his snow-white head, lets the old lower lip start to hang down, turns slowly, slowly, and suddenly I am hit by the Fear. What if . . . he turns into Liberty Valance right here and how? Starts to horse-whip Pam? Brings out the guns on me?

"We're just having one . . . little glass of white wine, Pam." Marvin says. "You understand?"

Pam smiles. She understands. She's seen Lee when he wasn't "well" before.

"I noticed something," I say to Marvin, feeling a little like Ransom Stoddard, attorney at law. "In that scene we just watched, the sense of menace you created was linked to . . . how much faster you move than everybody else. The rest of them are standing still. But Liberty is always dipping his shoulder, whirling around. Was that your idea or John Ford's?"

Marvin picks up his glass and takes a sip. He's relaxed again, back in his own skin. "It's one of the things I always do. I move faster onscreen. Creates a sense of danger . . . and ah. . . ."

Marvin doesn't finish his sentence. Though he's perfectly capable of going on in greatly detailed style about what he does, he often just lets things hang.

"I mean," Marvin says, looking at me through those glazed and slightly mad eyes, "you're in there, then do it and get the hell out."

"You mean," I say, picking up our thirteenth bottle of wine, "that fast movement isn't part of your subtle Stanislavskian approach to acting?"

"You ask me my motivation," Marvin says, moving back into his tough-guy persona again. "I say Thursday."

"Thursday?"

"Payday. That's it, Ward. Fuck all the other stuff. It's important not to think too much about what you do. Take Strasberg. I went to his joint once, back when I was first hanging out in New York, doing plays. I did a ten-minute scene in his class: the guy who had gangrene in his leg in *The Snows of Kilimanjaro*. After I did the scene, he starts in with, 'Well, you were going for the pain in your leg, but I didn't see it, so you didn't put it over and thus the scene failed.' I told him that he didn't know anything about gangrene. When it's in the terminal stage, there isn't any pain. What I was going for was that the guy was trying to feel pain, because if he had any pain, it meant he wasn't going to die. But he couldn't feel a damned thing. I know about that shit from the Pacific. Strasberg was furious when I corrected him. He threw me out, so I said 'fuck you' and walked. He's not my kind of guy at all. I didn't dig it when he came in using his acting-school reputation to get the creamy acting jobs that some other old actor who'd paid his dues might have really needed. Nah, you can have him. He's not in my outfit, pal."

Marvin nods his head. The old sense of menace darkens his brow. To begin to understand Marvin, you have to understand "his outfit," the one he signed on with when he was a kid during World War II and never really left—the Marines. But maybe you have to start somewhere else—with Lamont Waltman Marvin, Monty, his father, the Chief, the old man. Because when Marvin talks about the Marines, Monty, or the "screamers"—the directors he loved, like Lang and Ford—you realize they're all part of the same outfit. The authority that he loves and hates. A harsh judge, one he might never please but has spent a lot of his life trying to. The old man, the Marines, and the director. And all of them are joined by one artifact. One image that provides a common thread—the gun.

Marvin clicks on the videotape again. Ransom Stoddard is hauled into town by John Wayne. He ends up working with Vera Miles in the kitchen of this Old West restaurant, where the steaks are all ten-pounders and the skillets three times the normal size. Marvin is delighted by the props.

"Ford," he says reverentially. "Fucking Ford. You'll never see skillets and steaks like that in anybody else's picture. He's like the dickens. It's all about bigger than life. That's what the old guys understood about movies. If it's not bigger than life, put it on television.

"We got along from the start. Maybe I knew how to deal with him. The first day of *Liberty*, I was hanging around waiting for Ford to come in. Everybody told me how tough he was and not to say anything or he'd single you out and get on you the whole shoot. But as he walked in, I got up and saluted him. There was a dead silence. And then I said, 'Well, chief, when the admiral comes aboard, the first mate has to pipe him in.' He never got on me after that. He was a great lover of the navy, and he liked me because of it. He called me Washington. Because my family is descended from George Washington's brother, James. Which few people know or expect."

Which is an understatement. The standard guess on Marvin might best be summed up by a writer friend of mine who said, "He looks like he came out of nowhere. He had no father, no mother, just spawned out there in some gulch and has spent his whole life hating the world that vomited him up." Marvin would love that, for he's worked hard to create his image. People don't come over in bars with a glad hand and ruin his lunch. The reason is simple: They're afraid if they do, he'll kill them.

The facts are a bit more complex. Less legendary. Marvin grew up in New York during the Depression. The old man didn't shrink heads or shuck shells for a living but was an ad executive. His mother wasn't named Malvina or Bobbi Jean, and she didn't belch him out in a truck stop and then leave him for the wolves. Her name was Courtney, and she was a fashion editor for magazines like *Photoplay*, *Screenland*, *Silver Screen*. So Marvin had the old showbiz glamour in his life from the start. Upon hearing this tale, most people are disappointed. They want Marvin to be as mean and as lonely and as trashy as the characters he portrays. But put aside the working-class sentimentality and you find that in spite of his blue blood and his wealthy parents, Marvin was the victim of another classic American tragedy— uptight WASP puritanism. "My father," he told me in a bar in New York, "was the classic Puritan. Hold the emotions in check. Keep up appearances. Tight-assed. He had feelings, but he'd never show them to you. I remember once he told me about a bunch of horses he saw in World War I. They were twisted and dead from mustard gas. He cried talking about them. He had feelings. It took something like that to bring them out." Marvin's earliest memory of his father is so classic a case study that shrinks would stomp each other to get him on the couch.

"My father is shooting a gun. It's a movie he took of himself with a Kodak B, which was a very good camera in the twenties—16 mm. It was a film of him shooting near Randall's Island, where they had a firing range. So he's stripped down to the waist, with a .45 automatic—C98688 was the pistol number—that he got at Abercrombie and Fitch before he shipped out for World War I. And to watch him, the way he used to ride up, and in slow motion, when he fires, you see this ripple go up and down in his arm about four times, and then his shoulder moves like so, and then he starts to cock it, and up it comes like this, and it comes on in three waves, right on target, and this is on the speed targets. And he was nude from here up, with his hand on his waist. That's one of the first memories I have. That, and him letting me play with his gun. . . ."

When Marvin tells this story, he smiles a little, lets the jaw drop, and nods. He looks like the old cop on *M Squad*.

"Make of all that what you will," he says.

Of course, he knows what you'll make of it. He's told it in a way that is so highly erotic there can be no mistaking his intentions. Yet, if you ask him if he ever learned anything from three years of therapy, he smiles and says, no, it was a long time ago and it wasn't very useful.

Still, he will tell you candidly that he was his father's son. He barely mentions his mother. It's always his old man, the Chief. The Chief who went through World War I and then managed to get back into World War II.

"And it ruined him," Marvin says. "He came home from that half dead, totally broken. I was in the Marines at the time, after my bouts with prep schools."

And, of course, there were quite a few of those. One was a Quaker school, whose name he can no longer recall, in upstate New York. He was already seething, filled up with the Chief. One day he and some of his roommates were cleaning their room and one of the guys threw the dustpan out into the hall. Lee asked him why he did that. The guy called Marvin a son of a bitch. Marvin threw him out the window.

"It was on a hill. So nothing got broken. The Quakers didn't go for it much, though. They asked me to go home and commune with God and see the injustice of all this shit. . . ."

After the Quaker school, Marvin served time at Admiral Farragut Naval Academy near Toms River, New Jersey, which he recalls as "eleven hundred dollars' worth of uniforms in the Depression. God."

But soon enough, Marvin followed his father's footsteps. Right into the Marines. In a rare display of emotion, one that stunned Marvin when it happened and still stuns him now, the Chief, at age forty-seven, hitchhiked from his own army camp near Riverside down to San Diego, where his son was due to ship out with a raider group.

"The Marines put him up in the guard house," Marvin says. "They understood what he was about because he had his World War I stripes on his arm. The next morning I'm up at five o'clock for breakfast, and my old man walks in."

When Marvin tells this story, he gets quiet, and you can see the way it must have been. That act forever sealed his feeling for the Chief, bound it up with the war, with violence, with the gun.

"He gave me his .45 and said, 'Here, kid, and don't lose it in a crap game.' I carried it with me everywhere, with one in the chamber and seven in back of the clip, until one night, these Wrapees were standing there right at face level. I don't even remember unhooking the pistol, taking the safety off—there's my hand flying back. Didn't even hear it go off. And then to see this Jap just disappear."

Wrapees was the term Marines used for the Japanese because they had wrapping round their legs. In the morning, Marvin found the Wrapee he had shot with the Chief's pistol.

"I had got him one inch from the tit, straight into the heart. I rolled him over to see where it came out, and there was no big hole in the back. There were a lot of little pieces, pieces of lead and stuff. It was copper jack, had broken up as it hit those bones. And more than anything, I wanted a souvenir for my father, so I rolled him back, and he had gold teeth. I took out my knife, my Ka-Bar, and knocked his teeth out, but they fell into his throat. Meanwhile, rigor mortis had set in, so he was stiff, and I couldn't get 'em out. They said, 'Come on, Captain, let's go.' My nickname was Captain, though I was a private, first class. So I had to move out. But I spotted the body and I came back, but some son of a bitch had cut his throat and stolen the teeth. I think about it now. The way my old man came home a complete wreck from the war. He was never the same after that. I had wanted to give him something, something to make him proud. Gold teeth. Those teeth would have sent him around the bend forever. I tell you this story to show you how impossibly young I was."

It's so quiet that all you can hear is the click of the ice-cube machine in the background.

"That was my relationship with my father. Through the gun. Always the gun. Does that help explain Liberty Valance? And why I loved Jack Ford?"

Of course it does. It helps. The rage that Marvin has embodied, a man on the edge of eruption, is always a badly wounded man. The Chief wounded him, and after the Chief was through, the war added its own licks.

"I was a point man, like in *The Big Red One*," Marvin says. "It was at the Battle of Saipan. Me and another guy, Mike, were walking point. Now, a lot of people think that's the most dangerous position, but I've done a lot of thinking about it, and I realized I walked through a lot of the enemy that way. They don't want him and me. They want the whole platoon. That's what happened when we finally got hit. They let us get ahead of the outfit, then the rest of the guys came in. Only then did they shoot Mike and me. They got him first. I watched him drop. Then they shot me, right in the ass. They finished off the whole company in fifteen minutes. I ended up getting carried out of there, and when I came out of the morphine haze, I was in this cream-colored room, and outside the porthole I could hear 'Moonlight Serenade.' . . . A hospital troop ship. I felt crazy, like a coward. Because I didn't go running out there to get the enemy and die like a lot of my buddies. You know the old saying? They gave him a gun, and he never put it down? Well, that's true of me. Because there isn't a day that goes by that I don't think of that fire fight. Not all day, but every day of my life since."

"How does it connect to the acting?"

Marvin smiles.

"I'll tell you how. It was the Marines who taught me how to act. After that, pretending to be rough wasn't so hard. It was when they stopped rolling that it got rough."

Marvin has been aging well. Unlike the characters he plays, men who came from nowhere and, as he himself puts it, "go home to nobody." Lee Marvin has survived his own considerable boozing, his infamous palimony case, and the bad memories of both the Chief and the war.

At his Tucson hacienda he is a gracious host and a good neighbor. The kid from next door drops by and Marvin talks to him about the stunts in his latest film, *Death Hunt*. Just like plain folks. Later in the afternoon, Pam's son, Rod, his Japanese-black wife, Hideko, and their infant son, Morgan, visit. Marvin kisses the child and plays granddaddy.

Eventually the neighbors themselves make an appearance, everyone acting like Lee is a kindly white-haired retiree rather than an international movie star. Normality, domesticity, ease, in the blazing Arizona desert. It is his greatest performance to date. But late at night, when the wine eases him back into the chair, Marvin gets the haunted look we have loved and recognized as our own American terror since we first saw it on the screen in *You're in the Navy Now* in 1951. The fear of . . . Dad, of the war . . . yes, that . . . but something else . . . the fear that life is not being lived right here now. The fear that somewhere else it's really happening, somewhere just outside the confines of your own house, your own scene, your own brain.

"Ask me if I've had a midlife crisis, Ward," Marvin says.

"Have you?"

"No. Because I've always felt that way. Had to get to the next thing . . . had to find it. . . . They say that hits you when you're forty, but I can't remember feeling any other way. Ever. Some of it you can trace back to the war, but I don't get too Freudian about it; it's just the way we are. . . . You saw me today with the family. How did I do?"

"Oscar time."

"You saw that, then? I was detached. I wasn't really there. I was out, maybe in the Great Barrier Reef catching black marlin. Do you fish? No, you play basketball. But maybe it's the same thing: the moment when you push through the wall.

"It's like Jung in a way. I'll tell you, I used to deep-sea dive, but I felt like an interloper. It wasn't my world. I didn't want to be spying on them. So after a couple of years I gave it up. But what interested me more was the unknown. You drop the line just below the surface, see, and just a few feet below there is something strange that will hit it . . . like dropping into a dream. . . . Meanwhile, you're on the deck with everybody else, and nobody talks. It's the unwritten law. Nobody talks. Everybody is in his own dream . . . and then it hits . . . you see? Then everybody is in there working. You understand? No. Let me show you some films." Pam's daughter, Kerry, comes in. She's a freshman at college.

"B*ooooooo*ring," she says. "You aren't going to bore everyone with those marlin films again?"

I look over at Marvin, who gives her a slow study. Then he smiles and sounds defensive.

"Hey, they aren't that boring. I mean, the guy has to see it. Ah, what the hell."

A few minutes later, all the lights are out, and Marvin is watching himself, with white stubble of beard, being described by two Aussie newsmen, officious types who mumble things like, "To Lee Marvin, the mystery of the Barrier Reef is a challenge . . . man against fish. . . ."

Then they are interviewing him, and Marvin is making some heavy pronouncement like, "It's me versus the fish. One of us has to die."

"Jesus," Pam says. "That's awful, honey."

Pam's daughter goes into hysterics.

"It's *soooo baaaad*," she says. "It's so *baaad*."

"Shut the hell up," Lee Marvin says. "I know it's bad."

Then he looks over at me.

"This is bullshit," he says. "It wasn't my idea, really. My captain on the boat, Brazakka, he wanted me to do this Hemingway bit, with the white stubble, and he wanted the hero angle. It's not what fishing is really about at all. I don't know why I let them film it, fucking up the thing I loved."

Remember Marvin's father. Throughout all the stories of loss and pain with the Chief, there was barely a trace of emotion. Like his old man, he keeps it reined in, but when talking about fishing, a true regret seeps out. Betrayal . . . you can hear it . . . betraying the thing he loves for a cheap bit of film publicity. Yet there is something noble and even beautiful in Marvin's regret. At least he know what's been lost.

"Can't we turn this thing off?" Pam's daughter asks.

But Marvin puts his hand on her leg. He is straining toward the screen. It's almost as though he wants to dive into it.

"This is it," he says. "Wait. . . ."

Suddenly a huge, graceful black marlin leaps out of the water, sending a shower of water ten feet high. It is a marvelous moment, and you can almost see Marvin's mood change. He relaxes.

"It's there," he says, reaching for the wine bottle.

"I felt a little of it then," I say.

"No," Marvin says. "You can't know . . . you can't . . . unless. . . ."

He can barely get the words out. Everyone is sitting stock still. He seems possessed.

"Through the other side," Marvin says as the film runs out.

First light in the desert. The sound of birds, quail, even doves, make a wild grid of noise. It's like sleeping in an aviary. I turn over, look at the clock. It's six thirty . . . good, another couple of hours sleep before I trudge from Marvin's guest house up to the main place for an afternoon session. I fall back into a dream and then suddenly there is a tapping on the window just above my bed. I pull back the curtain. It's the original dog-assed heavy himself, smiling at me like Kid Shelleen in *Cat Ballou*.

"Get up, Ward. You've got to see the desert now."

"Yeah, man. That's a good idea," I say. "I don't want to oversleep. Christ, we've been zonked out for . . . like, two and a half hours. We could get weak . . . morally slack. . . . Come on, man. . . ."

But Marvin is holding up coffee.

"This will get you going. Hell, I've been up since five-thirty."

"Jesus."

I'm out of bed, Marvin coming in through the door now.

"Wait till you see it out there. It's what we were talking about last night. Through the wall. Oh, yeah. . . ."

Outside, sitting by his pool, we look out on the desert. It's everything he said it is. And Marvin never tires of looking at it or talking about it. When he does, there is a gentleness in his voice, a reflective and lovely quality that no movie he has been in has ever captured.

"Those are saguaro cactuses . . . the big ones . . . birds make holes in them and build their nests inside."

"And those?"

Marvin hops over the edge of his retaining wall, which he built.

"Well, this shorter cactus, with the golden tip, that's a barrel cactus. And this is an ocotillo, it's tall and fingery, see, with one red flower at the top. It's perfect. . . ."

"How about the animals? I heard what sounded like werewolves out there last night."

"Coyotes. But don't worry, they don't come down on people, though they will eat a dog now and then. But there also cottontail rabbit and jack rabbit and the Gambel's quail. There's one over there. . . ."

I look up and see a quail hustling along the road.

"The roadrunner?" I say, recognizing nature by a cartoon.

Marvin takes off his T-shirt and dives into his swimming pool. I dive in with him and swim to the bottom. The floor is inlaid with beautiful Mexican tile. Marvin himself cut the tiles. He likes when the sun glances off it from the top, because it looks like the black marlin.

When we come up, Marvin climbs out of the pool. His flesh is sagging a bit, but he is still trim and looks lean, sinewy and tough.

"Is it good to be here instead of in Hollywood?"

"Yeah," Marvin says. "Now it is, but there's a time when you have to be out there if you want to be in the business. Everybody puts it down, but it is what it is. There's no other place like it. You meet everybody and you have a good time."

"What other actors did you become friends with?"

"Not many. You don't make friends with the guys who are above you too much. Remember, I didn't make it until I was older, in my thirties. Up till then I was just a dog-assed heavy, one of the posse. My best friends were always stunt guys and extras. I've always seen myself as one of the masses. Besides, a lot of actors are just boring and pompous as hell."

"I've heard you put a few of them on."

"Well, yeah," Marvin says, his head cocked reflectively. When his head cocks, you can be sure he's going to let down the guard a bit, relax and tell a good tale.

"Like Rod Steiger. Now with Rod, you can't help but put him on. You tell yourself, 'Hey, this time 'round I won't do it,' but you can't help it. Like it was '65 when I was nominated for *Cat Ballou,* so I wasn't even going to go because I didn't think I had much of a chance to win. Steiger was nominated, and Richard Burton, and a lot of people in bigger movies. But I had won the British Award, Best Foreign Actor, so I went. Anyway, I get there early and—if you're nominated, they ask you to sit on the aisles. So I walk in and there's Rod, sitting and fidgeting on the aisle. So, like I say, I can't resist it. I go up behind him and I say, 'Hey, Rod, I see you're sitting on the aisle,' and he turns around real quick-like and his eyes are darting and he's dry-mouthed and he says, 'Yeah, so what, Lee?" and I smile *real* nice."

At this point Marvin gives his Liberty Valance smile, the kind that makes you wish you could disintegrate in front of him.

"So I say, 'Well, just this, Rod. If they call your name, and you get out of that chair, I'm going to break both your legs. You got that?' And of course, Rod, being Rod, goes for it a hundred percent; his mouth drops open and he says, '*What?*' So I just patted him kind-like on the shoulder and sat down. Every once in a while during the ceremony I'd look over at him and make a fist. You should have seen him. The guy was sweating. He was a wreck. I loved it. *Loved* it. Especially when I win. So I get up and do my acceptance speech, rah rah rah . . . and then we have the press taking pictures, and so a little later I'm in my limo and we're heading for the Beverly Hills Hotel for the big party, and we pull up to a light, and there, next to me, is Rod."

Marvin is totally into it now. He gives the greatest Lee Marvin big-teethed, killer-sadistic, gonna-eat-you-baby smile.

"He's sitting in the back seat, and I swear, he looks like he's crying. So I asked the driver to honk the horn, which he does, and Rod looks over. I held up the Oscar, and gave him a great big smile." You can almost feel old Rod wasting away.

Marvin sits down in his chair and sighs. He's settling back into his fifty-seven-year-old body. But while he was up there riffing about Steiger, he looked like he did in the *Big Heat*. Young and lean and mean as hell.

"Those were your drinking days, I take it."

"Yeah," Marvin says. "But I was never a world-class drinker. I tried, but I just couldn't keep up. Now the really great drinkers, well, let's see, Robert Newton . . . old Long John Silver himself . . . Jesus, he could drink . . . and, of late, the best contemporary drinker is Oliver Reed. Ollie is unbelievable. Let me tell you. We did a movie down in Durango—*Great Scout and Cat House Thursday*. So I get on the plane with Ollie and he's impeccably dressed and quite British, and we're flying down there, and I order a vodka martini, which was what I drank in those days, and which nearly did me in. And Ollie doesn't order anything. And I thought, 'This isn't the Oliver Reed I've heard about.' So we get off the plane and go into Durango. And I stop off in the bar to talk to the director. Well, Ollie comes in with me, and, just to feel him out, to be sure I've got the right guy, I order a double vodka martini. And Ollie says, 'Oh, I see, well, let me have two double vodka martinis.' So I said, 'Yeah, I'll have two too.' The director left then; he could see the impending catastrophe. So Ollie says, 'Christ, thank God we're off that bloody plane. I never drink on an aircraft.' And then we started in. . . . Jesus, this guy could drink. So after about an hour, we're really getting down into it, and I notice we're getting a bit loud. And there are these three or four very mean Mexicans sitting next to us. They have the serapes on, but I know they're packing iron, and they start insulting us. You can hear 'Gringos . . . fucking gringos.' So finally Ollie gets this mean look in his eyes, and I say, 'Now, Ollie, just look at me, just look at me, don't look over there,' and he says, 'Fuck it, they can't talk about me that way.' He gets up and goes over to their table and introduces himself, and he says, 'Hello, I'm Oliver Reed. Nice to meet you. I've heard the kind things you were saying about us. I just want you to know that I am not a goddamned gringo. I'm not North American. I am British. You understand? British. And I want you to understand one more thing as well. We sank your fucking Armada.' With that he sits down. Now these guys are going crazy. Jabbering away. And I tell Ollie, just look at me, because they just pulled out the *pistolas*. Christ, they've got their weapons out and they start shooting them into the ceiling. Bam bam bam . . . I mean, the whole hotel was going berserk. So Ollie gets up and looks at them and says, 'Very impressive. Well, watch this.' He then does a handstand on the arms of his bar chair. I mean, from a sitting position, he goes straight up. . . . That's a bitch. I mean, he's a bull, right? So these same Mexicans put their guns away and applaud him. But Ollie gets carried away. He says, 'That was nothing. Watch, one hand.' So he pulls off one hand; I guess he forgot he was supporting himself on the chair arms, because of course the minute he takes off one hand, the chair loses balance, tips over, and he falls straight down on his shoulder. Man, he was in pain. I had to carry him out of there. But he's the greatest drinker. He beats me by a long shot."

Pam smiles and shakes her head.

"I hate it when Ollie and Lee get together. They're both wonderful until they're drunk, but then . . . Jesus . . . it's unbelievable. He came to Phoenix once and we went up to see him, and they got so crazy that

I ended up trying to hitchhike home. I mean, I'm Mrs. Lee Marvin, and there I am out in the 102-degree sun, dressed to the nines, just trying to get away from them. . . . They were going really nuts that time."

"Yeah," Marvin says, laughing broadly. "I hate to see him show up, in a way. But I love the guy. He's the best."

Marvin sits back in his chair and stares out at the desert.

"Too many of the good old days," he says. "I can't make these scenes anymore. I've got to make them straight now. That's the only way I can handle it. I've got enough shit floating around in my head without feeling that bad anymore. You know, when I was younger, I used to make problems for myself, like it was too easy. I mean, the reality of it was, I had to go out and get on a horse, and ride in, shoot the gun—how hard was that, right? So I'd get a little juiced and tell myself that the horse was going to try to throw me, and make it dramatic. I thought I was getting my creativity from the booze. Man, it was there inside of me all the time. That's something I learned reading Jung . . . the collective unconscious. . . . I can tap into that. Understanding my own dreams had a lot to do with getting me off the juice. Here, come inside. I want to show you something."

Marvin and I leave the poolside and go into his dining room. In the wall are two paintings he did. One is blue with brown lines and a red splotch.

"I called this *Country Roads*," he says. "I dreamed it. It seemed like this country road . . . these lines . . . but later, on a trip down in Texas, I realized that these brown lines weren't roads at all. They were fire lanes. They were the machine-gun bullets coming from the ambush when my company got hit. I made this painting not to create art but to get it out. And this other one . . . I carved this one."

The second painting is a labyrinth.

"It's green and cream, like the hospitals after I was shot," he says. "And the labyrinth—I guess that's the wards, or different phases of my life. But it's closed off. In some ways I never got out of that unless realizing . . . well, that kind of seals it off. I think maybe I'm into another phase of my life now. I'm not a great thinker or anything, but as you get older, the journey becomes more mental."

"How will that affect your career?"

"Oh, I can still do it. I'm in good shape. In *Death Hunt* I was still able to put on the snowshoes and do it, except, you know, I'd suddenly find myself saying, 'Christ, do we have to go up the hill again? Let's go down once.' The body starts to give out on you a little, but you make up for it because you've got a perspective and you're cagey, and you know how to save yourself. You know there's a lot of crap people say, like, when the bulls are no longer good and the women aren't exciting, you should check out. Well, I say you should change your bulls and change your women. Life is too good to give up because it can't be like it was. That's why I don't live on memory lane. Too many trips down there can ruin you."

"Do you ever think about the palimony case?"

"No. I really don't. I knew I was going to win. I was declared innocent, and they said I should pay $104,000. We're appealing, because if you're innocent, why should you have to pay anything? But if you mean am I bitter about it, the answer is no. It was a long time ago. I knew it was coming for seven years. And by the time it was on trial, I was married to Pam. It's the same way with my movies. I do them, and I forget them. You can't bring them home with you. Pam helps with that, too."

Which is true. Pam Feeley was Marvin's old childhood sweetheart. He used to drive her to school once he came home from the Marines. Then they both went on to other marriages. After Marvin's affair with Michelle Triola, he went back to Woodstock, and, as he puts it, said, "Let's go." They've been together ever since.

The day I left, Marvin insisted on driving me to the airport. Despite his efforts to live in the present, he seemed haunted by the specter of his father. It was an early morning, and Marvin thinks best then. He is clear and full of energy.

"I remember this story about my father," Marvin says. "He went out to Denver to see his father, who was dying in the hospital. It was Valentine's Day, and they wouldn't let him see him because he was already dead. My father slipped the card he had under the door. He never saw him again. And when the Chief died . . . I went down to Florida. . . . He was in a coma. . . . I came over and I kissed him on the head and said, 'That's it, Chief. I'll see you down the line.' And then I got on a plane, and guess what was playing: *I Never Sang for My Father*. People hated it, man, but I loved it. It got it all out there . . . Gene Hackman and Douglas . . . Melvyn Douglas is amazing. What a great actor. One of the greatest of all time. I remember that after the movie, people were saying how depressing it was, and I started an argument with them. I was holding forth, man, to the whole plane. It was great. I got it out. Like that . . . I felt, you know, cleansed of it. . . ."

He smiles, but there is still that haunted look in his eye. It's as if he's testing me. How much of this shit do you believe? Can you catch me when I'm performing?

As we waited for my plane to come in, we stayed silent for a long time. A friendship had started between us. That morning Pam had hugged me and said, "You feel like family; come back again, just for the hell of it," and it was tough to break off. There were things unsaid about fathers and sons. People began moving toward the plane and Marvin said, "You can wait a minute. You know, Ward, I think I understand my father more every day. On some days I can almost. . . ."

He broke it off there. Like he broke off talking about the marlin, or the moment in acting that words can't reach, the moment when there is nothing that need be said because everything is right there, in sync.

Postscript

Of all the interviews I did Lee Marvin was by far the biggest surprise. I first saw Marvin when I was ten years old, living with my parents in Arlington, Virginia. My father was in an intelligence unit for the U.S. Navy, as he had been in World War II. So we went to movies at the naval base near Arlington. The movie we went to that Friday night in 1953 was *The Big Heat*. The star of the film was Glenn Ford, but I barely noticed him. What stuck in my mind were the two supporting actors, Gloria Grahame and Lee Marvin. The film has one of the most famous violent sequences of all time. Mobsters' moll, Gloria Grahame, talks to the cops about some gang goings-on and to repay her, Lee Marvin, a vicious gangster, throws red-hot coffee into her face. I had never seen anything like it before. Marvin's open-mouthed gangster was some kind of new species of vicious sadist. At the end of the movie Grahame gets him back by throwing coffee into *his* face, and very few things I've ever seen on the screen are that satisfying.

My father and I talked about Marvin all the way home. My mother said she didn't think I should see things like that. She was probably right.

After that film I was a Lee Marvin fan for life. As far as I was concerned he was the best bad guy in the history of the movies.

Though I knew, of course, that actors weren't the people they played, it never occurred to me that Lee Marvin would be much different than the guys he portrayed. I assumed he'd probably been born in a ditch somewhere, was raised by wolves, and had somehow gotten into the movies. Little did I know that Lee had actually been born into a wealthy family.

But, an even bigger shock. Not only was he a rich kid, but a kind one. We hit it off amazingly well, and started a real friendship. After my first trip to his place in Tucson we called one another on the telephone. Lee would stay up late, unable to sleep from the pains he had in his back. He would sometimes call me in the middle of the night, and say, "Hey, this is your reporter down in Tucson. What the hell are you doing anyway?"

I didn't care what time it was. I was always glad to hear from him.

When my novel *Red Baker* came out he called me at 4:30 A.M. and said, "Jesus Christ, this fucking novel of yours is like looking at a corpse. You don't want to but you can't help yourself. I just spent the whole fucking night reading it."

Coming from Lee, no comment could have been better.

Another time Lee called me in New York and said he was going to Russia to play the mink dealer baddie in *Gorky Park*. He announced that he'd be buying me dinner at the Palm, and told me not to try and pay for it or he'd have to work me over.

We met at the Palm in New York and had a great dinner. He'd been out of movies for a while and was thrilled to be playing a great part again. We ate steaks and of course people drifted over to get Lee's autograph. Every single time they did he said, "Hey, you have to get my friend's autograph too. He's written a great novel and trust me, you'll be glad you have it."

I was so embarrassed my face reddened but Lee kept it right up. I signed about ten autographs while we ate.

And when we were done Lee wouldn't hear about us splitting the check. That was the kind of guy he was, generous and kind. A sweetheart of a man.

And deeply sensitive.

I remember one phone call most of all. He called me at my girlfriend's place in D.C. It was around 2 A.M. Lee was upset, his voice cracking.

"Man," he said. "I just can't fucking believe myself. . . . Oh, man. . . ."

"What is it?" I said.

"This guy, he came up to me in the supermarket today. I was getting some steaks. He looks at me and says, 'Lee Marvin, you don't look so tough.'"

Lee stopped, and caught his breath.

"So?" I said.

"Well, I didn't do anything. I didn't slug him. I shoulda slugged him. I feel like such a fucking coward for not hitting him."

"Awww bullshit," I said. "You don't have to prove anything to an asshole like that. You did the right thing, Lee."

More silence.

"You think?"

"Fuckn A. Some asshole wants to feel big by taking on somebody who is really great. Fuck him."

"Ahhh, Bobby, you're all right."

"Hey man, you're my bud. Fuck that guy."

There was silence on both sides. He knew I loved him like a big brother, and I knew the feeling was mutual.

1985 was a huge year for me. *Red Baker* came out, and through a combination of good luck and hard work I ended up going to Hollywood and working on the television show *Hill Street Blues*. I was already over forty, had hardly a nickel in my pocket and this was the biggest break in my life. So when my wife and I moved to Laurel Canyon I spent my first year working night and day on the show. I often thought of Lee but I didn't call him except for a few times. I was obsessed with the show and making it in Hollywood. At forty-two I knew it was my last chance.

As the year wound down and I found out my contract was going to be renewed, I felt relaxed enough to get in touch with old friends again. I finally called Lee a couple of times and we talked but he was busy with guests at the house.

Almost six months more went by and one night I remembered how close we'd been and I gave him a call. He sounded even craggier than usual, and very tired.

"Hey, bud," I said. "I'm in Hollywood. Sorry, I haven't talked to you much of late but this has been a huge challenge, and all my energy is in it."

He said it was okay, that he had been busy too . . . busy fighting serious intestinal problems.

"Oh, shit," I said. "Is it bad?"

"They say it's curable, Bob, but I don't know if I believe them."

"Lee, you're gonna be okay," I said. "I *know* you are."

"Yeah, maybe. But, hey Bob, I can say one thing. No matter what happens at least I outlived that cocksucker Danny Kaye. He died last week, the prick."

We both cracked up. I had never known Kaye but he was legendary in Hollywood for being a bully, and attacking people lower on the pecking order than he was. Just the kind of guy generous and kind Lee would hate.

Not long after Lee died. Those were the last words I ever heard from him. Funny, and fitting.

In my opinion Lee was one of the greatest actors of all time. When he was on screen you couldn't look at anyone else.

But equally as important, he was a great guy, and a kind and generous friend. I did love him like a big brother, and miss him all the time.

Mr. Bad Taste
and Trouble Himself:
Robert Mitchum

*A big, crazy, sexy, sixty-five-year-old little boy who can't get used to
the idea that he's supposed to act like, like Ward Cleaver, you dig?*

Robert Mitchum is walking down this Kafkaesque hallway, holding
his arms straight out in front of him, crossed, as though they've been
manacled by the CBS production assistant who trucks along in front
of him. Mitchum staggers a bit. All he drinks nowadays is tequila—
and milk, though not together—and he had his first shot at one thirty
in the afternoon, and now it's ten thirty at night and he's been through
five interviews and a fifth of Cuervo Gold Especial and is fast moving
into that strange land between dreams and wakefulness.

Things are mightily askew but still manageable until someone
notices the glass partitions and the little wooden desks, which look
like interrogation booths, and yells, "Bob, look, we're in Czechoslova-
kia and they're going to bring out the fucking guards!"

This registers slowly behind Mitchum's lizard-lidded eyes, and
smiling his curling serpent's smile, he thrusts his hands forward as
though they are cuffed and booms in this deep, hilarious voice: "My

name is Robert Mitchum. My serial number is 2357982. My rank is private. I have nothing whatsoever to tell you. . . ."

Down these endless narrow hallways and out of these little rooms come women of all ages—twenty-three, forty-five, sixty-seven—each of them saying, "Hey, that's . . . that's Robert Mitchum," and each of them getting this *look* on her face. The *same* look. Lust! And helplessness. And yet, completely maternal. And sweet, like, "I've got to help that big, crazy, sexy, funky little boy who is sixty-five years old and has never gotten used to the idea that he has to act like a Ward Cleaver brand of grown-up."

Mitchum had drawn a similar response from a group of young businessmen as we'd left the Waldorf Hotel earlier. "There's Mitchum," one of them said. "He's all fucked up again." And the rest of them laughed and nodded. Thank God somebody is still wild.

"Where the hell is the goddamned makeup girl? I want to kiss her, okay?" he says now, as he runs through the halls. Yes, right here at CBS, is Mr. Bad Taste and Trouble himself. Yeah, he's got himself a pinstripe suit and dark Italian sunglasses like all the rest of those movie stars, but one look will convince you that here is a man *acting* like a civilized being. In a 1964 *Esquire* profile, the usually savage Helen Lawrenson said his personality had paralyzed her into wordlessness. D. H. Lawrence described it as the Life Force. But six-foot-one-inch, barrel-chested, ham-fisted, sleepy-eyed, speech-slurred Robert Mitchum gives off something that can't really be put into words at all. . . . Meanwhile, the makeup woman, a sixty-five-year-old gal herself, is literally buckling at the knees and wiping her brow and saying, "My, oh my, oh my . . . Robert Mitchum." The whole place cracks up, and Mitchum sweetly kisses her on the forehead.

A few minutes later, a few women and a few thousand feet of corridor later, Mitchum is in the taping room, meeting with the producers of *Nightwatch*: "Now, Mr. Mitchum, what is it you'd like to do?" Mitchum bobs and weaves, like he may sucker-punch this sap. But says, "Look, son, I'm a storyteller, all right? Just let me tell some stories, how 'bout that?" The guy puts on this shit-eating grin and says, "Well, just what kind of stories do you have in mind, Mr. Mitchum? After all, this is CBS."

"Forget it, man," Mitchum says. He does that when he's disappointed, when he's about to go over the crest, fly out there without the handgrips into the Mighty Tequila Pure Inspiration Good Time Void but is dragged back, as one inevitably is, by the Squares that Surround and Envelop and Enfold and Munch Away. He falls back on old '50s beat talk, like "*This producer cat is some down dude, Jim, you dig?*" Mitchum sags against a couch, stares at the lights and waits for the Interviewer—the sixth of the day—to show up. His friends are sitting across from the nifty little set with its green couches and fake bookcases, and out comes the Interviewer, Dapper Dan himself, in a three-piece suit. He sits down and looks warily at Mitchum, and admits that he has not yet had a chance to see *That Championship Season*, the movie Mitchum is starring in with Bruce Dern, Martin Sheen, Paul Sorvino, and Stacy Keach. "So, since we're not familiar with it, could you, ah, tell us the plot, Bob?"

Mitchum's pals look at each other in horror. This man is a storyteller, yes sir, but in his current shape, well, the plot might just be a little more than he's willing, or able, to do. But Mitchum remains cool and manages to tell the tale, which, briefly put, is about a team of high-school basketball players who won the Pennsylvania state championship in 1957 and have gathered to celebrate that one moment of glory twenty-four years later.

Mitchum also mentions that he is starring as U.S. Navy officer Victor "Pug" Henry in the ABC dramatization of Herman Wouk's *The Winds of War*, an eighteen-hour mini-series for which Mitchum received a cool million. Then he slides back on the couch, crosses his massive arms, and waits.

"Now, Mr. Mitchum, you say this is about a group of men, who had one shining moment and then everything else was downhill. Is that how you feel about your own life?"

Mitchum squints menacingly through his sunglasses. "No," he says flatly. "Why would I live like that?"

"Oh," the Interviewer says. "Well, Mr. Mitchum, do you think that you will become a cult star, a cult *hero* if you will, say, in the 1990s, like Bogart in the 1960s?"

Mitchum rolls his eyes and says loudly, "Hey, what year is it now, Jack?"

"It's 1982."

"Well, how would I know, man?" he says.

"Well, the 1990s are coming."

"That's deep," Mitchum says. "Thanks for telling me."

Mitchum's cronies are squealing with laughter, and the director is shooting threatening glares in their direction, and finally a technician says, "That's a wrap."

Mitchum looks around the darkened studio and, ignoring the host, yells at the top of his lungs, "Can I fart now?"

Stacy Keach, who plays a junior high school principal who takes orders for his friends and is always destined to be a second banana, is terrific in *That Championship Season*, but just now he would rather talk about Mitchum: "Bob's a legend, but he goes out of his way to make you feel completely at home. Not that he's ever comic, but he has just enough of the rebel in him, where you know there's a real character under there. And that character, I think, the guy who is at once a star but constantly laughs at it, undercuts it with humor, that's what comes across to his fans. The reason for all of that probably has to do with the way he was brought up. He came up in tough times. He doesn't make a big deal out of it. There's no pretension with Bob, but he had it tough."

Born in Bridegeport, Connecticut, on August 6, 1917, Mitchum never got to know his father, Jim, a railroad man who was "squashed to death" by two boxcars in Charleston, South Carolina, when Robert was eighteen months old, leaving Mitchum's mother, Ann Gunderson Mitchum, to care for three children—Robert; his older sister, Julie; and his younger brother, John. Mitchum's mother went to work as a linotype operator and fell in love with and married a newspaperman named Bill Clancy, who apparently had some other interests on the side.

"I'm coming down the steps one night," Mitchum says, a Pall Mall hanging out of the crack that is his mouth, as though he had been born smoking, "and I hear these guys talking. I look around the stairway, and I see Al Capone and another guy sitting in the living room having a beef about 'receipts.' I knew enough to go back upstairs."

At fifteen, he went south, riding in boxcars. ("I dug school. Truly. But not enough to hang around.") In Savannah, Georgia, a yard bull busted him "for being a suspicious character with no visible means of support." Two days later he was on a road gang and scared shitless. He smiles, puffs the Pall Mall, drinks the tequila. "I figured I was getting too good at that, so one day, when I had my first chance, I split."

He spent the next few months in the Civilian Conservation Corps, digging ditches for a living. He saved thirty dollars and hopped freight trains hobo-style to California. When he first hit LA, he met up with his sister, Julie, and his mother, who now was divorced from Clancy. She had remarried to a man named Hugh Cunningham-Morris and was pregnant with Mitchum's half sister, Carol. Julie was working in little theater groups, writing and acting. Mitchum, who had always wanted to be a writer like his idol, Thomas Wolfe, tried plays, stories, and acting. From 1934 to 1942, he was a busboy, a dishwasher, a truck driver, and a longshoreman. In 1940 he married Dorothy Spence and soon had two young sons, Jim and Chris, to support. An old foot wound was acting up, and he was unable to work much. After eight long, broke years, the situation was getting close to desperate.

When help did arrive, it came from an unlikely source. Years before Mitchum had landed in Hollywood, another young man had come to Tinseltown from Ohio. He was handsome, a good actor, pals with Clark Gable. His name was William Boyd. Unfortunately, before he found the right properties, he found vodka. Boyd drank a quart a day for ten years and was quietly fading into Nathanael West pink-stucco retirement when a producer decided he could get him cheap. Boyd and a crew travelled to Bakersfield, and the Hopalong Cassidy series was born.

Mitchum was pals with Boyd, and one day in the early '40s, he got a call telling him to get a bus up to Bakersfield to be in the movies. The twenty-five-year-old Mitchum could scarcely believe his luck. When he arrived a few hours later, the actors, crew, and directors were sitting on the veranda of the hotel, talking in low, hushed tones. Mitchum introduced himself, tried to look cheerful and ready for work. Boyd glumly told him to go over to makeup, which was housed in a little cabin across the road. When he entered the makeup cabin, Earl Mosher, a friendly prop guy, smiled slightly and gave him a cowboy suit. Chaps, shirt, bandanna, boots, and finally, a cowboy hat.

"This seems a little sticky," young Mitchum said.

"No problem," Mosher said. "See, the guy you're replacing, well, he was doing a stunt today, and he was pulled off his wagon, and the reins were lashed around his wrists, and, well, the wagon kept going back and forth over him, the horses went nuts, you know, when he fell, so what we got here is a little of his head blood in the hat. We'll take care of that fine, though."

Mosher took out a pen knife and scraped the blood off the hatband. "There," he said, smiling at the young actor, "that ought to fit just right now."

"That's how I broke into movies," Mitchum says now, as he belts down another tequila. "I got a dead guy's hat. And I've been selling horseshit ever since."

After racking up seven Hopalong Cassidy movies, Mitchum got himself an RKO contract for $350. After making three pictures for RKO, he starred in *The Story of G.I. Joe*, for which he was nominated for an Academy Award. Studio executives were talking about this hot new star. The guy had sleepy eyes and sex appeal, and what's more, under it all, he could really act.

Mitchum was thinking about the sweetness of all this one night, sitting on his front porch, just having a drink, looking at the stars, smoking a Pall Mall, when a car stops in front of his house, and a man starts running toward him and shines a light in his face.

Mitchum hit the man in the face, breaking his nose. The man was a member of the Los Angeles police force investigating a disturbance at such-and-such an address. He had the wrong address, but Mitchum came down the steps and demanded to be arrested.

"Hey," he shrugs, opening his leathery palms, "if the cops are going to come up to your porch and hassle you, then I wanted them to take it all the way. I mean, what the hell? Let's go through with it. Right?"

Or, as Mitchum's wife Dorothy puts it, "Robert sometimes has this little problem with authority."

Mitchum admits that leaping into the cop car and screaming, "Let's go downtown right now, motherfuckers," was probably a strategic error. One cop smashed him in the side with a billy club, breaking two ribs; the other cop—the one Mitchum had cold-cocked—used fists, knees, and his gun butt. By the time Mitchum arrived at headquarters, he was looking a bit like one of the soldiers in *G.I. Joe*. No fun.

When the RKO lawyer came prancing onto the scene, he told Mitchum that the trial was a lock. Just plead guilty, take a suspended sentence and a ten-dollar fine. Mitchum went along with the lawyer, only to receive a counteroffer from the judge—180 days in the slammer. At the trial, Mitchum said, "No . . . no . . . no way I can make that." The judge asked him why, and Mitchum said, because he was going into the army. The judge asked him when. Mitchum said, "Ummm, Tuesday." The judge smiled. He liked patriotic actors. That very afternoon, the same two cops who had given Mitchum the nice ride to the police station took him down to the draft board and let him enlist. Then it was back to jail for the weekend, and on the following Tuesday, America's hottest young actor was led, handcuffed, to the troop train.

Assigned to the medics, it was Mitchum's job to look up "the asshole of every GI in America. Just what was he supposed to be searching for? "Piles, hemorrhoids, bananas, grapes, dope . . . you name it."

After a year, Mitchum got out on a hardship case, and went back to making movies, only to discover that he had become something other than an actor. He had become *Robert Mitchum*. SEE HIM RAISE HELL ONSCREEN. READ ABOUT HIM RAISING HELL IN REAL LIFE.

Producers threw Mitchum into one forgettable action thriller after another—*Till the End of Time, The Locket, Pursued, Undercurrent, Desire Me, Rachel and the Stranger*.

There were some good pictures as well. Jacques Tourneur's *film noir* classic *Out of the Past* (Kirk Douglas's second film), with Jane Greer; *The Big Steal*, with Jane Greer; *Blood on the Moon*, with Barbara Bel Geddes. But for the most part, Mitchum, like all the other contract stars of the day, had to do what he was told. And he wasn't in any position to argue or hold out for better films. Mitchum never, *never* talks about this subject unless he's very under the weather. The most he usually says is, "I punch in, I punch out. I don't worry about the film." But privately he will say, "I would have done other things. But they weren't offering them to me. First I was unknown, different. . . . Then two weeks later, they're saying, 'Get me a Mitchum type.' That's it. The man tells you what to do. Not only that, in those days, the man took most of the money as well."

At the height of his earning power he was making over three thousand dollars a week. But with agents' fees, taxes, the Life of a Hollywood Star, and a family to feed, Mitchum didn't save a lot of the dough.

"Look, I'm not complaining," he says, over a drink at the Waldorf bar. "I got a great life out of the movies. I've been all over the world and met the most fantastic people. I don't really deserve all that I have gotten. It's a privileged life, and I know it. I didn't make what these young guys, the Spielbergs, are making. But I had a hell of a lot of fun. Working with all the great leading ladies of my day. Marilyn Monroe, and Jane Greer. I think she was the most underrated of them all. Working with guys like John Huston and Raoul Walsh.

"Hell, the first time I came on the set with Raoul, we did seventeen pages of dialogue in one day. He used to set up and roll cigarettes with his right hand, the side that had the eye patch. Because he couldn't see them, all the tobacco fell out, and he would immediately roll another one, take a puff or two and wonder how he'd smoked the damned thing so quickly. When he had us all ready, he used to turn his back to the shot and let the cameraman tell him when it was done. The thing was, he trusted us. He wouldn't have made the picture at all if he didn't."

It's the element of spontaneity and camaraderie that Mitchum finds missing in today's shooting.

"I know production values are better, sure, but are the scripts, are the pictures? I was on a set with De Niro, *The Last Tycoon*, and he takes forty minutes to get ready for a scene in his trailer. Ray Milland was in the movie, and he gets all upset. He asks Gage Kazan how come we didn't get that much time, and Kazan says, 'Hey, look, you guys don't need time like that. Come on, just say your lines, I got enough problems with him.' The thing is, it's a hell of a lot more work, and I don't see overall where the films are any better, really. You tell me."

One gets the feeling that Mitchum misses not only the spontaneity but the fun his generation had. Walsh was a great friend until his death, and John Huston, with whom he made *Heaven Knows, Mr. Allison*, remains one of Mitchum's closest buddies, and one of the few living directors he speaks lovingly of.

"John was relaxed, but he knows what he's doing all the time," Mitchum says now. "You want to do things for directors like that. He wasn't sitting around trying to create 'art.'"

But there was art to what he was doing?

"One hopes. Yeah, sure, but you don't go out there thinking like that. Where the hell would you be then? Look, take music. You can study it all you want, you can learn about time signatures, and you can know what legato means, and you can read it, and you can appreciate it, but if you haven't got an ear, if you're off-pitch, then that's it. I've always had an ear. Hey, it's like Bogart used to say, 'Say the lines and don't stumble over the furniture.'"

What he doesn't say is that he has always had complete dedication, despite the lousy movies he's had to endure. John Huston recalls in his autobiography, *An Open Book*, a time when he asked Mitchum to crawl across the grass on his elbows. The scene had to be shot three or four times, and when Mitchum stood up, he was covered with blood. He had been crawling across stinging nettles. When Huston asked him why he had done it, Mitchum only answered, "Because that's what you wanted."

One gets the sense that Mitchum has a high standard for people. If he trusts and respects you, he crawls through nettles. The same standard applies to Mitchum's leading ladies. He loves Betty Jane Greer because of her "great sense of the ridiculous." He loves Marilyn Monroe because she "had the guts of a lion."

Mitchum found out about Monroe's courage while on the set of *River of No Return*, a 1954 Preminger film. Monroe and he were about to go down some white water on a raft. When they got to the place where the shoot was to take place, the water was raging, and even the Mad Prussian was against sending Mitchum out. But Mitchum and Monroe thought they could make it. Halfway down the river, as they headed toward the rapids, the security line broke, and they were headed for some rocks. Mitchum signaled for the rescue boat—which started toward them. But Monroe wouldn't escape unless Mitchum got off at the same time.

"She was worried about me," Mitchum says now. "She kept saying, 'You're sick, you shouldn't even be out here with the flu. I don't get off until you do.' I told her, 'Look, this could be a matter of life and death. In another three minutes, we're going to be over those rapids and cut into forty pieces.' But she still wouldn't leave."

For a supposedly macho male, the two traits he likes best in women are a sense of humor and guts. His wife, Dorothy, has plenty of both. She is funny, and regularly deflates Mitchum when he gets on one of his sentimental, drunken storytelling jags. Mitchum takes her needling in the spirit in which it's intended and pours her another drink.

Robert Mitchum is a man who has made it in the toughest and most uncaring of businesses, and he has survived it all by staying one step out of it and pursuing other interests, like music. In 1939, he assisted Orson Welles, splicing together music for an oratorio for a Jewish refugee fundraiser that was performed at the Hollywood Bowl, which Welles directed and produced. In the '50s, he wrote the music and story for the film *Thunder Road*, which was originally supposed to star Elvis Presley. Instead, Mitchum recorded the title song and had a hit record. During the late '50s and early '60s, he spent a lot of time with oyster fishermen and the plain-spoken people of Maryland's Eastern Shore. Drinking, talking, hearing stories. He refused film after film simply because he didn't want work to become "all there was of me. I think that's pathetic.

"Listen," he says, "I always tell them, you don't want me. If you can get somebody better, please, by all means, get him. If you can get somebody cheaper, get him. I don't want to work much anyway."

One of Mitchum's most famous movies is *Cape Fear*. He turned it down at first and agreed to do it only because the producer sent him a case of liquor and some flowers. He called the guy up in the middle of the night and said, "I've smelled the flowers, and I've drunk the booze. I guess I have to do the picture."

Anyone who has seen Mitchum in *Cape Fear* will remember his performance. Perhaps the only other role he gave as much to is that of the crazed preacher in *The Night of the Hunter*. But if you talk to Mitchum about it now, he thinks the director, Charles Laughton, held him back.

"I wanted to take it all the way," he says. "I wanted to scare people to death. The book did that. It was ten times as frightening as the picture. But Charles had such good taste. He kept saying, 'I make my living reading the Bible. I can't do this sort of thing.' As it was, it was pretty good . . . I guess."

The public, however, probably remembers his pot bust in 1948 better than it remembers most of his films. Mitchum talks about it with a great ironic laugh.

"The guy who set me up for that bust was my ex–business manager. I wasn't even tried, you know, and in 1951 the jury apologized, but all people remember is that photo of me coming out of the cell. What they don't know is how close I came to killing the son of a bitch. I got a little hot one night, and I was telling a friend of mine that I was going down to the hardware store and I was going to buy a corncob, a can of gasoline, and a whip, and then I was going to go over to my ex-friend's home and stick the corncob up his ass, pour on the gasoline, light it, and whip his burning ass all the way down Sunset

Boulevard. My pal said, 'No . . . no, you're not. No way.' So I had a talk with the police about all the money he was stealing from me, and the guy went up to San Quentin. I don't mention his name anymore, he has kids and he paid. I had some pals who were in the joint, and I don't think the bastard got his head above water the whole time he was there. But I'll tell you what. He was lucky I didn't turn him over to the Mexicans."

"The Mexicans?"

"Yeah, when I was at Paramount there were these Mexican hard guys, gang guys I knew. They'd served as extras in one of my pictures, and after the bust and all the details came out in the papers, they used to meet me at the gate and say, 'Hey maaan, we know where this basteeeeerd leeeves. You geeve us the word, maaan, and weee go top heeeem for you. You deeeeg, man. We top heeeem!'"

"Top him?"

"Cut off his fucking head, Jack," Mitchum says, looking like the *Night of the Hunter* preacher. "You know what I mean?"

"It's the mystery of Mitchum as well as his charm," says actor Paul Sorvino, at a press conference for *That Championship Season*. "When I met him, I was in awe of him. And I think you're only in awe of someone who is mysterious, whom you can't read easily. In fact, we used that awe, all of us, in the movie, because the team members are supposed to have awe for the coach. Naturally, as you get to know Bob, some of that Screen Legend stuff diminishes, but I didn't want to let it go too easily, because it worked for the movie."

Mitchum himself is propped up against a wall, talking to two journalists. In his hand is a Bloody Mary, and his eyelids hang down his face like two broken blinds in a flophouse.

"You know what a Mitchum movie is," he says, as a woman reporter from *Newsweek* breaks into that sexual motherly smile. "It starts with a shot of a girl running across a beautiful open field. On the other side she sees this big gorilla. He waves to her. She runs toward him, smiling, with open arms. Then twelve guys come out and beat the gorilla over the head. He collapses on the grass. Scene Two: The girl meets the gorilla in a cabin. He's locked inside. She tries to get to him, but just as she opens the door, he's beaten over the head by twenty guys. Scene Three: a castle somewhere. The girl sees the gorilla in a turret. She climbs up, gets there, but again there're fifty guys beating him over the head. She finally takes his head in her arms and looks directly into the camera and says, 'He stinks and he's ugly but I like him.'"

Mitchum has told this story, oh, maybe fifty thousand times over the past forty years, but each time he gets a great laugh and a look of worship and admiration from whoever is around. Mitchum is, of course, the gorilla, and in his tale, he's being saved by the girl, who can't quite get to him in time. It perfectly illustrates the combination of bravado, real toughness, and a kind of lost-little-boy appeal that he has with women. Every woman who hears the story gets that look in her eyes. "If I were there, I'd save the big, helpless gorilla from the mobsters."

By the same token, it's quite possible to misconstrue the "sensitive heart within the gorilla body" angle. One evening, Mitchum invites me up to his room at the Waldorf. Both of us are having difficulty maneuvering down the flower-covered hallway, and Mitchum pretends to pick the flowers and eat them as he heads toward his room, laughing and staggering, cursing and picking imaginary flowers all at the same time.

When we get into his suite, he collapses on the couch and begins drinking tequila again.

"Still haven't eaten," he says. "No time to feed the gorilla. He's been on the chain gang."

"Hey," I say. "Let's call room service and get some hamburgers sent up and some milk, okay?"

"Nah," Mitchum says, looking down at his slightly bulging belly. "It's too late. Hell, I don't even need to eat."

"Hey," I say. "You do need it. I'm ordering you some food, for chrissakes."

"You think so?"

"Yeah, come on."

This is crazy, I think. Finally, reluctantly, he allows me to call room service and have them send him up a cheeseburger.

Meanwhile, I get out my tape recorder and set it up, and Mitchum smiles and talks about the making of *The Friends of Eddie Coyle*, which is one of his best and least-seen films.

"Up in Boston," he says, "these are some tough motherfuckers. I mean hard guys. You ever meet George Higgins? He and I are having dinner, and he says, 'Hey, Bob, did you ever think about committing suicide?' I said, 'Well, yeah, I guess, once or twice, but not really.' And he says, 'No, I mean with the gun in your mouth.' And I said, 'Well, yeah, but I always figured it would make too much of a mess for the other guys.' And Higgins smiles and says to me, 'No, I have that covered. I mean you do it in the shower, see? Then they can just sponge you off the walls.' Weird. See, I don't know why it is, but I attract weirdness."

"Maybe you like it."

"Yeah, hey, who the fuck are you, Sigmund Freud?"

Mitchum puts down another tequila, and I can feel the mood of the room changing. "There was this guy up there," he says. "Part of the Boston Mob. Reminded me of the guys who hung out at my father-in-law's house. Very natty dresser, very polite. He was a hit man for the mob. One night, see, this guy gets carried away just having fun in this Italian restaurant, and he takes out his piece and shoots a hole in the ceiling. You don't do that, you know? It's like shitting in the parlor. So he comes over to dinner at our house one day, and he's really down, and he say, 'You think you got problems, listen to this. You know what they made me do because of that little hole I blew in the ceiling? They made me go all the way out to San Francisco, get a hotel room, buy new suits, get a girlfriend to cover for me, spend days setting this guy up, and then I got to blow him away. All out of pocket! Can you believe that? I mean, would you consider that a fair thing to do?"

Mitchum laughs wildly at the story, as do I . . . but then the mood changes again.

"You getting this shit?" he says.

"Yeah. . . . Listen, maybe you don't need another drink, Bob."

"You're telling me?"

"No."

"That's good, because guys shouldn't push the gorilla too far. Sometimes in bars guys come on with stuff, you know. 'You think you're tough, or what?' I do like *this*. . . ."

Mitchum gets up and orders me to do the same. He comes over and stares down at me, his huge hands clamped firmly on my shoulders.

"You see, I don't fight clean. I gouge eyes, I break arms. I say to the guy, 'Listen, pal, if you really want to do this, you ready to go all the way? 'Cause that's what it's going to mean. You dig?'"

I feel myself trembling, but with Mitchum you don't back down. "What if they say, 'Fuck you, movie star?'"

Mitchum's eyes narrow.

"Then I do this!" he says.

Suddenly, he throws his whole body backward, still grasping my shoulders, and comes winging back toward me with his huge creased forehead. It's the old Irish forehead slammer trick and I stay perfectly still and pray that he's not too drunk to stop himself.

My prayers are answered, and Mitchum stops one millimeter from my head.

But he is still glowering at me, and I no longer have any idea whether he's acting or we've gone over into the Twilight Zone.

"If they aren't knocked out by that, I twist them around and break their arms, gouge their eyes. It's not the Marquis of fucking Queensberry rules, I want to tell you."

And at that moment the doorbell rings.

"Room service!" I say moving backward toward the door.

"Hey," Mitchum says, smiling, "I could use some food after all."

At the gala premiere of *That Championship Season*, surrounded by the Kennedys, Norman Mailer, Budd Schulberg, royalty from Greece, Robin Williams, and about a thousand other rich and famous people, Mitchum comes over to me and asks what I'm doing next. I tell him I am going home, back to work on my novel.

"Jesus Christ. You know, that's what I wanted to do. But I couldn't make that kind of commitment. Good luck with it. I mean it."

There is such real warmth and such actual concern in his voice that I feel touched, and can't resist giving him a hug.

"Listen," I say. "It's been great fun. Good luck and take care of yourself."

Mitchum smiles, looks at the little circle of people who are standing around and yells, "What? Five hundred dollars? You want to go to a motel with me? Jesus Christ, man, what kind of guy do you think I am? Get the hell out of here, kid! Some goddamned nerve!"

Then he pounds me on the back of the head with his big open hand and walks just behind his wife out of the room.

The Break

James Garner had long been one of my favorite actors, so when I got a chance to write a piece about him for Art Cooper at *GQ* I jumped at it. I was pretty sure he'd be great copy and I'd get a good piece.

Well, the piece turned out just fine. Garner was a willing and charming interview, though I don't think I hung with him long enough to get a piece worthy of being included in this volume.

But, that aside, going out to Vancouver to visit Garner while he was making the HBO version of Joseph Wambaugh's exciting cop novel *The Glitter Dome* turned out to be the biggest break in my career since I'd met Tom Wolfe way back at Hobart College.

Even now when I think back on it the whole story seems like some kind of miracle.

Not only was Jim Garner kind and forthcoming, all the people he worked with were the same way. Just great, funny, and brilliant people and it was no accident that they had all worked with Jim before.

Especially director Stuart Margolin, who used to play Angel, Rockford's on-again, off-again sidekick for years on Rockford. Now he was directing Jim's movie, and watching Stuart go about his business was very impressive. Soft-spoken, helpful, he led his cast in a subtle way. Margolin was also the least pompous director I've ever met. He made time for me, and was willing to talk to me about Garner and his craft. He was also a great reader of serious fiction and seemed interested in my novel writing.

One night Stuart; his wife, Pat, a beautiful and charming Texas woman, and I went out to dinner. Over drinks they asked me about my new novel, *Red Baker*, which was coming out in about seven months from Dial Press. I told them all about the book, how it was about a steel worker who had lost his job in Baltimore and how he couldn't find work and couldn't imagine that he could do anything else. The book was a dark, troubled drama, sometimes relieved by street humor. They seemed very interested in it, and Pat wrote the name of the book down on a postcard, along with the publisher's name, Dial Press, and my home phone number. She then dropped the card into her big handbag and said they would get it when it came out.

I told them I'd have one sent to them, but they insisted on buying it.

I felt a great warmth toward them. And hoped I'd somehow see them again.

A few months later *The Glitter Dome* was televised on HBO, and it was in every way a superior crime movie. I was impressed by the direction, by Garner, and by Margot Kidder, whom I had not yet met. (The days I was on the set she hadn't started yet.) But I knew how the business was. People meet on movie sets, form close, warm friendships, but once the shoot is over they never see one another again.

I never really expected to hear from Stuart and Pat again.

In 1985, *Red Baker* was published and got the best reviews of any novel I had ever published. Michiko Kakutani gave it a terrific review in the *New York Times*. Jonathan Yardley, a very tough Pulitzer Prize–winning critic who wrote for the *Washington Post*, loved the book, the

Saturday Review of Literature profiled me, and the *Village Voice* called it a classic working-class novel.

I had suffered heavily for *Red Baker*. It took me six years to write and I had received a mere ten grand for it. Still, I wrote it because I had to, not to make money. I never expected a book about an unemployed working man to make a lot of dough. In fact, I wondered if anyone would publish it at all.

But now that it was out, I seriously wondered what I was going to do next.

I was already forty-two years old and, materially speaking, I had almost nothing. My girlfriend Celeste Wesson and I lived in a one-bedroom place with a linoleum floor and exposed pipes in the kitchen. It was scary to think of the future. I couldn't spend another six years on a book, and besides, I didn't have another book in mind.

What should have been a joyous time—my reviews were truly wonderful—instead became a time of anxiety and fear. So I had written what some people thought was a great book? That was nice. Now all I needed was a subway token.

My wife was working at National Public Radio on the weekend news show, *All Things Considered*. I knew I could go on doing profiles, but I felt burned out from all that. I was so tired of travelling somewhere and hurriedly getting down my impressions of someone, then racing back and turning out five to ten thousand words on the subject. I just couldn't take it anymore.

Plus, a great change had come over the magazines I worked for. It had started in the early '80s. In the past we journalists could interview people and write whatever the hell we found. If they had big ears, we wrote that they had big ears. If they were loudmouthed jerk-offs we let them be loudmouth jerk-offs. But now a new element came into play. Publicists. In the '70s the publicist was just some guy the editor called to set up the interview. Now, however, independent publicists were a dying breed. Huge corporate publicists like Pickwick controlled all of the A-list people any magazine would want to interview. That meant they could dictate to the editors and writer what kind of piece was going to be written before the journalists got there. Of course, you could lie to them and write whatever the hell you wanted. But if you did that, you wouldn't be given access to any of their other clients. What it amounted to was censorship, American style.

I thought of all the things Sol had told me back in the '70s. It really was right out of the Marxist textbook. Get a monopoly and shut off the channels for information. Suddenly, writing funny and truthful pieces about well-known people was out of the question.

I thought of another piece I had done for a magazine and how suddenly the editors had red penciled all the interesting bits.

The whole New Journalism deal was over.

Anyway, I was burned out from it, and didn't much care. I was so tired and so broke I felt like giving up. Maybe I could get a job in publicity myself somewhere. Or maybe I could weasel my way back into teaching college, though the mere thought of that depressed me in the extreme. It meant that after all my work I had been defeated as an independent writer. I would be going back to the womb. God, the thought of it made me so depressed. Maybe I'd just start doping and drinking again until I freaking collapsed.

I should have been a happy guy after *Red Baker*, but when I realized it was the end of my career, well . . . it didn't seem so exciting anymore.

I was sitting around the house one Tuesday afternoon, wondering what the hell I'd do with my life, when the phone rang. I wearily picked it up.

"Hello."

"Hello," said a strangely familiar female voice. "Is this Robert Ward?"

"Yeah. It is." Hell, I thought, a bill collector.

"Well, this is Pat Margolin. I met you on *The Glitter Dome*?"

I really couldn't believe it. "Pat? Of course I remember you. How are you?"

"I'm fine. Just wanted to call you to tell you the damndest thing happened. I was cleaning out my purse. Remember that oversized purse I had in Vancouver?"

"Yes, sure."

"Well, I dumped all the stuff out of it on the table, lipstick, old pens, paperbacks, tissues, just everything and the last thing that falls out is this crumpled up postcard. I uncrumple it and read that it's your name, Robert Ward. And your novel, *Red Baker*, Dial Press. So I showed it to Stuart and he and I liked you so much we really wanted to read the book. So we called Dial Press and got it, and we both read it and it's just so wonderful."

"Thanks," I said. "Wow."

"And Stuart would like to make a deal with you. He wants to write the screenplay with you and then try and get the money together to make the movie. You'd get Writer's Guild minimum and split that with Stuart, but he really thinks he can make it."

That meant I'd get $17,500 for it. Hey, that was more than I got for the novel. Why not?

"You have a deal," I said. "But where would we write it?"

"Stuart will pay your way out to our place on Salt Spring Island, and you'd stay with us, if that's okay?"

"Sure, that would be fine."

"Great."

"Yeah, we can't wait to see you. This will be fun."

We both hung up. I felt like a guy waiting in the gas chamber who'd been given a last-minute reprieve.

In the next few months so much happened that I still can't quite believe it. First, Celeste Wesson and I got married at Stuart Mott's mansion near the capitol. It was about 100 degrees but the wedding was beautiful and Celeste looked like a goddess. After a brief honeymoon, which we really couldn't afford, we came back to D.C., and one day later I was off to Vancouver to write the script with Stuart at his dreamlike home on Salt Spring Island.

Our working relationship was about perfect and in three weeks, sticking closely to the novel, we had a script. I couldn't believe how well we worked together.

After the script was done I flew back to D.C., and my wife and I moved from Glover Park to Adams Morgan. It was a move I really wasn't crazy about. We had our own house in Adams Morgan but the street was rife with crime. A friend of mine who lived there had been mugged three times in one year.

Halfheartedly, I began working on a detective novel about smuggling in Baltimore Harbor when I got a call from Esther Newburg, my agent.

"Hey," she said. "Would you like to write television?"

The thought had never occurred to me.

"Sure," I said. "I mean if the show was any good."

"How would *Hill Street Blues* strike you?"

"That would be great," I said. "I'd also like to play center field for the Yankees but I think the job's taken."

"Well," she said. "I had dinner with David Milch and Jeffrey Lewis, two very smart guys, and I gave them your novel and your screenplay you wrote with Margolin. They're going to read the material and if they like it you're going to get a script offer."

"Wow," I said. Not a big "wow" because I was used to deals like this. So and so is going to read your work and if they fall in love with you they're going to call you and give you a billion dollars, sweetie.

"You don't sound excited," she said. "You should be fucking excited."

"I promise I'll get excited when they actually offer me a job," I said. "Thanks for giving it to them."

"Hey, stay positive," Esther said. "You're a hell of a writer."

I thanked her and hung up.

And felt such a jolt of anxiety I couldn't sit still. Instead, I picked up my guitar and played Muddy Waters for about two hours. That just about got my head straight.

When my wife got home I told her about the whole deal and she asked, "Well, when will you know?" Both of us were used to the glacial pace of publishing deals. I figured maybe a month and that's what I told her.

"God, that's a long time to wait," she said. "Don't let it make you crazy."

"Right," I said. Sure, no problem. I was already crazy.

It was about twelve noon the next day. The phone rang.

"Hello?"

"Hello?" said a woman's voice. "This is *Hill Street Blues*. I have Mr. Jeffrey Lewis and Mr. David Milch on a conference call for you."

I sat down at my desk, and felt my heart beat faster.

"Hi," said a voice. "This is Jeff."

"And this is David Milch. I've got to run out so I'll let Jeff tell you the details but basically we love your script and your novel and we want you to write a script for the show."

"Oh," I said. "That's . . . that's great."

David hung up the phone and Jeff Lewis asked me if I had any ideas for an hour episode.

"Oh yeah," I said. "I got a lot of them. But it's kind of hard to sort them out this second. I want to go through them. I mean there are so many, they're kind of jumbled all up in my mind now. You know what I mean."

"Sure," he said. "But we need to hear them soon. How about you fly out on Monday and tell them to us? Then if we like them you write the script. If we don't like them, well, you get a trip to Los Angeles."

"Oh, hey, you're going to like them," I said. "There's just so many and they're kind of jumbled up and. . . ."

I realized I was repeating myself and that I must have sounded retarded.

Lewis and I talked a little more, then they put me on with their assistant who booked my flight for me.

I couldn't believe it. Wow! What a break!

Except for one small fact. I had no ideas at all. Zero.

Trying not to panic, I called friends I had in the Baltimore Police Department. I was referred to a guy named (I kid you not) Detective Robert Ward. My mind was blown by this, but no more so than the way everything else had gone. It almost seemed fated.

I drove over to Baltimore and the two Wards went out to drink. Within ten minutes we had established a great rapport and Detective Ward told me an amazing story regarding a cop who had fallen in love with a woman, become like a father to her kid, but then panicked when she wanted to get married right away. Before he backed out, he couldn't resist going to her house and making love to her one more time. Then, after the hot sex session, he told her he was through. The woman went nuts, screamed, and threw things at him. Her son, already upset from her divorce, thought the cop was trying to kill his mom, picked up the cop's service revolver and shot the officer in the back. The cop staggered out to the lawn, called for help, but it was too late. Buy the time the ambulance had arrived the patrolman was dead.

When I heard that story I knew I was going to get the job. Ward gave me other stories too, a couple of comic ones, and as we riffed back and forth I invented a few funny things of my own.

We drank whiskey for three hours. I drove the forty miles back to D.C., loaded but confident.

Three days later I flew out to Los Angles. I was staying at the Sportsmen's Lodge in Studio City and I had to meet Milch and Lewis at the Wine Bistro right around the corner from MTM Studios. By the time I had driven the 1.2 miles down Ventura Boulevard I was sweating profusely, even in my air-conditioned car.

We sat at a table in the center of the restaurant and I put on my reporter's happy smile. After exchanging pleasantries about the trip out, Lewis asked me, "Well, what do you have for us?" I told him the story about the dying cop and waited. Jeff looked at Milch and they both smiled.

"You have any idea which character this story should be for?"

I told him Taurean Blaque, the black actor who played Detective Washington. They both smiled again and nodded their heads.

"You can write the script," Jeff said. "Congratulations."

They went on to say that if they liked the script I would be put on staff. I was so raw to the whole process I didn't even realize what 'on staff' meant. They explained that it meant I would move to Hollywood and come into the office every day and write the show with "the guys."

I smiled, and ate my lunch in a fog. I answered things and told funny stories and had no idea what anyone was saying. I had a script deal, and if they liked it. . . .

I couldn't even allow myself to say the rest of it again. It would be too crushing if they didn't.

I went home and started to write, and at once, I knew that I had nailed it. It was almost as if it was writing itself. The lines were fresh and the story was a killer.

I sent it to them via Federal Express and told myself they would probably get in touch with me in a week or two. (This was down from my earlier estimate of a month.)

I went to bed, woke up and went to the Washington YMCA in the morning. When I got back it was around two o'clock and the phone was ringing.

It was both David Milch and Jeff Lewis and they were laughing:

"This is the best freelance script we have ever read," David said. "You're on the staff."

Jeff Lewis said the same thing, and we all started laughing.

I was almost afraid to ask the next question.

"Ummm, could you ah tell me how much money I might make?"

David jumped right in:

"Well, you start at two hundred and fifty thousand a year but don't worry, with your script fees you end up making three or three and a quarter."

I had, remember, just made ten thousand dollars on my novel *Red Baker*. For six years work.

It was almost too much for me. I felt like I was going to faint.

"How much?" I said. I really had no idea of what television writers made. Milch laughed again and said: "Look, Robert, if it's not enough . . ."

"No, no, no. It's enough. Don't fire me!"

They both laughed and David came on again:

"I was going to say if it's not enough, don't worry. If you do well by the second year you'll make four or maybe even five hundred. That good enough for you?"

"Jesus Christ," I said. "When do you want me out there?"

"How about by Friday?" Jeff said. "You see, Bob, the season is already underway and you get paid by the week."

"I'll be there," I said.

They congratulated me again. I made travel arrangements with their secretary and fell back on my bed.

"Holy shit," I said. My heart was racing a thousand beats a minute. I actually thought I might have a heart attack I was so excited.

I called Celeste at NPR.

She was short with me, like she always is when she's busy.

"Sorry, honey. Can't talk. On deadline."

"I don't care," I said. "Deadline can wait."

"What? What is it?"

"We're moving to Hollywood," I said. "I just got the staff job on *Hill Street Blues*."

"WHAT?"

I heard people behind her say, "Is anything wrong?" She answered. "Robert got the job on *Hill Street Blues*. We're moving to Hollywood."

From behind her I heard cheering.

"On Friday," I yelled. "On Friday. We're moving to Hollywood. Holy fucking shit!"

So there it is. On Friday, August 8, 1985, I flew out to Los Angeles and we've been here ever since. My life changed forever from that script.

But really the entire thing started with my last magazine article. Well, the last one I wrote as a freelancer, anyway.

A couple of months later, sitting in my new office in Studio City, I wrote down a very improbable list:

1. I go to Vancouver to interview James Garner.
2. I meet Stuart and Pat Margolin and give them my name, phone number, and the name of my novel, *Red Baker*. On a postcard, which she throws into her bag.
3. Seven months later. Pat finds the card crumpled in the bottom of her old purse, and just happens to read what it says. What if she

had just tossed it without looking at it? There would have been no option of the book, no script, and no job. But she did look at it, and she did get the novel on her own and gave it to Stuart, who read it right away. As I subsequently learned, the odds of that happening are a million to one. No one reads anything in Hollywood. They have readers who read stuff for them and then tell them not to buy it. These people are terrified to option anything, because so few things get made. They are really paid to reject books. Most directors don't read either. I was lucky enough to get one who said he would and did.

4. Stuart and I write the script in record time.
5. My new agent Esther Newburg hears that Milch and Lewis are coming into town and want to find writers. She has had my script for about three days and read it already. What are the odds against that? Two million to one.
6. Esther meets David and Jeff at Elaine's, and tells them about me. She gives them the novel and the script.
7. They read both of them and call me the next day. I tell them I have tons of ideas. I have NO ideas.
8. I call the Baltimore Police Department and get my own namesake! He gives me the greatest story I've ever heard, perfect for the show.
9. I write the script and they give me the job. At the time I had five thousand bucks in the bank and I was forty-two years old.

When you think of all the things that could have gone wrong in that list it's truly humbling. It was almost like some kind of cosmic fate intervened and said, "You know, the guy worked on a novel about the working class for six years and got ten grand. Let's cut him a break."

I know that's naive and silly, but how else do you explain how so many things went right?

And there's one more thing as well. I finally did write the working-class novel I had tried to write in the early '70s when I was at Hobart.

Why couldn't I write it then? I believe because I hadn't suffered any setbacks. I had a nice cushy life as a professor, and even though I made little money it was, in the end, an easy gig. I had to test myself, put myself through a crucible of really making my living through writing, with no fallback position, before I could begin to understand what a working guy who lost his job went through. I just couldn't have truly imagined it before. And another thing. I didn't write a book about a good Revolutionary and a Bad Capitalist, but a simple, strong story about a real person, Red Baker, a man who is a mixture of good and bad, kindness and selfishness. By being beaten down and putting myself on the line I understood people better, in a way I'd never have done if I had stayed in academia.

That said, let me also say that I have many friends in academia today and some of them write very moving novels. Those that do don't need to put themselves through some trial by fire. Or maybe they've already done all that before they started teaching. But for many of the younger writers I've known teaching is a bad way to go. It's too soft, too easy, and cuts you off from workaday realities. Many of the so-called serious novels coming out of this world are lame, and lifeless.

Just like mine were before I left.

So it seemed I'd come full circle. I was finished with the wild life of the New Journalism, just as the era itself ended. It was a wild ride. I learned a ton about writing, and I met some of the most interesting people in the world.

And now, moving into Laurel Canyon in Hollywood I was off to a new era and a new challenge in my life. One that I learned would be far more daunting and tough than even the wild old journalism world.

But that's a subject for another book.

A bright woman friend of mine once asked me, "Bob, why do you always seem to interview wild men?"

"Those are just the assignments I get," I said. "No other reason than that."

She smiled at me and shook her head.

"Now we both know that's not true," she said. "Let me know when you have a better answer."

Maybe this last piece is part of the answer.

Son of the Invisible Man

My father was the Invisible Man. I feared his attacks. In my bed, I curled up beneath the covers and stared at the window, alert for any tremor of the cowboy curtains with "Bar-B Ranch" on them. I waited, biting down on the quilt, ready to laugh or scream at the first sight of his head. Suddenly there was a noise, a squeaking, and I jumped, banging my head on the end board. Terrified, I pushed the covers back slowly, waiting for the first sight of his towel-wrapped bandaged head, the fake nose made from cardboard, the dark sunglasses. My father was Griffin, the madman, out there among the dandelions and mulberry trees, stalking me, waiting. . . . I crawled to the end of the bed, giggling insanely, my heart beating through my Baltimore Colts T-shirt.

"I know you're in the yard," I said. "I know you're out there, Griffin!"

There was another noise, and I could bear it no longer. I picked up my Tom Corbett Ray Gun and waited on the end of the bed. From here, I'd see him approaching, and I could leap up, zap him.

"You can't fool me, Griffin," I said. Softly. "I've got you covered."

I moved closer to the window, and then there came from behind me a hideous, high-pitched laugh, and two hands clamped on my shoulders. I screamed, tried to pull away.

My father, the Invisible Man, picked me up by the waist and laughed wildly, turning me toward the hideous wrapped face.

"All right, you little fool," he said in his deepest voice. "You're dying to know who I am, aren't you? I begged you to leave me alone, never giving me any peace, prying and peeking into keyholes. You want to know who I am? I'll show you. . . ."

The Invisible Man set me down on the bed. I was screaming, howling, terrified, ecstatic. He loomed above me, and slowly, he began to unwrap the towel. All the while laughing, laughing, laughing . . .

Though we are good friends today, able to talk about politics, religion, sex, and the Orioles, my father, Robert Allan Ward, has always been a private man. This was doubly true when I was a child. Disillusioned first by the Depression, which knocked out his chances to be an artist, then by the Second World War, caught in a progression of jobs he could barely tolerate, my father sought relief in the fictional nightmares of others.

Though he read mature novels—Tolstoy, Thomas Mann, Kafka—his real allegiances were to the horror novels of his childhood, the books of Wilkie Collins, Lovecraft, Wakefield, Poe, Montague James, Algernon Blackwood, and anthologies like *Beyond the Wall of Sleep*. The great fun of having my father read these stories to me was his ability to imitate English lords, or earls sitting in men's clubs, asking the immortal question, "I say, Robbie, whatever *did* happen to old Bellamy?" At night, though, my father would suffer from dreams that were the raw material of horror stories. Often I would get up from my bed and hear him shuffling around in the kitchen. One night I heard him weeping, and when I saw him sitting beneath a cone of kitchen light he looked up, shook his head, and said, "It was just a dream, Bobby. But it was so real. I dreamt I killed my boss. I had my hands around his throat and I was choking him . . . I couldn't stop." He put his head in his hands and wept softly. Not knowing what to do, I walked to the bookcase and took out a volume of Poe. In a few minutes my father and I were lost in a terror more transcendent than the dull, brutish torments of his job.

The first horror movie I saw was *King Kong*. While he was serving in the Navy, my father took me to a PX theater, filled with sailors and their kids. I vowed that no matter how bad things got, no matter how much the ape scared me, I wouldn't cry or hang onto his arm.

Still, the thought of actually seeing the ape, fifty feet tall, rather than just hearing about him in a story . . . well, that was another place on the old terror map. I tugged my father's arm and said, "Hey, does he . . . come on right away?"

"Who?"

"The ape. You know, does he stare right out at you, right away? Are his teeth huge or what?"

My father patted my hand and smiled.

"It's a *story*," he said. "They have to get to the island first."

I sighed, and shook my head. Thank God there was a story. There was going to be time to get ready. Characters I could get to know and care about before I actually had to deal with horrible Kong!

Of course, the great shock of King Kong was, as it turned out, not the fear but the sympathy the monster instilled in me. By the end I was practically in tears, but certainly not for the reasons I had expected.

As I grew older my father and I fell away from each other. He had no use for either rock 'n' roll or sports, and no time for reading stories anymore. He worked long hours, came home exhausted, and spent hours alone, bathing behind a locked bathroom door. I realize now that he was perilously close to suffering a total nervous breakdown, but like his own father, a tugboat captain, he remained silent and secretive. Only during *Chiller Theater* could he relax, and we spent our best hours camped in front of late-night television watching Lon Chaney and Karloff and Lugosi howling and tromping and flying across the German Expressionist sets of the old classic horror flicks. My father acted as my own personal Rod Serling, guiding me through a land just one step beyond Baltimore row-house reality, into a twilight zone, where we could both breathe the heady air of the fantastic.

Of all the old movies that thrilled us, none was so wondrous as *The Invisible Man*, which my father and I watched again and again. He knew every single line in the picture, including those of the extras. He could converse with academic rigor on the difference between the book and the film. When the madman Griffin exacts revenge on the snotty scientist Kemp, we exulted, for we were glad to be rid of Kemp. He was, after all, a squealer, and in '50s Baltimore, there was no lower animal.

It was around that time that my father became the Invisible Man. He would dress up, raid my room, and scare the hell out of me. I found this change in him astonishing. It was as though he'd shed some inner reserve, and decided that in this one area, horror, it was okay to act like a kid again.

My father and I were never closer than when he could play Griffin, a character that somehow touched him. Like Griffin he was frustrated, brilliant, but unappreciated. Like Griffin, he had a fantasy of being an artist, a genius, and all of it was thwarted by "those fools" in the real world.

It was what we had between us, and it wasn't enough, but I made do. Somewhere along the line I understood, in some way beyond confessions, that my father loved me. I think, too, that playing Griffin may have saved his sanity.

Still, the years pushed us further apart. I spent every weekend with my gang of buddies in the Waverly Movie Theater, eating bagfuls of

Little Tavern Hamburgers and watching the new '50s horror films, like *Attack of the Crab Monsters, Earth vs. the Flying Saucers,* or *The Creeping Unknown.* Though most of these pictures were fun (especially the Hammer Films' *Blood of Dracula*), many of them were shot to look like '50s TV fare. The acting and the writing were usually stiff, with cardboard actors like John Agar and Richard Carlson battling monsters like the Creature from the Black Lagoon. Sometimes, while laughing at these flicks I would long for my father to be there with me. But he was always too tired, too angry, and probably felt too foolish to come.

By the late '60s I was married to a woman who had two young children. It was the Era of Innocence, in which we were supposed to be working on developing the child in all of us by listening to Simon and Garfunkel, blowing bubbles, and picking flowers. Nevertheless, I found that my two new children responded with innocent vigor to Jimi Hendrix, football, and late-night tellings of the good old "Red Lodge" by H. R. Wakefield. Soon we were all huddled on the couch together, watching *Chiller Theater.* I felt a strange ambivalence about my new role as guide to terror and fear. Unlike my father, who hadn't given it much thought, I had read enough criticism of violent movies to fear what they might do to my kids' minds and souls.

My sons loved the old pictures, just as I had, loved to hear the names of the old players, David Manners, Lionel Atwill, John Boles, and Colin Clive. I found that the classic pictures scared them just as they had me—in a way that was thrilling, but tinged with compassion. This was made eminently clear when I took them to their first horror movie in a theater—*King Kong,* of course.

Shannon, then six, fell in love immediately with the great ape and announced to everyone that he was King Kong. I looked at my wife and shook my head. Heartbreak up ahead. And sure enough, at the climax with the mighty Kong reeling from the airplane's machine-gun bullets, Kevin (five) was gripped with a wild fear for his big brother's

safety and screamed out, "Look out, Shannon. Here come the air-
planes. Duck! Duck!!"

There was a long, grand period in which we saw every new horror film made. *Halloween,* with its classic attention to detail, was the
last truly scary one. But unlike the carefully wrought villains of older
movies, its killer, a gigantic man in a white mask, had no other dimen-
sion than his desire to kill. More unfortunate, *Halloween* spawned a
mess of imitators (*Terror Train, Valentine's Day, Prom Night*) whose
monsters lacked even the humanity of the Creature from the Black
Lagoon. Horror directors became obsessed with special effects instead
of characters. Like mad scientists with a forbidden formula, they
boiled down everything to gore and violence. After a particularly
sadistic outing called *Mother's Day,* the boys and I agreed that we
weren't going to see any more pictures in which women were hacked
to death, in which the star of the picture was the killer's knife. As
Shannon noted, "You could feel sorry for the old werewolf. He was a
real monster. Who can feel sorry for a lot of chicken guts?"

A horror producer I met put it this way: "Just give them a good
dose of violence every three minutes and you'll make thirty million
dollars in two weeks."

This cowardly philosophy leaves us with movies like *The Evil Dead.*
The night I saw it I grew so bored I wandered out to the candy counter
where I met a member of the picture's "target audience," a black boy
of sixteen.

"Hey," I said, "you think this picture is scary?"

"Shit, man," he smiled. "This isn't even as scary as my neighborhood!"

He had that right. I left the candy line, wandered out onto Thirty-
fourth Street, and suddenly I had an intense desire to talk to my old
man. I went to a phone booth, dialed him down in Baltimore, ready
to bemoan the downfall of the horror flick. To my surprise, my father
was in a state of terrified ecstasy.

"Bobby," he said, "I just saw *Poltergeist*. Now there was one terrific horror story. Old Edgar Allan would have loved that movie. You coming down this summer, son?"

"Yeah," I said, "I was thinking about bringing the boys."

"Great . . . great . . . listen, I got a VHS. We'll set up a midnight screening of your favorite movie."

"Only if you do your Griffin routine."

"Hell, yes, . . . you fool," my father said. "You're dying to know who I am, aren't you? . . . Hahahahahaha."

Yeah, I thought when I put down the phone. I guess I still am.

The following essays were previously published in *New Times:*
"The Yawn Patrol"
"The Mount Kisco Sting"
"Marshal Ky Amongst the Roses"
"Grossing Out with Publishing's Hottest Hustler (or Flem Snopes in Skinland)"
"The Playboy of the Western Art World"
"The Bird Is the Word"
"Redneck Rock"

The following essays were previously published in *Rolling Stone*:
"Drinks with Liberty Valance: Lee Marvin Shoots from the Hip"
"Mr. Bad Taste and Trouble Himself: Robert Mitchum"

The following essays were previously published in *Sport*:
"Reggie Jackson in No-Man's Land"
"Pete Maravich Is Still Magic"
"The Oakland Raiders' Charming Assassin"

The following essays were previously published in *Crawdaddy*:
"Down at the End of Lonely Street"
"A Fistful of Critics"

The following essays were previously published in *GQ*:
"The Night the Lights Went Out in Baltimore"
"The Break"

"Son of the Invisible Man" was previously published in *The Movies*.
"The Passing of Baltimore's Block" was previously published in *Penthouse*.
"Zombies Every Sunday" was previously published in the *Village Voice*.